*POLITICAL QUOTATIONS*

# POLITICAL QUOTATIONS

*A Worldwide Dictionary of Thoughts
and Pronouncements from Politicians,
Literary Figures, Humorists and Others*

*compiled by*

MICHAEL C. THOMSETT

*and*

JEAN FREESTONE THOMSETT

McFarland & Company, Inc., Publishers
*Jefferson, North Carolina, and London*

British Library Cataloguing-in-Publication data are available


Library of Congress Cataloguing-in-Publication Data

Political quotations : a worldwide dictionary of thoughts and
    pronouncements from politicians, literary figures, humorists and
    others / compiled by Michael C. Thomsett and Jean F. Thomsett.
        p.   cm.
    Includes indexes.
    ISBN 0-89950-951-7 (lib. bdg. : 50#. alk. paper)
    1. Political science — Quotations, maxims, etc.  I. Thomsett,
Michael C.   II. Thomsett, Jean F., 1947- .
PN6084.P6P59   1994
808.88′2 — dc20                                                 93-41206
                                                                    CIP

Manufactured in the United States of America

*McFarland & Company, Inc., Publishers*
    *Box 611, Jefferson, North Carolina 28640*

# CONTENTS

# INTRODUCTION

In reading the opinions of politicians, philosophers, writers and revolutionaries throughout history, one might conclude that virtually everything is political. Some have said as much. There are political aspects to most activities and situations—business, education, the family, human relations, and anywhere people and institutions interact.

To narrow the focus of a book concerned only with "political" quotations, the compilers faced the question, Where should the line be drawn? The guideline used in this book was to provide the reader with information useful in political contexts. For example, a librarian or speechwriter will need to identify the author of a famous phrase; or identify the phrase knowing the author. Keeping the reader in mind has been the method for limiting the scope of this collection.

A quotation may be located in a number of ways in this book:

First, one may search the body of the book, which is arranged alphabetically by category. The categories are all listed in the contents, with "see" references from common alternative words or phrases to the heading under which they are gathered in this book.

Second, one may examine the Index of Authors, which cites entry numbers of all quotations uttered by a given individual that are included in this book. Author names are also cross-referenced by pen names when applicable.

Third, one may refer to the Index of Key Words in Context.

The book and its two indexes are arranged so as to be of practical use for the librarian, speechwriter, researcher and author.

The sequence of quotations within each category might appear arbitrary at first glance. However, it was done purposefully to achieve several effects. Complementary or contradictory statements are arranged in proximity, for the reader's insight and enjoyment. In some cases, the prevailing attitude of one age reverses itself in the next. This idea makes for greater usefulness than the predominant traditional method of arrangement, in which quotations within a classification are arranged in the life order of the individual being quoted.

(Thus, the ancient Greeks are always found together at the beginning of the section, and today's spokespersons are together at the end.) This tradition is awkward and artificial, in the compilers' view.

We recognize that many political maxims and sayings have been uttered by numerous people. We do not claim to have always used the first instance of any particular entry. However, we have often selected a version of a statement made by (a) a politician, (b) the most contemporary source, or (c) someone for whom the context of the statement is particularly ironic or interesting.

Modern writers and communicators are sensitive to the fact that men *and* women are involved in political and social issues. Unfortunately, this has not always been the case. Many traditional quotations refer to "man," "mankind," and other male players in the world of politics. It would be improper to edit quotations away from the original author's words, although it has been the intention to create as broad-based a compilation of political commentary as possible, for and by men and women.

Fall 1993

# THE QUOTATIONS

## Action *see* Political Action

───────── *Adages and Maxims* ─────────

1. If it ain't broke, don't fix it. —Bert Lance, in *Nation's Business*, May, 1977

2. Never make a defense or apology before you be accused. —Charles I, letter, September 3, 1636

3. Several excuses are always less convincing than one. —Aldous Huxley, *Point Counter Point*, 1928

4. Never complain and never explain. —Benjamin Disraeli, in J. Morley, *Life of William Ewart Gladstone*, 1903

5. Never explain. Your friends do not need it and your enemies will not believe you anyway. —Elbert Hubbard, *The Motto Book*, 1927

6. Never lose your temper with the press or the public, is a major rule of political life. —Christabel Pankhurst, *Unshackled*, 1959

7. Never forget posterity when devising a policy. Never think of posterity when making a speech. —Robert G. Menzies, *The Measure of the Years*, 1970

8. Experience suggests that the first rule of politics is never to say never. —William V. Shannon, in *New York Times*, March 3, 1968

9. Be nice to people on your way up because you'll meet 'em on your way down. —Wilson Mizner, in Alva Johnson, *The Legendary Mizners*, 1953

10. There is just one rule for politicians all over the world: Don't say in Power what you say in Opposition; if you do, you only have to carry out what the other fellows have found impossible. —John Galsworthy, *Maid in Waiting*, 1931

11. The proper memory for a politician is one that knows what to remember and what to forget. —John Morley, *Recollections*, 1917

12. The present moment is a powerful goddess. —Johann Wolfgang von Goethe, *Tasso*, 1790

13. A week is a long time in politics. —Harold Wilson, in Nigel Rees, *Sayings of the Century*, 1984

14. Always present your front to the world. —Molière, *L'Avare*, 1669

15. No pain, no palm; no thorns, no throne; no gall, no glory; no cross, no crown. —William Penn, *No Cross, No Crown*, 1669

16. No man can smile in the face of adversity and mean it. —Edgar Watson Howe, *Country Town Sayings*, 1911

17. For fools rush in where angels fear to tread. —Alexander Pope, *An Essay on Criticism*, 1711

18. When the going gets rough, remember to keep calm. —Horace, *Odes*, 1st c. B.C.

19. When the going gets tough, the tough get going. —Joseph P. Kennedy, in J. H. Cutler, *Honey Fitz*, 1962

20. Praise the Lord and pass the ammunition. —Howell Forgy, statement at Pearl Harbor, December 7, 1941

21. Damn the torpedoes! Full speed ahead. —David G. Farragut, statement, August 5, 1864

22. In skating over thin ice, our safety is in our speed. —Ralph Waldo Emerson, *Essays: First Series*, "Prudence," 1841

23. It is better to die on your feet than to live on your knees. —Dolores Ibarruri, speech, September 3, 1936

24. It is much easier to avoid disagreement than to remove discontents. —George Washington, letter, May 11, 1781

25. When in doubt, tell the truth. —Mark Twain, *Following the Equator*, 1897

26. You should never have your best trousers on when you turn out to fight for freedom and truth. —Henrik Ibsen, *An Enemy of the People*, 1882

27. Better break your word than do

worse by keeping it. — Thomas Fuller, M.D., *Gnomologia*, 1732

**28.** No one has a finer command of language than the person who keeps his mouth shut. — Sam Rayburn, in *Lawrence Daily Journal-World*, August 29, 1978

**29.** There is a homely adage which runs, "Speak softly and carry a big stick; you will go far." — Theodore Roosevelt, speech, September 2, 1901

**30.** It is much safer to be feared than to be loved, when you have to choose between the two. — Niccolò Machiavelli, *The Prince*, 1513

**31.** Among politicians the esteem of religion is profitable; the principles of it are troublesome. — Benjamin Whichcote, *Moral and Political Aphorisms*, 1703

**32.** He that resolves to deal with none but honest men must leave off dealing. — Thomas Fuller, M.D., *Gnomologia*, 1732

**33.** For a thing to remain undone nothing more is needed than to think it done. — Balthasar Gracián, *The Art of Worldly Wisdom*, 1647

**34.** If you're going to be a bridge, you've got to be prepared to be walked upon. — Roy A. West, in *Washington Post*, May 8, 1988

**35.** Nothing is easy to the unwilling. — Thomas Fuller, M.D., *Gnomologia*, 1732

**36.** Nothing is impossible for the man who doesn't have to do it himself. — A. H. Weiler, in *New York Times*, March 17, 1968

**37.** Every country has the government it deserves. — Josephe de Maistre, *Unpublished Letters and Pamphlets*, August 27, 1811

**38.** It is necessary for him who lays out a state and arranges laws for it to presuppose that all men are evil and that they are always going to act according to the wickedness of their spirits whenever they have free scope. — Niccolò Machiavelli, *Discourses on the First Ten Books of Titus Livius*, 1513–17

**39.** Everyone likes flattery; and when you come to Royalty, you should lay it on with a trowel. — Benjamin Disraeli, in G. W. E. Russell, *Collections and Recollections*, 1898

**40.** There is no other way for securing yourself against flatteries except that men understand that they do not offend you by telling you the truth; but when everybody can tell you the truth, you fail to get respect. — Niccolò Machiavelli, *The Prince*, 1513

**41.** [A politician] must get along with constituents who think all economies should be made at the expense of Somewhere Else, and also with the elected representatives of Somewhere Else whose constituents feel the same way. — Stimson Bullitt, *To Be a Politician*, 1977

**42.** In a serious struggle there is no worse cruelty than to be magnanimous at an inopportune time. — Leon Trotsky, *The Russian Revolution*, 1933

**43.** Strange to see how a good dinner and feasting reconciles everybody. — Samuel Pepys, *Diary*, November 9, 1665

**44.** You can always get the truth from an American statesman after he has turned seventy, or given up all hope of the Presidency. — Wendell Phillips, speech, November 7, 1860

**45.** Hindsight is always twenty-twenty. — Billy Wilder, in J. R. Columbo, *Wit and Wisdom of the Moviemakers*, 1979

**46.** In politics you should always leave an old bone behind for the critics to chew on. — Joseph Joubert, *Pensées*, 1842

**47.** In politics, your work is never visible enough. — Vaclav Havel, in *Vanity Fair*, August, 1991

**48.** A wise politician will never grudge a genuflexion or a rapture if it is expected of him by prevalent opinion. — Frederick Scott Oliver, *The Endless Adventure*, 1930

**49.** In this business, if you don't blow your own horn, there's no music. — Mario Cuomo, in *USA Today*, June 11, 1990

**50.** The biggest danger for a politician is to shake hands with a man who is physically stronger, has been drinking and is voting for the other guy. — William Proxmire, in *New York Herald Tribune,* February 16, 1964

# Advice and Advisors

**51.** Counsel, *n.* In American politics, a person who, having failed to secure an office from the people, is given one by the Administration on condition that he leave the country. — Ambrose Bierce, *The Devil's Dictionary,* 1906

**52.** Ineffective leaders often act on the advice and counsel of the last person they talked to. — Warren G. Bennis, speech, January 21, 1988

**53.** A politician has few friends and he is sure of hardly any except those he knew when he was still an unknown. — Stimson Bullitt, *To Be a Politician,* 1977

**54.** The best servants of the people, like the best valets, must whisper unpleasant truths in the master's ear. It is the court fool, not the foolish courtier, whom the king can least afford to lose. — Walter Lippmann, *A Preface to Politics,* 1914

**55.** A leader must have the courage to act against an expert's advice. — James Callaghan, in *Harvard Business Review,* November/December, 1986

**56.** The counselors of even the most bullheaded candidate do much to set a campaign's tone. The choice of level-headed, honorable advisers improves his chances to finish the race without regret or shame. — Stimson Bullitt, *To Be a Politician,* 1977

**57.** In the multitude of counselors there is safety. — Bible, *Proverbs 11:14*

**58.** Good words are worth much, and cost little. — George Herbert, *Jacula Prudentum,* 1651

**59.** If you hear that someone is speaking ill of you, instead of trying to defend yourself you should say: "He obviously does not know me very well, since there are so many other faults he could have mentioned." — Epictetus, *Enchiridion,* 2nd c.

**60.** The world will in the end, follow only those who have despised as well as served it. — Samuel Butler (II), *Notebooks,* 1912

**61.** In those days Mr. Baldwin was wiser than he is now; he used frequently to take my advice. — Winston S. Churchill, speech, May 22, 1935

**62.** The nine most terrifying words in the English language are, "I'm from the government and I'm here to help." Ronald Reagan, statement, August 12, 1986

# Ambition

## See also Fame; Greatness; Power

**63.** Ambition is the last refuge of the failure. — Oscar Wilde, "Phrases and Philosophies for the Use of the Young," 1894

**64.** Ambition is in fact the avarice of power. — Charles Caleb Colton, *Lacon,* 1820–22

**65.** Everybody in government is like a bunch of ants on a log floating down a river. Each one thinks he is guiding the log, but it's really just going with the flow. — Robert S. Strauss, in *Washington Post,* June 9, 1978

**66.** It has been the greatest fault of our politicians that they have all wanted to do something. — Anthony Trollope, *Phineas Finn,* 1869

**67.** To enter politics at the bottom

is easy and good sense. Competition is mild, and one may practice in an arena where unseasoned judgment is not fatal. — Stimson Bullitt, *To Be a Politician,* 1977

**68.** Public life is regarded as the crown of a career, and to young men it is the worthiest ambition. Politics is still the greatest and the most honorable adventure. — John Buchan, *Pilgrim's Way,* 1940

**69.** Great ambition unchecked by principle or the love of glory, is an unruly tyrant. — Alexander Hamilton, letter, January 16, 1801

**70.** A wise man is cured of ambition by ambition itself; his aim is so exalted that riches, office, fortune and favor cannot satisfy him. — Jean La Bruyère, *Characters,* "Of Personal Merit," 1688

**71.** Man in political life must be ambitious. — Rutherford B. Hayes, letter, June 27, 1888

**72.** We grow weary of those things (and perhaps soonest) which we most desire. — Samuel Butler (I), *Prose Observations,* 1660–80

**73.** Beaverbrook is so pleased to be in the Government that he is like the town tart who has finally married the Mayor! — Beverly Baxter, in Henry Channon, *Chips: The Diaries,* "June 12, 1940," 1967

**74.** Ambition, in a private man a vice, Is in a prince the virtue. — Philip Massinger, *The Bashful Lover,* 1936

**75.** All ambitions are lawful except those that climb upward on the miseries or credulities of mankind. — Joseph Conrad, *A Personal Record,* 1912

**76.** The rising unto place is laborious, and by pains men come to greater pains; and it is sometimes base, and by indignities men come to dignities. The standing is slippery, and the regress is either a downfall, or at least an eclipse. — Francis Bacon, *Essays,* "Of Great Place," 1625

**77.** A slave has but one master; an ambitious man has as many masters as there are people who may be useful in bettering his position. — Jean La Bruyère, *Characters,* "Of the Court," 1688

**78.** Men may be popular without being ambitious; but there is rarely an ambitious man who does not try to be popular. — Frederick North, speech, March, 1769

**79.** The oldest, wisest politician grows not more human so, but is merely a gray wharf rat at last. — Henry David Thoreau, *Journal,* 1853

**80.** I have climbed to the top of the greasy pole. — Benjamin Disraeli, in W. Montgomery and G. Buckle, *Life of Benjamin Disraeli,* 1916

**81.** All rising to great place is by a winding stair. — Francis Bacon, *Essays,* "Of Great Place," 1625

**82.** The ambitious climbs up high and perilous stairs, and never cares how to come down; the desire of rising hath swallowed up his fear of a fall. — Thomas Adams, *Diseases of the Soul,* 1616

**83.** Ambition can creep as well as soar. — Edmund Burke, *Letters on a Regicide Peace,* 1796–97

**84.** Ambition often puts men upon doing the meanest offices; so climbing is performed in the same posture with creeping. — Jonathan Swift, *Thoughts on Various Subjects,* 1711

**85.** And he that strives to touch the stars, Oft stumbles at a straw. — Edmund Spenser, *The Shepherd's Calendar,* 1579

**86.** There is no penalty for overachievement. — G. William Miller, in *Time,* July 17, 1978

**87.** There is no such thing as a great talent without great will-power. — Honoré de Balzac, *La Muse du Département,* 1843

**88.** O sacred hunger of ambitious minds. — Edmund Spenser, *The Faerie Queene,* 1596

**89.** To plunder, to lie, to show your arse, are three essentials for climbing high. — Aristophanes, *The Knights,* 424 B.C.

**90.** Politicians are to serve the people, not to direct them. — Woodrow Wilson, speech, October 18, 1912

**91.** Whom the gods wish to destroy they first call promising. — Cyril Connolly, *Enemies of Promise,* 1938

# *Anarchy*

## *See also* Order

**92.** Anarchism is a game at which the police can beat you. — George Bernard Shaw, *Misalliance,* 1914

**93.** Anarchy always brings about absolute power. — Napoleon I, speech, June 7, 1815

**94.** Hunger is the mother of anarchy. — Herbert Hoover, statement, January 1, 1919

**95.** In anarchy it's not just the king who loses his rights but the worker as well. — Max Weber, *Politics as Profession,* 1918–19

**96.** Anarchism . . . stands for the liberation of the human mind from the domination of religion; the liberation of the human body from the dominion of property; liberation from the shackles and restraints of government. — Emma Goldman, *Anarchism and Other Essays,* 1911

**97.** We started off trying to set up a small anarchist community, but people wouldn't obey the rules. — Alan Bennett, *Getting On,* 1972

**98.** Liberty unregulated by law degenerates into anarchy, which soon becomes the most horrid of all despotisms. — Millard Fillmore, message to Congress, December 5, 1852

**99.** Freedom and not servitude is the cure of anarchy; as religion, and not atheism, is the true remedy for superstition. — Edmund Burke, speech, March 22, 1775

**100.** Chaos and ineptitude are antihuman; but so too is a superlatively efficient government, equipped with all the products of a highly developed technology. — Aldous Huxley, *Tomorrow and Tomorrow and Tomorrow,* 1956

**101.** Government and co-operation are in all things the laws of life; anarchy and competition the laws of death. — John Ruskin, *Unto This Last,* 1862

**102.** The worst thing in this world, next to anarchy, is government. — Henry Ward Beecher, *Proverbs from Plymouth Pulpit,* 1887

**103.** The worst enemy of life, freedom, and the common decencies is total anarchy; the second worst enemy is total efficiency. — Aldous Huxley, *Adonis and the Alphabet,* 1956

**104.** Two dangers constantly threaten the world: order and disorder. — Paul Valéry, in *The Nation,* January 5, 1958

# *Argument*

**105.** One man's word is no man's word: we should quietly hear both sides. — Johann Wolfgang von Goethe, *Truth and Poetry,* 1811–22

**106.** There is no such thing as a convincing argument, although every man thinks he has one. — Edgar Watson Howe, *Country Town Sayings,* 1911

**107.** We may convince others by our arguments; but we can only persuade

them by their own. — Joseph Joubert, *Pensées,* 1810

**108.** One of the best ways to persuade others is with your ears — by listening to them. — Dean Rusk, in *Reader's Digest,* July, 1961

**109.** The most savage controversies are those about matters as to which there is no good evidence either way. — Bertrand Russell, *Unpopular Essays,* 1950

110. Disagreement shakes us out of our slumbers and forces us to see our own point of view through contrast with another person who does not share it. — R. D. Laing, *The Politics of Experience*, 1967

111. He who knows only his own side of the case knows little of that. — John Stuart Mill, *On Liberty*, 1859

112. Who can refute a sneer? — William Paley, *Principles of Moral and Political Philosophy*, 1785

113. We are most likely to get angry and excited in our opposition to some idea when we ourselves are not quite certain of our own position, and are inwardly tempted to take the other side. — Thomas Mann, *Buddenbrooks*, 1902

114. I dogmatise and am contradicted, and in this conflict of opinions and sentiments I find delight. — Samuel Johnson, in John Hawkins, *Life of Samuel Johnson*, 1787

115. A good life is a main argument. — Ben Jonson, *Timber; or Discoveries*, 1960

# Aristocracy

## See also Rulers and Ruling

116. There is a natural aristocracy among men. The grounds of this are virtue and talent. — Thomas Jefferson, letter, October 28, 1813

117. Thus our democracy was, from an early period, the most aristocratic, and our aristocracy the most democratic in the world. — Thomas Babington, *History of England*, 1849

118. The American aristocracy can be found in the lawyer's bar and the judge's bench. — Alexis de Tocqueville, *Democracy in America*, 1835

119. Democracy means government by the uneducated, while aristocracy means government by the badly educated. — Gilbert K. Chesterton, in *New York Times*, February 1, 1931

120. Aristocracy is always cruel. — Wendell Phillips, speech, 1861

121. An aristocracy is like cheese; the older it is the higher it becomes. — David Lloyd George, speech, December, 1910

122. An aristocracy in a republic is like a chicken whose head has been cut off; it may run about it a lovely way, but in fact it's dead. — Nancy Mitford, *Noblesse Oblige*, 1956

123. There is always more brass than brains in an aristocracy. — Oscar Wilde, *Vera, or The Nihilists*, 1883

124. There are no wise few. Every aristocracy that has ever existed has behaved, in all essential points, exactly like a small mob. — Gilbert K. Chesterton, *Heretics*, 1905

125. Sweet mercy is nobility's true badge. — William Shakespeare, *Titus Andronicus*, 1590

126. New nobility is but the act of power, but ancient nobility is the act of time. — Francis Bacon, *Essays*, "Of Nobility," 1625

127. A society without an aristocracy, without an elite minority, is not a society. — José Ortega y Gasset, *Invertebrate Spain*, 1922

# Authority

128. The best practical government is one that finds a working balance of liberty and authority. — M. Judd Harmon, *Political Thought*, 1964

129. The question before the human race is, whether the God of nature shall govern the world by his own laws, or whether priests and kings shall

rule it by fictitious miracles? — John Adams, letter, June 20, 1815

**130.** Authority is never without hate. — Euripides, *Ion,* ca. 415 B.C.

**131.** He who is firmly seated in authority soon learns to think security, and not progress, the highest lesson of statecraft. — James Russell Lowell, *Among My Books,* 1870

**132.** All political questions, by matters of right, are at bottom only questions of might. — August Bebel, speech, July 3, 1871

**133.** Who made thee a prince and a judge over us? — Bible, *Exodus 2:14*

**134.** Groups regard a political system as legitimate or illegitimate according to the way in which its values fit with theirs. — Seymour Martin Lipset, *Political Man,* 1981

**135.** Those who would combat general authority with particular opinion, must first establish themselves a reputation of understanding better than other men. — John Dryden, "Heroic Poetry and Heroic License," 1677

**136.** The first key to wisdom is this — constant and frequent questioning . . .

by doubting we are led to question and by questioning we arrive at the truth. — Pierre Abélard, *Sic et Non,* ca. 1120

**137.** Rome has spoken; the case is concluded. — Saint Augustine, 5th c., quoted in *Sermons,* 1702

**138.** Mere precedent is a dangerous source of authority. — Andrew Jackson, veto message, July 10, 1832

**139.** Stable authority is power plus legitimacy. — Seymour Martin Lipset, *Political Man,* 1981

**140.** He who has never learned to obey cannot be a good commander. — Aristotle, *Politics,* 4th c. B.C.

**141.** The best government rests on the people, and not on the few, on persons and not on property, on the free development of public opinion and not on authority. — George Bancroft, *The Office of the People in Art, Government, and Religion,* 1835

**142.** Rulers have no authority from God to do mischief. — Jonathan Mayhew, *A Discourse concerning Unlimited Submission and Non-Resistance to the Higher Powers,* 1750

# *Belief*

## *See also* **Dogma; Idealism; Ideas**

**143.** You may fight to the death for something in which you truly believe, but keep such commitments to a bare minimum. — Albert A. Grant, speech, May 30, 1988

**144.** One person with a belief is a social power equal to ninety-nine who have only interests. — John Stuart Mill, *Representative Government,* 1861

**145.** Men never do evil so completely and cheerfully as when they do it from religious conviction. — Blaise Pascal, *Pensées,* 1670

**146.** Religion . . . is the opium of the people. — Karl Marx, *A Contribution to the Critique of Hegel's Philosophy of Right,* 1843–44

**147.** Whenever you find yourself getting angry about a difference of opinion, be on your guard; you will probably find, on examination, that your belief is going beyond what the evidence warrants. — Bertrand Russell, *Unpopular Essays,* 1950

**148.** There are no atheists in the foxholes. — William Thomas Cummings, in Carlos P. Romulo, *I Saw the Fall of the Philippines,* 1943

**149.** For what a man would like to be true, that he more readily believes. — Francis Bacon, *Novum Organum,* 1620

**150.** Men are nearly always willing to believe what they wish. — Julius Caesar, *De Bello Gallico,* 1st c. B.C.

**151.** Castles in the air — they are so easy to take refuge in. And easy to build, too. — Henrik Ibsen, *The Master Builder*, 1892

**152.** What we call rational grounds for our beliefs are often extremely irrational attempts to justify our instincts. — T. H. Huxley, *On the Natural Inequality of Man*, 1890

**153.** All knowledge must be built on our intuitive beliefs; if they are rejected, nothing is left. — Bertrand Russell, *The Problems of Philosophy*, 1912

**154.** As a rule we believe as much as we can. We would believe everything if we could. — William James, *The Principles of Psychology*, 1890

**155.** It is always easier to believe than to deny. Our minds are naturally affirmative. — John Burroughs, *The Light of Day*, 1900

**156.** Optimism: the noble temptation to see too much in everything. — Gilbert K. Chesterton, in *Kansas City Star*, July 8, 1977

**157.** The place where optimism most flourishes is the lunatic asylum. — Havelock Ellis, *The Dance of Life*, 1923

**158.** Wisdom brings back the basic beliefs of eighteen. — Karl Shapiro, *The Bourgeois Poet*, 1964

**159.** It is always a relief to believe what is pleasant, but it is more important to believe what is true. — Hilaire Belloc, *The Silence of the Sea*, 1941

**160.** Doubt is not a pleasant condition, but certainty is absurd. — Voltaire, letter, November 28, 1770

**161.** To have doubted one's own first principles is the mark of a civilized man. — Oliver Wendell Holmes Jr., *Collected Legal Papers*, 1920

**162.** Doubt is the last vestibule which all must pass, before they can enter into the temple of truth. — Charles Caleb Colton, *Lacon*, 1820–22

**163.** One's belief in truth begins with a doubt of all the truths one has believed hitherto. — Friedrich Wilhelm Nietzsche, *Human, All Too Human*, 1878

**164.** Pessimism, when you get used to it, is just as agreeable as optimism.

— Enoch Arnold Bennett, *Things That Have Interested Me*, 1918

**165.** Just as no one can be forced into belief, so no one can be forced into unbelief. — Sigmund Freud, *The Ego and the Id*, 1923

**166.** What a man believes may be ascertained, not from his creed, but from the assumptions on which he habitually acts. — George Bernard Shaw, *Man and Superman*, 1903

**167.** If an individual wants to be a leader and isn't controversial, that means he never stood for anything. — Richard M. Nixon, in *Dallas Times-Herald*, December 10, 1978

**168.** Those who stand for nothing fall for anything. — Alex Hamilton, in *Listener*, November 9, 1978

**169.** Believe those who are seeking the truth; doubt those who have found it. — André Gide, *So Be It*, 1959

**170.** Never lay yourself open to what is called conviction; you might as well open your waistcoat to receive a knock-down blow. — Leigh Hunt, in *The Examiner*, March 6, 1808

**171.** In this world second thoughts, it seems, are best. — Euripides, *Hippolytus*, 428 B.C.

**172.** When I transfer my knowledge, I teach. When I transfer my beliefs, I indoctrinate. — Arthur Danto, *Analytic Philosophy of Knowledge*, 1968

**173.** Nothing changes so constantly than the past; for the past that influences our lives does not consist of what actually happened, but of what men believe happened. — Gerald White Johnson, *American Heroes and Hero-Worship*, 1943

**174.** In the matter of belief, we are all extremely conservative. — William James, *Pragmatism*, 1907

**175.** Men insist most vehemently upon their certainties when their hold upon them has been shaken. Frantic orthodoxy is a method for obscuring doubt. — Reinhold Niebuhr, *Does Civilization Need Religion?*, 1927

**176.** The heresy of one age becomes the orthodoxy of the next. — Helen Keller, *Optimism*, 1903

177. To accept an orthodoxy is always to inherit unresolved contradictions. — George Orwell, "Writers and Leviathan," 1948

178. Why, sometimes I've believed as many as six impossible things before breakfast. — Lewis Carroll, *Through the Looking-Glass*, 1872

# Budgets

## See also Economics; Taxes

179. He who has his thumb on the purse has the power. — Otto von Bismarck, speech, May 21, 1869

180. A budget is a statement of priorities, and there's no more political document. — Edward K. Hamilton, in *New York Times*, February 9, 1971

181. Too often our Washington reflex is to discover a problem and then throw money at it, hoping it will somehow go away. — Kenneth B. Keating, in *New York Times*, December 24, 1961

182. It is the highest impertinence and presumption . . . in kings and ministers to pretend to watch over the economy of private people, and to restrain their expense. — Adam Smith, *Wealth of Nations*, 1776

183. To contract new debts is not the way to pay old ones. — George Washington, letter, April 7, 1799

184. A national debt, if it is not excessive, will be to us a national blessing. — Alexander Hamilton, letter, April 30, 1781

185. I am one of those who do not believe that a national debt is a national blessing . . . it is calculated to raise around the administration a moneyed aristocracy dangerous to the liberties of the country. — Andrew Jackson, letter, April 26, 1824

186. Be not made a beggar by banqueting upon borrowing. — Bible: Apocrypha, *Ecclesiasticus 18:33*

187. I can get no remedy against this consumption of the purse: borrowing only lingers and lingers it out, but the disease is incurable. — William Shakespeare, *Henry IV, Part II*, 1597

188. The budget is a mythical bean bag. Congress votes mythical beans into it, and then tries to reach in and pull real beans out. — Will Rogers, *The Autobiography of Will Rogers*, 1949

189. Expenditure rises to meet income. — C. Northcote Parkinson, *The Law and the Profits*, 1960

190. Any jackass can draw up a balanced budget on paper. — Lane Kirkland, in *U.S. News & World Report*, May 19, 1980

191. All decent people live beyond their incomes nowadays, and those who aren't respectable live beyond other people's! — Saki, *Chronicles of Clovis*, 1911

192. I've had a tough time learning how to act like a congressman. Today I accidentally spent some of my own money. — Joseph P. Kennedy, in *Newsweek*, February 9, 1967

193. George Bush had been right all along. What they were advocating was "voodoo economics." — David A. Stockman, *The Triumph of Politics*, 1987

194. There is something worse than money in politics, and that's no money in politics. — Samuel Popkin, in *Christian Science Monitor*, March 5, 1992

195. Virtually everything is under federal control nowadays except the federal budget. — Herman E. Talmadge, in *American Legion Magazine*, August, 1975

# Bureaucracy

## See also Government, Forms of; Office

**196.** In a hierarchy every employee tends to rise to his level of incompetence. —Laurence J. Peter, *The Peter Principle*, 1969

**197.** Skewered through and through with office pens, and bound hand and foot with red tape. —Charles Dickens, *David Copperfield*, 1850

**198.** It's all papers and forms, the entire Civil Service is like a fortress made of papers, forms, and red tape. —Andrew Ostrovsky, *The Diary of a Scoundrel*, 1868

**199.** Bureaucracy, the rule of no one, has become the modern form of despotism. —Mary McCarthy, in *New Yorker*, October 18, 1958

**200.** The bureaucracy is what we all suffer from. —Otto von Bismarck, comment, December 12, 1891

**201.** The perfect bureaucrat everywhere is the man who manages to make no decisions and escape all responsibility. —Brooks Atkinson, *Once Around the Sun*, "September 9," 1951

**202.** Bureaucrats are the only people in the world who can say absolutely nothing and mean it. —Hugh Sidey, in *Time*, November 29, 1976

**203.** Committee—a group of men who individually can do nothing but as a group decide that nothing can be done. —Fred Allen, attributed

**204.** What is a committee? A group of the unwilling, picked from the unfit, to do the unnecessary. —Richard Harkness, in *New York Herald Tribune*, June 15, 1960

**205.** Meese had by now entombed himself beneath a pyramid of paper and disorganization. He never met a committee he didn't like. —David A Stockman, *The Triumph of Politics*, 1987

**206.** We always carry out by committee anything in which any one of us alone would be too reasonable to persist. —Frank Moore Colby, *The Colby Essays*, "Subsidizing Authors," 1926

**207.** A camel is a horse designed by a committee. —Alec Issigonis, in *Guardian*, January 14, 1991

**208.** Nothing is ever accomplished by a committee unless it consists of three members, one of whom happens to be sick and the others absent. —Hendrik van Loon, in *Reader's Digest*, June, 1934

**209.** Bureaucracy defends the status quo long past the time when the quo has lost its status. —Laurence J. Peter, in *San Francisco Chronicle*, January 29, 1978

**210.** When a bureaucrat makes a mistake and continues to make it, it usually becomes the new policy. —Hugh Sidey, in *Time*, November 29, 1976

**211.** There is something about a bureaucrat that does not like a poem. —Gore Vidal, *Sex, Death and Money*, 1968

**212.** As civilization advances, poetry almost necessarily declines. —Thomas Babington, *Essays Contributed to the Edinburgh Review*, 1843

**213.** A civil servant doesn't make jokes. —Eugene Ionesco, *Tueur sans gages*, 1958

**214.** Bureaucratization means…a decline of the arbitrary power of those in authority. By establishing norms of fair and equal treatment, and by reducing the unlimited power possessed by the leaders of many unbureaucratic organizations, bureaucracy may mean less rather than greater need to conform to superiors. —Seymour Martin Lipset, *Political Man*, 1981

**215.** Where there is officialdom every human relationship suffers. —E. M. Forster, *A Passage to India*, 1924

**216.** If you're going to sin, sin against God, not the bureaucracy. God will forgive you but the bureaucracy won't. —Hyman G. Rickover, in *New York Times*, November 3, 1986

217. It is not easy nowadays to remember anything so contrary to all appearances as that officials are the servants of the public; and the official must try not to foster the illusion that it is the other way around. — Ernest Gowers, *Plain Words,* 1948

218. If the SEC had jurisdiction over the White House, we might have all had time for a course in remedial economics at Allenwood Penitentiary. — David A. Stockman, *The Triumph of Politics,* 1987

219. This high official, all allow, Is grossly overpaid; There wasn't any Board, and now There isn't any trade. — A. P. Herbert, "The President of the Board of Trade," 1922

220. Institutions are just when no arbitrary distinctions are made between persons in the assigning of basic rights and duties and when the rules determine a proper balance between competing claims to the advantages of social life. — John Rawls, *A Theory of Justice,* 1971

221. Your public servants serve you right; indeed often they serve you better than your apathy and indifference deserve. — Adlai Stevenson, speech, September 11, 1952

222. Bureaucracies are designed to perform public business. But as soon as a bureaucracy is established, it develops autonomous spiritual life and comes to regard the public as its enemy. — Brooks Atkinson, *Once Around the Sun,* "September 9," 1951

223. The only thing that saves us from the bureaucracy is inefficiency. An efficient bureaucracy is the greatest threat to liberty. — Eugene J. McCarthy, in *Time,* February 12, 1979

224. Bureaucrats write memoranda both because they appear to be busy when they are writing and because the memos, once written, immediately become proof they were busy. — Charles Peters, *How Washington Really Works,* 1980

225. I learned in business that you had to be very careful when you told somebody that's working for you to do something, because the chances were very high he'd do it. In government, you don't have to worry about that. — George P. Shultz, in *New York Times,* October 14, 1984

226. Those who govern, having much business on their hands, do not generally like to take the trouble of considering and carrying into execution new projects. The best public measures are therefore seldom adopted from previous wisdom, but forced by the occasion. — Benjamin Franklin, *Autobiography,* 1791

227. The nearest approach to immortality on earth is a government bureaucracy. — James F. Byrnes, *Speaking Frankly,* 1947

228. Guidelines for bureaucrats: (1) When in charge, ponder. (2) When in trouble, delegate. (3) When in doubt, mumble. — James H. Boren, in *New York Times,* November 8, 1970

229. There was one catch and that was Catch-22, which specified that a concern for one's own safety in the face of dangers that were real and immediate was the process of a rational mind... one would be crazy to fly more missions and sane if he didn't, but if he was sane he had to fly them. If he flew them he was crazy and didn't have to; but if he didn't want to he was sane and had to. — Joseph Heller, *Catch-22,* 1961

230. The man whose life is devoted to paperwork has lost the initiative. He is dealing with things that are brought to his notice, having ceased to notice anything for himself. He has been essentially defeated by his job. — C. Northcote Parkinson, *In-Laws and Outlaws,* 1962

231. I see the woman with a scarf twisted round her hair and a cigarette in her mouth. She has put the tea tray down upon the file on which my future depends. — John Betjeman, *First and Last Loves,* 1952

232. The tedium of the bureaucracy does get to me. — James Webb, *Mc-Neil-Lehrer Report,* February 23, 1988

233. Millions are fascinated by the plan to transform the whole world into a

bureau, to make everybody a bureaucrat, and to wipe out any private initiative. —Ludwig Elder von Mises, *Bureaucracy,* 1944

**234.** Any argument worth making within the bureaucracy must be capable of being expressed in a simple declarative sentence that is obviously true once stated. —John McNaughton, in *Wall Street Journal,* March 3, 1974

**235.** The great question is therefore not how we can promote and hasten [bureaucracy] but what can we oppose to this machinery in order to keep a portion of mankind free from this parcelling-out of the soul, from this supreme mastery of the bureaucratic way of life. —Max Weber, in Reinhold Bendix, *Max Weber and German Politics,* 1960

**236.** Today, the man who is the real risk-taker is anonymous and nonheroic. He is the one trying to make institutions work. —John William Ward, in *Time,* November 17, 1955

**237.** You know what the trouble with peace is? No organization. —Bertolt Brecht, *Mutter Courage,* 1939

**238.** Constant emphasis on the need for objective criteria as the bases for settling conflicts enables bureaucratic institutions to play major mediating roles. —Seymour Martin Lipset, *Political Man,* 1981

**239.** We need to revise the old saying to read, Hell hath no fury like a bureaucrat scorned. —Milton Friedman, in *Newsweek,* December 29, 1975

**240.** Routine is not organization, any more than paralysis is order. —Arthur Helps, *Organization in Daily Life,* 1862

**241.** A certain amount of national wealth is likewise necessary to ensure a competent civil service. The poorer the country, the greater the emphasis on nepotism —support of kin and friends. And this in turn reduces the opportunity to develop the efficient bureaucracy which a modern democratic state requires. —Seymour Martin Lipset, *Political Man,* 1981

**242.** Time spent on any item of the agenda will be in inverse proportion to the sum involved. —C. Northcote Parkinson, *Parkinson's Law,* 1958

**243.** It's insane to carry timber to the forest. —Horace, *Satires,* 1st c. B.C.

**244.** The volume of paper expands to fill the available briefcases. —Edmund G. Brown, Jr., in *Wall Street Journal,* February 26, 1976

**245.** The measurement of the gestation period of an original thought in a bureaucracy is still pending. —Hugh Sidey, in *Time,* November 29, 1976

## Campaigns

### See also Voting and Elections; Winners and Losers

**246.** You can campaign in poetry. You govern in prose. —Mario Cuomo, in *New Republic,* April 8, 1985

**247.** In a Presidential campaign there is no such thing as an Off-Broadway production. —Theodore H. White, *The Making of the President 1968,* 1969

**248.** We love the blather and boast, the charge and countercharge of campaigning. Governing is a tougher deal. —Hugh Sidey, in *Time,* November 5, 1984

**249.** A President needs political understanding to *run* the government, but he may be *elected* without it. —Harry S Truman, *Memoirs,* 1955

**250.** A campaign is a revolving circus which bewilders actors and spectators alike. Blocks of votes are cast against (or for) a candidate for contradictory reasons, sometimes both wrong. —Stimson Bullitt, *To Be a Politician,* 1977

**251.** Political campaigns are designedly made into emotional orgies which endeavor to distract attention from the real issues involved, and they actually paralyze what slight powers of cerebration man can normally muster. —James H. Robinson, *The Human Comedy*, 1937

**252.** The problems seem so easy out there on the stump. Deficits shrink with a rhetorical flourish. —Hugh Sidey, in *Time*, November 5, 1984

**253.** Sometimes a candidate feels like a steer being groomed for a 4-H club contest. —Stimson Bullitt, *To Be a Politician*, 1977

**254.** The idea that you can merchandise candidates for high office like breakfast cereal—that you can gather votes like box tops—is, I think, the ultimate indignity to the democratic process. —Adlai Stevenson, speech, August 18, 1956

**255.** I didn't realize the system was so rotten. The thing that leaps out at you as a newcomer is that the process to select a president is totally irrelevant and disconnected from selecting a good person. It has everything to do with sound bites, whispers and innuendo. —H. Ross Perot, in *New York Times*, July 17, 1992

**256.** We were told our campaign wasn't sufficiently slick. We regard that as a compliment. —Margaret Thatcher, in *New York Times*, June 12, 1987

**257.** Politics has got so expensive that it takes lots of money to even get beat with. —Will Rogers, syndicated newspaper article, June 28, 1931

**258.** The game has become so expensive that 90 per cent of what a politician does today is raise money. —Joseph R. Cerrell, in *Los Angeles Times*, July 23, 1990

**259.** There are only three groups against public funding of campaigns—incumbents, challengers and the public. —Al Swift, in *USA Today*, August 1, 1990

**260.** I don't care who does the electing as long as I do the nominating. —William Marcy ("Boss") Tweed, attributed

**261.** A rigged convention is one with the other man's delegates in control. An open convention is when your delegates are in control. —James A. Farley, *Convention and Election Almanac*, 1964

**262.** In primaries, ambitions spurt from nowhere; unknown men carve their mark; old men are sent relentlessly to their political graves; bosses and leaders may be humiliated or unseated. At ward, county or state level, all primaries are fought with spurious family folksiness—and sharp knives. —Theodore H. White, *The Making of the President 1960*, 1961

**263.** Local public meetings held to enable the community to hear the candidates often waste the time of both audience and speaker. Each candidate is stalled for part of an evening waiting his turn to speak to a few people. He faces an audience numbed by the beating of incessant waves of oratory. —Stimson Bullitt, *To Be a Politician*, 1977

**264.** Prosperity is necessarily the first theme of a political campaign. —Woodrow Wilson, speech, September 4, 1912

**265.** A candidacy for any office is not simply the expression of individual ambition—any great candidacy is the gathering place of many men's ambitions. —Theodore H. White, *The Making of the President 1960*, 1961

**266.** If you think too much about being reelected, it is very difficult to be worth reelecting. —Woodrow Wilson, speech, October 25, 1913

**267.** I will praise any man that will praise me. —William Shakespeare, *Antony and Cleopatra*, 1606–07

**268.** I will not accept if nominated, and will not serve if elected. —William Sherman, telegram, 1884

**269.** My hat is in the ring. —Theodore Roosevelt, campaign announcement, 1912

**270.** Presidential candidates don't chew gum. —Theodore C. Sorenson, statement to John F. Kennedy, in Ralph G. Martin, *A Hero for Our Time*, 1983

**271.** I want you to know that I also will not make age an issue in this campaign. I am not going to exploit, for political purposes, my opponent's youth and inexperience. —Ronald Reagan, debate, October 21, 1984

# Capitalism

**272.** History suggests that capitalism is a necessary condition for political freedom. Clearly it is not a sufficient condition. — Milton Friedman, *Capitalism and Freedom,* 1962

**273.** The consumer society and the open society are not quite synonymous. Capitalism and democracy have a relationship, but it is something less than a marriage. — Benjamin R. Barber, in *Atlantic,* "Jihad vs. McWorld," March, 1992

**274.** The forces of a capitalist society, if left unchecked, tend to make the rich richer and the poor poorer. — Jawaharlal Nehru, in *New York Times,* September 7, 1958

**275.** The unpleasant and unacceptable face of capitalism. — Edward Heath, statement, May 15, 1973

**276.** The abortive Reagan Revolution proved that the American electorate wants a more moderate social democracy to shield it from capitalism's rougher edges. — David A. Stockman, *The Triumph of Politics,* 1987

**277.** Capitalism without bankruptcy is like Christianity without hell. — Frank Borman, in *US,* April 21, 1986

**278.** There is inherent in the capitalist system a tendency toward self-destruction. — Joseph A. Schumpeter, *Capitalism, Socialism and Democracy,* 1942

**279.** You cannot get white flour out of a coal sack, nor perfection out of human nature. — Charles Haddon Spurgeon, *John Ploughman's Talks,* 1869

**280.** It is the utmost folly to denounce capital. To do so is to undermine civilization, for capital is the first requisite of every social gain, educational, ecclesiastical, political, or other. — William Graham Sumner, *The Challenge of Facts,* 1880

**281.** The masters of the government of the United States are the combined capitalists and manufacturers of the United States. — Woodrow Wilson, speech, May 10, 1915

**282.** Capitalism inevitably and by virtue of the very logic of its civilization creates, educates and subsidizes a vested interest in social unrest. — Joseph A. Schumpeter, *Capitalism, Socialism and Democracy,* 1942

**283.** Capitalism needs and must have the prison to protect itself from the criminals it has created. — Eugene V. Debs, *Walls and Bars,* 1907

**284.** Capitalism and altruism cannot coexist in man or in the same society. — Ayn Rand, in *Time,* February 29, 1960

**285.** Imperialism is the monopoly stage of capitalism. — Lenin, *Imperialism as the Last Stage of Capitalism,* 1916

# Change

## See also **Reform**

**286.** Profound and powerful forces are shaking and remaking our world, and the urgent question of our time is whether we can make change our friend and not our enemy. — Bill Clinton, inaugural address, January 20, 1993

**287.** Change is the law of life. And those who look only to the past or present are certain to miss the future. — John F. Kennedy, speech, June 25, 1963

**288.** Change is inevitable in a progressive country. Change is constant. — Benjamin Disraeli, speech, October 29, 1867

**289.** Change is not made without inconvenience, even from worse to better. — Samuel Johnson, *A Dictionary of the English Language,* 1755

**290.** When it is not necessary to change, it is necessary not to change. — Lucius Cary, *Discourses of Infallibility,* 1660

**291.** We used to think that revolutions are the cause of change. Actually it is the other way around: change prepares the ground for revolution. — Eric Hoffer, *The Temper of Our Time,* "A Time for Juveniles," 1967

**292.** A man ought warily to begin changes which once begun will continue. — Francis Bacon, *Essays,* "Of Expense," 1625

**293.** The freethinking of one age is the common sense of the next. — Matthew Arnold, *God and the Bible,* 1875

**294.** Times change and we change with them. — Anonymous, 16th c.

**295.** All progress is based upon a universal desire on the part of every organism to live beyond its income. — Samuel Butler (II), *Notebooks,* 1912

**296.** The path of social advancement is, and must be, strewn with broken friendships. — H. G. Wells, *Kipps,* 1905

**297.** It is a folly second to none, To try to improve the world. — Molière, *The Misanthrope,* 1666

**298.** The one thing that does not change is that at any and every time it appears that there have been "great changes." — Marcel Proust, *Remembrance of Things Past,* 1913–26

**299.** The cause of change is always difficult to make. It is always easy to stay with a proven path, even if it is failure. It takes courage to change. — Bill Clinton, in *Christian Science Monitor,* September 28, 1992

**300.** When society requires to be rebuilt, there is no use in attempting to rebuild it on the old plan. — John Stuart Mill, *Dissertations and Discourses,* 1859

**301.** All growth is a leap in the dark, a spontaneous, unpremeditated act without the benefit of experience. — Henry Miller, *The Wisdom of the Heart,* 1941

**302.** Great political and social changes begin to be possible as soon as men are not afraid to risk their lives. — Thomas Masaryk, letter, March 16, 1917

**303.** If the changes we fear be thus irresistible, what remains but to acquiesce with silence, as in the other insurmountable distresses of humanity? It remains that we retard what we cannot repel, that we palliate what we cannot cure. — Samuel Johnson, *A Dictionary of the English Language,* 1755

**304.** A state without some means of change is without the means of its conservation. — Edmund Burke, *Reflections on the Revolution in France,* 1790

**305.** Mass movements can rise and spread without belief in a God, but never without belief in a devil. — Eric Hoffer, *The True Believer,* 1951

**306.** The present contains nothing more than the past, and what is found in the effect was already in the cause. — Henri Bergson, *L'Évolution créatrice,* 1907

**307.** Industries rise and fall, and in so doing bring about growth, technological advance, and rising general living standards. This is the phenomenon Joseph Schumpeter called "creative destruction." But the politician is by nature opposed to the cycle of creation and destruction of industry. He wants everything to be level, smooth, and unchanging. — David A. Stockman, *The Triumph of Politics,* 1987

**308.** We are so made that we can only derive intense enjoyment from a contrast, and only very little from a state of things. — Sigmund Freud, *Civilization and Its Discontents,* 1930

**309.** The philosophers have only interpreted the world in various ways; the point is to change it. — Karl Marx, *Theses on Feuerbach,* 1845

**310.** Every new adjustment is a crisis in self-esteem. — Eric Hoffer, *The Ordeal of Change,* 1964

**311.** To learn is to change. Education is a process that changes the learner. — George B. Leonard, *Education and Ecstasy,* 1968

**312.** A brave world, Sir, full of religion, knavery and change: we shall shortly see better days. — Aphra Behn, *The Roundheads,* 1682

**313.** Not a change for the better in our human housekeeping has ever taken place that wise and good men have not opposed it — have not prophesied that the world would wake up to find its throat cut in consequence. — James Russell Lowell, *Democracy and Other Addresses,* 1887

**314.** The quest for certainty blocks the search for meaning. Uncertainty is the very condition to impel man to unfold his powers. — Erich Fromm, *Man for Himself,* 1947

**315.** There is danger in reckless change; but greater danger in blind conservatism. — Henry George, *Social Problems,* 1884

**316.** Make haste slowly. — Augustus, 1st c., in Suetonius, *Lives of the Caesars*

**317.** The chief danger in life is that you may take too many precautions. — Alfred Adler, in *Kansas City Times,* January 24, 1977

**318.** There is a certain relief in change, even though it be from bad to worse...it is often a comfort to shift one's position and be bruised in a new place. — Washington Irving, *Tales of a Traveler,* 1824

**319.** The body politic, as well as the human body, begins to die as soon as it is born, and carries in itself the causes of its destruction. — Jean-Jacques Rousseau, *The Social Contract,* 1762

**320.** We had better wait and see. — Herbert Asquith, phrase in speeches, 1910

---

# *Character*

## *See also* **Honesty; Morality; Virtue and Vice**

**321.** You can tell a lot about a fellow's character by his way of eating jelly beans. — Ronald Reagan, in *New York Times,* January 15, 1981

**322.** Small things make base men proud. — William Shakespeare, *Henry VI, Part II,* 1592

**323.** I reject the idea that holding public men and women to a high standard of behavior means that no one will want to run for president. I think it means we can look forward to a better crop than we have had before. — Cal Thomas, in *Washington Times,* October 2, 1987

**324.** The more things a man is ashamed of, the more respectable he is. — George Bernard Shaw, *Man and Superman,* 1903

**325.** No American leader, certainly not Washington or Lincoln, not Jackson or Jefferson at the height of their power, was thought to be above criticism or even above a certain degree of legitimate suspicion. — D. W. Brogan, *The American Character,* 1944

**326.** Thomas Jefferson was treated especially harshly by elements of the early American press. Jefferson's attempt, while young and single, to seduce a neighbor's wife, became a "character issue" for a viciously partisan press. — Larry J. Sabato, *Feeding Frenzy,* 1991

**327.** Some high-ranking politicians are promiscuous with women. After long neglect, their wives tend to cool toward them. They are away from home much of the time and often drink enough to forget some of their duties when an opportunity comes to hand...[but] they take women not for pleasure but as one of the signs of success, like exclusive club memberships and addressing big shots by their first names. — Stimson Bullitt, *To Be a Politician,* 1977

**328.** I don't care if a public official goes home and sleeps with a sheep, unless he's on the agricultural committee dealing with sheep subsidies. — Andrew Lack, in Larry J. Sabato, *Feeding Frenzy,* 1991

329. No man can climb out beyond the limitations of his own character. — John Morley, *Critical Miscellanies,* "Robespierre," 1908

330. It's a delightful thing to think of perfection; but it's vastly more amusing to talk of errors and absurdities. — Fanny Burney, *Camilla,* 1796

331. Only a mediocre person is always at his best. — W. Somerset Maugham, in *Forbes,* August 1, 1977

332. No one ever became extremely wicked suddenly. — Juvenal, *Satires,* ca. 110

333. A person who is fundamentally honest doesn't need a code of ethics. The Ten Commandments and The Sermon on the Mount are all the ethical codes anybody needs. — Harry S Truman, remark, July 10, 1958

334. The measure of any man's virtue is what he would do if he had neither the laws nor public opinion, nor even his own prejudices, to control him. — William Hazlitt, *Characteristics,* 1823

335. The greatest thing in the world is to know how to be oneself. — Michel Eyquem de Montaigne, *Essays,* 1580

336. Honor, without money, is just a disease. — Jean Racine, *Les Plaideurs,* 1668

337. Among politicians one finds cowardice, dishonesty, and pride, but little sloth, lust, cruelty or greed. — Stimson Bullitt, *To Be a Politician,* 1977

338. The appearance of character makes the State unnecessary. The wise man is the State. — Ralph Waldo Emerson, *Essays: Second Series,* "Politics," 1844

339. No government is better than the men who compose it. — John F. Kennedy, speech, October 17, 1960

340. The candidate stands for whatever his pollster tells him the public wants to hear at the moment. The question is not what his party stands for because party is irrelevant.... And so the central issue in a campaign must be the character of the person running for office.

— Brooks Jackson, in Larry J. Sabato, *Feeding Frenzy,* 1991

341. People are always blaming their circumstances for what they are. I don't believe in circumstances. The people who get on in this world are the people who get up and look for the circumstances they want, and if they can't find them, make them. — George Bernard Shaw, *Mrs. Warren's Profession,* 1893

342. Even a child is known by his doings. — Bible, *Proverbs 20:11*

343. It is easy for the strong man to be strong, as it is for the weak to be weak. — Ralph Waldo Emerson, *Essays: First Series,* "Self-Reliance," 1841

344. Talent is best nurtured in solitude; character is best formed in the stormy billows of the world. — Johann Wolfgang von Goethe, *Torquato Tasso,* 1790

345. We are told that talent creates its own opportunities. But it sometimes seems that intense desire creates not only its own opportunities, but its own talents. — Eric Hoffer, *The Passionate State of Mind,* 1954

346. To me, politics is the only area of human life where it's bad form to be ambitious. — Bill Clinton, in *Newsweek,* March 9, 1992

347. A politician may yield to evidence, logic, temptation, or pressure, but he will not do much wrong to help the money-making of a friend. — Stimson Bullitt, *To Be a Politician,* 1977

348. Beware the fury of a patient man. — John Dryden, *Absalom and Achitophel,* 1681

349. I cannot and will not cut my conscience to fit this year's fashions. — Lillian Hellman, letter, May 19, 1952

350. It is public scandal that constitutes offense, and to sin in secret is not to sin at all. — Molière, *Le Tartuffe,* 1669

351. It is in private life that we find the great characters. They are too great to get into the public world. — Gilbert K. Chesterton, *Charles Dickens,* 1906

352. He who says there is no such thing as an honest man, you may be sure

is himself a knave. — George Berkeley, *Maxims Concerning Patriotism,* 1740

**353.** It is not he who has many possessions that you should call blessed: he more rightly deserves that name who knows how to use the gods' gifts wisely and to endure harsh poverty, and who fears dishonor more than death. — Horace, *Odes,* 1st c. B.C.

**354.** We must know how to commit such foolishness as our character demands. — Sébastien Roch Nicholas Chamfort, *Maximes et pensées,* 1805

**355.** I know of no higher fortitude than stubbornness in the face of overwhelming odds. — Louis Nizer, *My Life in Court,* 1962

**356.** 'Tis pride that pulls the country down. — William Shakespeare, *Othello,* 1602–04

**357.** Political courage reads well in editorials, but it doesn't translate into political reality. — Henry Hyde, in *Newsweek,* October 15, 1990

**358.** Does one's integrity ever lie in what he is not able to do? I think that usually it does, for free will does not mean one will, but many wills conflicting in one man. Freedom cannot be conceived simply. — Flannery O'Connor, *Wise Blood,* 1952

**359.** Nixon without Watergate is an absurd proposition. It's like Macbeth without the murder. — Stephen Ambrose, in *Los Angeles Times,* July 17, 1990

## Citizenship

### *See also* Followers; the People

**360.** From a very early age I had imbibed the opinion that it was every man's duty to do all that lay in his power to leave his country as good as he had found it. — William Cobbett, in *Political Register,* December 22, 1832

**361.** It is not always the same thing to be a good man and a good citizen. — Aristotle, *Nicomachean Ethics,* 4th c. B.C.

**362.** The first requisite of a good citizen in this republic of ours is that he shall be able and willing to pull his weight. — Theodore Roosevelt, speech, November 11, 1902

**363.** Everyone who receives the protection of society owes a return for the benefit. — John Stuart Mill, *On Liberty,* 1859

**364.** There are three classes of citizens. The first are the rich, who are indolent and yet always crave more. The second are the poor, who have nothing, are full of envy, hate the rich, and are easily led by demagogues. Between the two extremes lie those who make the state secure and uphold the laws. — Euripides, *The Suppliants,* ca. 420 B.C.

**365.** The citizen is influenced by principle in direct proportion to his distance from the political situation. — Milton Rakove, in *Virginia Quarterly Review,* Summer, 1965

**366.** The citizen who criticizes his country is paying it an implied tribute. — J. William Fulbright, speech, April 28, 1966

**367.** It is the duty of every citizen according to his best capacities to give validity to his convictions in political affairs. — Albert Einstein, *Treasury for the Free World,* 1946

**368.** As citizens of this democracy, you are the rulers and the ruled, the lawgivers and the law-abiding, the beginning and the end. — Adlai Stevenson, speech, September 29, 1952

**369.** Self-governing requires qualities of self-denial and restraint. — John F. Kennedy, speech, September 20, 1960

**370.** Political society exists for the sake of noble actions, and not of mere companionship. — Aristotle, *Politics,* 4th c. B.C.

**371.** In this country . . . the individual subject . . . "has nothing to do with the laws but to obey them." — Samuel Horsley, statement, November 13, 1795

**372.** As soon as public service ceases to be the chief business of the citizens, and they would rather serve with their money than with their persons, the State is not far from its fall. — Jean-Jacques Rousseau, *The Social Contract,* 1762

**373.** The true test of civilization is not the census, nor the size of cities, nor the crops — no, but the kind of man the country turns out. — Ralph Waldo Emerson, *Society and Solitude,* "Civilization," 1870

**374.** It is not the function of our Government to keep the citizen from falling into error; it is the function of the citizen to keep the Government from falling into error. — Robert H. Jackson, *American Communications Association v. Douds,* 1950

**375.** A community is like a ship; everyone ought to be prepared to take the helm. — Henrik Ibsen, *An Enemy of the People,* 1882

# Civil Disobedience *see* Dissent; Law; Order

# *Class*

## See also Haves and Have Nots; Masses and Elites

**376.** The ruling ideas of each age have ever been the ideas of its ruling class. — Karl Marx and Friedrich Engels, *Communist Manifesto,* 1848

**377.** The danger is not that a particular class is unfit to govern. Every class is unfit to govern. — John E. E. Dalberg, letter, April 24, 1881

**378.** The history of all hitherto existing society is the history of class struggles. — Karl Marx and Friedrich Engels, *Communist Manifesto,* 1848

**379.** How right the working classes are in their "materialism." How right they are to realize that the belly comes before the soul. — George Orwell, *Looking Back on the Spanish War,* 1945

**380.** Riches are a good handmaid, but the worst mistress. — Francis Bacon, *De Dignitate et Augmentis Scientiarum,* 1623

**381.** There is a good deal of solemn cant about the common interests of capital and labor. As matters stand, their only common interest is that of cutting each other's throat. — Brooks Atkinson, *Once Around the Sun,* "September 7," 1951

**382.** The class struggle necessarily leads to the dictatorship of the proletariat. — Karl Marx, letter, March 5, 1852

**383.** Our object in the construction of the state is the greatest happiness of the whole, and not that of any one class. — Plato, *The Republic,* ca. 370 B.C.

**384.** Rousseau was the first militant lowbrow. — Isaiah Berlin, in *Observer,* November 9, 1952

**385.** The order of nobility is of great use, too, not only in what it creates, but in what it prevents. It prevents the rule of wealth — the religion of gold. This is the obvious and natural idol of the Anglo-Saxon. — Walter Bagehot, *The English Constitution,* "The House of Lords," 1867

**386.** Inequality has the natural and necessary effect, under the present circumstances, of materializing our upper class, vulgarizing our middle class, and brutalizing our lower class. — Matthew Arnold, *Mixed Essays,* "Equality," 1879

**387.** While there is a lower class, I am in it; while there is a criminal element, I am in it; while there is a soul in prison, I am not free. — Eugene V. Debs, speech, September 14, 1918

**388.** The real working class, though they hate war and are immune to jingoism, are never really pacifist, because their life teaches them something different. — George Orwell, "No, Not One," 1941

**389.** The executive of the modern state is but a committee for managing the common affairs of the whole bourgeoisie. — Karl Marx and Friedrich Engels, *Communist Manifesto,* 1848

**390.** The State is an instrument in the hands of the ruling class used to break the resistance of the adversaries of that class. — Joseph Stalin, *Foundations of Leninism,* 1924

**391.** From shirtsleeves to shirtsleeves in three generations. — Anonymous, 20th c.

**392.** To have a horror of the bourgeois is bourgeois. — Jules Renard, *Journal,* 1889

**393.** Destroy him as you will, the bourgeois always bounces up — execute him, expropriate him, starve him out *en masse,* and he reappears in your children. — Cyril Connolly, in *Observer,* March 7, 1937

**394.** The best political community is formed by citizens of the middle class...those states are likely to be well administered in which the middle class is large. — Aristotle, *Politics,* 4th c. B.C.

**395.** The bourgeois prefers comfort to pleasure, convenience to liberty, and a pleasant temperature to the deathly inner consuming fire. — Hermann Hesse, *Der Steppenwolf,* 1927

**396.** Bourgeois...is an epithet which the riff-raff apply to what is respectable, and the aristocracy to what is decent. — Anthony Hope, *The Dolly Dialogues,* 1894

**397.** You must shock the bourgeois. — Charles Baudelaire, attributed

**398.** The bourgeois are other people. — Jules Renard, *Journal,* January, 1890

**399.** What a horrible invention, the bourgeois, don't you think? — Gustave Flaubert, letter, September 22, 1846

# Cold War

## See also Communism; War

**400.** We are today in the midst of a cold war. — Bernard Baruch, speech, April 16, 1947

**401.** The former Soviet Union may become a democratic federation, or it may just grow into an anarchic and weak conglomeration of markets for other nations' goods and services. — Benjamin R. Barber, *Atlantic,* "Jihad vs. McWorld," March, 1992

**402.** The Communist world understands unity, but not liberty, while the free world understands liberty, but not unity. Eventually the victory may be won by the first of the two sides to achieve the synthesis of both liberty and unity. — Salvador de Madariaga, in *New Yorker,* June 18, 1960

**403.** A Communist has no right to be a mere onlooker. — Nikita S. Khrushchev, report, February 14, 1956

**404.** Marxian Socialism must always remain a portent to the historians of opinion — how a doctrine so illogical and so dull can have exercised so powerful and enduring an influence on the minds of men, and, through them, the events of history. — John Maynard Keynes, *The End of Laissez-Faire,* 1926

**405.** *Glasnost* will go and *perestroika* — defined as privatization and an opening of markets to Western bidders —

will stay. — Benjamin R. Barber, *Atlantic,* "Jihad vs. McWorld," March, 1992

**406.** . . . an evil empire. — Ronald Reagan, speech, March 8, 1983

**407.** Far from being a classless society, Communism is governed by an elite as steadfast in its determination to maintain its prerogatives as any oligarchy known to history. — Robert F. Kennedy, *The Pursuit of Justice,* "Berlin East and West," 1964

**408.** From Stettin in the Baltic to Trieste in the Adriatic an Iron Curtain has descended across the Continent. — Winston S. Churchill, speech, March 5, 1946

**409.** The Iron Curtain still stretches from Stettin to Trieste. But it's a rusting curtain. — George Bush, speech, October 18, 1988

**410.** Khrushchev reminds me of the tiger hunter who has picked a place on the wall to hang the tiger's skin long before he has caught the tiger. The tiger has other ideas. — John F. Kennedy, in *New York Times,* December 24, 1961

**411.** There is no political or ideological difference between the Soviet Union and the United States — nothing which either side would like, or would hope, to achieve at the expense of the other — that would be worth the risks and sacrifices of a military encounter. — George F. Kennan, *The Cloud of Danger,* 1977

**412.** In 1990, Gorbachev is definitely going to have troubles with the military establishment in the Soviet Union. . . . Two things are going on in Gorbachev's chest that make me very apprehensive. . . . Physical assassination is not an impossibility. — Joan Quigley, *What Does Joan Say,* 1990

**413.** We're eyeball to eyeball and I think the other fellow just blinked. — Dean Rusk, in *Saturday Evening Post,* December 8, 1962

## *Common Interests*

**414.** What is common to the greatest number has the least care bestowed upon it. Everyone thinks chiefly of his own, hardly at all of the common interest. — Aristotle, *Politics,* 4th c. B.C.

**415.** The business of everybody is the business of nobody. — Thomas Babington, *Essays Contributed to the Edinburgh Review,* 1843

**416.** There appears then, to be some truth in the conservative dictum that everybody's property is nobody's property. Wealth that is free for all is valued by no one because he who is foolhardy enough to wait for its proper time of use will only find that it has been taken by another . . . The fish in the sea are valueless to the fisherman, because there is no assurance that they will be there for him tomorrow if they are left behind today. — H. Scott Gordon, *Journal of Political Economy, Vol. 64,* "The Economic Theory of a Common-Property Research: The Fishery," 1954

**417.** Unless the number of individuals is quite small, or unless there is coercion or some other special device to make individuals act in their common interest, *national, self-interested individuals will not act to achieve their common or group interests.* — Mancur Olson, Jr., *The Logic of Collective Action,* 1965

**418.** A resolute minority has usually prevailed over an easygoing or wobbly majority whose prime purpose was to be left alone. — James Reston, *Sketches in the Sand,* 1967

**419.** The shortest and best way to make your fortune is to let people see clearly that it is in their best interests to promote yours. — Jean La Bruyère, *Characters,* "Of the Gifts of Fortune," 1688

**420.** You can't get four people to agree on too many things. — Charles T. Vaughn, Jr., in *Inc. Magazine,* March, 1988

**421.** For it is your business, when the wall next door catches fire. — Horace, *Epistles*, 1st c. B.C.

**422.** "The Tragedy of the Commons." — Garrett Hardin, in *Science, Vol. 162*, article title, 1968

**423.** For even among just men, once goods are indivisible over large numbers of individuals, their actions decided upon in isolation from one another will not lead to the general good. — John Rawls, *A Theory of Justice*, 1971

**424.** Because I don't trust him, we are friends. — Bertolt Brecht, *Mutter Courage*, 1939

**425.** There can be hope only for a society which acts as one big family, and not as many separate ones. — Anwar al-Sadat, *In Search of Identity*, 1978

**426.** A democracy is more than a form of government; it is primarily a mode of associated living, of conjoint communicated experience. — John Dewey, *Democracy and Education*, 1916

**427.** The only way by which anyone divests himself of his natural liberty and puts on the bonds of civil society is by agreeing with other men to join and unite into a community. — John Locke, *Second Treatise of Civil Government*, 1690

**428.** We must all hang together, or assuredly we shall all hang separately. — Benjamin Franklin, statement, July 4, 1776

# *Communism*

## *See also* Capitalism; Cold War; Property

**429.** Communism is the corruption of a dream of justice. — Adlai Stevenson, speech, 1951

**430.** Communism is a Russian autocracy turned upside down. — Alexander Ivanovich Hertzen, *The Development of Revolutionary Ideas in Russia*, 1851

**431.** Communism is Soviet power plus the electrification of the whole country. — Lenin, report to Congress, 1920

**432.** Communism is like prohibition, it's a good idea but it won't work. — Will Rogers, *Weekly Articles*, 1927

**433.** Communism is not love. Communism is a hammer which we use to crush the enemy. — Mao Zedong, in *Time*, December 18, 1950

**434.** Christian theology is the grandmother of Bolshevism. — Oswald Spengler, *The Hour of Decision*, 1934

**435.** Every Communist must grasp the truth: "Political power grows out of the barrel of a gun." — Mao Zedong, *Selected Works of Mao Zedong*, 1965

**436.** The most alarming spectacle today is not the spectacle of the atomic bomb in an unfederated world, it is the spectacle of the Americans beginning to accept the device of loyalty oaths and witchhunts, beginning to call anybody they don't like a Communist. — E. B. White, letter, April 27, 1952

**437.** The objection to a Communist always resolves itself into the fact that he is not a gentleman. — H. L. Mencken, *Minority Report*, 1956

**438.** I am a good friend to Communists abroad but I do not like them at home. — Souvanna Phouma, in *Life*, November 3, 1961

**439.** I thank heaven for a man like Adolf Hitler, who built a front line of defense against the anti-Christ of Communism. — Frank Buchman, in *New York World-Telegram*, August 26, 1936

**440.** You cannot deal with rattlesnakes and you cannot deal with Communist governments. — Jesse Helms, in *Los Angeles Times*, June 6, 1989

**441.** Convergence between the two

ostensibly different industrial systems occurs at all fundamental points... Those who speak for the unbridgeable gulf that divides the free world from the Communist world... can survive the evidence only for a time. — John Kenneth Galbraith, *The New Industrial State,* 1967

**442.** Communism's collapse has called forth old animosities and new dangers. — Bill Clinton, inaugural address, January 20, 1993

**443.** Communist charity does not even allow its enemies to die an honorable death. — Raymond Aron, *The Great Debate, The Opium of the Intellectuals,* 1965

**444.** A red is any son-of-a-bitch who wants thirty cents an hour when we're payin' twenty-five! — John Steinbeck, *The Grapes of Wrath,* 1939

**445.** No Communist country has ever solved the problem of succession. — Henry Kissinger, in *Time,* March 12, 1979

**446.** All I know is that I am not a Marxist. — Karl Marx, attributed

**447.** Marxism is essentially a product of the bourgeois mind. — Joseph Schumpeter, *Capitalism, Socialism and Democracy,* 1942

# Competence

**448.** Every man loves what he is good at. — Thomas Shadwell, *A True Widow,* 1679

**449.** Man is not the sum of what he has but the totality of what he does not yet have, of what he might have. — Jean-Paul Sartre, *Situations,* 1939

**450.** Perfection has one grave defect: it is apt to be dull. — W. Somerset Maugham, *The Summing Up,* 1938

**451.** You know what charm is: a way of getting the answer yes without having asked any clear question. — Albert Camus, *The Fall,* 1956

**452.** The sad truth is that excellence makes people nervous. — Shana Alexander, *The Feminist Eye,* 1970

**453.** The single most exciting thing you encounter in government is competence, because it's so rare. — Daniel P. Moynihan, in *New York Times,* March 2, 1976

**454.** Everyone is bound to bear patiently the results of his own example. — Phaedrus, *Fables,* ca. 10 B.C.

**455.** Unless a man has the talents to make something of himself, freedom is an irksome burden. — Eric Hoffer, *The True Believer,* 1951

**456.** There is no substitute for talent. Industry and all the virtues are of no avail. — Aldous Huxley, *Point Counter Point,* 1928

**457.** There is the same difference between talent and genius that there is between a stone mason and a sculptor. — Robert G. Ingersoll, *Shakespeare,* 1891

**458.** When a true genius appears in the world, you may know him by this sign, that the dunces are all in confederacy against him. — Jonathan Swift, *Thoughts on Various Subjects,* 1711

**459.** Mediocrity knows nothing higher than itself, but talent instantly recognizes genius. — Arthur Conan Doyle, *The Valley of Fear,* 1914

**460.** If every man worked at that for which nature fitted him, the cows would be well tended. — Jean Pierre Claris de Florian, *La Vacher de la Garde-chasse,* 1792

**461.** There's no such hell on earth as that of the man who knows himself doomed to mediocrity in the work he loves. — Philip Barry, *You and I,* 1922

# Compromise

**462.** Compromise is but the sacrifice of one right or good in the hope of retaining another, too often ending in the loss of both. — Tryon Edwards, *The New Dictionary of Thought*, 1957

**463.** Compromise may be man's best friend. — George Will, in *Washington Post*, February 28, 1988

**464.** Truth is the glue that holds governments together. Compromise is the oil that makes governments go. — Gerald R. Ford, statement, November 15, 1973

**465.** It is well known what a middleman is: he is a man who bamboozles one party and plunders the other. — Benjamin Disraeli, speech, April 11, 1845

**466.** All government — indeed, every human benefit and enjoyment, every virtue and every prudent act — is founded on compromise and barter. — Edmund Burke, speech, March 22, 1775

**467.** The heart of man is made to reconcile the most glaring contradictions. — David Hume, *Essays, Moral, Political, and Literary*, 1741–42

**468.** Some say that we were brought to the verge of war. Of course we were . . . We walked to the brink and we looked it in the face. — John Foster Dulles, in *Life*, January 16, 1956

**469.** Our swords shall play the orators for us. — Christopher Marlowe, *Tamburlaine the Great*, 1590

**470.** The interesting question in connection with compromise obviously turns upon the placing of the boundary that divides wise suspense in forming opinions, wise reserve in expressing them, and wise tardiness in trying to realize them, from unavowed disingenuousness and self-illusion, from voluntary dissimulation and from indolence and pusillanimity. — John Morley, *On Compromise*, 1874

**471.** By uniting we stand, by dividing we fall. — John Dickinson, "The Liberty Song," 1768

**472.** For how agree the kettle and the earthen pot together. — Bible: Apocrypha, *Ecclesiasticus 13:2*

**473.** The uncompromising attitude is more indicative of an inner uncertainty than of deep conviction. — Eric Hoffer, *The Passionate State of Mind*, 1954

**474.** I don't say "never" to anything. — Richard M. Bressler, in *Business Week*, August 3, 1987

# Conflict

## *See also* Enemies

**475.** I guess there are two schools of thought about this — yours and mine. — Ernest Gallo, in *New York Times*, May 2, 1988

**476.** Adversity is sometimes hard upon a man; but for one man who can stand prosperity, there are a hundred that will stand adversity. — Thomas Carlyle, *On Heroes, Hero-Worship, and the Heroic*, 1841

**477.** No mortal man has ever served at the same time his passions and his best interests. — Sallust, *The War with Catiline*, ca. 40 B.C.

**478.** Let us learn to respect sincerity of conviction in our opponents. — Otto von Bismarck, speech, December 18, 1863

**479.** The opposition is indispensable. A good statesman, like any other sensible human being, always learns more from his opponents than from his fervent supporters. — Walter Lippmann, in *Atlantic,* August, 1939

**480.** When the Government of the day and the Opposition of the day take the same side, one can be almost sure that some great wrong is at hand. — George William Erskine Russell, *One Look Back,* 1912

**481.** Opposition, *n.* In politics the party that prevents the Government from running amuck by hamstringing it. — Ambrose Bierce, *The Devil's Dictionary,* 1906

**482.** I am grateful for even the sharpest criticism, as long as it sticks to the point. — Otto von Bismarck, speech, November 30, 1874

**483.** Each generation of critics does nothing but take the opposite of the truths accepted by their predecessors. — Marcel Proust, *Remembrance of Things Past,* 1913–26

**484.** I always cheer up immediately if an attack is particularly wounding because I think, well, if they attack one personally, it means they have not a single political argument left. — Margaret Thatcher, in *Daily Telegraph,* March 21, 1986

**485.** I hate victims who respect their executioners. — Jean-Paul Sartre, *The Confinement of Altona,* 1960

**486.** How often we should stop in the pursuit of folly, if it were not for the difficulties that continually beckon us onwards. — Arthur Helps, *Thoughts in the Cloister and the Crowd,* 1835

**487.** The dignity of truth is lost with much protesting. — Ben Jonson, *Catiline's Conspiracy,* 1611

**488.** There is no good in arguing with the inevitable. The only argument available with an east wind is to put on your overcoat. — James Russell Lowell, *Democracy and Other Addresses,* 1887

**489.** If you fear making anyone mad, then you ultimately probe for the lowest common denominator of human achievement. — Jimmy Carter, speech, November 9, 1978

**490.** Insofar as it represents a genuine reconciliation of differences, a consensus is a fine thing; insofar as it represents a concealment of differences, it is a miscarriage of democratic procedure. — J. William Fulbright, speech, October 22, 1965

**491.** "A house divided against itself cannot stand." I believe this government cannot endure permanently, half slave and half free. — Abraham Lincoln, speech, June 16, 1858

**492.** When in the course of human events, it becomes necessary for one people to dissolve the political bonds which have connected them with another, and to assume among the powers of the earth the separate and equal station to which the laws of nature and of Nature's God entitle them, a decent respect to the opinions of mankind requires that they should declare the causes which impel them to the separation. — Thomas Jefferson, *Declaration of Independence,* July 4, 1776

**493.** All history is only one long story to this effect: men have struggled for power over their fellow-men in order that they might win the joys of earth at the expense of others, and might shift the burdens of life from their own shoulders upon those of others. — William Graham Sumner, *The Forgotten Man,* 1883

**494.** I respect only those who resist me, but I cannot tolerate them. — Charles de Gaulle, in *New York Times,* May 12, 1968

**495.** The first blow is half the battle. — Oliver Goldsmith, *She Stoops to Conquer,* 1773

**496.** Speaking generally, punishment hardens and numbs, it produces concentration, it sharpens the consciousness of alienation, it strengthens the power of resistance. — Friedrich Wilhelm Nietzsche, *The Genealogy of Morals,* 1887

**497.** A man that studieth revenge keeps his own wounds green. — Francis Bacon, *Essays,* "Of Revenge," 1625

**498.** When bad men combine, the good must associate; else they will fall, one by one, an unpitied sacrifice in a contemptible struggle. — Edmund Burke,

*Thoughts on the Cause of the Present Discontent,* 1770

**499.** Many can bear adversity but few contempt. — Thomas Fuller, M.D., *Gnomologia,* 1732

**500.** Better to have him [J. Edgar Hoover] inside the tent pissing out, than outside pissing in. — Lyndon B. Johnson, in David Halbersham, *The Best and the Brightest,* 1972

**501.** Calumnies are answered best with silence. — Ben Jonson, *Volpone,* 1605

**502.** The essence of a free government consists in an effectual control of rivalries. — John Adams, *Discourses on Davila,* 1789

**503.** Hatred is a tonic, it makes one live, it inspires vengeance; but pity kills, it makes our weakness weaker. — Honoré de Balzac, *La Peau de Chagrin,* 1831

**504.** Holy Deadlock. — A. P. Herbert, book title, 1934

**505.** Come not between the dragon and his wrath. — William Shakespeare, *King Lear,* 1605–06

**506.** Difference of opinion leads to inquiry, and inquiry to truth. — Thomas Jefferson, letter, March 13, 1815

# *Conformity*

## *See also* Conservatives

**507.** Conformity is the philosophy of indifference. — Dagobert D. Runes, *Treasury of Thought,* 1966

**508.** Conformity is the jailer of freedom and the enemy of growth. — John F. Kennedy, speech, September 25, 1961

**509.** When we lose the right to be different, we lose the privilege to be free. — Charles Evans Hughes, speech, June 17, 1925

**510.** Unity is desirable, but it can too easily become the goal, and complete unity can only be gained at the cost of individual liberty. — M. Judd Harmon, *Political Thought,* 1964

**511.** The degree of non-conformity present — and tolerated — in a society might be looked upon as a symptom of its state of health. — Ben Shahn, *The Shape of Content,* 1957

**512.** Every society honors its live conformists and its dead troublemakers. — Mignon McLaughlin, *The Neurotic's Notebook,* 1963

**513.** True individualists tend to be quite unobservant; it is the snob, the would-be sophisticate, the frightened conformist, who keeps a fascinated or worried eye on what is in the wind. — Louis Kronenberger, *Company Manners,* 1954

**514.** Man is a rebel. He is committed by his biology not to conform. — Robert M. Lindner, *Must You Conform?,* 1956

**515.** We are, of course, a nation of differences. Those differences don't make us weak. They're the same source of our strength. — Jimmy Carter, speech, October 21, 1976

**516.** The voice of protest, of warning, of appeal is never more needed than when the clamor of fife and drum, echoed by the press and too often by the pulpit, is bidding all men fall in and keep step and obey in silence the tyrannous word of command. Then, more than ever, it is the duty of the good citizen not to be silent. — Charles Eliot Norton, *True Patriotism,* 1898

**517.** We are half ruined by conformity, but we should be wholly ruined without it. — Charles Dudley Warner, *My Summer in a Garden,* "Eighteenth Week," 1871

**518.** Our society cannot have it both ways: to maintain a conformist and ignoble system *and* to have skillful and spirited men to man that system. — Paul Goodman, *Growing Up Absurd,* 1960

**519.** No society in which eccentricity is a matter of reproach can be in a wholesome state. — John Stuart Mill, *Principle of Political Economy,* 1848

520. We seldom judge a man to be sensible unless his ideas agree with ours. — François de La Rochefoucauld, *Maxims,* 1665

# Congress *see* Legislatures

# *Conscience*

## *See also* Morality

521. Conscience is but a word that cowards use, Devised at first to keep the strong in awe. — William Shakespeare, *Richard III,* 1591

522. A good conscience is the best divinity. — Thomas Fuller, M.D., *Gnomologia,* 1732

523. Wild liberty breeds iron conscience; natures with great impulses have great resources, and return from afar. — Ralph Waldo Emerson, *The Conduct of Life,* "Power," 1860

524. No people can be truly happy, though under the greatest Enjoyment of Civil Liberties, if abridged of the Freedom of their Consciences. — William Penn, *Charter of Liberties,* 1701

525. Never do anything against conscience even if the state demands it. — Albert Einstein, in *Saturday Review,* April 30, 1955

526. Good men must not obey the laws too well. — Ralph Waldo Emerson, *Essays: Second Series,* "Politics," 1844

527. When I refuse to obey an unjust law, I do not contest the right of the majority to command, but I simply appeal from the sovereignty of the people to the sovereignty of mankind. — Alexis de Tocqueville, *Democracy in America,* 1835

528. Conscience has no more to do with gallantry than it has to do with politics. — Richard Brinsley Sheridan, *The Duenna,* 1775

529. Wholesome of life and free of crimes. — Horace, *Odes,* 1st c. B.C.

530. No one can rule guiltlessly, and least of all those whom history compels to hurry. — Edgar Snow, *Journey to the Beginning,* 1958

531. There is one thing alone that stands the brunt of life throughout its course: a quiet conscience. — Euripides, *Hippolytus,* 428 B.C.

532. Suspicion always haunts the guilty mind; The thief doth fear each bush an officer. — William Shakespeare, *Henry VI, Part III,* 1592

533. Give me the liberty to know, to utter, and to argue freely according to conscience, above all liberties. — John Milton, *Areopagitica,* 1644

534. Most people sell their souls and live with a good conscience on the proceeds. — Logan Pearsall Smith, *Afterthoughts,* 1931

# *Conservatives*

## *See also* Conformity; Liberals

535. A conservative is someone who admires radicals a century after they're dead. — Anonymous

536. A conservative is a liberal who was mugged the night before. — Frank L. Rizzo, in *American Opinion,* November, 1975

537. The Conservatives . . . being

by the law of their existence the stupidest party. — John Stuart Mill, *Representative Government,* 1861

**538.** A Conservative is a man with two perfectly good legs who, however, has never learned how to walk forward. — Franklin D. Roosevelt, radio address, October 26, 1939

**539.** Conservative, *n.* A statesman who is enamoured of existing evils, as distinguished from the Liberal, who wishes to replace them with others. — Ambrose Bierce, *The Devil's Dictionary,* 1906

**540.** [Conservatives] define themselves in terms of what they oppose. — George Will, in *Newsweek,* September 30, 1974

**541.** One might say that the only difference between old-school liberals and conservatives is that the former would destroy the market through public means and the latter through private means. — Theodore Lowi, in *American Political Science Review,* March, 1967

**542.** The true conservative is the man who has a real concern for injustices and takes thought against the day of reckoning. — Franklin D. Roosevelt, speech, September 29, 1936

**543.** The democrat is a young conservative; the conservative an old democrat. The aristocrat is the democrat ripe and gone to seed. — Ralph Waldo Emerson, *Representative Men,* "Napoleon; or, The Man of the World," 1850

**544.** A conservative is a man who is too cowardly to fight and too fat to run. — Elbert Hubbard, *The Note Book,* 1927

**545.** Conservatism is distrust of the people tempered by fear. — William E. Gladstone, speech, 1878

**546.** Conservatives do not believe that the political struggle is the most important thing in life. . . The simplest of them prefer fox-hunting — the wisest religion. — Quinton Hogg, *The Case for Conservatism,* 1947

**547.** Men are of a predominantly conservative temper. They prefer the familiar difficulties to the possible benefits of the unknown. — M. Judd Harmon, *Political Thought,* 1964

**548.** The healthy stomach is nothing if not conservative. Few radicals have good digestions. — Samuel Butler (II), *Notebooks,* 1912

**549.** Stupid people can only see their own side to a question: they cannot even imagine any other side possible. So, as a rule, stupid people are Conservative. — Charles Grant Allen, in *Westminister Gazette,* 1894

**550.** When a nation's young men are conservative, its funeral bell is already rung. — Henry Ward Beecher, *Proverbs from Plymouth Pulpit,* 1887

**551.** It is one of the surprising things about youth that it can so easily be the most conservative of all ages. — Randolph Bourne, *Youth and Life,* 1913

**552.** Come, come, my conservative friend, wipe the dew off your spectacles, and see that the world is moving. — Elizabeth Cady Stanton, *The Woman's Bible,* 1895

**553.** I do not know which makes a man more conservative — to know nothing but the present, or nothing but the past. — John Maynard Keynes, *The End of Laissez-Faire,* 1926

**554.** What is conservatism? Is it not adherence to the old and tried against the new and untried? — Abraham Lincoln, speech, February 27, 1860

**555.** Conservatism is a lump, is a euphemism for selfishness. — Charles Grant Allen, in *Westminister Gazette,* 1894

**556.** America — a conservative country without any conservative ideology. — C. Wright Mills, *The Power Elite,* 1956

**557.** Being an intellectual of the right continued to strike me as an oxymoron. But if one got to the minimalist government of the right through cynicism — the unmarking of the parochial claims behind the alleged good works of government — the trek was more acceptable. — David A. Stockman, *The Triumph of Politics,* 1987

**558.** How can wealth persuade poverty to use its political freedom to keep wealth in power? Here lies the whole art of Conservative politics in the twentieth century. — Aneurin Bevan, *In Place of Fear,* 1952

**559.** From my conservative viewpoint and my conservative ideology, the more Congress is messed up, the better the country is. — Dan Quayle, in *USA Today,* April 28, 1992

**560.** All conservatism is based upon the idea that if you leave things alone you leave them as they are. But you do not. If you leave a thing alone you leave it to a torrent of change. — Gilbert K. Chesterton, *Orthodoxy,* 1908

**561.** Success breeds conservatism, and that means a love affair with the status quo and an aversion to change. — Frank Popoff, in *New York Times,* November 22, 1987

**562.** There is always a certain meanness in the argument of conservatism, joined with a certain superiority in its facts. — Ralph Waldo Emerson, *The Conservative,* 1842

**563.** Conservatism discards Prescription, shrinks from Principle, disavows Progress; having rejected all respect for antiquity, it offers no redress for the present, and makes no preparation for the future. — Benjamin Disraeli, *Coningsby,* 1844

**564.** Revolutionaries are more formalistic than conservatives. — Italo Calvino, *Il Barone Rampante,* 1957

**565.** Conservatism goes for comfort, reform for truth. — Ralph Waldo Emerson, lecture, December 9, 1841

**566.** It seems to be a barren thing, this Conservatism — an unhappy crossbreed, the mule of politics that engenders nothing. — Benjamin Disraeli, *Coningsby,* 1844

# *Consistency*

**567.** Consistency is a jewel; and, as is the case of other jewels, we may marvel at the price that some people will pay for it. — George Santayana, *Character and Opinion in the United States,* 1920

**568.** Inconsistency — the only thing in which men are consistent. — Horace Smith, *The Tin Trumpet,* 1836

**569.** Democracy is the recurrent suspicion that more than half of the people are right more than half of the time. — E. B. White, *The Wild Flag,* 1946

**570.** The consistent thinker, the consistently moral man, is either a walking mummy or else, if he has not succeeded in stifling all his vitality, a fanatical monomaniac. — Aldous Huxley, *Do What You Will,* 1929

**571.** I believe that all of us have the capacity for one adventure inside us, but great adventure is facing responsibility day after day. — William Gordon, in *Time,* November 19, 1965

**572.** Every central government worships uniformity; uniformity relieves it from inquiry into an infinity of details, which must be attended to if rules have to be adapted to different men, instead of indiscriminately subjecting all men to the same rule. — Alexis de Tocqueville, *Democracy in America,* 1835

**573.** The brute necessity of believing something so long as life lasts does not justify any belief in particular. — George Santayana, *Scepticism and Animal Faith,* 1923

**574.** Mediocre men often have the most acquired knowledge. — Claude Bernard, *Introduction to the Study of Experimental Medicine,* 1865

**575.** It is also said of me that I now and then contradict myself. Yes, I improve wonderfully as time goes on. — George Jean Nathan, *The Theater in the Fifties,* 1953

**576.** Too much consistency is as bad for the mind as it is for the body. Consistency is contrary to nature, contrary to life. The only completely consistent people are the dead. — Aldous Huxley, *Do What You Will,* 1929

# Constitution

## See also Law; Rights

577. Constitutions should be short and vague. — Napoleon I, conference, January 29, 1803

578. The principles of a free constitution are irrevocably lost, when the legislative power is nominated by the executive. — Edward Gibbon, *Decline and Fall of the Roman Empire,* 1776–88

579. Freedom of religion; freedom of the press, and freedom of person under the protection of *habeas corpus,* and trial by juries impartially selected. These principles form the bright constellation which has gone before us, and guided our steps through an age of revolution and reformation. — Thomas Jefferson, inaugural address, March 4, 1801

580. We are under a Constitution, but the Constitution is what the judges say it is, and the judiciary is the safeguard of our liberty and of our property under the Constitution. — Charles Evans Hughes, speech, May 3, 1907

581. The Constitution is not neutral. It was designed to take the government off the backs of people. — William O. Douglas, *The Court Years 1939–75,* 1980

582. Most faults are not in our Constitution, but in ourselves. — Ramsey Clark, in *Washington Post,* November 12, 1970

583. The layman's constitutional view is that what he likes is constitutional, and that which he doesn't like is unconstitutional. — Hugo L. Black, in *New York Times,* February 26, 1971

584. Each public officer who takes an oath to support the constitution swears that he will support it as he understands it, and not as it is understood by others. — Andrew Jackson, message, July 10, 1832

585. I invoke the genius of the Constitution. — William Pitt (I), speech, November 18, 1777

586. Liberty cannot lie apart from constitutional principle. — Woodrow Wilson, in *Political Science Quarterly,* June, 1887

587. A government of laws, and not of men. — John Adams, in *Boston Gazette,* 1774

# Corruption

## See also Dirty Politics; Morality; Virtue and Vice

588. Wrongdoing can only be avoided if those who are not wronged feel the same indignation at it as those who are. — Solon, ca. 600 B.C.

589. Among a people generally corrupt, liberty cannot long exist. — Edmund Burke, *Letter to the Sheriffs of Bristol,* 1777

590. Our worst enemies here are not the ignorant and the simple, however cruel; our worst enemies are the intelligent and corrupt. — Graham Greene, *The Human Factor,* 1978

591. There is nothing more agreeable in this life than to make peace with the Establishment — and nothing more corrupting. — A. J. P. Taylor, *New Statesman,* 1953

592. Those who corrupt the public mind are just as evil as those who steal from the public purse. — Adlai Stevenson, speech, September 12, 1952

593. Corruption, the most infallible symptom of constitutional liberty. — Edward Gibbon, *Decline and Fall of the Roman Empire,* 1776–88

**594.** Democracy substitutes election by the incompetent many for appointment by the corrupt few. — George Bernard Shaw, *Man and Superman,* 1903

**595.** The more corrupt the State the more numerous the laws. — Cornelius Tacitus, *Annals,* 2nd c.

**596.** Contradiction is the salt which keeps truth from corruption. — John Lancaster Spalding, *Means and Ends of Education,* 1895

**597.** So long as selfishness makes government needful at all, it must make every government corrupt, save one in which all men are represented. — Herbert Spencer, *Social Statics,* 1851

**598.** The taking of a bribe or gratuity should be punished with as severe penalties as the defrauding of the State. — William Penn, *Some Fruits of Solitude,* 1693

**599.** For if it is supposed that institutions are reasonably just, then it is of great importance that the authorities should be impartial and not influenced by personal, monetary, or other irrelevant considerations in their handling of particular cases. — John Rawls, *A Theory of Justice,* 1971

**600.** Government is more than the sum of all the interests; it is the paramount interest, the public interest. It must be the efficient, effective agent of a responsible citizenry, not the shelter of the incompetent and the corrupt. — Adlai Stevenson, speech, 1948

**601.** Corruption wins not more than honesty. — William Shakespeare, *Henry VIII,* 1613

**602.** The American way is to seduce a man by bribery and make a prostitute of him. Or else to ignore him, starve him into submission and make a hack out of him. — Henry Miller, *The Air-Conditioned Nightmare,* 1945

**603.** I think I can say, and say with pride, that we have some legislatures that bring higher prices than any in the world. — Mark Twain, in *Chicago Daily News,* October 9, 1882

**604.** Anybody who gets away with something will come back to get away with a little bit more. — Harold Schonberg, in *New York Times,* October 8, 1972

**605.** Everybody has a little bit of Watergate in him. — Billy Graham, remark, February 3, 1974

**606.** It was beautiful and simple as all truly great swindles are. — O. Henry, *Gentle Grafter,* 1908

## Crisis

**607.** When written in Chinese, the word *crisis* is composed of two characters. One represents danger and the other represents opportunity. — John F. Kennedy, speech, April 12, 1959

**608.** These are the times that try men's souls. — Thomas Paine, *The American Crisis,* 1776–83

**609.** Political crises are moral crises. — Octavio Paz, *Postscript,* 1970

**610.** A crisis of legitimacy is a crisis of change. — Seymour Martin Lipset, *Political Man,* 1981

**611.** In crisis the most daring course is often safest. — Henry Kissinger, *Years of Upheaval,* 1982

**612.** Seizure of power is the point of the uprising; its political task will be clarified after the seizure. To delay action is the same as death. — Lenin, letter, November 6, 1917

**613.** Next week there can't be any crisis. My schedule is already full. — Henry Kissinger, in *New York Times,* October 28, 1973

**614.** It is exciting to have a real crisis on your hands, when you have spent half your political life dealing with humdrum issues like the environment. — Margaret Thatcher, speech, May 14, 1982

**615.** You can't learn too soon that

the most useful thing about a principle is that it can always be sacrificed to expediency. — W. Somerset Maugham, *The Circle,* 1921

**616.** No man is justified in doing evil on the ground of expediency. — Theodore Roosevelt, *The Strenuous Life: Essays and Addresses,* 1900

**617.** Sometimes in life situations develop that only the half-crazy can get out of. — François de La Rochefoucauld, *Maxims,* 1665

**618.** Depend upon it sir, when a man knows he is to be hanged in a fortnight, it concentrates his mind wonderfully. — Samuel Johnson, in James Boswell, *Life of Samuel Johnson,* 1791

**619.** In politics, there is no use looking beyond the next fortnight. — Joseph Chamberlain, in A. J. Balfour, *Chapters of Autobiography,* 1930

## Cynics and Skeptics

**620.** I have named the destroyers of nations: comfort, plenty and security— out of which grows a bored and slothful cynicism, in which rebellion against the world as it is, and myself as I am, are submerged in listless self-satisfaction. —John Steinbeck, *America and Americans,* 1966

**621.** Cynicism is intellectual dandyism. — George Meredith, *The Egoist,* 1879

**622.** Cynicism is a luxury and is something that people who have real needs can't afford. I can't afford to be cynical because it is hope that keeps the people alive. — Jesse Jackson, in *Los Angeles Times,* May 15, 1992

**623.** Cynicism is, after all, simply idealism gone sour. — Will Herberg, *Judaism and Modern Man,* 1951

**624.** The only deadly sin I know is cynicism. — Henry Lewis Stimson, *On Active Service in Peace and War,* 1948

**625.** Cynics know the answers without having penetrated deeply enough to know the questions. When challenged by mysterious truths, they marshall "facts." — Marilyn Ferguson, *The Aquarian Conspiracy,* 1980

**626.** Skeptic always rhymes with septic; the spirit died of intellectual poisoning. — Franz Werfel, *Realism and Inwardness,* 1930

**627.** I am too much of a skeptic to deny the possibility of anything. — T. H. Huxley, letter, March 22, 1886

**628.** Scepticism is the chastity of the intellect. — George Santayana, *Scepticism and Animal Faith,* 1923

**629.** The path to sound credence is through the thick forest of skepticism. — George Jean Nathan, *Materia Critica,* 1924

**630.** Skepticism, riddling the faith of yesterday, prepares the way for the faith of tomorrow. — Romain Rolland, *Jean Christophe,* 1904–12

**631.** What has not been examined impartially has not been well examined. Skepticism is therefore the first step toward truth. — Denis Diderot, *Pensées Philosophiques,* 1746

**632.** The civilized man has a moral obligation to be skeptical, to demand the credentials of all statements that claim to be facts. — Bergen Evans, *The Natural History of Nonsense,* 1946

**633.** We should never accept anything reverently without asking it a great many very searching questions. —George Bernard Shaw, *The Apple Cart,* 1930

**634.** Rough work, iconoclasm— but the only way to get at truth. — Oliver Wendell Holmes, Sr., *The Professor at the Breakfast-Table,* 1860

**635.** Man is an animal who lifts his head to the sky and does not see the spiders on his ceiling. — Jules Renard, *Journal*, April, 1894

**636.** The optimist proclaims that we live in the best of all possible worlds; and the pessimist fears this is true. — James B. Cabell, *The Silver Stallion*, 1926

**637.** "Do you know what a pessimist is?" "A man who thinks everybody is as nasty as himself, and hates them for it." — George Bernard Shaw, *An Unsocial Socialist*, 1887

**638.** An election is coming. Universal peace is declared, and the foxes have a sincere interest in prolonging the lives of the poultry. — George Eliot, *Felix Holt*, 1866

**639.** Every day, in every way, things are getting worse and worse. — William F. Buckley, Jr., in *National Review*, July 2, 1963

**640.** If an historian were to relate truthfully all the crimes, weaknesses and disorders of mankind, his readers would take his work for satire rather than for history. — Pierre Bayle, *Historical and Critical Dictionary*, 1697

**641.** It's hard not to write satire. — Juvenal, *Satires*, ca. 110

---

# *Decisions*

## *See also* Problems and Solutions

**642.** We have to make some hard choices. . . Elected officials back away from this like a dog backs away from an angry cat. They're worried about getting scratched in the face by some angry special interest. — H. Ross Perot, *United We Stand*, 1992

**643.** One man that has a mind and knows it can always beat ten men who haven't and don't. — George Bernard Shaw, *The Apple Cart*, 1930

**644.** I never sit on a fence. I am either on one side or another. — Harry S Truman, speech, October 30, 1948

**645.** People who dislike doubt often get into worse trouble by committing themselves to an immature and untenable decision. — Charles Horton Cooley, *Life and the Student*, 1931

**646.** It is better to stir up a question without deciding it, than to decide it without stirring it up. — Joseph Joubert, *Pensées*, 1810

**647.** Some people, however long their experience or strong their intellect, are temperamentally incapable of reaching firm decisions. — James Callaghan, in *Harvard Business Review*, November/December, 1986

**648.** There is no more miserable human being than one in whom nothing is habitual but indecision. — William James, *The Principles of Psychology*, 1890

**649.** My sad conviction is that people can only agree about what they're not really interested in. — Bertrand Russell, *New Statesman*, 1939

**650.** One cool judgment is worth a thousand hasty councils. The thing to do is to supply light and not heat. — Woodrow Wilson, speech, January 29, 1916

**651.** The ability to arrive at complex decisions is the hallmark of the educated person. — Jean Mayer, in *People Weekly*, November 15, 1976

**652.** The man who is denied the opportunity of making decisions of importance begins to regard as important the decisions he is allowed to make. — C. Northcote Parkinson, *Parkinson's Law*, 1958

**653.** Philosophical decisions are nothing but the reflections of common life, methodized and corrected. — David Hume, *An Enquiry Concerning Human Understanding*, 1748

**654.** It is seldom that statesmen have the option of choosing between a good and an evil. — Charles Caleb Colton, *Lacon*, 1820–22

**655.** Decision making isn't a matter of arriving at a right or wrong answer, it's a matter of selecting the most effective course of action from among less effective courses of action. — Philip Marvin, *Developing Decisions for Action,* 1971

**656.** The plain fact is that there are no conclusions. — James Jeans, *Physics and Philosophy,* 1942

**657.** Example is always more efficacious than precept. — Samuel Johnson, *Rasselas,* 1759

**658.** Circumstances rule men; men do not rule circumstances. — Herodotus, *The History,* ca. 450 B.C.

**659.** The offhanded decision of some commonplace mind high in office at a critical moment influences the course of events for a hundred years. — Thomas Hardy, in F. E. Hardy, *The Early Years of Thomas Hardy,* 1928

**660.** If someone tells you he is going to make "a realistic decision," you immediately understand that he has resolved to do something bad. — Mary McCarthy, *On the Contrary,* 1962

**661.** Intractable problems are usually not intractable because there are no solutions, but because there are no solutions without severe side effects. — Lester C. Thurow, *The Zero-Sum Society,* 1980

**662.** Don't wait for the Last Judgment. It takes place every day. — Albert Camus, *The Fall,* 1956

---

# Democracy

## *See also* Government, Forms of

**663.** All the ills of democracy can be cured by more democracy. — Alfred E. Smith, speech, June 27, 1935

**664.** My anchor is democracy — and more democracy. — Franklin D. Roosevelt, speech, August 18, 1937

**665.** Nothing but a permanent body can check the imprudence of democracy. — Alexander Hamilton, speech, June 18, 1787

**666.** The ultimate rulers of our democracy are not a president and senators and congressmen and government officials, but the voters of this country. — Franklin D. Roosevelt, speech, July 8, 1938

**667.** Man's capacity for justice makes democracy possible, but man's inclination to injustice makes democracy necessary. — Reinhold Niebuhr, *The Children of Light and the Children of Darkness,* 1944

**668.** If we are to keep our democracy, there must be one commandment: Thou shalt not ration justice. — Learned Hand, speech, February 16, 1951

**669.** Today we frankly recognize that democracy can be no more than aspiration, and have rule not so much by the people as by the cleverest people; not an aristocracy of birth, not a plutocracy of wealth, but a true meritocracy of talent. — Michael Young, *The Rise of the Meritocracy,* 1958

**670.** As a matter of practical necessity, socialist democracy may eventually turn out to be more of a sham than capitalist democracy ever was. — Joseph Schumpeter, *Capitalism, Socialism and Democracy,* 1942

**671.** Envy is the basis of democracy. — Bertrand Russell, *The Conquest of Happiness,* 1930

**672.** In democracies, nothing is more great or more brilliant than commerce. — Alexis de Tocqueville, *Democracy in America,* 1835

**673.** A great democracy must be progressive or it will soon cease to be great or a democracy. — Theodore Roosevelt, speech, November 5, 1910

**674.** The experience of democracy is like the experience of life itself — always changing, infinite in its varieties, sometimes turbulent and all the more valuable for having been tested by adversity. — Jimmy Carter, speech, January 2, 1978

**675.** In the strict sense of the term, a true democracy has never existed, and will never exist. It is against natural order that the great number should govern and that the few should be governed. — Jean-Jacques Rousseau, *The Social Contract,* 1762

**676.** Political democracy, as it exists and practically works in America, with all its threatening evils, supplies a training school for making first-class men. It is life's gymnasium, not of good only, but of all. — Walt Whitman, *Democratic Vistas,* 1871

**677.** Democratic institutions generally give men a lofty notion of their country and themselves. — Alexis de Tocqueville, *Democracy in America,* 1835

**678.** Puritanism, believing itself quick with the seed of religious liberty, laid, without knowing it, the egg of democracy. — James Russell Lowell, *Literary Essays, Vol. II,* "New England Two Centuries Ago," 1870–90

**679.** Self-criticism is the secret weapon of democracy, and candor and confession are good for the political soul. — Adlai Stevenson, speech, July 21, 1952

**680.** Democracy, which shuts the past against the poet, opens the future before him. — Alexis de Tocqueville, *Democracy in America,* 1835

**681.** A democracy smugly disdainful of new ideas would be a sick democracy. — Dwight D. Eisenhower, letter, June 14, 1953

**682.** Were there a people of gods, their government would be democratic. So perfect a government is not for me. — Jean-Jacques Rousseau, *The Social Contract,* 1762

**683.** No one pretends that democracy is perfect or all-wise. Indeed, it has been said that democracy is the worst form of Government except all those other forms that have been tried from

time to time. — Winston S. Churchill, speech, November 11, 1947

**684.** Two cheers for Democracy: one because it admits variety and two because it permits criticism. Two cheers are quite enough: there is no occasion to give three. — E. M. Forster, *Two Cheers for Democracy,* 1951

**685.** I have always been of the mind that in a democracy manners are the only effective weapons against the Bowie knife. — James Russell Lowell, letter, March 4, 1873

**686.** Under democracy one party always devotes its chief energies to trying to prove that the other party is unfit to rule — and both commonly succeed, and are right. — H. L. Mencken, *Minority Report,* 1956

**687.** I'm tired of hearing it said that democracy doesn't work. Of course it doesn't work. It isn't supposed to work. We are supposed to work it. — Alexander Woollcott, in *Kansas City Times,* January 4, 1977

**688.** Secrecy and a free, democratic government don't mix. — Harry S Truman, in Mark Miller, *Plain Speaking: An Oral Biography of Harry S Truman,* 1974

**689.** Democracy requires institutions which support conflict and disagreement as well as those which sustain legitimacy and consensus. — Seymour Martin Lipset, *Political Man,* 1981

**690.** If this nation is not truly democratic, then she must die. — Alexander Crummell, speech, November 20, 1888

**691.** The world must be made safe for democracy. Its peace must be planted on the tested foundations of political liberty. — Woodrow Wilson, speech, April 2, 1917

**692.** We must be the great arsenal of democracy. — Franklin D. Roosevelt, radio address, December 29, 1940

**693.** If democracy loses its touch, then no great war will be needed to overwhelm it. If it keeps and enhances its strength, no great war need come again. — Vannevar Bush, *Modern Arms and Free Men,* 1949

**694.** The tendencies of democracies are, in all things, to mediocrity, since the tastes, knowledge, and principles of the majority form the tribunal of appeal. —James Fenimore Cooper, *The American Democrat*, 1838

**695.** It is the American vice, the democratic disease, which expresses its tyranny by reducing everything unique to the level of the herd. —Henry Miller, *The Wisdom of the Heart*, 1941

**696.** Television is democracy at its ugliest. —Paddy Chayefsky, in *New York Times*, November 14, 1976

**697.** The taste of democracy becomes a bitter taste when the fullness of democracy is denied. —Max Lerner, *Actions and Passions*, 1949

**698.** If we cannot say that a "high" level of education is a *sufficient* condition for democracy, the available evidence suggests that it comes close to being a *necessary* one. —Seymour Martin Lipset, *Political Man*, 1981

**699.** That a peasant may become king does not render the kingdom democratic. —Woodrow Wilson, speech, August 31, 1910

**700.** Democracy needs cleavage within linguistic or religious groups, not between them. —Seymour Martin Lipset, *Political Man*, 1981

**701.** Democratic nations care but little for what has been, but they are haunted by visions of what will be. —Alexis de Tocqueville, *Democracy in America*, 1835

**702.** Democracy grows from the bottom up and cannot be imposed from the top down. . . Democrats need to seek out indigenous democratic impulses. . . Typically, democracy in a hurry often looks something like France in 1794 or China in 1989. —Benjamin R. Barber, in *Atlantic*, "Jihad vs. McWorld," March, 1992

**703.** Democracy is the form of government in which the free are rulers. —Aristotle, *Politics*, 4th c. B.C.

**704.** Democracy in a complex society may be defined as a political system which supplies regular constitutional opportunities for changing the governing officials, and a social mechanism which permits the largest possible part of the population to influence major decisions by choosing among contenders for political office. —Seymour Martin Lipset, *Political Man*, 1981

**705.** Democracy is not a static thing. It is an everlasting march. —Franklin D. Roosevelt, speech, October 1, 1935

**706.** Democracy is the most difficult of all forms of government, since it requires the widest spread of intelligence. —Will Durant and Ariel Durant, *The Lessons of History*, 1968

**707.** Democracy, the practice of self-government, is a covenant among free men to respect the rights and liberties of their fellows. —Franklin D. Roosevelt, State of the Union Address, January 4, 1939

**708.** Democracy is the superior form of government, because it is based on a respect for man as a reasonable being. —John F. Kennedy, *Why England Slept*, 1940

**709.** Democracy is the worst form of government. It is the most inefficient, the most clumsy, the most unpractical. . . Yet democracy is the only form of social order admissible, because it is the only one consistent with justice. —Robert Briffault, *Rational Evolution*, 1930

**710.** Democracy is a form of government which may be rationally defended not as being good, but as being less bad than any other. —William Ralph Inge, *Outspoken Essays: First Series*, 1919

**711.** Democracy is good. I say this because other systems are worse. —Jawaharlal Nehru, in *New York Times*, January 25, 1961

**712.** Democracy is not only or even primarily a means through which different groups can attain their ends or seek the good society; it is the good society itself in operation. —Martin Seymour Lipset, *Political Man*, 1981

**713.** A democracy is the most difficult kind of government to operate. It represents the last flowering, really, of the human experience. — John F. Kennedy, speech, September 6, 1960

**714.** Democracy is not a fragile flower; still it needs cultivating. — Ronald Reagan, speech, June 8, 1982

**715.** Democracy is not so much a form of government as a set of principles. — Woodrow Wilson, in *Atlantic*, March, 1901

**716.** It is almost universally felt that when we call a country democratic we are praising it: consequently the defenders of every kind of regime claim that it is a democracy, and fear that they might have to stop using the word if it were tied down to any one meaning. — George Orwell, *Shooting an Elephant*, 1950

**717.** [In the lexicon of 1968] *Democracy* is a phoney word to be sneered at unless carefully modified by such phrases as *democracy of the streets, democracy of direct action* or *participatory democracy*. — Theodore H. White, *The Making of the President 1968*, 1969

**718.** Democracy means government by discussion but it is only effective if you can stop people talking. — Clement Attlee, *Anatomy of Britain*, 1962

**719.** Democracy is the name we give to the people each time we need them. — Robert de Flers, *L'Habit vert*, 1912

**720.** Democracy is the theory that the common people know what they want, and deserve to get it good and hard. — H. L. Mencken, *A Little Book in C Major*, 1916

**721.** Democracy is, by the nature of it, a self-canceling business; and gives in the long run a net result of zero. — Thomas Carlyle, *Chartism*, 1839

**722.** Democracy is...the worship of jackals by jackasses. — H. L. Mencken, *A Book of Burlesques*, "Sententiae," 1920

**723.** A perfect democracy is therefore the most shameless thing in the world. — Edmund Burke, *Reflections on the Revolution in France*, 1790

**724.** Democracy is that system of government under which the people, having 35,717,342 native-born adult whites to choose from, including thousands who are handsome and many who are wise, pick out a Coolidge to be head of the State. — H. L. Mencken, *Prejudices, Fifth Series*, 1926

# Despotism

## See also Rulers and Ruling; Tyranny

**725.** We are not to expect to be translated from despotism to liberty in a featherbed. — Thomas Jefferson, letter, April 2, 1790

**726.** If Despotism failed only for want of a capable benevolent despot, what chance has Democracy, which requires a whole population of capable voters. — George Bernard Shaw, *Man and Superman*, 1903

**727.** Democracy passes into despotism. — Plato, *The Republic*, ca. 370 B.C.

**728.** A state too extensive in itself, or by virtue of its dependencies, ulti-

mately falls into decay; its free government is transformed into a tyranny; it disregards the principles which it should preserve, and finally degenerates into despotism. — Simón Bolívar, letter, summer, 1815

**729.** The fundamental article of my political creed is that despotism, or unlimited sovereignty, or absolute power, is the same in a majority of a popular assembly, an aristocratical council, an oligarchical junto, and a single emperor. — John Adams, letter, November 13, 1815

**730.** Man is about the same, in the main, whether with despotism, or whether with freedom. — Walt Whitman, *Notes Left Over,* 1881

**731.** The benevolent despot who sees himself as a shepherd of the people still demands from others the submissiveness of sheep. — Eric Hoffer, *The Ordeal of Change,* 1964

**732.** To have the welfare and the lives of millions placed at our disposal, is a sort of warrant, a challenge to squander them without mercy. — William Hazlitt, "On the Spirit of Monarchy," 1823

**733.** The possession of unlimited power will make a despot of almost any man. There is a possible Nero in the gentlest human creature that walks. — Thomas Bailey Aldrich, *Ponkapog Papers,* 1903

**734.** It sometimes happens that he who would not hurt a fly will hurt a nation. — Henry Taylor, *The Statesman,* 1836

**735.** A country governed by a despot is an inverted cone. — Samuel Johnson, in James Boswell, *Life of Samuel Johnson,* 1791

**736.** Despotism accomplishes great things illegally; liberty doesn't even go to the trouble of accomplishing small things legally. — Honoré de Balzac, *La Peau de chagrin,* 1831

**737.** Whenever you have an efficient government you have a dictatorship. — Harry S Truman, speech, April 28, 1959

**738.** It can be laid down as a rule that those who speak most of liberty are least inclined to use it.... The general who tells his troops...that they are in the forefront of the fight for freedom is a man who has always submitted happily to army discipline. — John Kenneth Galbraith, *The New Industrial State,* 1967

**739.** The greatest dangers to liberty lurk in insidious encroachments by men of zeal, well-meaning but without understanding. — Louis D. Brandeis, *Olmstead v. United States,* 1928

**740.** The tree of liberty only grows when watered by the blood of tyrants. — Bertrand Barère de Vieuzac, speech, January 16, 1793

**741.** O freedom, what liberties are taken in thy name! — Daniel George, *The Perpetual Pessimist,* 1963

**742.** We know that the road to freedom has always been stalked by death. — Angela Davis, in *Daily World,* August 25, 1971

**743.** The cause of liberty becomes a mockery if the price to be paid is the wholesale destruction of those who are to enjoy liberty. — Mohandas K. Gandhi, *Non-Violence in Peace and War,* 1948

**744.** No matter how noble the objectives of a government, if it blurs decency and kindness, cheapens human life, and breeds ill will and suspicion — it is an evil government. — Eric Hoffer, *The Passionate State of Mind,* 1954

**745.** When power feels itself totally justified and approved it immediately destroys whatever freedom we have left; and that is fascism. — Luis Buñuel, in *New York Times Magazine,* March 11, 1973

**746.** Every despotism has a specially keen and hostile instinct for whatever keeps up human dignity and independence. — Henri-Frédérick Amiel, *Journal,* 1852

**747.** You have not converted a man because you have silenced him. — John Morley, *On Compromise,* 1874

**748.** Freedom suppressed and again regained bites with keener fangs than freedom never endangered. — Cicero, *De Officiis,* ca. 44 B.C.

**749.** Totalitarianism is bad, gangsterism is worse, but capitulationism is the worst of all. — Daniel P. Moynihan, in *Time,* January 26, 1976

**750.** Totalitarianism spells simplification: an enormous reduction in the variety of aims, motives, interests, human types, and, above all, in the categories and units of power. — Eric Hoffer, *The Ordeal of Change,* 1964

**751.** It is the common failing of totalitarian regimes that they cannot really understand the nature of our democracy. They mistake dissent for disloyalty. They mistake restlessness for a rejection of policy. They mistake a few committees for a country. They mistake individual speeches for public policy. —Lyndon B. Johnson, speech, September 29, 1967

752. If one man offers you democracy and another offers you a bag of grain, at what stage of starvation will you prefer the grain to the vote? —Bertrand Russell, *Silhouettes in Satire,* 1958

753. A police state finds it cannot command the grain to grow. —John F. Kennedy, State of the Union Address, January 14, 1963

754. It is true that you cannot eat freedom and you cannot power machinery with democracy. But then neither can political prisoners turn on the light in the cells of a dictatorship. —Corazon C. Aquino, in *Washington Post,* June 29, 1992

755. Where it is a duty to worship the sun it is pretty sure to be a crime to examine the laws of heat. —John Morley, *Voltaire,* 1872

756. Everywhere the sun is setting on the day of the dictator. And for the dictators across the world, democracy is the greatest revenge. —Banazir Bhutto, in *Los Angeles Times,* June 8, 1989

757. Power is not a means, it is an end. One does not establish a dictatorship in order to safeguard a revolution; one makes the revolution in order to establish the dictatorship. —George Orwell, *1984,* 1949

758. I don't mind dictatorships abroad provided they are pro–American. —George Wallace, in *Time,* October 27, 1975

759. Dictators ride to and fro upon tigers which they dare not dismount. And the tigers are getting hungry. —Winston S. Churchill, *While England Slept,* 1936

760. When you stop a dictator there are always risks. But there are greater risks in not stopping a dictator. —Margaret Thatcher, interview, April 5, 1982

761. The cost of liberty is less than the price of repression. —W. E. B. DuBois, *John Brown,* 1909

762. It Can't Happen Here. —Sinclair Lewis, novel title, 1935

763. Big Brother is watching you. —George Orwell, *1984,* 1949

# Diplomacy

## See also Government, Roles and Functions of

764. All diplomacy is a continuation of war by other means. —Zhau Enlai, in *Saturday Evening Post,* March 27, 1954

765. To jaw-jaw is better than to war-war. —Winston S. Churchill, speech, June 26, 1954

766. War is regarded as nothing but the continuation of state policy with other means. —Karl von Clausewitz, *On War,* 1833

767. War is not the continuation of policy. It is the breakdown of policy. —Hans von Seeckt, *Thoughts of a Soldier,* 1929

768. Our patience will achieve more than our force. —Edmund Burke, *Reflections on the Revolution in France,* 1790

769. Diplomacy is to do and say the nastiest thing in the nicest way. —Isaac Goldberg, *The Reflex,* 1930

770. Diplomacy is letting someone else have your way. —Lester B. Pearson, in *Vancouver Sun,* March 18, 1965

771. A diplomat is a person who can tell you to go to hell in such a way that you actually look forward to the trip. —Caskie Stinnett, *Out of the Red,* 1960

772. The trick of statesmanship is

to turn the inevitable to one's own advantage. — Christopher Layne, in *Atlantic,* June, 1989

**773.** Diplomats write Notes, because they wouldn't have the nerve to tell the same thing to each other's face. — Will Rogers, *The Autobiography of Will Rogers,* 1949

**774.** Conferences at the top level are always courteous. Name-calling is left to the foreign ministers. — W. Averell Harriman, news summaries, August 1, 1955

**775.** In ninety-nine cases out of a hundred, when there is a quarrel between two states, it is generally occasioned by some blunder of a ministry. — Benjamin Disraeli, speech, February 19, 1858

**776.** The statesman must weigh the rewards of success against the penalties of failure. And he is permitted only one guess. — Henry Kissinger, in *Newsweek,* October 22, 1990

**777.** Vacillation and inconsistency are as incompatible with successful diplomacy as they are with the national dignity. — Benjamin Harrison, speech, September 11, 1888

**778.** The statesman's duty is to bridge the gap between his nation's experience and his vision. — Henry Kissinger, *Years of Upheaval,* 1982

**779.** Statesman, yet friend to Truth! of soul sincere, In action faithful, and in honor clear; Who broke no promise, served no private end, Who gained no title, and who lost no friend. — Alexander Pope, *Epistles to Several Persons,* 1720

**780.** Foreign relations are like human relations. They are endless. The solution of one problem usually leads to another. — James Reston, *Sketches in the Sand,* 1967

**781.** Men are linked in friendship. Nations are linked only by interests. — Rolf Hochhuth, *The Soldiers,* 1967

**782.** I asked Tom if countries always apologized when they had done wrong, and he says: "Yes; the little ones does." — Mark Twain, *Tom Sawyer Abroad,* 1894

**783.** If the United Nations is a country unto itself, then the commodity it exports most is words. — Esther B. Fein, in *New York Times,* October 14, 1985

**784.** There is nothing more likely to start disagreement among people or countries than an agreement. — E. B. White, *One Man's Meat,* 1944

**785.** All political decisions are taken under great pressure, and if a treaty serves its turn for ten or twenty years, the wisdom of its framers is sufficiently confirmed. — H. A. L. Fisher, *Political Prophecies,* 1918

**786.** Treaties, you see, are like girls and roses: they last while they last. — Charles de Gaulle, speech, July 2, 1963

**787.** Personally, I feel happier now that we have no allies to be polite to and to pamper. — George VI, statement, June 27, 1940

**788.** The first requirement of a statesman is that he be dull. — Dean Acheson, in *Observer,* June 21, 1970

**789.** A diplomat these days is nothing but a head-waiter who's allowed to sit down occasionally. — Peter Ustinov, *Romanoff and Juliet,* 1956

**790.** Diplomats are useful only in fair weather. As soon as it rains they drown in every drop. — Charles de Gaulle, in *Newsweek,* October 1, 1962

**791.** The only real diplomacy ever performed by a diplomat is in deceiving their own people after their dumbness has got them into a war. — Will Rogers, *The Autobiography of Will Rogers,* 1949

**792.** An ambassador is an honest man sent to lie abroad for the good of his country. — Henry Wotton, in Izaak Walton, *Reliquiae Wottonianae,* 1651

**793.** It is good to be on your guard against an Englishman who speaks French perfectly; he is very likely to be a card-sharper or an attache in the diplomatic service. — W. Somerset Maugham, *The Summing Up,* 1938

**794.** In statesmanship get formalities right, never mind about the moralities. — Mark Twain, *Following the Equator,* 1897

**795.** The difference between being

an elder statesman And posing successfully as an elder statesman Is practically negligible. — T. S. Eliot, *The Elder Statesman*, 1958

**796.** Diplomacy . . . the art of nearly deceiving all your friends, but not quite deceiving all your enemies. — Kufi Busia, interview, February 2, 1970

**797.** Watching foreign affairs is sometimes like watching a magician; the eye is drawn to the hand performing the dramatic flourishes, leaving the other hand — the one doing the important job — unnoticed. — David K. Shipler, in *New York Times*, March 15, 1987

---

# Dirty Politics

## See also Corruption; Politics

**798.** Those people who treat politics and morality separately will never understand either of them. — Jean-Jacques Rousseau, *Emile*, 1762

**799.** We do many things at the federal level that would be considered dishonest and illegal if done in the private sector. — Donald T. Regan, in *New York Times*, August 25, 1986

**800.** In politics nothing is contemptible. — Benjamin Disraeli, *Vivian Grey*, 1826

**801.** The choice in politics isn't usually between black and white. It's between two horrible shades of gray. — Peter Thorneycroft, in *London Sunday Telegraph*, February 11, 1979

**802.** Vain hope to make men happy by politics! — Thomas Carlyle, *Journal*, 1831

**803.** Politics ruins the character. — Otto von Bismarck, attributed

**804.** Politics, where fat, bald, disagreeable men, unable to be candidates themselves, teach a president how to act on a public stage. — Jimmy Breslin, *Table Money*, 1986

**805.** Politics, as the word is commonly understood, are nothing but corruptions. — Jonathan Swift, *Thoughts on Various Subjects*, 1711

**806.** Politics, and the fate of mankind, are shaped by men without ideals and without greatness. — Albert Camus, *Notebooks 1935–1942*, 1962

**807.** Than politics the American citizen knows no higher profession — for it is the most lucrative. — Alexis de Tocqueville, *Democracy in America*, 1835

**808.** The flood of money that gushes into politics today is a pollution of democracy. — Theodore H. White, in *Time*, November 19, 1984

**809.** People have got to know whether or not their president is a crook. Well, I'm not a crook. I earned everything I've got. — Richard M. Nixon, statement, November 17, 1973

**810.** Politics is supposed to be the second oldest profession. I have come to realize that it bears a very close resemblance to the first. — Ronald Reagan, statement, March 2, 1977

**811.** Politics makes strange bedfellows. — Charles Dudley Warner, *My Summer in a Garden*, 1870

**812.** Strange bedfellows makes politics. — J. M. Freestone, remark, 1977

**813.** Political language . . . is designed to make lies sound truthful and murder respectable, and to give an appearance of solidity to pure wind. — George Orwell, *Shooting an Elephant*, 1950

**814.** There can be no whitewash at the White House. — Richard M. Nixon, speech, April 30, 1973

**815.** Once the toothpaste is out of the tube, it is awfully hard to get it back in. — H. R. Haldeman, statement, April 8, 1973

**816.** If you're in politics, you're a

whore anyhow. It doesn't make any difference who you sleep with. — Robert S. Strauss, in *Texas Monthly,* February, 1978

**817.** Politics are now nothing more than means of rising in the world. — Samuel Johnson, in James Boswell, *Life of Samuel Johnson,* 1791

**818.** You never really win anything in politics. All you get is a chance to play for higher stakes and perform at a higher level. — John Sears, in *Time,* January 21, 1980

**819.** The argument of the broken window pane is the most valuable argument in modern politics. — Emmeline Pankhurst, in George Dangerfield, *The Strange Death of Liberal England,* 1936

**820.** All issues are political issues, and politics itself is a mass of lies, evasions, folly, hatred and schizophrenia.

— George Orwell, *Shooting an Elephant,* 1950

**821.** Politics are vulgar when they are not liberalized by history, and history fades into mere literature when it loses sight of its relation to practical politics. — John Seeley, *The Expansion of England,* 1883

**822.** I have always noticed in politics how often men are ruined by having too good a memory. — Alexis de Tocqueville, *Recollections,* 1893

**823.** Great blunders are often made, like large ropes, of a multitude of fibers. — Victor Hugo, *Les Misérables,* 1862

**824.** [Watergate] was worse than a crime, it was a blunder. — Richard M. Nixon, in *Observer,* December 3, 1978 (paraphrasing Tallyrand, "It is worse than a crime, it is a blunder")

# *Dissent*

## *See also* Freedom of Speech

**825.** In a democracy dissent is an act of faith. — J. William Fulbright, *The Arrogance of Power,* 1966

**826.** Dissent...is a right essential to any concept of the dignity and freedom of the individual; it is essential to the search for truth in a world wherein no authority is infallible. — Norman Thomas, in *New York Times Magazine,* November 15, 1959

**827.** The dissenter is every human being at those moments of his life when he resigns momentarily from the herd and thinks for himself. — Archibald MacLeish, in *The Nation,* December 4, 1937

**828.** Discussion in America means dissent. — James Thurber, *Lanterns and Lances,* "The Duchess and the Bugs," 1961

**829.** We must not confuse dissent with disloyalty. — Edward R. Murrow, broadcast, March 7, 1954

**830.** Here in America we are descended in blood and in spirit from revolutionists and rebels — men and women who dared to dissent from accepted doctrine. As their heirs, we may never confuse honest dissent with disloyal subversion. — Dwight D. Eisenhower, speech, May 31, 1954

**831.** Mere unorthodoxy or dissent from the prevailing mores is not to be condemned. The absence of such voices would be a symptom of grave illness in our society. — Earl Warren, *Sweezy v. New Hampshire,* 1957

**832.** In the end it is worse to suppress dissent than to run the risk of heresy. — Learned Hand, lecture, 1958

**833.** Persecution is the first law of society because it is always easier to suppress criticism than to meet it. — Howard Mumford Jones, *Primer of Intellectual Freedom,* 1949

**834.** A free society is a society where

it is safe to be unpopular. — Adlai Stevenson, speech, October 7, 1952

**835.** He that goeth about to persuade a multitude that they are not so well governed as they ought to be, shall never want attentive and favorable hearers. — Richard Hooker, *Ecclesiastical Polity*, 1593

**836.** It is much easier to be critical than to be correct. — Benjamin Disraeli, speech, January 24, 1860

# Dogma

## See also Belief

**837.** The modern world is filled with men who hold dogmas so strongly that they do not even know that they are dogmas. — Gilbert K. Chesterton, *Heretics*, 1905

**838.** The mind petrifies if a circle be drawn around it, and it can hardly be denied that dogma draws a circle round the mind. — George Moore, *Confessions of a Young Man*, 1888

**839.** At least two-thirds of our miseries spring from human stupidity, human malice and those great motivators and justifiers of malice and stupidity, idealism, dogmatism and proselytizing zeal on behalf of religious or political idols. — Aldous Huxley, *Tomorrow and Tomorrow and Tomorrow*, 1956

**840.** Men still want the crutch of dogma, of beliefs fixed by authority, to relieve them of the trouble of thinking and responsibility of directing their activity by thought. — John Dewey, *Democracy and Education*, 1916

**841.** Truths turn into dogmas the moment they are disputed. — Gilbert K. Chesterton, *Heretics*, 1905

**842.** When people are least sure, they are often most dogmatic. — John Kenneth Galbraith, *The Great Crash, 1929*, 1955

**843.** If you have nothing to say, or rather, something extremely stupid and obvious, say it, but in a "plonking" tone of voice — i.e. roundly, but hollowly and dogmatically. — Stephen Potter, *Lifemanship*, 1950

**844.** The wave of the future is not the conquest of the world by a single dogmatic creed but the liberation of the diverse energies of free nations and free men. — John F. Kennedy, speech, March 23, 1962

**845.** Dogmatism is puppyism come to its full growth. — Douglas Jerrold, *A Man Made of Money*, 1849

**846.** Any stigma, as the old say is, will serve to beat a dogma. — Philip Guedalla, *Masters and Men*, 1923

# Duty

## See also Patriotism

**847.** My duty is to speak; I have no wish to be an accomplice. — Émile Zola, letter, January 15, 1898

**848.** Do your duty, and leave the outcome to the Gods. — Pierre Corneille, *Horace*, 1640

**849.** The strongest is never strong enough to be always the master, unless he transfers strength into right, and obedience into duty. — Jean-Jacques Rousseau, *The Social Contract*, 1762

**850.** A sense of duty is moral glue,

constantly subject to stress. — William Safire, in *New York Times,* May 23, 1986

**851.** To renounce liberty is to renounce being a man, to surrender the rights of humanity and even its duties. — Jean-Jacques Rousseau, *The Social Contract,* 1762

**852.** The first duty of government is to see that people have food, fuel and clothes. The second, that they have means of moral and intellectual education. — John Ruskin, *Fors Clavigera,* 1876

**853.** The State seeks to hinder every free activity by its censorship, its supervision, its police; and holds this hindering to be its duty, because it is in truth a duty of self-preservation. — Max Stirner, *The Ego and His Own,* 1845

**854.** When a stupid man is doing something he is ashamed of he always declares that it is his duty. — George Bernard Shaw, *Caesar and Cleopatra,* 1901

**855.** I therefore believe it is my duty to my country to love it, to support its Constitution, to obey its laws, to respect its flag, and to defend it against all enemies. — William Tyler Page, "The American's Creed," adopted by Congress April 3, 1918

**856.** Every subject's duty is the king's; but every subject's soul is his own. — William Shakespeare, *Henry V,* 1598–1600

# Economic Freedom

## See also Economics

**857.** Markets are enemies of parochialism, isolation, fractiousness, war. — Benjamin R. Barber, *Atlantic,* "Jihad vs. McWorld," March, 1992

**858.** The populace doesn't want to be fed; it wants more freedom to graze on its own. — Irving Kristol, in *Esquire,* May 23, 1978

**859.** Civilization and profits go hand in hand. — Calvin Coolidge, speech, November 27, 1920

**860.** Extinguish free enterprise and you extinguish liberty. — Margaret Thatcher, in *Time,* May 14, 1979

**861.** What I want to see above all is that this country remains a country where someone can always get rich. That's the one thing we have and that must be preserved. — Ronald Reagan, press conference, 1983

**862.** We have always known that heedless self-interest was bad morals; we know now that it is bad economics. — Franklin D. Roosevelt, inaugural address, January 20, 1937

**863.** Money is coined liberty, and so it is ten times dearer to a man who is deprived of freedom. If money is jingling in his pocket, he is half consoled, even though he cannot spend it. — Fyodor Dostoyevski, *House of the Dead,* 1862

**864.** A free economy demands engagement in the economic mainstream. Isolation and protectionism doom its practitioners to degradation and want. — George Bush, speech, August 1, 1991

**865.** Everything that is really great and inspiring is created by the individual who can labor in freedom. — Albert Einstein, *Out of My Later Years,* 1950

**866.** The best social program in this country is a job for every single American, especially young people who have not seen their parents or their grandparents work. — Michael R. White, in *Christian Science Monitor,* August 12, 1991

**867.** The State rests on the *slavery of labor.* If *labor* becomes *free,* the State is lost. — Max Stirner, *The Ego and His Own,* 1845

**868.** Liberty produces wealth and

wealth destroys liberty. — Henry Demarest Lloyd, *Wealth Against Commonwealth,* 1894

**869.** Lippmann had been right: Economic controls are the malignant cancer of state power. — David A. Stockman, *The Triumph of Politics,* 1987

**870.** Liberty and monopoly cannot live together. — Henry Demarest Lloyd, *Wealth Against Commonwealth,* 1894

**871.** There can be no liberty unless there is economic liberty. — Margaret Thatcher, in *Time,* May 14, 1979

**872.** Market competition is the only form of organization which can afford a large measure of freedom to the individual. — Frank Hyneman Knight, *Freedom and Reform,* 1947

**873.** There can be no real freedom without the freedom to fail. — Eric Hoffer, *The Ordeal of Change,* 1964

**874.** Democracy is clearly most appropriate for countries which enjoy an economic surplus and least appropriate for countries where there is an economic insufficiency. — David Morris Potter, *People of Plenty: Economic Abundance and the American Character,* 1954

**875.** It is a mistake to believe that a just and good society must wait upon a high material standard of life. What men want is meaningful work in free association with others. — John Rawls, *A Theory of Justice,* 1971

**876.** Only when he has ceased to need things can a man truly be his own master and so really exist. — Anwar al-Sadat, *In Search of Identity,* 1978

**877.** The love of money is the root of all evil. — Bible, *I Timothy, 6:10*

**878.** Lack of money is the root of all evil. — George Bernard Shaw, *Man and Superman,* 1903

**879.** A criminal is a person with predatory instincts who has not sufficient capital to form a corporation. — Howard Scott, *The New Dictionary of Thought,* 1957

--------- *Economics* ---------

## See also Budgets; Capitalism; Class; Economic Freedom; Haves and Have Nots; Inflation

**880.** Once demystified, the dismal science is nothing less than the study of power. — Richard J. Barnet, in *New York Times,* September 16, 1973

**881.** Politics is not a level field. It systematically disrupts the natural economic terrain, using the fiscal and legal powers of the state to grant privileges, subsidies, protections, and advantages unattainable in the competitive market. — David A. Stockman, *The Triumph of Politics,* 1987

**882.** Commerce is the greatest of all political interests. — Joseph Chamberlain, speech, November 13, 1896

**883.** The pulse of modern life is economic and the fundamental principle of economic production is individual independence. — Ch'en Tu-hsiu, in *The New Youth,* December, 1916

**884.** The state is or can be master of money, but in a free society it is master of very little else. — William H. Beveridge, *Voluntary Action,* 1948

**885.** Political institutions are a superstructure resting on an economic foundation. — Lenin, *The Three Sources and Three Constituent Parts of Marxism,* 1913

**886.** No nation was ever ruined by trade. — Benjamin Franklin, *Thoughts on Commercial Subjects,* ca. 1780

**887.** In every well-governed state, wealth is a sacred thing; in democracies it is the only sacred thing. — Anatole France, *L'Île des pingouins,* 1908

**888.** The chief business of the American people is business. — Calvin Coolidge, speech, January 17, 1925

**889.** The moral flabbiness born of

the exclusive worship of the bitch-goddess *success*. That — with the squalid cash interpretation put on the word success — is our national disease. — William James, letter, September 11, 1906

**890.** The almighty dollar, that great object of universal devotion. — Washington Irving, *Wolfert's Roost*, 1855

**891.** People of the same trade seldom meet together, even for merriment and diversion, but the conversation ends in a conspiracy against the public, or in some contrivance to raise prices. It is impossible indeed to prevent such meetings by any law which either could be executed, or would be consistent with liberty and justice. — Adam Smith, *Wealth of Nations, Vol. I, Book I,* 1776

**892.** These capitalists generally act harmoniously, and in concert, to fleece the people. — Abraham Lincoln, speech, January 11, 1837

**893.** God is on everyone's side. . . . And, in the final analysis, he is on the side of those with plenty of money and large armies. — Jean Anouilh, *L'Alouette,* 1953

**894.** There can be no economy where there is no efficiency. — Benjamin Disraeli, speech, October 1, 1868

**895.** Nixon and his Treasury Secretary John Connolly. . . had turned Republican economics on its head, imposed wage and price controls, and abolished the gold standard. It was perverse. Everything the free market scholars said would happen — shortages, bottlenecks, investment distortions, waste, irrationality, and more inflation — did happen before my eyes. — David A. Stockman, *The Triumph of Politics,* 1987

**896.** If ignorance paid dividends, most Americans could make a fortune out of what they don't know about economics. — Luther Hodges, in *Wall Street Journal,* March 14, 1962

**897.** There are two problems in my life. The political ones are insoluble and the economic ones are incomprehensi-

ble. — Alec Douglas-Home, in *New York Times,* January 9, 1964

**898.** One of the greatest pieces of economic wisdom is to know what you do not know. — John Kenneth Galbraith, in *Time,* March 3, 1961

**899.** Most of the economics as taught is a form of brain damage. — Ernst F. Schumacher, in *The Reader,* March 25, 1977

**900.** The instability of the economy is equaled only by the instability of economists. — John Henry Williams, in *New York Times,* June 2, 1956

**901.** In all recorded history there has not been one economist who had to worry about where the next meal was coming from. — Peter F. Drucker, in *New York Times,* May 16, 1976

**902.** Economy is going without something you do want in case you should, some day, want something you probably won't want. — Anthony Hope, *The Dolly Dialogues,* 1894

**903.** It's a recession when your neighbor loses his job; it's a depression when you lose your own. — Harry S Truman, in *Observer,* April 6, 1958

**904.** When more and more people are thrown out of work, unemployment results. — Calvin Coolidge, attributed

**905.** Call a thing immoral or ugly, soul-destroying or a degradation of man, a peril to the peace of the world or to the well-being of future generations: as long as you have not shown it to be "uneconomic" you have not really questioned its right to exist, grow, and prosper. — Ernst F. Schumacher, *Small Is Beautiful,* 1973

**906.** The notion that big business and big labor and big government can sit down around a table somewhere and work out the direction of the American economy is at complete variance with the reality of where the American economy is headed. I mean, it's like dinosaurs gathering to talk about the evolution of a new generation of mammals. — Bruce Babbitt, in *Inc. Magazine,* August, 1987

# Education

## See also Intellectuals; Knowledge; Wisdom

**907.** What is the first part of politics? Education. The second? Education. And the third? Education. — Jules Michelot, *Le Peuple,* 1846

**908.** Education is a state-controlled manufacturing of echoes. — Norman Douglas, *How About Europe?,* 1930

**909.** Almost all education has a political motive: it aims at strengthening some group, national or religious or even social, in the competition with other groups. — Bertrand Russell, *Principles of Social Reconstruction,* "Education," 1916

**910.** The aim of education is the knowledge not of facts but of values. — William Ralph Inge, "The Training of the Reason," in A. C. Benson, *Cambridge Essays on Education,* 1917

**911.** Human history becomes more and more a race between education and catastrophe. — H. G. Wells, *The Outline of History,* 1920

**912.** A well-instructed people alone can be permanently a free people. — James Madison, message to Congress, December 5, 1810

**913.** Education makes a people easy to lead, but difficult to drive; easy to govern but impossible to enslave. — Henry Peter Brougham, speech, January 29, 1828

**914.** Upon the education of the people of this country the fate of this country depends. — Benjamin Disraeli, speech, June 15, 1874

**915.** When we talk of our political goals, we admit the right of every man to be a ruler. When we talk of our educational program, we see no inconsistency in saying that only a few have the capacity to get the education that rulers ought to have. — Robert M. Hutchins, *The Conflict in Education in a Democratic Society,* 1953

**916.** Mankind have been created for the sake of one another. Either instruct them, therefore, or endure them. — Marcus Aurelius, *Meditations,* 2nd c.

**917.** Chance favors the trained mind. — Louis Pasteur, speech, December 7, 1854

**918.** The proper method for hastening the decay of error is . . . by teaching every man to think for himself. — William Godwin, *An Enquiry Concerning Political Justice,* 1793

**919.** Let us dare to read, think, speak and write. — John Adams, *Dissertation on the Canon and the Feudal Law,* 1765

**920.** Learning is discovering that something is possible. — Fritz Perls, in *Omni,* November, 1979

**921.** Minds are like parachutes. They only function when they are open. — James Dewar, attributed

**922.** If a man will begin with certainties, he shall end in doubts; but if he will be content to begin with doubts, he shall end in certainties. — Francis Bacon, *The Advancement of Learning,* 1605

**923.** The interrogation of custom at all points is an inevitable stage in the growth of every superior mind. — Ralph Waldo Emerson, *Representative Man,* "Montaigne," 1850

**924.** Education is the result of contact. A great people is produced by contact with great minds. — Calvin Coolidge, speech, January 21, 1923

**925.** To be able to be caught up into the world of thought — that is educated. — Edith Hamilton, in *Saturday Evening Post,* September 27, 1958

**926.** Stay at home in your mind. Don't recite other people's opinions. — Ralph Waldo Emerson, *Letters and Social Aims,* "Social Aims," 1876

**927.** Personally I'm always ready to learn, although I do not always like being taught. — Winston S. Churchill, speech, November 4, 1952

928. Men are not narrow in their intellectual interests by nature; it takes special and vigorous training to accomplish that end. —Jacob Viner, *Scholarship in Graduate Training*, 1953

929. Intelligence appears to be the thing that enables a man to get along without education. Education appears to be the thing that enables a man to get along without the use of his intelligence. —Albert Edward Wiggam, *The New Decalogue of Science*, 1923

930. Pedantry is the unseasonable ostentation of learning. —Samuel Johnson, *The Rambler*, 1750–52

931. We are faced with the paradoxical fact that education has become one of the chief obstacles to intelligence and freedom of thought. —Bertrand Russell, *Sceptical Essays*, 1928

932. It is a very great thing to be able to think as you like; but, after all, an important question remains: *what* you think. —Matthew Arnold, *Democracy*, 1861

933. It is not enough to have a good mind. The main thing is to use it well. —René Descartes, *Discourse on the Method*, 1637

934. Both teachers and learners go to sleep at their post, as soon as there is no enemy in the field. —John Stuart Mill, *On Liberty*, 1859

935. We may prevent people from learning, but we cannot make them unlearn. —Ludwig Bourne, *Aphorisms and Fragments*, 1840

936. The mind is slow in unlearning what it has been long in learning. —Seneca, *Troades*, ca. 60

937. There is nothing makes a man suspect much, more than to know little. —Francis Bacon, *Essays*, "Of Suspicion," 1625

938. Some people will never learn anything, for this reason, because they understand everything too soon. —Alexander Pope, *Thoughts on Various Subjects*, 1727

939. Common sense is the best distributed commodity in the world, for every man is convinced that he is well supplied with it. —René Descartes, *Discourse on the Method*, 1637

940. The philosophy of one century is the common sense of the next. —Henry Ward Beecher, *Life Thoughts*, 1858

941. Never learn anything until you find you have been made uncomfortable for a long time by not knowing it. —Samuel Butler (II), *The Way of All Flesh*, 1903

942. I had not the advantage of a classical education, and no man should, in my judgment, accept a degree he cannot read. —Millard Fillmore, statement upon refusing an honorary degree from Oxford University, 1855

# Elections *see* Campaigns; Voting and Elections; Winners and Losers

## *Ends and Means*

943. If a prince succeeds in establishing and maintaining his authority, the means will always be judged honorable and be approved by everyone. —Niccolò Machiavelli, *The Prince*, 1513

944. The end justifies the means. —Hermann Busenbaum, *Medulla Theologiae Moralis*, 1650

945. The end must justify the means. —Matthew Prior, *Hans Carvel*, 1700

946. The end directs and sanctifies the means. —John Eardley Wilmot, *Collins v. Blantem*, 1767

947. Wisdom denotes the pursuing of the best ends by the best means. —Fran-

cis Hutcheson, *An Inquiry into the Origin of Our Ideas of Beauty and Virtue,* 1725

**948.** The state employs evil weapons to subjugate evil, and is alike contaminated by the objects with which it deals, and the means by which it works. — Herbert Spencer, *Social Statics, Part II,* 1851

**949.** Let us have faith that right makes might, and in that faith let us to the end do our duty as we understand it. — Abraham Lincoln, speech, February 27, 1860

**950.** Politics can be relatively fair in the breathing spaces of history; at its crucial turning points there is no other rule possible than the old one, that the end justifies the means. — Arthur Koestler, *Darkness at Noon,* 1940

**951.** Economics is the science which studies human behavior as a relationship between ends and scarce means which have alternative uses. — Lionel C. Robbins, *Essay on the Nature and Significance of Economic Science,* 1932

**952.** I work for a Government I despise for ends I think criminal. — John Maynard Keynes, letter, December 15, 1917

**953.** The end cannot justify the means for the simple and obvious reason that the means employed determine the nature of the ends produced. — Aldous Huxley, *Ends and Means,* 1937

**954.** Democracy and socialism are means to an end, not the end itself. — Jawaharlal Nehru, in *New York Times,* September 7, 1958

**955.** Greatness is not manifested by unlimited pragmatism, which places such a high premium on the end justifying any means and any method. — Margaret Chase Smith, speech, April 16, 1962

**956.** The means by which we live have outdistanced the ends for which we live. Our scientific power has outrun our spiritual power. We have guided missiles and misguided men. — Martin Luther King Jr., *Strength to Love,* 1963

**957.** The free way of life proposes ends, but it does not prescribe means. — Robert F. Kennedy, *The Pursuit of Justice,* "Berlin East and West," 1964

---

# Enemies

## See also Conflict; War

**958.** Don't worry about your enemies, it's your allies who will do you in. — James Abourezk, in *Playboy,* "Life Inside the Congressional Cookie Jar," March, 1979

**959.** And now, what will become of us without the barbarians? Those people were a kind of solution. — Constantine Cavafy, "Waiting for the Barbarians," 1904

**960.** He that would make his own liberty secure, must guard even his enemy from oppression; for if he violates this duty, he establishes a precedent that will reach to himself. — Thomas Paine, *Dissertation on First Principles of Government,* 1795

**961.** The truth is forced upon us, very quickly, by a foe. — Aristophanes, *The Birds,* ca. 415 B.C.

**962.** He who has not forgiven an enemy has not yet tasted one of the most sublime enjoyments of life. — Johann Kaspar Lavater, *Aphorisms on Man,* 1788

**963.** All our foes are mortal. — Paul Valéry, *Tel Quel,* 1943

**964.** Friends may come and go, but enemies accumulate. — Thomas Jones, in *Wall Street Journal,* February 20, 1975

**965.** A man cannot be too careful in the choice of his enemies. — Oscar Wilde, *The Picture of Dorian Gray,* 1891

**966.** You shall judge of a man by

his foes as well as by his friends. —Joseph Conrad, *Lord Jim*, 1900

**967.** There is no little enemy. —Benjamin Franklin, *Poor Richard's Almanac*, 1733–58

**968.** One enemy is too much. —George Herbert, *Jacula Prudentum*, 1651

**969.** Even a paranoid has some real enemies. —Henry Kissinger, in *Newsweek*, June 13, 1983

**970.** As for me, I think anyone, whoever he may be, who has done nothing for liberty, or has not done all he could, deserves to be counted as an enemy to it. —Joseph-Pierre Fayau, speech, November 26, 1793

**971.** In all ages of the world, priests have been enemies of liberty. —David Hume, *Essays, Moral, Political, and Literary*, 1741–42

**972.** The enemies of Freedom do not argue; they shout and shoot. —William Ralph Inge, *End of an Age*, 1948

## Environment *see* Common Interests

## —————— *Equality* ——————
### *See also* Masses and Elites; Natural Law; Rights

**973.** Democracy, which is a charming form of government, full of variety and disorder, and dispensing a sort of equality to equals and unequals alike. —Plato, *The Republic*, ca. 370 B.C.

**974.** If a man is genuinely superior to his fellows the first thing that he believes is in the equality of man. —Gilbert K. Chesterton, *Heretics*, 1905

**975.** Intellect has nothing to do with equality except to respect it as a sublime convention. —Jacques Barzun, *The House of Intellect*, 1959

**976.** However distinguished by rank or property, in the rights of freedom we are all equal. —Junius, in *Public Advertiser*, March 19, 1770

**977.** I am proud up to the point of equality: everything above or below that appears to me arrant impertinence or abject meanness. —William Hazlitt, *The Round Table*, "Commonplaces," 1817

**978.** The general conception of justice as fairness requires that all primary social goods be distributed equally unless an unequal distribution would be to everyone's advantage. —John Rawls, *A Theory of Justice*, 1971

**979.** Democratic institutions awaken and foster a passion for equality which they can never satisfy. —Alexis de Tocqueville, *Democracy in America*, 1835

**980.** Equality would be a heaven, if we could attain it. —Anthony Trollope, *The Prime Minister*, 1876

**981.** The democrats think that as they are equal they ought to be equal in all things. —Aristotle, *Politics*, 4th c. B.C.

**982.** Democracy and socialism have nothing in common but one word: equality. But notice the difference: while democracy seeks equality in liberty, socialism seeks equality in restraint and servitude. —Alexis de Tocqueville, speech, September 12, 1848

**983.** What is a Communist? one who hath yearnings For equal division of unequal earnings. —Ebenezer Elliott, *Poetical Works*, 1846

**984.** We wish, in a word, equality —equality in fact as corollary, or rather, as primordial condition of liberty. From each according to his faculties, to each according to his needs; that is what we wish sincerely and energetically. —Michael Bakunin, statement at trial, 1870

**985.** Equality may perhaps be a

right, but no power on earth can ever turn it into a fact. — Honoré de Balzac, *La Duchesse de Langeais,* 1834

**986.** Equality — the informing soul of Freedom! — James A. Garfield, *Maxims,* 1880

**987.** Inequality is the inevitable consequence of liberty. — Salvador de Madariaga, *Anarchy or Hierarchy,* 1937

**988.** Liberty without equality is a name of noble sound and squalid result. — Leonard Hobhouse, *Liberalism,* 1911

**989.** Inequality is as dear to the American heart as liberty itself. — William Dean Howells, in *Time,* December 19, 1960

**990.** The Constitution does not provide for first and second class citizens. — Wendell L. Willkie, *An American Program,* 1944

**991.** We conclude that in the field of public education the doctrine of "separate but equal" has no place. — Earl Warren, *Brown v. Board of Education,* May 17, 1954

**992.** Equality is the result of human organization. We are not born equal. — Hannah Arendt, *The Origins of Totalitarianism,* 1973

**993.** Free market arrangements must be set within a framework of political and legal institutions which regulates the overall trends of economic events and preserves the social conditions necessary for fair equality of opportunity. — John Rawls, *A Theory of Justice,* 1971

**994.** Distinctions in society will always exist under every just government. Equality of talents, of education, or of wealth can not be produced by human institutions. — Andrew Jackson, veto message, July 10, 1832

**995.** It is a wise man who said that there is no greater inequality than the equal treatment of unequals. — Felix Frankfurter, *Dennis v. United States,* 1949

**996.** Men are created different; they lose their social freedom and their individual autonomy in seeking to be-

come like each other. — David Riesman, *The Lonely Crowd,* 1950

**997.** The principle of equality does not destroy the imagination, but lowers its flight to the level of the earth. — Alexis de Tocqueville, *Democracy in America,* 1835

**998.** The general tendency of things throughout the world is to render mediocrity the ascendent power among mankind. — John Stuart Mill, *On Liberty,* 1859

**999.** We who are liberal and progressive know that the poor are our equals in every sense except that of being equal to us. — Lionel Trilling, *The Liberal Imagination,* 1950

**1000.** All animals are equal, but some animals are more equal than others. — George Orwell, *Animal Farm,* 1945

**1001.** That all men are equal is a proposition to which, in ordinary times, no sane individual has ever given his assent. — Aldous Huxley, *Proper Studies,* 1927

**1002.** In America everybody is of opinion that he has no social superiors, since all men are equal, but he does not admit that he has no social inferiors. — Bertrand Russell, *Unpopular Essays,* 1950

**1003.** There is no merit in equality, unless it be equality with the best. — John Lancaster Spalding, *Thoughts and Theories of Life and Education,* 1897

**1004.** What makes equality such a difficult business is that we only want it with our superiors. — Henry Becque, *Querelles littéraires,* 1890

**1005.** We clamor for equality chiefly in matters in which we ourselves cannot hope to obtain excellence. — Eric Hoffer, *The Passionate State of Mind,* 1954

**1006.** Inferiors revolt in order that they may be equal, and equals so that they may be superior. — Aristotle, *Politics,* 4th c. B.C.

**1007.** Whatever may be the general endeavor of a community to render its members equal and alike, the personal pride of individuals will always seek to rise above the line, and to form somewhere an inequality to their own advantage. — Alexis de Tocqueville, *Democracy in America*, 1835

**1008.** It is better that some should be unhappy than that none should be happy, which would be the case in a general state of equality. — Samuel Johnson, in James Boswell, *Life of Samuel Johnson*, 1791

**1009.** Equality is a mortuary word. — Christopher Fry, *Venus Observed*, 1950

## Ethics *see* Character; Honesty; Morality; Office; Virtue and Vice

## Extremism

### *See also* Moderation; Radicals and Reactionaries; Rebellion; Revolutionaries

**1010.** Political extremism involves two prime ingredients: an excessively simple diagnosis of the world's ills and a conviction that there are identifiable villains back of it all. — John W. Gardner, *No Easy Victories*, 1968

**1011.** A fanatic is a man that does what he thinks th' Lord wud do if He knew th' facts iv th' case. — Finley Peter Dunne, *Mr. Dooley's Philosophy*, "Casual Observations," 1900

**1012.** It is part of the nature of fanaticism that it loses sight of the totality of evil and rushes like a bull at the red cloth instead of at the man who holds it. — Dietrich Bonhoeffer, *Ethics*, 1955

**1013.** Foolish fanatics...the men who form the lunatic fringe in all reform movements. — Theodore Roosevelt, *Autobiography*, 1913

**1014.** Fanaticism consists in redoubling your effort when you have forgotten your aims. — George Santayana, *The Life of Reason*, 1905–06

**1015.** There is nobody as enslaved as the fanatic, the person in whom one impulse, one value, has assumed ascendency over all others. — Milton R. Sapirstein, *Paradoxes of Everyday Life*, 1955

**1016.** An infallible method of making fanatics is to persuade before you instruct. — Voltaire, *Philosophical Dictionary*, "Oracles," 1764

**1017.** There is a danger in being persuaded before one understands. — Thomas Wilson, *Maxims of Piety and of Christianity*, 1755

**1018.** Zeal without knowledge is a runaway horse. — Henry Davidoff, *A World Treasury of Proverbs*, 1946

**1019.** There is only one step from fanaticism to barbarism. — Denis Diderot, "Essai sue le mérite de la vertu," 1745

**1020.** Before doing someone a favor, make sure that he isn't a madman. — Eugène Labiche, *Le voyage de M. Perrichon*, 1860

**1021.** Extremists think "communication" means agreeing with them. — Leo Rosten, *A Trumpet for Reason*, 1970

**1022.** Violent men reel from one extremity to another. — Thomas Fuller, D.D., *The Holy State and the Profane State*, 1642

# Facts

## See also Lies; Opinion, Difference of; Truth

**1023.** There seems to me very few facts, at least ascertainable facts, in politics. — Robert Peel, letter, 1846

**1024.** Facts speak for themselves. — Terence, *The Eunuch,* 161 B.C.

**1025.** Facts are stubborn things. — Alain René Lesage, *Gil Blas,* 1735

**1026.** Comment is free, but facts are sacred. — C. P. Scott, in *Manchester Guardian,* May 6, 1926

**1027.** Facts do not cease to exist because they are ignored. — Aldous Huxley, *Proper Studies,* 1927

**1028.** There are no eternal facts, as there are no absolute truths. — Friedrich Wilhelm Nietzsche, *Human, All Too Human,* 1878

**1029.** People don't ask for facts in making up their minds. They would rather have one good, soul-satisfying emotion than a dozen facts. — Robert Keith Leavitt, *Voyages and Discourses,* 1939

**1030.** This is one of those cases in which the imagination is baffled by the facts. — Winston S. Churchill, remark concerning the defection of Rudolf Hess, May 13, 1941

**1031.** Principles become modified in practice by facts. — James Fenimore Cooper, *The American Democrat,* 1838

**1032.** The trouble with facts is that there are so many of them. — Samuel McChord Crothers, *The Gentle Reader,* 1903

**1033.** I was brought up to believe that the only thing worth doing was to add to the sum of accurate information in the world. — Margaret Mead, in *New York Times,* August 9, 1964

**1034.** Information's pretty thin stuff, unless mixed with experience. — Clarence Day, *The Crow's Nest,* "The Three Tigers," 1921

**1035.** It is facts that are needed. Facts, Facts, Facts. When facts have been supplied, each of us can try to reason

from them. — James Bryce, *Modern Democracies,* 1922

**1036.** The greatest American superstition is belief in facts. — Hermann A. Keyserling, in *Kansas City Times,* January 25, 1977

**1037.** Do not become archivists of facts. Try to penetrate to the secret of their occurrence, persistently search for the laws which govern them. — Ivan Pavlov, *To the Academic Youth of Russia,* February 27, 1936

**1038.** What are facts but compromises? A fact merely marks the point where we have agreed to let investigation cease. — Bliss Carman, in *Atlantic,* May, 1906

**1039.** Facts are never neutral; they are impregnated with value judgments. — Peter Gay, *Style in History,* 1974

**1040.** A myth is, of course, not a fairy story. It is the presentation of facts belonging to one category in the idioms appropriate to another. To explode a myth is accordingly not to deny the facts but to reallocate them. — Gilbert Ryle, *The Concept of Mind,* 1949

**1041.** One of the most untruthful things possible, you know, is a collection of facts, because they can be made to appear so many different ways. — Karl A. Menninger, *A Psychiatrist's World,* 1959

**1042.** Facts are ventriloquists' dummies. Sitting on a wise man's knee they may be made to utter words of wisdom; elsewhere they say nothing or talk nonsense. — Aldous Huxley, *Time Must Have a Stop,* 1944

**1043.** When the mind withdraws into itself and dispenses with facts it makes only chaos. — Edith Hamilton, *The Greek Way,* 1930

**1044.** True opinions can prevail only if the facts to which they refer are known; if they are not known, false ideas are just as effective as true ones, if not a little more effective. — Walter Lippmann, *Liberty and the News*, 1920

**1045.** Every man has a right to his opinion, but no man has a right to be wrong in his facts. — Bernard Baruch, in *Reader's Digest*, March, 1948

--------------------------------- *Fame* ---------------------------------

### *See also* Ambition; Greatness; Office; Power

**1046.** The desire for glory clings even to the best men longer than any other passion. — Cornelius Tacitus, *Histories*, ca. 95

**1047.** Fame and tranquility can never be bedfellows. — Michel Eyquem de Montaigne, *Essays*, 1580

**1048.** Fame is so sweet that we love anything with which we connect it, even death. — Blaise Pascal, *Pensées*, 1670

**1049.** Glory is like a circle in the water, Which never ceaseth to enlarge itself, Till by broad spreading it disperse to nought. — William Shakespeare, *Henry VI, Part I*, 1592

**1050.** Contempt of fame begets contempt of virtue. — Ben Jonson, *Sejanus*, 1605

**1051.** Popularity is a crime from the moment it is sought; it is only a virtue where men have it whether they will or no. — George Savile, *Political, Moral, and Miscellaneous Reflections*, 1750

**1052.** Fame usually comes to those who are thinking about something else. — Oliver Wendell Holmes Sr., *The Autocrat of the Breakfast Table*, 1858

**1053.** Most celebrated men live in a condition of prostitution. — Charles Augustin Sainte-Beuve, *Notebooks*, 1876

**1054.** Martyrdom...the only way in which a man can become famous without ability. — George Bernard Shaw, *The Devil's Disciple*, 1901

**1055.** Every country is renewed out of the unknown ranks and not out of the ranks of those already famous and powerful and in control. — Woodrow Wilson, speech, October 28, 1912

**1056.** Why long for glory which one despises as soon as one has it? But that is precisely what the ambitious man wants: having it in order to be able to despise it. — Jean Rostand, *De la vanité*, 1925

## Fanaticism *see* Extremism

--------------------------------- *Fear* ---------------------------------

**1057.** Fear is the foundation of most governments. — John Adams, *Thoughts on Government*, 1776

**1058.** It is when power is wedded to chronic fear that it becomes formidable. — Eric Hoffer, *The Passionate State of Mind*, 1954

**1059.** The King said, "Power does not corrupt. Fear corrupts, perhaps the fear of a loss of power." — John Steinbeck, *The Short Reign of Pippin IV*, 1957

**1060.** To be feared is to fear: no one has been able to strike terror into others and at the same time enjoy peace of mind himself. — Seneca, *Epistles*, 1st c.

**1061.** Who is all-powerful should fear everything. — Pierre Corneille, *Cinna*, 1640

**1062.** Nothing is more despicable than respect based on fear. — Albert Camus, *Notebooks 1935–1942*, 1962

**1063.** You must keep people scared every day. — Peter Grace, in *Financial World*, April 5, 1988

**1064.** Human beings are perhaps never more frightened than when they are convinced beyond doubt that they are right. — Laurens Van der Post, *The Lost World of the Kalahari,* 1958

**1065.** We prate of freedom; we are in deadly fear of life. — Learned Hand, speech, March 20, 1930

**1066.** No passion so effectively robs the mind of all its powers of acting and reasoning as fear. — Edmund Burke, *On the Sublime and Beautiful,* 1756

**1067.** The only thing we have to fear is fear itself. — Franklin D. Roosevelt, inaugural address, March 4, 1933

**1068.** True nobility is exempt from fear. — William Shakespeare, *Henry VI, Part II,* 1592

**1069.** As a rule people are afraid of truth. Each truth we discover in nature or social life destroys the crutches on which we used to lean. — Ernst Toller, in *Saturday Review of Literature,* May 20, 1944

**1070.** Prosperity is not without many fears and distastes; and adversity is not without comforts and hopes. — Francis Bacon, *Essays,* "Of Adversity," 1625

---

# *Followers*

## *See also* Citizenship; Leaders; Masses and Elites; the People

**1071.** Good followers do not become good leaders. — Laurence J. Peter, *The Peter Principle,* 1969

**1072.** The followers of a great man often put their eyes out, so that they may be the better able to sing his praise. — Friedrich Wilhelm Nietzsche, *Miscellaneous Maxims and Opinions,* 1879

**1073.** Ah! I am their leader, I really had to follow them. — Alexandre Ledru-Rollin, in E. de Mirecourt, *Les Contemporains,* 1857

**1074.** A political leader must keep looking over his shoulder all the time to see if the boys are still there. If they aren't still there, he's no longer a political leader. — Bernard Baruch, in *New York Times,* June 21, 1965

**1075.** For the most part our leaders are merely following out in front; they do but marshal us the way that we are going. — Bergen Evans, *The Spoor of Spooks and Other Nonsense,* 1954

**1076.** No man is great enough or wise enough for any of us to surrender our destiny to. The only way in which any one can lead us is to restore to us the belief in our own guidance. — Henry Miller, *The Wisdom of the Heart,* 1941

**1077.** It is for men to choose whether they will govern themselves or be governed. — Henry Ward Beecher, *Proverbs from Plymouth Pulpit,* 1887

**1078.** The job of party leaders is often to persuade their followers that the traditional policy is still being carried out, even when this is demonstrably not true. — R. H. S. Crossman, in *Encounter,* "On Political Neurosis," May, 1954

**1079.** The weaknesses of the many make the leader possible. — Elbert Hubbard, *The Note Book,* 1927

**1080.** People are more easily led than driven. — David Harold Fink, *Release from Nervous Tension,* 1943

**1081.** The death of democracy is not likely to be an assassination from ambush. It will be a slow extinction from apathy, indifference, and undernourishment. — Robert M. Hutchins, *Great Books,* 1954

**1082.** Unless you can find some sort of loyalty, you cannot find unity and peace in your active living. — Josiah Royce, *The Philosophy of Loyalty,* 1907–08

**1083.** What I want is men who will support me when I am in the wrong. — William Lamb, in D. Cecil, *Lord M,* 1954

**1084.** I don't want loyalty. I want

*loyalty,* I want him to kiss my ass in Macy's window at high noon and tell me it smells like roses. I want his pecker in my pocket. — Lyndon B. Johnson, in David Halbersham, *The Best and the Brightest,* 1972

# Fools

## *See also* Ignorance; Wisdom

**1085.** I ain't never seen no head so level that it could bear the lettin' in of politics. It makes a fool of a man and a worse fool of a fool. — Ellen Glasgow, *The Voice of the People,* 1900

**1086.** A person does not deserve, and cannot long enjoy, the title of politician unless he conceals any feelings of disgust with knaves or impatience with fools. — Stimson Bullitt, *To Be a Politician,* 1977

**1087.** You cannot accomplish good for the people unless you face up to the weak and the foolish. — Napoleon I, letter, December 15, 1806

**1088.** Many politicians of our time are in the habit of laying it down as a self-evident proposition that no people ought to be free till they are fit to use their freedom. The maxim is worthy of the fool in the old story, who resolved not to go into the water till he had learnt to swim. If men are to wait for liberty till they become wise and good in slavery, they may indeed wait forever. — Thomas Babington, *Essays Contributed to the Edinburgh Review,* 1843

**1089.** Strong and sharp as our wit may be, it is not so strong as the memory of fools, nor so keen as their resentment. — Charles Caleb Colton, *Lacon,* 1820–22

**1090.** A great deal of learning can be packed into an empty head. — Karl Kraus, *Aphorisms and More Aphorisms,* 1909

**1091.** Let a fool be made serviceable according to his folly. — Joseph Conrad, *Under Western Eyes,* 1911

**1092.** An intelligent man on one plane can be a fool on others. — Albert Camus, *Notebooks 1935–1942,* 1962

**1093.** Fools and intelligent people are equally harmless. It is half-fools and the half-intelligent who are the most dangerous. — Johann Wolfgang von Goethe, *Proverbs in Prose,* 1819

**1094.** The haste of a fool is the slowest thing in the world. — Thomas Shadwell, *A True Widow,* 1679

**1095.** A fool can always find a greater fool to admire him. — Nicholas Boileau, *The Art of Poetry,* 1674

**1096.** Among wise men, the wisest knows that he knows least; among fools, the most foolish thinks he knows most. — Antonio de Guevara, *Libro Llamado Relox de Principes,* 1529

**1097.** A fool uttereth all his mind. — Bible, *Proverbs 29:11*

**1098.** He dares to be a fool, and that is the first step in the direction of wisdom. — James G. Huneker, *Pathos of Distance,* 1913

**1099.** Every man is a damn fool for at least five minutes every day. Wisdom consists in not exceeding the limit. — Elbert Hubbard, *Roycroft Dictionary and Book of Epigrams,* 1923

**1100.** Man is wise only while in search of wisdom; when he imagines he has attained it, he is a fool. — Solomon Ibn Gabirol, *Choice of Pearls,* ca. 1050

**1101.** The little foolery that wise men have makes a great show. — William Shakespeare, *As You Like It,* 1599

**1102.** Mix a little foolishness with your prudence: it's good to be silly at the right moment. — Horace, *Odes,* 1st c. B.C.

**1103.** To find a young fellow that is neither a wit in his own eye nor a fool in the eye of the world, is a very hard task. — William Congreve, *Love for Love,* 1695

**1104.** There are well turned-out follies, just as there are smartly-dressed fools. — Sébastien Roch Nicholas Chamfort, *Maxims et pensées*, 1805

**1105.** If all fooles wore white Caps, wee should seeme a flock of geese. — George Herbert, *Outlandish Proverbs*, 1640

**1106.** Silence is the virtue of fools. — Francis Bacon, *De Dignitate et Augmentis Scientiarum*, 1623

**1107.** Let a fool hold his tongue and he will pass for a sage. — Publilius Syrus, *Maxims*, 1st c. B.C.

**1108.** Logical consequences are the scarecrows of fools and the beacons of wise men. — T. H. Huxley, *Science and Culture and Other Essays*, "On the Hypothesis That Animals Are Automata," 1881

--------------------- *Force* ---------------------

## *See also* Diplomacy; Violence; War

**1109.** The purification of politics is an iridescent dream. Government is force. — John J. Ingalls, in *New York World*, 1890

**1110.** There will always be a government of force where men are selfish. — Ralph Waldo Emerson, *Essays: Second Series*, "Politics," 1844

**1111.** Force works on servile nations, not the free. — Ben Jonson, *Every Man in His Humor*, 1598

**1112.** Force has no place where there is need of skill. — Herodotus, *The History*, ca. 450 B.C.

**1113.** One must know the limitations of force; one must know when to blend force with a maneuver, a blow with an agreement. — Leon Trotsky, *What Next?*, 1932

**1114.** Nothing is so weak and unstable as a reputation for power not based on force. — Cornelius Tacitus, *Annals*, 2nd c.

**1115.** Civilization is nothing more than the effort to reduce the use of force to the last resort. — José Ortega y Gasset, *The Revolt of the Masses*, 1930

**1116.** Those entrusted with arms ...should be persons of some substance and stake in the country. — William Windham, speech, July 22, 1807

**1117.** Battle, *n*. A method for untying with the teeth a political knot that would not yield to the tongue. — Ambrose Bierce, *The Devil's Dictionary*, 1906

**1118.** Eleven men well armed will certainly subdue one single man in his shirt. — Jonathan Swift, *Drapier's Letters*, 1724

**1119.** Force, and fraud, are in war the two cardinal virtues. — Thomas Hobbes, *Leviathan*, 1651

**1120.** Force is not a remedy. — John Bright, speech, November 16, 1880

--------------------- *Freedom* ---------------------

## *See also* Freedom of Speech; Freedom of the Press; Liberty

**1121.** I wish that every human life might be pure transparent freedom. — Simone de Beauvoir, *The Blood of Others*, 1946

**1122.** I only ask to be free. The butterflies are free. — Charles Dickens, *Bleak House*, 1852

**1123.** As long as possible live free and uncommitted. It makes but little difference whether you are committed to a farm or the county jail. — Henry David Thoreau, *Walden*, "Where I Lived, and What I Lived For," 1854

**1124.** We *know* our will is free, and

*there's* an end on't. — Samuel Johnson, in James Boswell, *Life of Samuel Johnson,* 1791

**1125.** We must be free not because we claim freedom, but because we practice it. — William Faulkner, in *Harper's Magazine,* June, 1956

**1126.** A Country can get more real joy out of just Hollering for their Freedom than they can if they get it. — Will Rogers, *The Autobiography of Will Rogers,* 1949

**1127.** The weakness of political programs — Five Year Plans and the like — is that they can be achieved. But human freedom can never be achieved because human freedom is a continuously evolving condition. — Archibald MacLeish, in *New York Times,* May 30, 1960

**1128.** Nothing has ever been more insurmountable for a man and a human society than freedom. — Fyodor Dostoyevski, *The Brothers Karamazov,* 1880

**1129.** I am condemned to be free. — Jean-Paul Sartre, *Being and Nothingness,* 1943

**1130.** We have confused the free with the free and easy. — Adlai Stevenson, *Putting First Things First,* 1960

**1131.** The history of American freedom is, in no small measure, the history of procedure. — Felix Frankfurter, *Malinski v. New York,* 1945

**1132.** Although discipline and freedom seem antithetical, each without the other destroys itself. — Donard Barr, *Who Pushed Humpty Dumpty?,* 1971

**1133.** There is no substitute for a militant freedom. — Calvin Coolidge, speech, April 27, 1922

**1134.** Those who expect to reap the blessings of freedom must, like men, undergo the fatigue of supporting it. — Thomas Paine, *The American Crisis,* 1776–83

**1135.** If a nation values anything more than freedom, it will lose its freedom; and the irony of it is that if it is comfort or money that it values more, it will lose that too. — W. Somerset Maugham, *Strictly Personal,* 1941

**1136.** We must plan for freedom, and not only for security, if for no other reason than that only freedom can make security secure. — Karl R. Popper, *The Open Society and Its Enemies,* 1945

**1137.** Only the educated are free. — Epictetus, *Discourses,* 2nd c.

**1138.** I believe there are more instances of the abridgment of the freedom of the people by gradual and silent encroachments of those in power than by violent and sudden usurpations. — James Madison, speech, June 16, 1788

**1139.** The biggest menace to American freedom is the intelligence community. — I. F. Stone, in *Wilson Library Bulletin,* September, 1976

**1140.** When people are free to do as they please, they usually imitate each other. — Eric Hoffer, *The Passionate State of Mind,* 1954

**1141.** So long as man remains free he strives for nothing so incessantly and so painfully as to find someone to worship. — Fyodor Dostoyevski, *The Brothers Karamazov,* 1880

**1142.** It is doubtful if the oppressed ever fight for freedom. They fight for pride and for power — power to oppress others. The oppressed want above all to imitate their oppressors; they want to retaliate. — Eric Hoffer, *The True Believer,* 1951

**1143.** What man wants is simply *independent* choice, whatever that independence may cost and wherever it may lead. — Fyodor Dostoyevski, *Notes from Underground,* 1864

**1144.** Perfect freedom is reserved for the man who lives by his own work and in that work does what he wants to do. — R. G. Collingwood, *Speculum Mentis,* 1924

**1145.** What is it that every man seeks? To be secure, to be happy, to do what he pleases without restraint and without compulsion. — Epictetus, *Discourses,* 2nd c.

**1146.** Freedom belongs to the strong. — Richard Wright, *Long Black Song,* 1936

**1147.** It is the business of the very few to be independent; it is a privilege of the strong. — Friedrich Wilhelm Nietzsche, *Beyond Good and Evil,* 1886

**1148.** It is necessary to grow accustomed to freedom before one may walk in it sure-footedly. — Suzanne LaFollette, *Concerning Women,* 1926

**1149.** Freedom is the greatest fruit of self-sufficiency. — Epicurus, *Letters, Principal Doctrines, and Vatican Sayings,* 3rd c. B.C.

**1150.** What is the freedom of the most free? To do what is right! — Johann Wolfgang von Goethe, *Egmont,* 1788

**1151.** Freedom is nothing but the recognition and adoption of such universal objects as right and law, and the production of a reality that is accordant with the State. — Georg Wilhelm Friedrich Hegel, *The Philosophy of Right,* 1821

**1152.** But what is Freedom? Rightly understood, A universal license to be good. — Hartley Coleridge, "Liberty," 1833

**1153.** Freedom is the will to be responsible to ourselves. — Friedrich Wilhelm Nietzsche, *Twilight of the Idols,* 1888

**1154.** Freedom is the supreme good — freedom from self-imposed limitation. — Elbert Hubbard, *The Note Book,* 1927

**1155.** Our freedom is but a light that breaks through from another world. — Nikolai Gumilev, "The Tram That Lost Its Way," 1921

**1156.** Freedom is a condition of mind, and the best way to secure it is to breed it. — Elbert Hubbard, *The Note Book,* 1927

**1157.** Freedom is not worth fighting for if it means no more than license for everyone to get as much as he can for himself. — Dorothy Canfield Fisher, *Seasoned Timber,* 1939

**1158.** Freedom is not worth having if it does not connote freedom to err. — Mohandas K. Gandhi, in *Saturday Review,* March 1, 1959

**1159.** Freedom is an indivisible word. If we want to enjoy it, and fight for it, we must be prepared to extend it to everyone. — Wendell L. Willkie, *One World,* 1943

**1160.** Freedom is a hard-bought thing. — Paul Robeson, *Here I Stand,* 1958

**1161.** Freedom is not choosing; that is merely the move that we make when all is already lost. Freedom is knowing and understanding and respecting things quite other than ourselves. — Iris Murdoch, in *Yale Review,* 1959

**1162.** Freedom is nothing else but a chance to be better, whereas enslavement is a certainty of the worse. — Albert Camus, *Resistance, Rebellion, and Death,* 1960

**1163.** Freedom is not something that anybody can be given; freedom is something people take and people are as free as they want to be. — James Baldwin, *Nobody Knows My Name,* 1961

**1164.** Freedom is the freedom to say that two plus two make four. If that is granted, all else follows. — George Orwell, *1984,* 1949

---

# Freedom of Speech

## See also Freedom of the Press; Gossip; Language; Liberty; Press and Media; Rights; Speech; Tolerance

**1165.** Liberty of speech inviteth and provoketh liberty to be used again, and so bringeth much to a man's knowledge. — Francis Bacon, *The Advancement of Learning,* 1605

**1166.** We owe almost all our knowledge not to those who have agreed, but to those who have differed. — Charles Caleb Colton, *Lacon,* 1820–22

**1167.** Free speech is to a great people what winds are to oceans and malarial regions, which waft away the elements of disease, and brings new elements of health. Where free speech is stopped miasma is bred, and death comes fast. — Henry Ward Beecher, *Royal Truths,* 1862

**1168.** It is by the goodness of God that in our country we have those three unspeakably precious things: freedom of speech, freedom of conscience, and the prudence never to practice either of them. — Mark Twain, *Following the Equator,* 1897

**1169.** Free speech does not live many hours after free industry and free commerce die. — Herbert Hoover, speech, October 22, 1928

**1170.** Freedom of expression is the matrix, the indispensable condition, of nearly every other form of freedom. — Benjamin N. Cardozo, *Palko v. Connecticut,* 1937

**1171.** The first principle of a free society is an untrammeled flow of words in an open forum. — Adlai Stevenson, in *New York Times,* January 19, 1962

**1172.** If men's minds were as easily controlled as their tongues, every king would sit safely on his throne, and government by compulsion would cease. — Baruch Spinoza, *Tractatus Theologicus-Politicus,* 1670

**1173.** Restriction of free thought and free speech is the most dangerous of all subversions. It is the one un–American act that could most easily defeat us. — William O. Douglas, speech, December 3, 1952

**1174.** Thought that is silenced is always rebellious. — Alan Barth, *The Loyalty of Free Men,* 1951

**1175.** Freedom of speech and freedom of action are meaningless without freedom of thought without doubts. — Bergen Evans, *The Natural History of Nonsense,* 1946

**1176.** Where men cannot freely convey their thoughts to one another, no other liberty is secure. — William Ernest Hocking, *Freedom of the Press,* 1947

**1177.** The very aim and end of our institutions is just this: that we may think what we like and say what we think.

— Oliver Wendell Holmes Sr., *The Professor at the Breakfast Table,* 1860

**1178.** It is our attitude toward free thought and free expression that will determine our fate. There must be no limit on the range of temperate discussion, no limits on thoughts. No subject must be taboo. No censor must preside at our assemblies. — William O. Douglas, speech, December 3, 1952

**1179.** Opinions become dangerous to a state only when persecution makes it necessary for the people to communicate their ideas under the bond of secrecy. — Charles James Fox, speech, May, 1797

**1180.** If all mankind minus one were of one opinion, and only one person were of the contrary opinion, mankind would be no more justified in silencing that one person, than he, if he had the power, would be justified in silencing mankind. — John Stuart Mill, *On Liberty,* 1859

**1181.** The problem of freedom in America is that of maintaining a competition of ideas, and you do not achieve that by silencing one brand of ideas. — Max Lerner, *Actions and Passions,* 1949

**1182.** The only way to make sure people you agree with can speak is to support the rights of people you don't agree with. — Eleanor Holmes Norton, in *New York Post,* March 28, 1970

**1183.** Government should be concerned with anti-social conduct, not with utterances. — William O. Douglas, *Roth v. United States,* June 24, 1957

**1184.** Whoever deprives another of the right to state unpopular views necessarily deprives others of the right to listen to those views. — C. Vann Woodward, in *New York Times,* January 28, 1975

**1185.** There is no nation so poor that it cannot afford free speech, but there are few elites which will put up with the bother of it. — Daniel P. Moynihan, in *Time,* January 26, 1976

**1186.** Free speech is about as good a cause as the world has ever known. But, like the poor, it is always with us and gets shoved aside in favor of things more vital. — Heywood Broun, in *New York World,* October 23, 1926

**1187.** By placing discretion in the hands of an official to grant or deny a license, such a statute creates a threat of censorship that by its very existence chills free speech. — Harry A. Blackmun, *Roe v. Wade; Doe v. Bolton,* 1973

**1188.** Everyone is in favor of free speech ... but some people's idea of it is that they are free to say what they like, but if anyone says anything back, that is an outrage. — Winston S. Churchill, speech, October 13, 1943

**1189.** Experience informs us that the first defense of weak minds is to recriminate. — Samuel Taylor Coleridge, *Biographia Literaria,* 1817

**1190.** Every man has a right to utter what he thinks truth, and every other man has a right to knock him down for it. Martyrdom is the test. — Samuel Johnson, in James Boswell, *Life of Samuel Johnson,* 1791

**1191.** The right to be heard does not automatically include the right to be taken seriously. — Hubert H. Humphrey, speech, August 23, 1965

**1192.** The wisest thing to do with a fool is to encourage him to hire a hall and discourse to his fellow-citizens. Nothing chills nonsense like exposure to the air. — Woodrow Wilson, *Constitutional Government,* 1908

**1193.** Almost nobody means precisely what he says when he makes the declaration, "I'm in favor of free speech." — Heywood Broun, in *New York World,* October 23, 1926

**1194.** The American feels so rich in his opportunities for free expression that he often no longer knows what he is free from. Neither does he know where he is not free; he does not recognize his native autocrats when he sees them. — Erik H. Erikson, *Childhood and Society,* 1950

**1195.** "No comment" is a splendid expression. I am using it again and again. — Winston S. Churchill, statement to reporters, February 12, 1946

# Freedom of the Press

## See also Freedom of Speech; Liberty; Press and Media; Rights

**1196.** The liberty of the press is the *Palladium* of all the civil, political, and religious rights of an Englishman. — Junius, *The Letters of Junius,* 1772

**1197.** The freedom of the press is one of the great bulwarks of liberty, and can never be restrained but by despotic governments. — George Mason, *Virginia Bill of Rights,* June 12, 1776

**1198.** Freedom of the press is not an end in itself but a means to the end of a free society. — Felix Frankfurter, in *New York Times,* November 28, 1954

**1199.** To be able to think freely, a man must be certain that no consequences will follow whatever he writes. — Ernest Renan, *The Christian Church,* 1879

**1200.** The chief danger which threatens the influence and honor of the press is the tendency of its liberty to degenerate into license. — James A. Garfield, speech, July 11, 1878

**1201.** Freedom of the press is perhaps the freedom that has suffered the most from the gradual degradation of the idea of liberty. — Albert Camus, *Resistance, Rebellion, and Death,* 1960

**1202.** The liberty of the press is most generally approved when it takes liberties with the other fellow, and leaves us alone. — Edgar Watson Howe, *Country Town Sayings,* 1911

**1203.** A free press can of course be good or bad, but most certainly, without freedom it will never be anything but bad. — Albert Camus, *Resistance, Rebellion, and Death,* 1960

**1204.** The liberty of the press is always bound to favorable opportunities, and accordingly will never be an absolute liberty; Not *in* the State, but only *against* it can the liberty of the press be carried through. — Max Stirner, *The Ego and His Own,* 1845

**1205.** Despotism can no more exist in a nation until the liberty of the press be destroyed than night can happen before the sun is set. — Charles Caleb Colton, *Lacon,* 1820–22

**1206.** When a person goes to a country and finds their newspapers filled with nothing but good news, he can bet there are good men in jail. — Daniel P. Moynihan, in *University Daily Kansan,* February 16, 1977

**1207.** The price of justice is eternal publicity. — Arnold Bennett, *Things That Have Interested Me,* "Secret Trials," 1923

**1208.** In order to enjoy the inestimable benefits that the liberty of the press ensures, it is necessary to submit to the inevitable evils that it creates. — Alexis de Tocqueville, *Democracy in America,* 1835

**1209.** We have all of us at times suffered from the liberty of the press, but we have to take the good with the bad. — Theodore Roosevelt, speech, March 27, 1883

**1210.** I have lent myself willingly as the subject of a great experiment... to demonstrate the falsehood of the pretext that freedom of the press is incompatible with orderly government. — Thomas Jefferson, letter, February 11, 1807

**1211.** The essence of the free press is the reliable, reasonable and moral nature of freedom. The character of the censored press is the nondescript confusion of tyranny. — Karl Marx, in *Neue Rheinische Zeitung,* May 13, 1842

**1212.** Wherever books will be burned, men also, in the end, are burned. — Heinrich Heine, *Almansor,* 1823

**1213.** Don't join the book burners. Don't think you are going to conceal faults by concealing evidence that they ever existed. — Dwight D. Eisenhower, speech, June 14, 1953

**1214.** In general, we have as natural a right to make use of our pens as of our tongue, at our peril, risk, and hazard. I know many books which have bored their readers, but I know of none which has done real evil. — Voltaire, *Philosophical Dictionary,* "Liberty of the Press," 1764

**1215.** The censor's sword pierces deeply into the heart of free expression. — Earl Warren, *Times Film Corporation v. City of Chicago,* January 23, 1961

**1216.** I'm with you on the free press. It's the newspapers I can't stand. — Tom Stoppard, *Night and Day,* 1978

**1217.** Freedom of the press is guaranteed to those who own one. — A. J. Liebling, in *New Yorker,* May 14, 1960

## *Future*

### See also **Progress; Security**

**1218.** Future, *n.* That period of time in which our affairs prosper, our friends are true, and our happiness is assured. — Ambrose Bierce, *The Devil's Dictionary,* 1906

**1219.** To renew America, we must be bold. We must do what no generation has had to do before. — Bill Clinton, inaugural address, January 20, 1993

**1220.** ...to boldly go where no man has gone before. — Gene Roddenberry, *Star Trek,* 1966

**1221.** Posterity is likely to be as wrong as anybody else. — Heywood Broun, *Sitting on the World,* 1924

**1222.** When we are planning for posterity, we ought to remember that virtue is not hereditary. — Thomas Paine, *Common Sense,* 1776

**1223.** It is a bad plan that admits no modification. — Publilius Syrus, *Maxims,* 1st c. B.C.

**1224.** The reason why everybody likes planning is because nobody has to do anything. —Edmund G. Brown Jr., in *The Coevolution Quarterly,* Summer, 1976

**1225.** While we're talking, envious time is fleeing; seize the day, put no trust in the future. —Horace, *Odes,* 1st c. B.C.

**1226.** For present joys are more to flesh and blood Than a dull prospect of a distant good. —John Dryden, *The Hind and the Panther,* 1687

**1227.** How different the new order would be if we could consult the veteran instead of the politician. —Henry Miller, *The Wisdom of the Heart,* 1941

**1228.** You can never plan the future by the past. —Edmund Burke, *Letter to a Member of the National Assembly,* 1791

**1229.** It is a mistake to look too far ahead. Only one link of the chain of destiny can be handled at a time. —Winston S. Churchill, speech, February 27, 1945

**1230.** Our Madisonian government of checks and balances, three branches, two legislative houses, and infinitely splintered power is conservative, not radical. It shuffles into the future one step at a time. —David A. Stockman, *The Triumph of Politics,* 1987

**1231.** There is reason to expect that stable democratic institutions in which political freedom is great and even increasing...will continue to characterize the mature industrialized Western societies. —Seymour Martin Lipset, *Political Man,* 1981

**1232.** The test of political institutions is the condition of the country whose future they regulate. —Benjamin Disraeli, speech, April 3, 1872

**1233.** I have but one lamp by which my feet are guided, and that is the lamp of experience. —Patrick Henry, speech, March 23, 1775

**1234.** To complain of the age we live in, to murmur at the present possessors of power, to lament the past, to conceive extravagant hopes of the future, are the common dispositions of the greater part of mankind. —Edmund Burke, *Thoughts on the Cause of the Present Discontent,* 1770

**1235.** He that liveth in hope danceth without music. —George Herbert, *Outlandish Proverbs,* 1640

**1236.** Do not let your plans for a new world divert your energies from saving what is left of the old. —Winston S. Churchill, memorandum, January 6, 1941

**1237.** One is better prepared for politics by a background in business than by a background in law because business and political decisions both deal with possible future events, while arguments before a court look mainly to the past. —Stimson Bullitt, *To Be a Politician,* 1977

**1238.** If you do not think about the future, you cannot have one. —John Galsworthy, *Swan Song,* 1928

**1239.** There is, I think, nothing in the world more futile than the attempt to find out how a task should be done when one has not yet decided what the task is. —Alexander Meiklejohn, *Education Between Two Worlds,* 1942

**1240.** The tragedy of life doesn't lie in not reaching your goal. The tragedy lies in having no goal to reach. —Benjamin E. Mays, in *New York Times,* May 16, 1985

**1241.** For each age is a dream that is dying, Or one that is coming to birth. —Arthur O'Shaughnessy, "Ode," 1874

**1242.** A dying people tolerates the present, rejects the future, and finds its satisfactions in past greatness and half-remembered glory. —John Steinbeck, *America and Americans,* 1966

**1243.** Nations are formed and are kept alive by the fact that they have a program for tomorrow. —José Ortega y Gasset, *Invertebrate Spain,* 1922

**1244.** The empires of the future are the empires of the mind. —Winston S. Churchill, speech, September 6, 1943

**1245.** Vision is the art of seeing things invisible. —Jonathan Swift, *Thoughts on Various Subjects,* 1711

**1246.** Where there is no vision, the people perish. —Bible, *Proverbs 29:18*

**1247.** We are a pragmatic society. We distrust ideas, ideology. We distrust people with visions; we distrust abstractions. — Richard H. Pells, in *Los Angeles Times,* March 4, 1990

**1248.** The vision thing. — George Bush, remark, 1988 (dismissing the importance of the future and apologizing that he lacked "the vision thing.")

**1249.** Among all forms of mistake, prophecy is the most gratuitous. — George Eliot, *Middlemarch,* 1871–72

**1250.** A hopeful disposition is not the sole qualification to be a prophet.

— Winston S. Churchill, speech, April 30, 1927

**1251.** There are two classes of people who tell what is going to happen in the future: Those who don't know, and those who don't know they don't know. — John Kenneth Galbraith, in *Washington Post,* February 28, 1988

**1252.** Heaven knows what seeming nonsense may not tomorrow be demonstrated truth. — Alfred North Whitehead, *Science and the Modern World,* 1925

**1253.** You cannot fight against the future. Time is on our side. — William E. Gladstone, speech, April 27, 1866

# Gossip and Publicity

## *See also* Character; Corruption; Lies; Opinion, Difference of; Press and Media

**1254.** I know that's a secret, for it's whispered everywhere. — William Congreve, *Love for Love,* 1695

**1255.** I joked about every prominent man in my lifetime, but I never met one I didn't like. — Will Rogers, epitaph

**1256.** There is only one thing in the world worse than being talked about, and that is not being talked about. — Oscar Wilde, *The Picture of Dorian Gray,* 1891

**1257.** Public men are bees working in a glass hive; and curious spectators enjoy themselves in watching every secret movement, as if it were a study in natural history. — Henry Ward Beecher, *Proverbs from Plymouth Pulpit,* 1887

**1258.** This is a free country, madam. We have a right to share your privacy in a public place. — Peter Ustinov, *Romanoff and Juliet,* 1956

**1259.** No one gossips about other people's secret virtues. — Bertrand Russell, *On Education,* 1926

**1260.** Even those who do not display any acuteness and acumen in other respects are experts in the algebra of other people's affairs. — Arthur Schopenhauer, *Parerga and Paralipomena,* "Counsels and Maxims," 1851

**1261.** I set it down as a fact that if all men knew what each said of the other, there would not be four friends in the world. — Blaise Pascal, *Pensées,* 1670

**1262.** Heaven knows what would become of our sociality if we never visited people we speak ill of: we should live, like Egyptian hermits, in crowded solitude. — George Eliot, *Scenes of Clerical Life,* 1858

**1263.** There are persons who, when they cease to shock us, cease to interest us. — F. H. Bradley, *Aphorisms,* 1930

**1264.** Gossip, unlike river water, flows both ways. — Michael Korda, in *Reader's Digest,* June, 1976

**1265.** Why is it that when political ammunition runs low, inevitably the rusty artillery of abuse is always wheeled into action? — Adlai Stevenson, speech, September 22, 1952

**1266.** When two men communicate with each other by word of mouth, there is a twofold hazard in that communication. — Sam Ervin, in *New York Times*, July 13, 1973

**1267.** The belief that fashion alone should dominate opinion has great advantages. It makes thought unnecessary and puts the highest intelligence within the reach of everyone. — Bertrand Russell, *Unpopular Essays*, 1950

**1268.** The public have an insatiable curiosity to know everything except what is worth knowing. — Oscar Wilde, *The Soul of Man Under Socialism*, 1895

**1269.** Tale-bearers are as bad as the tale-makers. — Richard Brinsley Sheridan, *The School for Scandal*, 1777

**1270.** Publicity is one of the purifying elements of politics.... Nothing checks all the bad practices of politics as public exposure. — Woodrow Wilson, in William B. Hale, *The New Freedom*, 1913

**1271.** The sweetest of all sounds is praise. — Xenophon, *Hiero*, ca. 373 B.C.

**1272.** What really flatters a man is that you think him worth flattering. — George Bernard Shaw, *John Bull's Other Island*, 1907

**1273.** We seek our happiness outside ourselves, and in the opinion of men whom we know to be flatterers, insincere, unjust, full of envy, caprice and prejudice. How absurd! — Jean La Bruyère, *Characters,* "Of Mankind," 1688

**1274.** To be happy we must not be too concerned with others. — Albert Camus, *The Fall*, 1956

**1275.** I do not believe the people who tell me that they do not care a row of pins for the opinions of their fellows. It is the bravado of ignorance. — W. Somerset Maugham, *The Summing Up*, 1938

**1276.** Falsehood has a perennial spring. — Edmund Burke, *On American Taxation*, 1775

**1277.** If you give me six sentences written by the most innocent of men, I will find something in them with which to hang him. — Armand Jean du Plessis, *Mirame*, ca. 1625

**1278.** How is the world ruled and how do wars start? Diplomats tell lies to journalists and then believe what they read. — Karl Kraus, *Aphorisms and More Aphorisms*, 1909

**1279.** The man in political life must come to expect the smear and to know that, generally, the best thing to do about it is ignore it — and hope that it will fade away. — Richard M. Nixon, *Six Crises,* 1962

**1280.** It is pure illusion to think that an opinion which passes down from century to century, from generation to generation, may not be entirely false. — Pierre Bayle, *Thoughts on the Comet,* 1682

**1281.** Repetition does not transform a lie into a truth. — Franklin D. Roosevelt, radio address, October 26, 1939

**1282.** What I tell you three times is true. — Lewis Carroll, *The Hunting of the Snark,* 1876

---

# Government

## *See also* Bureaucracy; Government, Roles and Functions of; Haves and Have Nots; Office; the People; State; Welfare

**1283.** The greatest need a people have is for government; their greatest happiness is having good government. — Joseph Joubert, *Pensées,* 1842

**1284.** That government which thinks in terms of humanity will continue. — Franklin D. Roosevelt, speech, October 17, 1936

**1285.** A good government remains the greatest of human blessings, and no nation has ever enjoyed it. — William Ralph Inge, *Outspoken Essays: Second Series,* 1922

**1286.** There is only one thing better than good government, and that is government in which all the people have a part. — Walter H. Page, *Life and Letters, Vol. III,* 1922–25

**1287.** Mankind, when left to themselves, are unfit for their own government. — George Washington, letter, October 31, 1786

**1288.** So they [the government] go on in strange paradox, decided only to be undecided, resolved to be irresolute, adamant to drift, solid for fluidity, all-powerful to be impotent. — Winston S. Churchill, speech, November 12, 1936

**1289.** It is safe to assert that no government proper ever had a provision in its organic law for its own termination. — Abraham Lincoln, inaugural address, March 4, 1861

**1290.** Governments need both shepherds and butchers. — Voltaire, "The Piccini Notebooks," ca. 1750

**1291.** The four pillars of government...(which are religion, justice, counsel, and treasure). — Francis Bacon, *Essays,* "Of Seditions and Troubles," 1625

**1292.** A cabinet is a combining committee—a *hyphen* which joins, a *buckle* which fastens, the legislative part of the state to the executive part of the state. — Walter Bagehot, *The English Constitution,* "The Cabinet," 1867

**1293.** Governance, I was learning, consisted not so much of a tidal wave but of endless smaller waves of angry Lilliputians. — David A. Stockman, *The Triumph of Politics,* 1987

**1294.** The Crown is, according to the saying, the "fountain of honor"; but the Treasury is the spring of business. — Walter Bagehot, *The English Constitution,* "The Cabinet," 1867

**1295.** In the councils of government, we must guard against the acquisition of unwarranted influence, whether sought or unsought, by the military-industrial complex. The potential for the disastrous rise of misplaced power exists and will persist. — Dwight D. Eisenhower, farewell address, January 17, 1961

**1296.** It is very easy to accuse a government of imperfection, for all mortal things are full of it. — Michel Eyquem de Montaigne, *Essays,* 1580

**1297.** To govern is always to choose among disadvantages. — Charles de Gaulle, in *New York Times,* November 14, 1965

**1298.** A government never loses anything by mildness and forbearance to its own citizens, more especially when the consequences of an opposite course may be the shedding of blood. — John Tyler, letter, May 9, 1842

**1299.** In the long-run every government is the exact symbol of its people, with their wisdom and unwisdom. — Thomas Carlyle, *Past and Present,* 1843

**1300.** Governments are more the effect than the cause of that which we are. — Samuel Taylor Coleridge, letter, April, 1798

**1301.** The guilt of a government is the crime of a whole country. — Thomas Paine, *The American Crisis,* 1776–83

**1302.** There are no necessary evils in government. Its evils exist only in its abuses. — Andrew Jackson, veto of the Bank Bill, July 10, 1832

**1303.** Governments arise either out of the people or over the people. — Thomas Paine, *The Rights of Man,* 1791

**1304.** Under a government which imprisons any unjustly, the true place for a just man is also a prison...the only house in a slave State in which a free man can abide with honor. — Henry David Thoreau, *Civil Disobedience,* 1849

**1305.** You have the God-given right to kick the government around. Don't hesitate to do so. — Edmund S. Muskie, speech, September 11, 1968

**1306.** Lay then the axe to the root, and teach governments humanity. — Thomas Paine, *The Rights of Man,* 1791

**1307.** A decent and manly examination of the acts of government should be not only tolerated, but encouraged. —William Henry Harrison, inaugural address, March 4, 1841

**1308.** The pleasure of governing must certainly be exquisite, if we may judge from the vast numbers who are eager to be concerned with it. —Voltaire, *Philosophical Dictionary*, "Government," 1764

**1309.** The less government we have, the better—the fewer laws, and the less confided power. —Ralph Waldo Emerson, *Essays: Second Series*, "Politics," 1844

**1310.** Every time the government attempts to handle our affairs, it costs more and the results are worse than if we had handled them ourselves. —Benjamin Constant, *Cours de politique constitutionelle*, 1818–20

**1311.** Government has a tendency to push itself into all sorts of realms where it worsens situations instead of improving them. —William Bulger, in *Wall Street Journal*, July 12, 1989

**1312.** Anything that the private sector can do, the government can do it worse. —Dixy Lee Ray, in *Mother Jones*, May, 1977

**1313.** In our complex world, there cannot be fruitful initiative without government, but unfortunately there can be government without initiative. —Bertrand Russell, *Authority and the Individual*, 1949

**1314.** Giving money and power to government is like giving whiskey and car keys to teenage boys. —P. J. O'Rourke, *Parliament of Whores*, 1991

**1315.** Accountancy, that is government. —Louis D. Brandeis, statement, January 30, 1914

**1316.** Government, after all, is a very simple thing. —Warren G. Harding, speech, May 27, 1920

**1317.** Government is not an exact science. —Louis D. Brandeis, *Truax v. Corrigan*, 1921

**1318.** The best government is that which governs least. —John L. O'Sullivan, in *United States Magazine and Democratic Review*, 1837

**1319.** It is perfectly true that that government is best which governs least. It is equally true that that government is best which provides most. —Walter Lippmann, *A Preface to Politics*, 1914

**1320.** That government is not best which best secures mere life and property—there is a more valuable thing—manhood. —Mark Twain, *Notebook*, 1935

**1321.** A government that is big enough to give you all you want is big enough to take it all away. —Barry Goldwater, speech, October 21, 1964

**1322.** Society in every state is a blessing, but government, even in its best state, is but a necessary evil; in its worst state an intolerable one. —Thomas Paine, *Common Sense*, 1776

**1323.** Government is at best but an expedient; but most governments are usually, and all governments are sometimes, inexpedient. —Henry David Thoreau, *Civil Disobedience*, 1849

**1324.** Society is produced by our wants and government by our wickedness. —Thomas Paine, *Common Sense*, 1776

**1325.** All government is ultimately and essentially absolute. —Samuel Johnson, *Taxation No Tyranny*, 1775

**1326.** The government of man by man (under whatever name it be disguised) is oppression. —Pierre Joseph Proudhon, *What Is Property?*, 1840

**1327.** It is unquestionably true that Government is begotten of aggression and by aggression. —Herbert Spencer, *The Man Versus the State*, "The Sins of Legislators," 1884

**1328.** The art of government is the organization of idolatry. —George Bernard Shaw, *Man and Superman*, 1903

**1329.** The only good government... is a bad one in a hell of a fright. —Joyce Cary, *The Horse's Mouth*, 1944

**1330.** The government's like a mule, it's slow and it's sure; it's slow to turn, and it's sure to turn the way you don't want it. —Ellen Glasgow, *The Voice of the People*, 1900

**1331.** Our Government is the potent,

the omnipresent teacher. For good or for ill, it teaches the whole people by its example. — Louis D. Brandeis, *Olmstead v. United States,* 1928

**1332.** Our government is based on the belief that a people can be both strong and free, that civilized men need no restraint but that imposed by themselves against abuse of freedom.

— Franklin D. Roosevelt, speech, September 18, 1936

**1333.** Government. . . is neither business nor technology, nor applied science. It is the art of making men live together in peace and with reasonable happiness. — Felix Frankfurter, in *New Republic,* October 31, 1928

---

# Government, Forms of

## See also Bureaucracy; Democracy; Despotism; Monarchy; Revolution; Socialism; Tyranny

**1334.** Any system of government will work when everything is going well. It's the system that functions in the pinches that survives. — John F. Kennedy, *Why England Slept,* 1940

**1335.** Of governments, that of the mob is the most sanguinary, that of soldiers the most expensive, and that of civilians the most vexatious. — Charles Caleb Colton, *Lacon,* 1820–22

**1336.** Which is the best government? That which teaches us to govern ourselves. — Johann Wolfgang von Goethe, in Bailey Saunders, *The Maxims and Reflections of Goethe,* 1893

**1337.** Governments are best classified by considering who are the "somebodies" they are in fact endeavoring to satisfy. — Alfred North Whitehead, *Adventures of Ideas,* 1933

**1338.** For forms of government let fools contest; Whate'er is best administered is best. — Alexander Pope, *An Essay on Man,* 1733

**1339.** The best frame of government is that which is most likely to prevent the greatest sum of evil. — James Monroe, "Observations of the Federal Government," 1789

**1340.** When, in countries that are called civilized, we see age going to the workhouse and youth to the gallows, something must be wrong in the system

of government. — Thomas Paine, *The Rights of Man, Part 2,* 1792

**1341.** A government of statesmen or of clerks? of Humbug or Humdrum? — Benjamin Disraeli, *Coningsby,* 1844

**1342.** The form of government which prevails is the expression of what cultivation exists in the population which permits it. The law is only a memorandum. — Ralph Waldo Emerson, *Essays: Second Series,* "Politics," 1844

**1343.** Popular government has not yet been proved to guarantee, always and everywhere, good government. — Walter Lippmann, *The Public Philosophy,* 1955

**1344.** The art of government has grown from its seeds in the tiny city-states of Greece to become the political mode of half the world. So let us dream of a world in which all states, great and small, work together for the peaceful flowering of the republic of man. — Adlai Stevenson, speech, June 17, 1965

**1345.** The Republican form of government is the highest form of government: but because of this it requires the highest type of human nature — a type nowhere at present existing. — Herbert Spencer, *Essays,* "The Americans," 1891

**1346.** The essence of a republican government is not command. It is consent. — Adlai Stevenson, speech, August 14, 1952

**1347.** In a republic the governing power, being wholly secularized, loses much of its prestige; it is stripped, if one prefers, of all the illusions of intrinsic majesty. — Walter Lippmann, *The Public Philosophy*, 1955

**1348.** I would not give half a guinea to live under one form of government rather than another. It is of no moment to the happiness of an individual. — Samuel Johnson, in James Boswell, *Life of Samuel Johnson*, 1791

# —— *Government, Roles and Functions of* ——

## *See also* Bureaucracy; Diplomacy; Government; Leadership; the People; Welfare

**1349.** The happiness of society is the end of government. — John Adams, *Thoughts on Government*, 1776

**1350.** The only orthodox object of the institution of government is to secure the greatest degree of happiness possible to the general mass of those associated under it. — Thomas Jefferson, letter, March 22, 1812

**1351.** Government is, or ought to be instituted for the common benefit, protection, and security of the people, nation, or community; of all the various modes and forms of government, that is best which is capable of producing the greatest degree of happiness and safety, and is most effectually shared against the danger of maladministration. — George Mason, *Virginia Bill of Rights,* June 12, 1776

**1352.** The object of government in peace and in war is not the glory of rulers or of races, but the happiness of the common man. — William H. Beveridge, *Social Insurance and Allied Services,* 1942

**1353.** The office of government is not to confer happiness, but to give men opportunity to work out happiness for themselves. — William Ellery Channing, in *Christian Examiner,* September/October, 1827

**1354.** The care of human life and happiness, and not their destruction, is the first and only legitimate object of good government. — Thomas Jefferson, *To the Republican Citizens of Wash-*

*ington County, Maryland,* March 31, 1809

**1355.** The final end of government is not to exert restraint but to do good. — Rufus Choate, speech, July 2, 1841

**1356.** The function of a government is to calm, rather than to excite agitation. — Henry John Temple, in Philip Guedella, *Gladstone and Palmerston,* 1928

**1357.** The only sure bulwark of continuing liberty is a government strong enough to protect the interests of the people, and a people strong enough and well enough informed to maintain its sovereign control over its government. — Franklin D. Roosevelt, radio address, April 14, 1938

**1358.** Even to observe neutrality you must have a strong government. — Alexander Hamilton, speech, June 29, 1787

**1359.** Government's role should be to support business: creating jobs and creating taxpayers. — H. Ross Perot, *United We Stand,* 1992

**1360.** The lessons of paternalism ought to be unlearned and the better lesson taught that, while the people should patriotically and cheerfully support their government, its functions do not include the support of the people. — Grover Cleveland, inaugural address, March 4, 1893

**1361.** We get the fundamental confusion that government, since it can correct much abuse, can also create righteousness. — Herbert Hoover, letter, December 30, 1929

**1362.** The important thing for Government is not to do things which individuals are doing already, and to do them a little better or a little worse; but to do those things which at present are not done at all. — John Maynard Keynes, *The End of Laissez-Faire,* 1926

**1363.** Government exists to protect us from each other. Where Government has gone beyond its limits is in deciding to protect us from ourselves. — Ronald Reagan, in *New York Times,* April 13, 1980

**1364.** Since government, even in its best state is an evil, the object principally to be aimed at is that we should have as little of it as the general peace of human society will permit. — William Godwin, *An Enquiry Concerning Political Justice,* 1793

**1365.** See that government weighs as little as possible and does not unnecessarily burden the people. — Napoleon I, letter, January 1, 1809

**1366.** Government was intended to suppress injustice, but its effect has been to embody and perpetuate it. — William Godwin, *An Enquiry Concerning Political Justice,* 1793

**1367.** It is a function of government to invent philosophies to explain the demands of its own convenience. — Murray Kempton, *America Comes of Middle Age,* 1963

**1368.** What is a Government for except to dictate! If it does not dictate, then it is not a Government. — David Lloyd George, *War Memories,* 1933–36

---

## *Greatness*

### *See also* Ambition; Fame; Leaders; Leadership

**1369.** Few great men could pass Personnel. — Paul Goodman, *Growing Up Absurd,* 1960

**1370.** Greatness of soul is never apparent, for it conceals itself; a little originality is usually all that shows. Greatness of soul is more frequent than one would suppose. — Stendhal, *Love,* 1822

**1371.** Great men are the guideposts and landmarks in the state. — Edmund Burke, speech, April 19, 1774

**1372.** A great man does enough for us when he refrains from doing us harm. — Pierre de Beaumarchais, *The Barber of Seville,* 1775

**1373.** Greatness is usually the result of a natural equilibrium among opposite qualities. — Denis Diderot, *Rameau's Nephew,* 1761

**1374.** Great offices will have great talents. — William Cowper, *The Task,* 1785

**1375.** An institution is the length-ened shadow of one man. — Ralph Waldo Emerson, *Essays: First Series,* "Self-Reliance," 1841

**1376.** There is much difference between imitating a good man, and counterfeiting him. — Benjamin Franklin, *Poor Richard's Almanac,* 1733–58

**1377.** No man was ever great by imitation. — Samuel Johnson, *Rasselas,* 1759

**1378.** The essence of greatness is the perception that virtue is enough. — Ralph Waldo Emerson, *Essays: First Series,* "Heroism," 1841

**1379.** Those who believe that they are exclusively in the right are generally those who achieve something. — Aldous Huxley, *Proper Studies,* 1927

**1380.** Greatness knows itself. — William Shakespeare, *Henry IV, Part I,* 1597

**1381.** He who comes up to his own idea of greatness must always have had a very low standard of it in his mind.

—William Hazlitt, *The Plain Speaker,* 1826

1382. To be great is to be misunderstood. — Ralph Waldo Emerson, *Essays: First Series,* "Self-Reliance," 1841

1383. You can calculate the worth of a man by the number of his enemies, and the importance of a work of art by the harm that is spoken of it. — Gustave Flaubert, letter, June 14, 1853

1384. A great man's failures to understand define him. — André Gide, *Pretexts,* 1903

1385. Great men, like great cities, have many crooked arts, and dark alleys in their hearts whereby he that knows them may save himself much time and trouble. — Charles Caleb Colton, *Lacon,* 1820–22

1386. If two or three persons should come with a high spiritual aim and with great powers, the world would fall into their hands like a ripe peach. — Ralph Waldo Emerson, *Journals,* 1844

1387. A citizen, first in war, first in peace, and first in the hearts of his countrymen. — Henry Lee, funeral oration for George Washington, 1800

1388. Courtesy is the politic witchery of great personages. — Balthasar Gracián, *The Art of Worldly Wisdom,* 1647

1389. The civilities of the great are never thrown away. — Samuel Johnson, *Memories of the King of Prussia,* 1756

1390. I would sooner fail than not be among the greatest. — John Keats, letter, October 9, 1818

1391. No man is truly great who is great only in his lifetime. The test of greatness is the page of history. — William Hazlitt, *Table Talk,* "The Indian Jugglers," 1821–22

1392. A great man's greatest good luck is to die at the right time. — Eric Hoffer, *The Passionate State of Mind,* 1954

1393. No great man is ever born too soon or too late. — Norman Douglas, *South Wind,* 1917

1394. Heroes are created by popular demand, sometimes out of the scantiest materials, or none at all. — Gerald White Johnson, *American Heroes and Hero-Worship,* 1943

1395. Show me a hero and I will write you a tragedy. — F. Scott Fitzgerald, *The Crack-Up,* 1945

1396. The privilege of the great is to see catastrophes from the terrace. — Jean Giraudoux, *Tiger at the Gates,* 1935

1397. It is not the clear-sighted who rule the world. Great achievements are accomplished in a blessed, warm mental fog. — Joseph Conrad, *Victory,* 1915

1398. Great minds tend toward banality. — André Gide, *Pretexts,* 1903

1399. Men are seldom more commonplace than on supreme occasions. — Samuel Butler (II), *Notebooks,* 1912

1400. We have, I fear, confused power with greatness. — Stewart L. Udall, speech, June 13, 1965

1401. Great men are but life-sized. Most of them, indeed, are rather short. — Max Beerbohm, *And Even Now,* 1921

# Haves and Have Nots

## See also Class; Masses and Elites; Poverty; Welfare

1402. There are only two families in the world, the Haves and the Have-Nots. — Miguel de Cervantes, *Don Quixote,* 1615

1403. "Two nations; between whom there is no intercourse and no sympathy; who are as ignorant of each other's habits, thoughts, and feelings, as if they were dwellers in different zones, or inhabitants of different planets; who are formed by a different breeding, are fed by a different food, are ordered by different manners, and are not governed by the same laws." "You speak of—" said Egremont, hesitatingly, "The rich and the poor."—Benjamin Disraeli, *Sybil*, 1845

**1404.** Let me tell you about the very rich. They are different from you and me.—F. Scott Fitzgerald, *All the Sad Young Men*, 1926

**1405.** The worst discrimination on Earth is the rich and powerful against the poor and weak.—Jimmy Carter, in *Los Angeles Times*, May 26, 1992

**1406.** A man thinks differently in a palace than in a hut.—Ludwig Feuerbach, *The Essence of Religion*, 1845

**1407.** It is not the consciousness of men that determines their existence, but on the contrary it is their social existence that determines their consciousness. —Karl Marx, *Critique of Political Economy*, 1859

**1408.** Man was formed by society.—William Blackstone, *Commentaries on the Laws of England*, 1765

**1409.** Economic development, producing increased income, greater economic security, and widespread higher education, largely determines the form of "class struggle," by permitting those in the lower strata to develop longer time perspectives and more complex and gradualist views of politics.—Seymour Martin Lipset, *Political Man*, 1981

**1410.** The two greatest obstacles to democracy in the United States are, first, the widespread delusion among the poor that we have a democracy, and second, the chronic terror among the rich, lest we get it.—Edward Dowling, in *Chicago Daily News*, August 28, 1941

**1411.** The distribution of wealth is the most important source of interest-conflict in complex societies. At the opposite pole is the institution of the family: the integrator par excellence. —Seymour Martin Lipset, *Political Man*, 1981

**1412.** You are a king by your own fireside, as much as any monarch in his throne.—Miguel de Cervantes, *Don Quixote*, 1615

**1413.** The world of the happy is quite different from that of the unhappy.—Ludwig Wittenstein, *Tractatus Logico-Philosophicus*, 1922

**1414.** I can sympathize with people's pain, but not with their pleasures. There is something curiously boring about somebody else's happiness. — Aldous Huxley, *Limbo*, "Cynthia," 1920

**1415.** What difference does it make to the dead, the orphans and the homeless, whether the mad destruction is wrought under the name of totalitarianism or the holy name of liberty and democracy?—Mohandas K. Gandhi, *Non-Violence in Peace and War*, 1948

**1416.** I see one-third of a nation ill-housed, ill-clad, ill-nourished.—Franklin D. Roosevelt, inaugural address, January 20, 1937

**1417.** Of all the preposterous assumptions of humanity over humanity, nothing exceeds most of the criticisms made on the habits of the poor by the well-housed, well-warmed, and well-fed.—Herman Melville, "Poor Man's Pudding and Rich Man's Crumbs," 1854

**1418.** The law, in its majestic equality, forbids the rich as well as the poor to sleep under bridges, to beg in the streets, and to steal bread.—Anatole France, *Le Lys rouge*, 1894

**1419.** Great wealth always supports the party in power, no matter how corrupt it may be. It never exerts itself for reform for it instinctively fears change. —Henry George, *Social Problems*, 1884

**1420.** Civil government . . . is in reality instituted for the defense of the rich against the poor, or of those who have some property against those who have none at all.—Adam Smith, *The Wealth of Nations, Vol. II*, 1776

**1421.** In revolutionary times the rich are always the people who are most afraid.—Gerald White Johnson, *American Freedom and the Press*, 1958

**1422.** If the French noblesse had been capable of playing cricket with their peasants, their chateaux would never have been burnt.—G. M. Trevelyan, *English Social History*, 1942

1423. There is always more misery among the lower classes than there is humanity in the higher. —Victor Hugo, *Les Misérables*, 1862

1424. The danger of success is that it makes us forget the world's dreadful injustice. —Jules Renard, *Journal*, 1908

1425. Wealth is the relentless enemy of understanding. —John Kenneth Galbraith, *The Affluent Society*, 1958

1426. Whereas it has long been known and declared that the poor have no right to the property of the rich, I wish it also to be known and declared that the rich have no right to the property of the poor. —John Ruskin, *Unto This Last*, 1862

1427. During the whole period of written history, it is not the workers but the robbers who have been in control of the world. —Scott Nearing, *From Capitalism to Communism*, 1946

1428. Never contend with a man who has nothing to lose. —Balthasar Gracián, *The Art of Worldly Wisdom*, 1647

1429. Extreme hopes are born of extreme misery. —Bertrand Russell, *Unpopular Essays*, 1950

1430. A hungry stomach cannot hear. —Jean de La Fontaine, *Fables Book*, 1678–79

1431. In a word, we desire to throw no one into the shade, but we also demand our own place in the sun. Bernhard von Bülow, speech, December 6, 1897

1432. He that wants money, means and content is without three good friends. —William Shakespeare, *As You Like It*, 1599

1433. The want of a thing is perplexing enough, but the possession of it is intolerable. —John Vanbrugh, *The Confederacy*, 1705

1434. Most people seek after what they do not possess and are thus enslaved by the very things they want to acquire. —Anwar al-Sadat, *In Search of Identity*, 1978

1435. A beggar amidst great riches. —Horace, *Odes*, 1st c. B.C.

1436. The poor have little, beggars none, the rich too much, enough not one. —Benjamin Franklin, *Poor Richard's Almanac*, 1733–58

1437. Untaught to bear poverty. —Horace, *Odes*, 1st c. B.C.

1438. There are three ways by which an individual can get wealth—by work, by gift, and by theft. And, clearly, the reason why the workers get so little is that beggars and thieves get too much. —Henry George, *Social Problems*, 1884

1439. An ounce of enterprise is worth a pound of privilege. —Frederic R. Marvin, *The Companionship of Books*, 1905

## History

1440. History teaches us that men and nations behave wisely once they have exhausted all other alternatives. —Abba Eban, speech, December 16, 1970

1441. Unlike presidential administrations, problems rarely have terminal dates. —Dwight D. Eisenhower, State of the Union Address, January 12, 1961

1442. History knows no resting places and no plateaus. —Henry Kissinger, *White House Years*, 1979

1443. An honest man can feel no pleasure in the exercise of power over his fellow citizens. —Thomas Jefferson, letter, January 13, 1813

1444. The history of the world is the record of a man in quest of his daily bread and butter. —Hendrik Van Loon, *The Story of Mankind*, 1921

1445. History is the crystallisation of popular beliefs. —Donn Piatt, *Memories of Men Who Saved the Union*, "Abraham Lincoln," 1887

1446. Political history is far too

criminal and pathological to be a fit subject of study for the young. Children should acquire their heroes and villains from fiction. — W. H. Auden, *A Certain World*, 1971

**1447.** A lot of history is just dirty politics cleaned up for the consumption of children and other innocents. — Richard Reeves, in *Detroit Free Press*, November 4, 1982

**1448.** History is the transformation of tumultuous conquerors into silent footnotes. — Paul Eldridge, *Maxims for a Modern Man*, 1965

**1449.** The history of the great events of this world is scarcely more than the history of crimes. — Voltaire, *Essay on the Morals and the Spirit of Nations*, 1756

**1450.** Man is a history-making creature who can neither repeat his past nor leave it behind. — W. H. Auden, *The Dyer's Hand*, "D. H. Lawrence," 1962

**1451.** History is a vast early warning system. — Norman Cousins, in *Saturday Review*, April 15, 1978

**1452.** Those who cannot remember the past are condemned to repeat it. — George Santayana, *The Life of Reason*, 1905–06

**1453.** People and governments have never learned anything from history, or acted on principles deduced from it. — Georg Wilhelm Friedrich Hegel, *Philosophy of History*, 1832

**1454.** Difficulty is the excuse history never accepts. — Edward R. Murrow, remark, October 19, 1959

**1455.** Life has to be lived forwards; but it can only be understood backwards. — Aldous Huxley, *Mortal Coils*, 1922

**1456.** Those men and women are fortunate who are born at a time when a great struggle for human freedom is in progress. — Emmeline Pankhurst, *My Own Story*, 1914

**1457.** I claim not to have controlled events, but confess plainly that events have controlled me. — Abraham Lincoln, letter, April 4, 1864

**1458.** There is no history of mankind, there are only many histories of all kinds of aspects of human life. And one of these is the history of political power. This is elevated into the history of the world. — Karl R. Popper, *The Open Society and Its Enemies*, 1945

**1459.** History can be well written only in a free country. — Voltaire, letter, May 27, 1737

**1460.** Whosoever, in writing a modern history, shall follow truth too near the heels, it may happily strike out its teeth. — Walter Ralegh, *The History of the World*, 1614

**1461.** History gets thicker as it approaches recent times. — A. J. P. Taylor, *English History 1914–45*, 1965

**1462.** History does not unfold; it piles up. — Robert M. Adams, *Bad Mouth*, 1977

**1463.** I should contend that "men are free to make history," but that some men are indeed much freer than others. — C. Wright Mills, *The Power Elite*, 1956

**1464.** History is a distillation of rumor. — Thomas Carlyle, *History of the French Revolution*, 1837

**1465.** History is a gallery of pictures in which there are few originals and many copies. — Alexis de Tocqueville, *The Old Regime*, 1856

**1466.** The world's history is the world's judgment. — Friedrich von Schiller, "Resignation," 1786

**1467.** Yesterday's miracle is today's intolerable condition. — Lewis D. Eigen, *Microcomputers for Executive Decision-Making*, 1985

**1468.** The certainties of one age are the problems of the next. — R. H. Tawney, *Religion and the Rise of Capitalism*, 1926

**1469.** History is principally the inaccurate narration of events which ought not to have happened. — Ernest Albert Hooten, *Twilight of Man*, 1939

**1470.** Human blunders usually do more to shape history than human wickedness. — A. J. P. Taylor, *The Origins of the Second World War*, 1961

**1471.** Just as philosophy is the study of other people's misconceptions, so history is the study of other people's mistakes. — Philip Guedalla, *Supers and Supermen,* 1920

**1472.** Might and right do differ frightfully from hour to hour; but give them centuries to try it in, they are found to be identical. — Thomas Carlyle, *Chartism,* 1839

**1473.** What is history after all? History is facts which become lies in the end; legends are lies which become history in the end. — Jean Cocteau, in *Observer,* September 22, 1957

**1474.** History is more or less bunk. — Henry Ford, testimony, July 15, 1919

**1475.** The history of the world is a farce. — Gustave Flaubert, *Intimate Notebook, 1840–1841,* 1967

**1476.** That great dust-heap called history. — Augustine Birrell, *Obiter Dicta,* "Carlyle," 1884

**1477.** I tell you the past is a bucket of ashes. — Carl Sandberg, *Cornhuskers,* "Prairie," 1918

**1478.** With history one can never be certain, but [if Khrushchev had been assassinated instead of Kennedy] I think I can safely say that Aristotle Onassis would not have married Mrs. Khrushchev. — Gore Vidal, in *Sunday Times,* June 4, 1989

# Honesty

## See also Character; Hypocrisy; Lies; Truth

**1479.** It happens that intellectual honesty is not the coin of the realm in politics. — Edward Koch, in *New York Times,* October 23, 1979

**1480.** You cannot adopt politics as a profession and remain honest. — Louis McHenry Howe, speech, January 17, 1933

**1481.** The trouble with this country is that there are too many politicians who believe, with a conviction based on experience, that you can fool all of the people all of the time. — Franklin P. Adams, *Nods and Becks,* 1944

**1482.** If experience teaches us anything at all, it teaches us this: that a good politician, under democracy, is quite as unthinkable as an honest burglar. — H. L. Mencken, *Prejudices: Fourth Series,* 1924

**1483.** For de little stealin' dey gits you in jail soon or late. For de big stealin' dey makes you emperor and puts you in de Hall o' Fame when you croaks. — Eugene O'Neill, *The Emperor Jones,* 1920

**1484.** Found a Society of Honest Men, and all the thieves will join it. — Alain, *Propos d'un Normand,* 1906–14

**1485.** Dishonesty is never an accident. Good men, like good women, never see temptation when they meet it. — John Peers, *1,001 Logical Laws,* 1979

**1486.** What we need is appointive positions in men of knowledge and experience who have sufficient character to resist temptations. — Calvin Coolidge, *Autobiography,* 1929

**1487.** It is easier for a camel to go through the eye of a needle, or for a rich man to enter the kingdom of heaven, than for a politician to lay aside disguise. — James Caulfeild, letter, January, 1867

**1488.** Politicians tend to live "in character," and many a public figure has come to imitate the journalism which describes him. — Walter Lippmann, *A Preface to Politics,* 1914

**1489.** Some members of Congress are the best actors in the world. — Shirley Chisholm, *Unbought and Unbossed,* 1970

**1490.** Since a politician never believes what he says, he is surprised when others believe him. — Charles de Gaulle, in *Newsweek,* October 1, 1962

**1491.** It is impossible that a man who is false to his friends and neighbors should be true to the public. — George Berkeley, *Maxims Concerning Patriotism*, 1740

**1492.** We are inclined to believe those whom we do not know because they have never deceived us. — Samuel Johnson, *The Idler*, 1758

**1493.** Shrewdness in Public Life all over the World is always honored, while honesty in Public Life is generally attributed to Dumbness and is seldom rewarded. — Will Rogers, *The Autobiography of Will Rogers*, 1949

**1494.** Our great democracies still tend to think that a stupid man is more likely to be honest than a clever man, and our politicians take advantage of this prejudice by pretending to be more stupid than nature made them. — Bertrand Russell, *New Hope for a Changing World*, 1951

**1495.** The cure for bad politics is the same as the cure for tuberculosis. It is living in the open space. — Woodrow Wilson, speech, September 18, 1912

**1496.** In politics nothing is just save what is honest; nothing is useful except that is just. — Maximilien Robespierre, speech, May, 1791

**1497.** An honest God is the noblest work of man. — Robert G. Ingersoll, *The Gods*, 1876

**1498.** Leaders often just do not realize what they can cause if they permit the impression to exist that there is room for dishonesty in any form in their world. Fuses are lit all over the place. Who knows where they will lead? — Philip B. Crosby, *Running Things*, 1986

**1499.** Political thinking consists in deciding upon the conclusion first and then finding good arguments for it. An open mind is considered irresponsible — and perhaps it really is. — R. H. S. Crossman, *Diary*, November 13, 1951

**1500.** "But the Emperor has nothing on at all!" cried a little child. — Hans Christian Andersen, *Danish Fairy Legends and Tales*, "The Emperor's New Clothes," 1846

**1501.** The whole of government consists in the art of being honest. — Thomas Jefferson, *Works, Vol. VI*, 1804–05

---

# Hypocrisy

## *See also* Character; Honesty; Lies

**1502.** Honesty is praised and left to shiver. — Juvenal, *Satires*, ca. 110

**1503.** Hateful to me as the gates of Hades is that man who hides one thing in his heart and speaks another. — Homer, *The Iliad*, ca. 700 B.C.

**1504.** Be a hypocrite, if you like, but don't talk like one! — Denis Diderot, *Rameau's Nephew*, 1761

**1505.** Do not ask me to be kind; just ask me to act as though I were. — Jules Renard, *Journal*, 1898

**1506.** The only vice that cannot be forgiven is hypocrisy. The repentance of a hypocrite is itself hypocrisy. — William Hazlitt, *Characteristics*, 1823

**1507.** Hypocrisy is the most difficult and nerve-racking vice that any man can pursue; it needs an unceasing vigilance and a rare detachment of spirit. It cannot, like adultery or gluttony, be practiced at spare moments; it is a whole-time job. — W. Somerset Maugham, *Cakes and Ale*, 1930

**1508.** We have, in fact, two kinds of morality side by side; one which we preach but do not practice, and another which we practice but seldom preach. — Bertrand Russell, *Sceptical Essays*, 1928

**1509.** In all ages, hypocrites, called priests, have put crowns upon the heads of thieves, called kings. — Robert G. Ingersoll, *Prose-Poems and Selections,* 1884

**1510.** Put not your trust in princes. — Bible, *Psalms 146:3*

**1511.** The louder he talked of his honor, the faster we counted our spoons. — Ralph Waldo Emerson, *The Conduct of Life,* "Worship," 1860

**1512.** No man, for any considerable period, can wear one face to himself, and another to the multitude, without finally getting bewildered as to which may be the true. — Nathaniel Hawthorne, *The Scarlet Letter,* 1850

**1513.** Those who profess outrageous zeal for the liberty and prosperity of their country, and at the same time infringe her laws, affront her religion and debauch her people, are but despicable quacks. — Soame Jenyns, *A Free Enquiry into the Nature and Origin of Evil,* 1757

**1514.** Those who have given themselves the most concern about the happiness of peoples have made their neighbors very miserable. — Anatole France, *The Crime of Sylvestre Bonnard,* 1881

**1515.** The greatest superstition now entertained by public men is that hypocrisy is the royal road to success. — Robert G. Ingersoll, speech, December 13, 1886

**1516.** A Conservative Government is an organized hypocrisy. — Benjamin Disraeli, speech, March 17, 1845

**1517.** Democracy is hypocrisy without limitation. — Iskander Mirza, in *Time,* October 20, 1958

**1518.** No man is a hypocrite in his pleasures. — Samuel Johnson, in James Boswell, *Life of Samuel Johnson,* 1791

**1519.** We ought to see far enough into a hypocrite to see even his sincerity. — Gilbert K. Chesterton, *Heretics,* 1905

**1520.** A plague of opinion! A man may wear it on both sides, like a leather jerkin. — William Shakespeare, *Troilus and Cressida,* 1602

**1521.** What kind of truth is this which is true on one side of a mountain and false on the other? — Michel Eyquem de Montaigne, *Essays,* 1580

**1522.** How long halt ye between two opinions? — Bible, *I Kings, 18:21*

**1523.** All I say is, if you cannot ride two horses, you have no right in the circus. — James Maxton, in *Daily Herald,* January 12, 1931

# *Idealism*

## *See also* **Belief; Ideas; Intellectuals**

**1524.** To say that a man is an idealist is merely to say that he is a man. — Gilbert K. Chesterton, *Heretics,* 1905

**1525.** The ideals of yesterday are the truths of today. — William McKinley, speech, September 1, 1901

**1526.** Young people should remain idealistic all their lives. If you have to choose between being Don Quixote and Sancho Panza, for heaven's sake, be the Don. — Ramsey Clark, in *Detroit News,* April 28, 1978

**1527.** Sometimes people call me an idealist. Well, that is the way I know I am an American. America is the only idealistic nation in the world. — Woodrow Wilson, speech, September 8, 1919

**1528.** Americans ought ever be asking themselves about their concept of the ideal republic. — Warren G. Harding, speech, June 22, 1923

**1529.** Our bodies can be mobilized by law and police and men with guns, if necessary — but where shall we find that which will make us believe in what we must do, so that we can fight through to victory? — Pearl S. Buck, *What America Means to Me,* 1943

**1530.** Nations are not truly great solely because the individuals composing them are numerous, free, and active; but they are great when these numbers, this freedom, and this activity are employed in the service of an ideal higher than that of an ordinary man, taken by himself. —Matthew Arnold, *Democracy,* 1861

**1531.** Idealism springs from deep feelings, but feelings are nothing without the formulated idea that keeps them whole. —Jacques Barzun, *The House of Intellect,* 1959

**1532.** Everything in our political life tends to hide from us that there is anything wiser than our ordinary selves. —Matthew Arnold, *Culture and Anarchy,* 1869

**1533.** Ideals are an imaginative understanding of that which is desirable in that which is possible. —Walter Lippmann, *A Preface to Morals,* 1929

**1534.** An ideal is a port toward which we resolve to steer. —Felix Adler, *Life and Destiny,* 1903

**1535.** Ideal perfection is not the true basis of English legislation. We look at the attainable; we look at the practical. —William E. Gladstone, speech, February 28, 1884

**1536.** All idealism is falsehood in the face of necessity. —Friedrich Wilhelm Nietzsche, *Ecce Homo, Part II,* 1908

**1537.** The road from political idealism to political realism is strewn with the corpses of our dead selves. —André Malraux, in *Saturday Review,* December 9, 1961

**1538.** The uncommitted life isn't worth living. —Marshall W. Fishwick, in *Saturday Review,* December 21, 1963

**1539.** If a man hasn't discovered something that he will die for, he isn't fit to live. —Martin Luther King Jr., speech, June 23, 1963

**1540.** To die for an idea; it is unquestionably noble. But how much nobler it would be if men died for ideas that were true! —H. L. Mencken, *Prejudices, First Series,* 1919

**1541.** To die for an idea is to place a pretty high price upon conjectures. —Anatole France, *La Révolte des Anges,* 1914

**1542.** All men are prepared to accomplish the incredible if their ideals are threatened. —Hermann Hesse, *Demian,* 1919

**1543.** When hopes and dreams are loose in the streets, it is well for the timid to lock doors, shutter windows and lie low until the wrath has passed. —Eric Hoffer, *The True Believer,* 1951

**1544.** It is not materialism that is the chief curse of the world, as pastors teach, but idealism. Men get into trouble by taking their visions and hallucinations too seriously. —H. L. Mencken, *Minority Report,* 1956

**1545.** Every age and every condition indulges some daring fallacy; every man amuses himself with projects which he knows to be improbable, and which, therefore, he resolves to pursue without daring to examine them. —Samuel Johnson, *The Adventurer,* 1753

**1546.** Every form of addiction is bad, no matter whether the narcotic be alcohol or morphine or idealism. —Carl Jung, *Memory, Dreams, Thought,* 1962

**1547.** When they come downstairs from their Ivory Towers, Idealists are apt to walk straight into the gutter. —Logan Pearsall Smith, *Afterthoughts,* 1931

**1548.** A man gazing on the stars is proverbially at the mercy of the puddles in the road. —Alexander Smith, *Dreamthorp,* "Men of Letters," 1863

**1549.** The idealist is incorrigible: if he be thrown out of his Heaven, he makes himself a suitable, ideal out of Hell. —Friedrich Wilhelm Nietzsche, *Miscellaneous Maxims and Opinions,* 1879

**1550.** It is always with the best intentions that the worst work is done. —Oscar Wilde, *Intentions,* 1891

**1551.** Don't use that foreign word "ideals." We have that excellent native word "lies." —Henrik Ibsen, *The Wild Duck,* 1884

**1552.** In our ideals we unwittingly reveal our vices. —Jean Rostand, *Julien ou une conscience,* 1928

**1553.** Society often forgives the criminal, it never forgives the dreamer. — Oscar Wilde, *Oscariana*, 1911

**1554.** Idealism is the despot of thought, just as politics is the despot of will. — Michael Bakunin, "A Circular Letter to My Friends in Italy," 1871

**1555.** Idealism is the noble toga that political gentlemen drape over the will to power. — Aldous Huxley, in *New York Herald Tribune*, November 24, 1963

**1556.** It seems to be the fate of idealists to obtain what they have struggled for in a form which destroys their ideals. — Bertrand Russell, *Marriage and Morals*, "The Liberation of Women," 1929

**1557.** You can tell the ideals of a nation by its advertisements. — Norman Douglas, *South Wind*, 1917

**1558.** An idealist is one who, on noticing that a rose smells better than a cabbage, concludes that it will also make better soup. — H. L. Mencken, *A Book of Burlesques*, "Sententiae," 1920

---

# *Ideas*

## See also Belief; Education; Idealism; Knowledge; Thought

**1559.** An invasion of armies can be resisted, but not an idea whose time has come. — Victor Hugo, *Histoire d'un Crime*, 1852

**1560.** There would seem to be a law operating in human experience by which the mind once suddenly aware of a verity for the first time immediately invents it again. — Agnes Sligh Turnbull, *The Golden Journey*, 1955

**1561.** There is nothing so powerful as an old idea whose time has come again. — Ben Wattenberg, in *Washingtonian*, November, 1979

**1562.** A powerful idea communicates some of its power to the man who contradicts it. — Marcel Proust, *Remembrance of Things Past*, 1913–26

**1563.** Ideas are not always the mere signs and effects of social circumstances, they are themselves a power in history. — John Stuart Mill, "Tocqueville on Democracy in America," 1835

**1564.** One of the greatest pains to human nature is the pain of a new idea. — Walter Bagehot, *Physics and Politics*, 1869

**1565.** Every new idea has something of the pain and peril of childbirth about it. — Samuel Butler (II), *Notebooks*, 1912

**1566.** All great deeds and great thoughts have a ridiculous beginning. — Albert Camus, *The Myth of Sisyphus*, 1955

**1567.** A new idea is delicate. It can be killed by a sneer or a yawn; it can be stabbed to death by a quip and worried to death by a frown on the right man's brow. — Charles Brower, in *Advertising Age*, August 10, 1959

**1568.** If we watch ourselves honestly, we shall often find that we have begun to argue against a new idea even before it has been completely stated. — Arthur Koestler, *The Act of Creation*, 1964

**1569.** Every new idea is obscure at first. It is or it wouldn't be new. — Robert Irwin, in *Newsweek*, December 29, 1976

**1570.** An idea can turn into dust or magic, depending on the talent that rubs against it. — William Bernbach, in *New York Times*, October 6, 1982

**1571.** As soon as an idea is accepted it is time to reject it. — Holbrook Jackson, *Platitudes in the Making*, 1911

**1572.** The thinker dies, but his thoughts are beyond the reach of destruction. Men are mortals; but ideas are immortal. — Walter Lippmann, *A Preface to Morals*, 1929

1573. The most effective way of shutting our minds against a great man's ideas is to take them for granted and admit he was great and have done with him. — George Bernard Shaw, *The Quintessence of Ibsenism,* 1913

1574. A society made up of individuals who were capable of original thought would probably be unendurable. The pressure of ideas would simply drive it frantic. — H. L. Mencken, *Minority Report,* 1956

1575. The test of a first-rate intelligence is the ability to hold two opposed ideas in the mind at the same time, and still retain the ability to function. — F. Scott Fitzgerald, *The Crack-Up,* 1945

1576. *Doublethink* means the power of holding two contradictory beliefs in one's mind simultaneously, and accepting both of them. — George Orwell, *1984,* 1949

1577. In this new rhetoric, normal contradictions of thought vanish. Thus, the old virtues of tolerance and free speech become *repressive tolerance,* a sinister effort by the *establishment* to smother the truth by indulgence; this, apparently, justifies the denial of free speech to those who disagree. — Theodore H. White, *The Making of the President 1968,* 1969

1578. There never was an idea stated that woke up men out of their stupid indifference but its originator was spoken of as a crank. — Oliver Wendell Holmes Sr., *Over the Teacups,* 1891

1579. A man is not necessarily intelligent because he has plenty of ideas, any more than he is a good general because he has plenty of soldiers. — Sébastien Roch Nicholas Chamfort, *Maxims et pensées,* 1805

1580. The value of an idea lies in the using of it. — Thomas Alva Edison, in *Government Executive,* 1987

1581. A "new thinker," when studied closely, is merely a man who does not know what other people have thought. — Frank Moore Colby, *The Margin of Hesitation,* 1921

1582. The best ideas are common property. — Seneca, *Epistles,* 1st c.

1583. Democracy, more than any other form of government, depends upon ideas. — Barbara A. Mikulski, in *Washington Post,* March 28, 1990

1584. There is no connection between the political ideas of our educated class and the deep places of the imagination. — Lionel Trilling, *The Liberal Imagination,* 1950

1585. In the American political system, you're only allowed to have real ideas if it's absolutely guaranteed that you can't win an election. — P. J. O'Rourke, *Parliament of Whores,* 1991

1586. Orthodoxy: That peculiar condition where the patient can neither eliminate an old idea nor absorb a new one. — Elbert Hubbard, *The Note Book,* 1927

1587. No grand idea was ever born in a conference, but a lot of foolish ideas have died there. — F. Scott Fitzgerald, *The Crack-Up,* 1945

1588. Human history is in essence a history of ideas. — H. G. Wells, *The Outline of History,* 1920

1589. General notions are generally wrong. — Mary Wortley Montagu, letter, March 28, 1710

1590. General and abstract ideas are the source of the greatest errors of mankind. — Jean-Jacques Rousseau, *Émile,* 1762

1591. We do not sell ideas if they are not good. Ideas are not salami. — Nikita S. Khrushchev, in *New York Herald Tribune,* February 11, 1960

1592. All ideas are to some extent inevitably subversive.... Christianity was subversive to paganism. — Albert Guérard, *Testament of a Liberal,* 1956

1593. All great ideas are dangerous. — Oscar Wilde, *De Profundis,* 1905

1594. Ideas are dangerous, but the man to whom they are least dangerous is the man of ideas. — Gilbert K. Chesterton, *Heretics,* 1905

1595. An idea that is not dangerous is unworthy of being called an idea at all. — Oscar Wilde, "The Critic as Artist," 1890

**1596.** Nothing is more dangerous than an idea, when a man has only one idea. — Alain, *Propos sur la religion*, 1938

**1597.** A fixed idea ends in madness or heroism. — Victor Hugo, *Quatre-vingt-treize*, 1879

**1598.** If there is anything more dangerous to the life of the mind than having no independent commitment to ideas, it is having an excess of commitment to some special and constricting idea. — Richard Hofstadter, *Anti-Intellectualism in American Life*, 1963

**1599.** Mr. Kremlin himself was distinguished for ignorance, for he had only one idea, — and that was wrong. — Benjamin Disraeli, *Sybil*, 1845

**1600.** Ideas are indeed the most dangerous weapons in the world. Our ideas of freedom are the most powerful political weapons man has ever forged. — William O. Douglas, *An Almanac of Liberty*, 1954

**1601.** Throughout history the world has been laid waste to ensure the triumph of conceptions that are now as dead as the men that died for them. — Henry de Montherlant, *Notebooks*, 1930–44

**1602.** The enemy of conventional wisdom is not ideas but the march of events. — John Kenneth Galbraith, *The Affluent Society*, 1958

**1603.** Not to engage in the pursuit of ideas is to live like ants instead of like men. — Mortimer J. Adler, in *Saturday Review*, November 22, 1958

**1604.** It is better to entertain an idea than to take it home to live with you for the rest of your life. — Randall Jarrell, *Pictures from an Institution*, 1954

# Ideology *see* Dogma; Idealism; Intellectuals; Theory

# *Ignorance*

## *See also* Fools; Knowledge; Wisdom

**1605.** Ignorance is an evil weed, which dictators may cultivate among their dupes, but which no democracy can afford among its citizens. — William H. Beveridge, *Full Employment in a Free Society*, 1944

**1606.** The free man cannot be long an ignorant man. — William McKinley, speech, November 3, 1897

**1607.** There is no slavery but ignorance. — Robert G. Ingersoll, *The Liberty of Man, Woman and Child*, 1877

**1608.** If a nation expects to be ignorant and free, in a state of civilization, it expects what never was and never will be. — Thomas Jefferson, letter, January 6, 1816

**1609.** Ignorance never settles a question. — Benjamin Disraeli, speech, May 14, 1866

**1610.** It pays to be ignorant, for when you're smart you already know it can't be done. — Jeno F. Paulucci, in *New York Times*, November 7, 1976

**1611.** Never tell a young person that anything cannot be done. God may have been waiting for centuries for someone ignorant enough of the impossible to do that very thing. — John Andrew Holmes, *Wisdom in Small Doses*, 1927

**1612.** Ignorance is a voluntary misfortune. — Nicholas Ling, *Politeaphuia*, 1669

**1613.** He that voluntarily continues in ignorance, is guilty of all the crimes which ignorance produces. — Samuel Johnson, letter, August 13, 1766

**1614.** While all complain of our ignorance and error, everyone exempts himself. — Joseph Glanvill, *The Vanity of Dogmatizing*, 1661

**1615.** Those who enter politics late

in life, and start in high office, are led by ignorance into errors which are avoided by those who realize the nature and significance of the work done by people down the line. — Stimson Bullitt, *To Be a Politician,* 1977

**1616.** Those which knowe nothing, think they knowe all things, and holde their ignorance for wisdome. — Stefano Gujazzo, *Civil Conversation,* 1574

**1617.** Only the ignorant know everything. — Dagobert D. Runes, *Treasury of Thought,* 1966

**1618.** He that knows little often repeats it. — Thomas Fuller, M.D., *Gnomologia,* 1732

**1619.** I never met a man so ignorant that I could not learn something from him. — Galileo Galilei, *Dialogues concerning Two New Sciences,* 1638

**1620.** There is nothing more frightful than ignorance in action. — Johann Wolfgang von Goethe, *Proverbs in Prose,* 1819

**1621.** Nothing in the world is more dangerous than a sincere ignorance and conscientious stupidity. — Martin Luther King Jr., *Strength to Love,* 1963

**1622.** Ignorance per se is not nearly as dangerous as ignorance of ignorance. — Sydney J. Harris, *Pieces of Eight,* 1982

**1623.** The ignorant man always adores what he cannot understand. — Cesare Lombrosio, *The Man of Genius,* 1889

**1624.** Ignorance is not bliss — it is oblivion. — Philip Wylie, *Generation of Vipers,* 1942

**1625.** If ignorance is indeed bliss, it is a very low grade of the article. — Tehyi Hsieh, *Chinese Epigrams Inside Out and Proverbs,* 1948

**1626.** Happy people are ignoramuses and glory is nothing else but success, but to achieve it one only has to be cunning. — Mikhail Lermontov, *A Hero of Our Time,* 1840

**1627.** Ignorance is the first requisite of the historian — ignorance, which simplifies and clarifies, which selects and omits, with a placid perfection unattainable by the highest art. — Lytton Strachey, *Eminent Victorians,* 1918

**1628.** Our knowledge can only be finite, while our ignorance must necessarily be infinite. — Karl R. Popper, *Conjectures and Refutations,* 1968

**1629.** To know anything well involves a profound sensation of ignorance. — John Ruskin, *Modern Painters, Vol. I,* 1843

**1630.** The greater our knowledge increases, the greater our ignorance unfolds. — John F. Kennedy, speech, September 12, 1962

**1631.** In expanding the field of knowledge we but increase the horizon of ignorance. — Henry Miller, *The Wisdom of the Heart,* 1941

**1632.** A man only becomes wise when he begins to calculate the approximate depth of his ignorance. — Gian Carlo Menotti, in *New York Times,* April 14, 1974

**1633.** Ignorance lies at the bottom of all human knowledge, and the deeper we penetrate, the nearer we arrive unto it. — Charles Caleb Colton, *Lacon,* 1820–22

**1634.** Ignorance gives one a large range of probabilities. — George Eliot, *Daniel Deronda,* 1876

---

## *Individualism*

### *See also* Freedom; Liberty; The Political Animal

**1635.** Whatever crushes individuality is despotism, by whatever name it may be called. — John Stuart Mill, *On Liberty,* 1859

**1636.** The American system of rugged individualism. — Herbert Hoover, speech, October 22, 1928

**1637.** Individuality is the aim of

political liberty. — James Fenimore Cooper, *The American Democrat*, 1838

**1638.** The right to be let alone is indeed the beginning of all freedom. — William O. Douglas, *Public Utilities Commission v. Pollak*, May 26, 1952

**1639.** The man who walks alone is soon trailed by the F.B.I. — Wright Morris, *A Bill of Rites, A Bill of Wrongs, A Bill of Goods*, 1967

**1640.** When you soar like an eagle, you attract the hunters. — Milton S. Gould, in *Time*, December 8, 1967

**1641.** The greater intellect one has, the more originality one finds in men. Ordinary persons find no differences between men. — Blaise Pascal, *Pensées*, 1670

**1642.** The individual is not accountable to society for his actions, insofar as these concern the interests of no person but himself. — John Stuart Mill, *On Liberty*, 1859

**1643.** If individuality has no play, society does not advance; if individuality breaks out of all bounds, society perishes. — T. H. Huxley, *Administrative Nihilism*, 1871

**1644.** Like the leaves on a tree, we are all alike and yet all different. — Dagobert D. Runes, *Treasury of Thought*, 1966

**1645.** The definition of the individual was: a multitude of one million divided by one million. — Arthur Koestler, *Darkness at Noon*, 1940

**1646.** Seriously to contemplate one's abject personal triteness is probably the most painful act a man can perform. — Robert M. Adams, *Bad Mouth*, 1977

**1647.** Individualism is rather like innocence; there must be something unconscious about it. — Louis Kronenberger, *Company Manners*, 1954

**1648.** Man is a masterpiece of creation, if only because no amount of determinism can prevent him from believing that he acts as a free being. — Georg Christoph Lichtenberg, *Aphorisms*, 1764–99

**1649.** Freedom is always and exclusively freedom for the one who thinks differently. — Rosa Luxemburg, *The Russian Revolution*, 1918

**1650.** This I believe: that the free, exploring mind of the individual human is the most valuable thing in the world. And this I would fight for: the freedom of the mind to take any direction it wishes, undirected. And this I must fight against: any idea, religion, or government which limits or destroys the individual. — John Steinbeck, *East of Eden*, 1952

# Inflation

## See also Economics

**1651.** What this country needs is a really good 5-cent cigar. — Thomas R. Marshall, in *New York Tribune*, January 4, 1920

**1652.** What this country needs is a good five-cent nickel. — Franklin P. Adams, in *Liberty*, January 2, 1943

**1653.** Inflation might be called prosperity with high blood pressure. — Arnold H. Glasgow, in *Reader's Digest*, September, 1966

**1654.** Steel prices cause inflation like wet sidewalks cause rain. — Roger Blough, in *Forbes*, August 1, 1967

**1655.** Nothing so weakens a government as persistent inflation. — John Kenneth Galbraith, *The Affluent Society*, 1958

**1656.** Inflation is like sin; every government denounces it and every government practices it. — Frederick Leith-Ross, in *Observer*, June 30, 1957

**1657.** The wage-price program clearly demonstrated that the impossibility of controlling the markets feeds bureaucratic expansion, coercion, and caprice at a staggering rate, once the erroneous enterprise is launched. — David A. Stockman, *The Triumph of Politics,* 1987

**1658.** Lenin was right. There is no subtler, no surer means of overturning the existing basis of society than to debauch the currency. The process engages all the hidden forces of economic law on the side of destruction, and does it in a manner which not one man in a million is able to diagnose. — John Maynard Keynes, *The Economic Consequences of the Peace,* 1919

**1659.** Inflation is a great conservatizing issue. — George Will, in *Newsweek,* November 7, 1977

**1660.** Inflation is as violent as a mugger, as frightening as an armed robber and as deadly as a hit man. — Ronald Reagan, in *Los Angeles Times,* October 20, 1978

# Intellectuals

## See also Education; Knowledge; Theory; Thought

**1661.** It is always the task of the intellectual to "think otherwise." This is not just a perverse idiosyncrasy. It is an absolutely essential feature of a society. — Harvey Cox, *The Secular City,* 1966

**1662.** Intellectual slavery of whatever nature it may be, will always have as a natural result both political and social slavery. — Michael Bakunin, *Federalism, Socialism and Anti-Theologism,* 1868

**1663.** Beware when the great God lets loose a thinker on this planet. Then all things are at risk. — Ralph Waldo Emerson, *Essays: First Series,* "Circles," 1841

**1664.** Every thinker puts some new portion of an apparently stable world in peril. — John Dewey, *Characters and Events,* 1929

**1665.** Every intellectual revolution which has ever stirred humanity into greatness has been a passionate protest against inert ideas. — Alfred North Whitehead, *The Aims of Education,* 1929

**1666.** The highest intellectuals, like the tops of mountains, are the first to catch and to reflect the dawn. — Thomas Babington, *Essays Contributed to the Edinburgh Review,* 1843

**1667.** It is ironic that the United States should have been founded by intellectuals; for throughout most of our political history the intellectual has been for the most part either an outsider, a servant, or a scapegoat. — Richard Hofstadter, *Anti-Intellectualism in American Life,* 1963

**1668.** To be surprised, to wonder, is to begin to understand. This is the sport, the luxury, special to the intellectual man. — José Ortega y Gasset, *The Revolt of the Masses,* 1930

**1669.** The intellectual is a middle-class product; if he is not born into the class he must soon insert himself into it, in order to exist. He is the fine nervous flower of the bourgeoisie. — Louise Bogan, *Solicited Criticism,* "Some Notes on Popular and Unpopular Art," 1955

**1670.** All intellectual improvement arises from leisure. — Samuel Johnson, in James Boswell, *Life of Samuel Johnson,* 1791

**1671.** Curiosity is one of the permanent and certain characteristics of a vigorous intellect. — Samuel Johnson, *The Rambler,* 1750–52

**1672.** Intellectualism, though by no means confined to doubters, is often the sole piety of the skeptic. — Richard Hofstadter, *Anti-Intellectualism in American Life,* 1963

**1673.** An intellectual is someone whose mind watches itself. I am happy to be both halves, the watcher and the watched. — Albert Camus, *Notebooks 1935–1942,* 1962

**1674.** The trouble with me is, I belong to a vanishing race. I'm one of the intellectuals. — Robert E. Sherwood, *The Petrified Forest,* 1934

**1675.** He who anticipates his century is generally persecuted when living, and is always pilfered when dead. — Benjamin Disraeli, *Vivian Gray,* 1826

**1676.** No real English gentleman, in his secret soul, was ever sorry for the death of a political economist. — Walter Bagehot, *Estimates of Some Englishmen and Scotchmen,* "The First Edinburgh Reviewers," 1858

**1677.** The intellectuals' chief cause of anguish is one another's works. — Jacques Barzun, *The House of Intellect,* 1959

**1678.** An intellectual hatred is the worst. — William Butler Yeats, "A Prayer for My Daughter," 1919

**1679.** Our culture peculiarly honors the act of blaming, which it takes as the sign of virtue and intellect. — Lionel Trilling, *The Liberal Imagination,* 1950

**1680.** In the practical use of our intellect, forgetting is as important as remembering. — William James, *The Principles of Psychology,* 1890

**1681.** The greatest minds are capable of the greatest vices as well as of the greatest virtues. — René Descartes, *Discourse on the Method,* 1637

**1682.** Observe how the greatest minds yield in some degree to the superstitions of their age. — Henry David Thoreau, *Journal,* 1853

**1683.** Intellect obscures more than it illumines. — Israel Zangwill, *Children of the Ghetto,* 1892

**1684.** The intelligent are to the intelligentsia what a gentleman is to a gent. — Stanley Baldwin, in G. M. Young, *Stanley Baldwin,* 1952

**1685.** Marxism is the opium of the intellectuals. — Edmund Wilson, *Memoirs of Hecate County,* 1949

**1686.** Intellectuals are people who believe that ideas are more important than values. That is to say, their own ideas and other people's values. — Gerald Brenan, *Thoughts in a Dry Season,* "Life," 1978

**1687.** It's among the intelligentsia, and especially among those who like to play with thoughts and concepts without really taking part in the cultural endeavors of their epoch that we often find the glib compulsion to explain everything and to understand nothing. — Joost A. M. Meerloo, *The Rape of the Mind,* 1956

**1688.** The function of the intellectual has always been confined, in the main, to embellishing the bored existence of the bourgeoisie, to consoling the rich in the trivial troubles of their lives. — Marksim Gorki, *To American Intellectuals,* 1922

**1689.** The intellectual world is divided into two classes — dilettantes, on the one hand, and pedants, on the other. — Miguel de Unamuno, *The Tragic Sense of Life,* 1912

**1690.** Scratch an intellectual and you find a would-be aristocrat who loathes the sight, the sound and the smell of common folk. — Eric Hoffer, *First Things, Last Things,* 1970

**1691.** A spirit of nation masochism prevails, encouraged by an effete corps of impudent snobs who characterize themselves as intellectuals. — Spiro T. Agnew, in *New York Times,* October 20, 1969

**1692.** The best university that can be recommended to a man of ideas is the gauntlet of the mob. — Ralph Waldo Emerson, *Society and Solitude,* 1870

**1693.** Let's face it: Intellectual achievement and the intellectual elite are alien to the main stream of American society. They are off to the side in a subsection of esoteric isolation labeled "oddball," "high brow," "egghead," "double-dome." — Elmo Roper, in *Publishers Weekly,* "Roadblocks to Bookbuying," June 16, 1958

**1694.** The intellectual is constantly betrayed by his vanity. God-like, he blandly assumes that he can express everything in words; whereas the things one loves, lives, and dies for are not, in the last analysis, completely expressible in words. — Anne Morrow Lindburgh, *The Wave of the Future*, 1940

**1695.** Intelligence is not all that important in the exercise of power and is often, in point of fact, useless. — Henry Kissinger, in *Esquire*, June, 1975

**1696.** One who chooses politics may have a first-rate mind but rarely is a deep thinker about ultimates and almost never is trained in philosophy. — Stimson Bullitt, *To Be a Politician*, 1977

**1697.** Farming looks mighty easy when your plow is a pencil and you're a thousand miles from a cornfield. — Dwight D. Eisenhower, speech, September 25, 1956

**1698.** The democratic class struggle will continue, but it will be a fight without ideologies, without red flags, without May Day parades. This naturally upsets many intellectuals who can participate only as ideologists or major critics of the *status quo.* — Seymour Martin Lipset, *Political Man*, 1981

**1699.** The question ceased to be what should be done, and became what *could* be done. It is the question politicians ask, not idealogues. — David A. Stockman, *The Triumph of Politics*, 1987

# International Relations

## See also Diplomacy

**1700.** Nations touch at their summits. — Walter Bagehot, *The English Constitution*, "The House of Lords," 1867

**1701.** Nations, like individuals, have to limit their objectives or take the consequences. — James Reston, *Sketches in the Sand*, 1967

**1702.** Every government is in some respects a problem for every other government, and it will always be this way so long as the sovereign state, with its supremely self-centered rationale, remains the basis of international life. — George F. Kennan, *Russia and the West Under Lenin and Stalin*, 1961

**1703.** At bottom, every state regards another as a gang of robbers who will fall upon it as soon as there is an opportunity. — Arthur Schopenhauer, *Parerga and Paralipomena*, "On Jurisprudence and Politics," 1851

**1704.** The management of a balance of power is a permanent undertaking, not an exertion that has a foreseeable end. — Henry Kissinger, *White House Years*, 1979

**1705.** In the field of world policy I would dedicate this nation to the policy of the good neighbor. — Franklin D. Roosevelt, inaugural address, March 4, 1933

**1706.** The responsibility of the great states is to serve and not to dominate the world. — Harry S Truman, message to Congress, April 16, 1945

**1707.** We Americans have no commission from God to police the world. — Benjamin Harrison, speech, 1888

**1708.** The foreign policy adopted by our government is to do justice to all, and to submit to wrong by none. — Andrew Jackson, inaugural address, March 4, 1833

**1709.** Making foreign policy is a little bit like making pornographic movies. It's more fun doing it than watching it. — William P. Rogers, in *Chicago Sun-Times*, June 29, 1976

**1710.** [The] American temptation [is] to believe that foreign policy is a subdivision of psychiatry. — Henry Kissinger, in *Time*, June 17, 1985

**1711.** Every nation determines its

policies in terms of its own interests. —John F. Kennedy, speech, September 26, 1963

**1712.** What a country calls its vital economic interests are not the things which enable its citizens to live, but the things which enable it to make war. Gasoline is much more likely than wheat to be a cause of international conflict. —Simone Weil, *The Need for Roots,* 1949

**1713.** No small country can depend for its existence on the loyalty of its capitalists. International interests may require the sacrifice of the lesser loyalty of patriotism. Only in dominant nations is the loyalty of capitalists ensured. —George Grant, *Lament for a Nation: The Defeat of Canadian Nationalism,* 1965

**1714.** No nation is wise enough to rule another. —Helen Keller, *Let Us Have Faith,* 1940

**1715.** I am not aware that any community has a right to force another to be civilized. —John Stuart Mill, *On Liberty,* 1859

**1716.** These wretched colonies will all be independent, too, in a few years, and are a millstone round our necks. —Benjamin Disraeli, letter, August 13, 1852

**1717.** Colonies do not cease to be colonies because they are independent. —Benjamin Disraeli, speech, February 5, 1863

**1718.** Gratitude, like love, is never a dependable international emotion. —Joseph Alsop, in *Observer,* November 30, 1952

**1719.** Small nations are like indecently dressed women. They tempt the evil-minded. —Julius Nyerere, in *Reporter,* April 9, 1964

**1720.** The great nations have always acted like gangsters, and the small nations like prostitutes. —Stanley Kubrick, in *Guardian,* June 5, 1963

**1721.** Alliance, *n.* In international politics, the union of two thieves who have their hands so deeply inserted in each other's pocket that they cannot separately plunder a third. —Ambrose Bierce, *The Devil's Dictionary,* 1906

**1722.** If you wish to avoid foreign collision, you had better abandon the ocean. —Henry Clay, speech, January 22, 1812

**1723.** When myth meets myth, the collision is very real. —Stanislaw Lec, *Unkempt Thoughts,* 1962

**1724.** There is still a real need for political analysis, ideology, and controversy within the world community, if not within Western democracies. —Seymour Martin Lipset, *Political Man,* 1981

**1725.** The new electronic interdependence recreates the world in the image of a global village. —Marshall McLuhan, *The Gutenberg Galaxy,* 1962

**1726.** We hope that the world will not narrow into a neighborhood before it has broadened into a brotherhood. —Lyndon B. Johnson, speech, December 22, 1963

**1727.** The tendencies of what I am here calling the forces of Jihad and the forces of McWorld operate with equal strength in opposite directions, the one driven by parochial hatreds, the other by universaling markets, the one recreating ancient subnational and ethnic borders from within, the other making national borders porous from without. —Benjamin R. Barber, *Atlantic,* "Jihad vs. McWorld," March, 1992

---

# Judgment

**1728.** Judgment comes from experience, and great judgment comes from bad experience. —Bob Packwood, in *New York Times,* May 30, 1986

**1729.** Your representative owes you, not his industry only, but his judgment; and he betrays instead of serving you if he sacrifices it to your opinion. —Edmund Burke, speech, November 3, 1774

1730. Power-worship blurs political judgment because it leads, almost unavoidably, to the belief that present trends will continue. Whoever is winning at the moment will always seem to be invincible. — George Orwell, *Shooting an Elephant*, 1950

1731. I have noted that persons with bad judgment are more insistent that we do what they think best. — Lionel Abel, *Important Nonsense*, 1986

1732. Diff'ring judgments serve but to declare That Truth lies somewhere, if he knew but where. — William Cowper, *Hope*, 1781

1733. Obviously, a man's judgment cannot be better than the information on which he has based it. — Arthur Hays Sulzberger, speech, August 30, 1948

1734. He hath a good judgment that relieth not wholly on his own. — Thomas Fuller, M.D., *Gnomologia*, 1732

1735. You can't depend on your judgment when your imagination is out of focus. — Mark Twain, *Notebook*, 1935

1736. The better part of valor is discretion. — William Shakespeare, *Henry IV, Part I*, 1597

1737. Judgments too quickly formed are dangerous. — Sophocles, *Oedipus Rex*, ca. 430 B.C.

1738. It is the property of fools, to be always judging. — Thomas Fuller, M.D., *Gnomologia*, 1732

1739. Whoever undertakes to set himself up as judge in the field of Truth and Knowledge is shipwrecked by the laughter of the gods. — Albert Einstein, *Ideas and Opinions*, 1954

1740. One should look long and carefully at oneself before one considers judging others. — Molière, *Le Misanthrope*, 1666

1741. Judge not, that ye be not judged. — Bible, *Matthew 7:1*

# Justice

## See also Judgment; Law; Truth

1742. Justice is the end of government. It is the end of society. — James Madison, *The Federalist*, 1788

1743. Justice is truth in action. — Benjamin Disraeli, speech, February 11, 1851

1744. Let justice be done, though the world perish. — Ferdinand I, motto, 16th c.

1745. *Fiat justitia, pereat coelum* [Let justice be done, though heaven fall]. My toast would be, may our country be always successful, but whether successful or otherwise, always right. — John Quincy Adams, letter, August 1, 1816

1746. All virtue is summed up in dealing justly. — Aristotle, *Nicomachean Ethics*, ca. 325 B.C.

1747. Justice is like a train that's nearly always late. — Yevgeny Yevtushenko, *A Precocious Autobiography*, 1963

1748. Justice delayed is democracy denied. — Robert F. Kennedy, *The Pursuit of Justice*, 1964

1749. Justice is the constant and perpetual wish to render to everyone his due. — Justinian, *Institutes*, 6th c.

1750. Fairness is what justice really is. — Potter Stewart, in *Time*, October 20, 1958

1751. The circumstances of justice obtain whenever mutually disinterested persons put forward conflicting claims to the division of social advantages under conditions of moderate scarcity. — John Rawls, *A Theory of Justice*, 1971

1752. The firm basis of government is justice, not pity. — Woodrow Wilson, inaugural address, March 4, 1913

1753. Men are not hanged for stealing horses, but that horses may not be stolen. — George Savile, *Political, Moral, and Miscellaneous Thoughts and Reflections*, 1750

**1754.** There are different kinds of wrong. The people sinned against are not always the best. — Ivy Compton-Burnett, *The Mighty and Their Fall*, 1961

**1755.** The injustice done to an individual is sometimes of service to the public. — Junius, in *Public Advertiser*, November 14, 1770

**1756.** There are some acts of justice which corrupt those who perform them. — Joseph Joubert, *Pensées*, 1842

**1757.** We start from this rule — it is never right to do any injustice, or to do injustice in return, or, when one is evilly treated, to defend oneself by doing evil in return. — Plato, *Crito*, ca. 370 B.C.

**1758.** Once the laws are just, then men will be just. — Anatole France, *Monsieur Bergeret à Paris*, 1900

**1759.** The great mistake is that of looking upon men as virtuous, or thinking that they can be made so by laws. — Henry St. John, comment (ca. 1728), in Joseph Spence, *Observations, Anecdotes, and Characters*, 1820

**1760.** The administration of justice lies at the foundation of government. — William H. Taft, speech, July 28, 1908

**1761.** A government without justice is a great robbery. — Saint Augustine, *The City of God*, 415

**1762.** Justice is the first virtue of social institutions, as truth is of systems of thought. A theory, however elegant and economical, must be rejected or revised if it is untrue; likewise laws and institutions, no matter how efficient and well-arranged, must be reformed or abolished if they are unjust. — John Rawls, *A Theory of Justice*, 1971

**1763.** There is no authority without justice. — Napoleon I, remark, March 12, 1803

**1764.** He that judges without informing himself to the utmost that he is capable, cannot acquit himself of judging amiss. — John Locke, *An Essay Concerning Human Understanding*, 1690

**1765.** There is no injustice in the greater benefits earned by a few, provided that the situation of persons not so fortunate is thereby improved. — John Rawls, *A Theory of Justice*, 1971

**1766.** Justice is the sanction used to support established injustices. — Anatole France, "Crainquebille," 1905

**1767.** How fond men are of justice when it comes to judging the crimes of former generations. — Armand Salacrou, *Boulevard Durand*, 1961

**1768.** The slave begins by demanding justice and ends by wanting to wear a crown. — Albert Camus, *The Rebel*, 1951

**1769.** The strictest justice is sometimes the greatest injustice. — Terence, *Heauton Timorumenos*, 163 B.C.

**1770.** The severest justice may not always be the best policy. — Abraham Lincoln, message to Congress, July 17, 1862

**1771.** The remedy is worse than the disease. — Francis Bacon, *Essays*, "Of Seditions and Troubles," 1625

**1772.** It is better that ten guilty persons escape than one innocent suffer. — William Blackstone, *Commentaries on the Laws of England*, 1765

**1773.** National injustice is the surest road to national downfall. — William E. Gladstone, speech, 1878

**1774.** Injustice anywhere is a threat to justice everywhere. — Martin Luther King Jr., letter, April 16, 1963

**1775.** Those who are fond of setting things to right have no great objection to seeing them wrong. There is often a good deal of spleen at the bottom of benevolence. — William Hazlitt, *Characteristics*, 1823

**1776.** Justice and good will will outlast passion. — James A. Garfield, letter, July 12, 1880

**1777.** This is the first of punishments, that no guilty man is acquitted if judged by himself. — Juvenal, *Satires*, ca. 110

**1778.** To show resentment at a reproach is to acknowledge that one may have deserved it. — Cornelius Tacitus, *Annals*, 2nd c.

**1779.** Get out of the way of Justice. She is blind. — Stanislaw Lec, *More Unkempt Thoughts*, 1968

**1780.** Indeed, I tremble for my

country when I reflect that God is just. — Thomas Jefferson, *Notes on the State of Virginia,* 1781–85

**1781.** No man can be just who is not free. — Woodrow Wilson, speech, July 7, 1912

**1782.** Without justice courage is weak. — Benjamin Franklin, *Poor Richard's Almanac,* 1733–58

**1783.** Absolute freedom mocks at justice. Absolute justice denies freedom. — Albert Camus, *The Rebel,* 1951

**1784.** And liberty plucks justice by the nose. — William Shakespeare, *Measure for Measure,* 1604

**1785.** Living well is the best revenge. — George Herbert, *Jacula Prudentum,* 1651

## Knowledge

### *See also* Education; Facts; Ideas; Ignorance; Intellectuals; Thought; Truth; Wisdom

**1786.** "Knowledge—do you say it is power?" "...yes, most mighty of all powers." — Plato, *The Republic,* ca. 370 B.C.

**1787.** Knowledge itself is power. — Francis Bacon, *Religious Meditations,* "Of Heresies," 1597

**1788.** In a time of turbulence and change, it is more true than ever that knowledge is power. — John F. Kennedy, speech, March 23, 1962

**1789.** Human knowledge and human power meet in one; when the cause is not known the effect cannot be produced. — Francis Bacon, *Novum Organum,* 1620

**1790.** The preservation of the means of knowledge among the lowest ranks is of more importance to the public than all the property of all the rich men in the country. — John Adams, *Dissertation on the Canon and the Federal Law,* 1765

**1791.** This is the bitterest pain among men, to have much knowledge but no power. — Herodotus, *The History,* ca. 450 B.C.

**1792.** Riches, knowledge and honor are but several sorts of power. — Thomas Hobbes, *Leviathan,* 1651

**1793.** The desire of power in excess caused the angels to fall; the desire of knowledge in excess caused man to fall. — Francis Bacon, *Essays,* "Of Goodness and Goodness of Nature," 1625

**1794.** Knowledge will forever govern ignorance; and a people who mean to be their own Governors must arm themselves with the power which knowledge gives. — James Madison, letter, August 4, 1822

**1795.** Knowledge is not a loose-leaf notebook of facts. — Jacob Bronowski, *The Ascent of Man,* 1973

**1796.** If we value the pursuit of knowledge, we must be free to follow wherever that search may lead us. The free mind is no barking dog, to be tethered on a ten-foot chain. — Adlai Stevenson, speech, October 8, 1952

**1797.** A little learning is a dangerous thing. — Alexander Pope, *An Essay on Criticism,* 1711

**1798.** If a little knowledge is dangerous, where is the man who has so much as to be out of danger? — T. H. Huxley, *Collected Essays,* "On Elementary Instruction in Physiology," 1895

**1799.** It is neither possible for man to know the truth fully nor to avoid the error of pretending that he does. — Reinhold Niebuhr, *Human Destiny,* 1943

**1800.** If you are sure you understand everything that is going on, you are hopelessly confused. — Walter Mondale, in *Poughkeepsie Journal,* March 26, 1978

**1801.** The greatest obstacle to discovery is not ignorance—it is the illusion of knowledge. — Daniel J. Boorstin, in *Washington Post*, January 29, 1984

**1802.** The most certain way to hide from others the limits of our knowledge is not to go beyond them. — Giacomo Leopardi, *Pensieri*, 1834–37

**1803.** Pedantry is the dotage of knowledge. — Holbrook Jackson, *The Anatomy of Bibliomania*, 1930

**1804.** Woe unto you, lawyers! for ye have taken away the key of knowledge. — Bible, *Luke 11:52*

**1805.** To be conscious that you are ignorant is a great step to knowledge. — Benjamin Disraeli, *Sybil*, 1845

**1806.** Only the shallow know themselves. — Oscar Wilde, "Phrases and Philosophies for the Use of the Young," 1894

**1807.** To know a little less and to understand a little more: that, it seems to me, is our greatest need. — James Ramsey Ullmann, *The White Tower*, 1945

**1808.** Knowledge shrinks as wisdom grows. — Alfred North Whitehead, *Aims of Education*, 1929

**1809.** It takes a lot of knowledge to understand how little we know. — Dagobert D. Runes, *Treasury of Thought*, 1966

**1810.** It is in the matter of knowledge that a man is most haunted with a sense of inevitable limitation. — Joseph Farrell, *Lectures of a Certain Professor*, 1877

**1811.** From contemplation one may become wise, but knowledge comes only from study. — A. Edward Newton, *A Magnificent Farce*, 1921

**1812.** Knowledge is not enough, unless it leads you to understanding and, in turn, to wisdom. — David Sarnoff, in *Youth in a Changing World*, June 12, 1954

**1813.** Knowledge is the distilled essence of our intuitions, corroborated by experience. — Elbert Hubbard, *The Note Book*, 1927

**1814.** All men by nature have a desire to know. — Aristotle, *Metaphysics*, 3rd c. B.C.

**1815.** It is the peculiarity of knowledge that those who really thirst for it always get it. — Richard Jeffries, *Country Literature*, ca. 1880

**1816.** An honest heart being the first blessing, a knowing head is the second. — Thomas Jefferson, letter, August 19, 1785

**1817.** Knowledge is always accompanied with accessories of emotion and purpose. — Alfred North Whitehead, *Adventures of Ideas*, 1933

**1818.** The greatest intellectual capacities are only found in connection with a vehement and passionate will. — Arthur Schopenhauer, *The World as Will and Idea*, 1819

**1819.** We are least open to precise knowledge concerning the things we are most vehement about. — Eric Hoffer, *The Passionate State of Mind*, 1954

**1820.** Liberty cannot be preserved without a general knowledge among the people. — John Adams, *Dissertation on the Canon and the Federal Law*, 1765

**1821.** In order that knowledge be properly digested, it must have been swallowed with a good appetite. — Anatole France, *The Crime of Sylvestre Bonnard*, 1881

**1822.** The desire of knowledge, like the thirst of riches, increases ever with the acquisition of it. — Laurence Sterne, *Tristram Shandy*, 1760

**1823.** The larger the island of knowledge, the longer the shore line of wonder. — Ralph W. Sockman, *Now to Live!*, 1946

**1824.** Wonder, rather than doubt, is the root of knowledge. — Abraham Heschel, *Man Is Not Alone*, 1951

**1825.** What is all our knowledge? We do not even know what weather it will be tomorrow. — Berthold Auerbach, *On the Heights*, 1865

**1826.** All knowledge resolves itself into probability. — David Hume, *A Treatise of Human Nature*, 1739

**1827.** Knowledge is twofold, and consists not only in an affirmation of what is true, but in the negation of that which is false. — Charles Caleb Colton, *Lacon*, 1820–22

**1828.** There is no new knowledge without a new problem. —Leo Baeck, *Judaism and Science,* 1949

**1829.** If we would have new knowledge, we must get a whole world of new questions. —Susanne K. Langer, *Philosophy in a New Key,* 1957

**1830.** The pursuit of knowledge can never be anything but a leap in the dark, and a leap in the dark is a very un-comfortable thing. —Samuel Butler (II), *Notebooks,* 1912

**1831.** Knowledge does not keep any better than fish. —Alfred North Whitehead, *The Aims of Education,* 1929

**1832.** We're drowning in information and starving for knowledge. —Rutherford D. Rogers, in *New York Times,* 1985

——————— *Language* ———————

## See also Ideas; Speech

**1833.** Syllables govern the world. —John Selden, *Table Talk,* "Power," 1689

**1834.** Words wound. But as a veteran of twelve years in the United States Senate, I happily attest that they do not kill. —Lyndon B. Johnson, speech, August 26, 1966

**1835.** Many have fallen by the edge of the sword: but not so many as have fallen by the tongue. —Bible: Apocrypha, *Ecclesiasticus 28:18*

**1836.** Words can be treasonable as well as deeds. —Baruch Spinoza, *Tractatus Theologicus-Politicus,* 1670

**1837.** From politics, it was an easy step to silence. —Jane Austen, *Northanger Abbey,* 1818

**1838.** A riot is at bottom the language of the unheard. —Martin Luther King Jr., *Where Do We Go from Here?,* 1967

**1839.** I strive to be brief, and I become obscure. —Horace, *Ars Poetica,* 1st c. B.C.

**1840.** Bushspeak. —Douglas Harbrecht and Howard Gleckman, describing President George Bush's method of communicating, in *Business Week,* August 24, 1992

**1841.** A plurality of words does not necessarily represent a plurality of things. —Joseph Albo, *Book of Principles,* 1428

**1842.** Against the misuse of words every editorial prejudice should be fixed in concrete. —Ellery Sedgwick, *The Happy Profession,* 1946

**1843.** He that useth too many words for the explaining any subject, doth, like the cuttle fish, hide himself for the most part in his own ink. —John Ray, *On Creation,* ca. 1700

**1844.** Ours is the age of substitutes; instead of language, we have jargon; instead of principles, slogans; instead of genuine ideas, Bright ideas. —Eric Bentley, *The Dramatic Event,* 1954

**1845.** In our time, political speech and writing are largely the defense of the indefensible. —George Orwell, *Shooting an Elephant,* 1950

**1846.** Some of mankind's most terrible misdeeds have been committed under the spell of certain magic words or phrases. —James Bryant Conant, speech, June, 1934

**1847.** A good catchword can obscure analysis for fifty years. —Johan Huizinga, *The Waning of the Middle Ages,* 1924

**1848.** If I take refuge in ambiguity, I assure you that it's quite intentional. —Kingman Brewster, in *New York Herald,* October 14, 1963

**1849.** A candidate for office can have no greater advantage than muddled syntax; no greater liability than a command of language. —Marya Mannes, *More in Anger,* 1958

**1850.** No one means all he says, and yet very few say all they mean, for words are slippery and thought is viscous. — Henry Brooks Adams, *The Education of Henry Adams,* 1907

**1851.** "Then you should say what you mean," the March Hare went on. "I do," Alice hastily replied; "At least I mean what I say — that's the same thing, you know." "Not the same thing a bit!" said the Hatter. "Why, you might just as well say that 'I see what I eat' is the same thing as 'I eat what I see'!" — Lewis Carroll, *Alice's Adventures in Wonderland,* 1865

**1852.** Unless one is a genius, it is best to aim at being intelligible. — Anthony Hope, *The Dolly Dialogues,* 1894

**1853.** Nowadays to be intelligible is to be found out. — Oscar Wilde, *Lady Windermere's Fan,* 1892

**1854.** It is easier to be impressed than to be instructed, and the public is very ready to believe that where there is noble language not without obscurity there must be profound knowledge. — George Santayana, *The Sense of Beauty,* 1896

**1855.** There is no means by which men so powerfully elude their ignorance, disguise it from themselves and others as by words. — Gamaliel Bradford, *Letters,* 1934

**1856.** Abuse of words has been the great instrument of sophistry and chicanery, of party faction, and division of society. — John Adams, *Dissertation on the Canon and the Federal Law,* 1765

**1857.** The power of words is such that they have prevented our learning some of the most important events in the world's history. — Norman Angell, *Let the People Know,* "Words That Are Assassins," 1943

**1858.** Words form the thread on which we string our experiences. — Aldous Huxley, *The Olive Tree,* "Words and Behavior," 1937

**1859.** How often misused words generate misleading thoughts. — Herbert Spencer, *Principles of Ethics,* 1892–93

**1860.** Millions of peasants are robbed of their farms and sent trudging along the roads with no more than they can carry: this is called *transfer of population* or *rectification of frontiers.* . . . Such phraseology is needed if one wants to name things without calling up mental pictures of them. — George Orwell, *Shooting an Elephant,* 1950

**1861.** Words may varnish facts, they cannot alter them. — Harry James Smith, *Mrs. Bumpstead-Leigh,* 1911

**1862.** Words are weapons, and it is dangerous in speculation, as in politics, to borrow them from our enemies. — George Santayana, *Obiter Scripta,* 1936

**1863.** The logic of words should yield to the logic of realities. — Louis D. Brandeis, *DeSanto v. Pennsylvania,* 1926

**1864.** For an answer which cannot be expressed, the question too cannot be expressed. — Ludwig Wittenstein, *Tractatus Logico-Philosophicus,* 1922

**1865.** Any general statement is like a check drawn on a bank. Its value depends on what is there to meet it. — Ezra Pound, *The ABC of Reading,* 1934

**1866.** Glittering generalities! They are blazing ubiquities. — Ralph Waldo Emerson, attributed

**1867.** Every word or concept, clear as it may be, has only a limited range of applicability. — Werner Heisenberg, *Physics and Beyond,* 1971

**1868.** The word *Fascism* has now no meaning except insofar as it signifies "something not desirable." — George Orwell, *Shooting an Elephant,* 1950

**1869.** All our words from loose using have lost their edge. — Ernest Hemingway, *Death in the Afternoon,* 1932

**1870.** Hold fast the form of sound words. — Bible, *II Timothy,* 1:13

**1871.** Don't talk to me of your Archimedes' lever. . . . Give me the right word and the right accent, and I will move the world. — Joseph Conrad, *A Personal Record,* 1912

**1872.** Every word is a preconceived judgment. — Friedrich Wilhelm Nietzsche, *Human, All Too Human,* 1878

**1873.** All words are pegs to hang ideas on. — Henry Ward Beecher, *Proverbs from Plymouth Pulpit,* 1887

**1874.** We should have a great many fewer disputes in the world, if words were taken for what they are, the signs of our ideas only. —John Locke, *An Essay Concerning Human Understanding,* 1690

**1875.** Ever since the first great battle between Federalists and anti–Federalists the American people have viewed politicians with suspicion, and the word itself has a derogatory significance in the United States which it lacks in England. —H. L. Mencken, *The American Language, Supplement I,* 1945

**1876.** Thatcher's liberal enemies ...dismissed her supporters as taxi drivers and rich butchers. Lady Warnock...of Girton College, Cambridge was more forthright still.... Margaret Thatcher is rather "common." That is a word whose nuances are almost impossible to explain to an American audience...but that is still crucial in England. —Geoffrey Wheatcroft, in *Atlantic,* December, 1991

**1877.** This is the sort of English up with which I will not put. —Winston S. Churchill, in Ernest Gowers, *Plain Words,* 1948

---

# Law

## See also Constitution; Justice; Natural Law; Order

**1878.** Where good laws are, much people flock thither. —Benjamin Franklin, *Poor Richard's Almanac,* 1733–58

**1879.** The good of the people is the supreme law. —Cicero, *De Legibus,* ca. 52 B.C.

**1880.** The only purpose for which power can be rightfully exercised over any member of a civilized community, against his will, is to prevent harm to others. His own good, either physical or moral, is not a sufficient warrant. —John Stuart Mill, *On Liberty,* 1859

**1881.** Government implies the power of making laws. It is essential to the idea of a law, that it be attended with a sanction; or, in other words, a penalty or punishment for disobedience. —Alexander Hamilton, *The Federalist,* 1787–88

**1882.** Where the laws are not supreme, there demagogues spring up. —Aristotle, *Politics,* 4th c. B.C.

**1883.** Unlimited power is apt to corrupt the minds of those who possess it; and this I know, my lords, that where laws end, tyranny begins. —William Pitt (I), speech, January 9, 1770

**1884.** In civilized life, law floats in a sea of ethics. —Earl Warren, in *New York Times,* November 12, 1962

**1885.** Moral principle is the foundation of law. —Ronald D. Dworkin, *Law's Empire,* 1986

**1886.** A precedent embalms a principle. —William Scott, opinion, 1788

**1887.** How long soever it hath continued, if it be against reason, it is of no force in law. —Edward Coke, *The First Part of the Institutes of the Laws of England,* 1628

**1888.** Custom, that unwritten law, By which the people keep even kings in awe. —Charles D'Avenant, *Circe,* 1677

**1889.** True freedom in society can be achieved only if men participate in making the laws which they are compelled to obey. —M. Judd Harmon, *Political Thought,* 1964

**1890.** The end of law is, not to abolish or restrain, but to preserve and enlarge freedom. —John Locke, *Second Treatise of Civil Government,* 1690

**1891.** Permissive legislation is the characteristic of a free people. —Benjamin Disraeli, speech, June 18, 1875

**1892.** Good laws lead to the making of better ones; bad ones bring about worse. —Jean-Jacques Rousseau, *The Social Contract,* 1762

**1893.** Government can easily exist

without law, but law cannot exist without government. — Bertrand Russell, *Unpopular Essays,* 1950

**1894.** There is hardly a political question in the United States which does not sooner or later turn into a judicial one. — Alexis de Tocqueville, *Democracy in America,* 1835

**1895.** Our long national nightmare is over. Our Constitution works; our great Republic is a government of laws and not of men. — Gerald R. Ford, statement upon assuming office, August 9, 1974

**1896.** What is constitutional may still be unwise. — Zechariah Chaffee Jr., in *The Nation,* July 28, 1952

**1897.** No rule is so general, which admits not some exception. — Robert Burton, *The Anatomy of Melancholy,* 1651

**1898.** There are times when national interest is more important than the law. — Henry Kissinger, in *New York Times Magazine,* October 31, 1976

**1899.** Laws are silent in time of war. — Cicero, *Pro Milone,* 1st c. B.C.

**1900.** Men of most renowned virtue have sometimes by transgressing most truly kept the law. — John Milton, *Tetrachordon,* 1644–45

**1901.** Laws were made to be broken. — Christopher North, in *Blackwood's Magazine,* May, 1830

**1902.** The best use of laws is to teach men to trample bad laws under their feet. — Wendell Phillips, speech, April 12, 1852

**1903.** People crushed by law have no hopes but from power. If laws are their enemies, they will be enemies to law. — Edmund Burke, letter, October 8, 1777

**1904.** It is the right of our people to organize to oppose any law and any part of the Constitution with which they are not in sympathy. — Alfred E. Smith, speech, December 2, 1927

**1905.** It is not desirable to cultivate a respect for the law, so much as for the right. — Henry David Thoreau, *Civil Disobedience,* 1849

**1906.** Laws too gentle are seldom obeyed; too severe, seldom executed. — Benjamin Franklin, *Poor Richard's Almanac,* 1733–58

**1907.** I know no method to secure the repeal of bad or obnoxious laws so effective as their stringent execution. — Ulysses S. Grant, inaugural address, March 4, 1869

**1908.** Courts are, unquestionably, the seats of politeness and good-breeding; were they not so, they would be the seats of slaughter and desolation. — Philip D. Stanhope, *Letters,* 1749

**1909.** The closeness of the decision attests the measure of the doubt. — Benjamin N. Cardozo, *People ex. rel. Hayes v. McLaughlin,* 1927

**1910.** As in law so in war, the longest purse finally wins. — Mohandas K. Gandhi, lecture, September 17, 1917

**1911.** A lawyer with his briefcase can steal more than a hundred men with guns. — Mario Puzo, *The Godfather,* 1969

**1912.** Laws grind the poor, and rich men rule the law. — Oliver Goldsmith, *The Traveler,* 1765

**1913.** Law is a bottomless pit. — John Arbuthnot, *The History of John Bull,* 1712

**1914.** Laws are like cobwebs, which may catch small flies, but let wasps and hornets break through. — Jonathan Swift, *A Critical Essay Upon the Faculties of the Mind,* 1709

**1915.** Do what thou wilt shall be the whole of the Law. — Aleister Crowley, *Book of the Law,* 1909

**1916.** For where no law is, there is no transgression. — Bible, *Romans 4:15*

**1917.** I am ashamed the law is such an ass. — George Chapman, *Revenge for Honor,* 1654

**1918.** Laws are like sausages. You should never watch them being made. — Honoré Mirabeau, attributed

# Leaders

## *See also* Followers; Greatness; Leadership; U.S. Presidency

**1919.** Leaders help personify the political system, and thus provide us with handles on a reality which might otherwise be overwhelming in its complexity. — Roger Gibbins, *Conflict and Unity,* 1985

**1920.** The first function of a political leader is advocacy. It is he who must make articulate the wants, the frustration, and the aspiration of the masses. — Aneurin Bevan, *In Place of Fear,* 1952

**1921.** A leader has to lead, or otherwise he has no business in politics. — Harry S Truman, in Mark Miller, *Plain Speaking: An Oral Biography of Harry S Truman,* 1974

**1922.** They should rule who are able to rule best. — Aristotle, *Politics,* 4th c. B.C.

**1923.** There are men who, by their sympathetic attractions, carry nations with them, and lead the activity of the human race. — Ralph Waldo Emerson, *The Conduct of Life,* "Power," 1860

**1924.** You are uneasy; you never sailed with *me* before, I see. — Andrew Jackson, in James Parton, *Life of Jackson,* 1860

**1925.** It must be that to govern a nation you need a specific talent and that this may very well exist without general ability. — W. Somerset Maugham, *The Summing Up,* 1938

**1926.** The art of governing is a great metier, requiring the whole man, and it is therefore not well for a ruler to have too strong tendencies for other affairs. — Johann Wolfgang von Goethe, in Johann P. Eckermann, *Conversations with Goethe,* February 18, 1831

**1927.** Charisma becomes the undoing of leaders. It makes them inflexible, convinced of their own infallibility, unable to change. — Peter F. Drucker, in *Wall Street Journal,* January 6, 1988

**1928.** The genius of a good leader is to leave behind him a situation which common sense, without the grace of genius, can deal with successfully. — Walter Lippmann, column, April 14, 1945

**1929.** There is no indispensable man. — Franklin D. Roosevelt, speech, November 3, 1932

**1930.** The graveyards are full of indispensable men. — Charles de Gaulle, attributed

**1931.** Anyone can hold the helm when the sea is calm. — Publilius Syrus, *Maxims,* 1st c. B.C.

**1932.** To rule is not so much a question of the heavy hand as the firm seat. — José Ortega y Gasset, *The Revolt of the Masses,* 1930

**1933.** People ask the difference between a leader and a boss. . . . The leader leads, and the boss drives. — Theodore Roosevelt, speech, October 24, 1910

**1934.** The real leader has no need to lead — he is content to point the way. — Henry Miller, *The Wisdom of the Heart,* 1941

**1935.** A leader should not get too far in front of his troops or he will be shot in the ass. — Joseph Clark, in *Washingtonian,* November, 1979

**1936.** Unlucky the country that needs a hero. — Bertolt Brecht, *Leben des Galilei,* 1943

**1937.** It is not well that there should be many masters; one man must be supreme. — Homer, *The Iliad,* ca. 700 B.C.

**1938.** We need supermen to rule us — the job is so vast and the need for wise judgment is so urgent. But, alas, there are no supermen. — Brooks Atkinson, *Once Around the Sun,* "January 27," 1951

**1939.** If you're strong enough, there *are* no precedents. — F. Scott Fitzgerald, *The Crack-Up,* 1945

1940. Men are of no importance. What counts is who commands. — Charles de Gaulle, in *New York Times Magazine,* May 12, 1968

1941. Ill can he rule the great that cannot reach the small. — Edmund Spenser, *The Faerie Queene,* 1596

1942. Leadership should be born out of the understanding of the needs of those who would be affected by it. — Marian Anderson, in *New York Times,* July 22, 1951

1943. The leader is a stimulus, but he is also a response. — Eduard C. Lindeman, *Social Discovery,* 1924

1944. I have never accepted what many people have kindly said — namely that I inspired the nation. Their will was resolute and remorseless, and as it is proved, unconquerable. It fell to me to express it. — Winston S. Churchill, speech, November 30, 1954

1945. He that would govern others, first should be Master of himself. — Philip Massinger, *The Bondman,* 1624

1946. One can't reign and be innocent. — Louis Antoine Léon de Saint-Just, speech, November 13, 1792

1947. A man has made great progress in cunning when he does not seem too clever to others. — Jean La Bruyère, *Characters,* "Of the Court," 1688

1948. A leader of whom it is said, "he's a nice man," is lost. — Napoleon I, letter, April 19, 1807

1949. The most important quality in a leader is that of being acknowledged as such. All leaders whose fitness is questioned are clearly lacking in force. — André Maurois, *The Art of Living,* 1939

1950. Woe to the land that's governed by a child! — William Shakespeare, *Richard III,* 1591

1951. People sense weakness, and step in and try to take control. — H. Ross Perot, in *Washington Post,* November 22, 1987

1952. You can't lead a cavalry charge if you think you look funny on a horse. — John Peers, *1,001 Logical Laws,* 1979

1953. Leaders make mistakes when they're too tired and overwhelmed with paper. — James Callaghan, in *Harvard Business Review,* November/December, 1986

1954. If the blind lead the blind, both shall fall into the ditch. — Bible, *Matthew 15:14*

1955. The blind lead the blind. It's the democratic way. — Henry Miller, *The Air-Conditioned Nightmare,* 1945

# Leadership

## See also Followers; Government, Roles and Functions of; Greatness; Leaders; U.S. Presidency

1956. Whether a man is burdened by power or enjoys power; whether he is trapped by responsibility or made free by it; whether he is moved by other people and outer forces or moves them — this is of the essence of leadership. — Theodore H. White, *The Making of the President 1960,* 1961

1957. I start with the premise that the function of leadership is to produce more leaders, not more followers. — Ralph Nader, in *Time,* November 8, 1976

1958. Herein lies political genius, in the identification of an individual with a principle. — Georg Wilhelm Friedrich Hegel, *The German Constitution,* 1802

1959. The final test of a leader is that he leaves behind him in other men the conviction and the will to carry on. — Walter Lippmann, in *New York Herald Tribune,* April 14, 1945

1960. You know what makes leadership? It is the ability to get men to do what they don't want to do, and like it.

—Harry S Truman, in *Time*, November 8, 1976

**1961.** Skill is a superb and necessary instrument, but it functions at its highest level only when it is guided by a mature mind and an exalted spirit. —Richard H. Guggenheimer, *Creative Vision*, 1950

**1962.** The only real training for leadership is leadership. —Antony Jay, *Management and Machiavelli*, 1968

**1963.** What we really need is a Constitutional amendment that says, "There shall be some spine in our national leaders." —Robert C. Byrd, in *Washington Post*, June 11, 1992

**1964.** The superior man is easy to serve and difficult to please. —Confucius, *Analects*, 6th c. B.C.

**1965.** Charlatanism of some degree is indispensable to effective leadership. —Eric Hoffer, *The True Believer*, 1951

**1966.** The modern world is not given to uncritical admiration. It expects its idols to have feet of clay, and can be reasonably sure that press and camera will report their exact dimensions. —Barbara Ward, in *Saturday Review*, September 30, 1961

**1967.** Leadership and learning are indispensable to each other. —John F. Kennedy, notes for scheduled speech, November 22, 1963

**1968.** For just experience tells; in every soil That those that think must govern those that toil. —Oliver Goldsmith, *The Traveler*, 1765

**1969.** We all know that Prime Ministers are wedded to the truth, but like other married couples they sometimes live apart. —Saki, *The Unbearable Bassington*, 1912

**1970.** What grimaces, what capers, leaps and chuckles prime ministers, presidents, and kings must indulge in, in the privacy of their bedrooms, so as to avenge their systems of the daylong strain imposed on them! —Paul Valéry, *Tel Quel*, 1943

**1971.** The man with a host of friends who slaps the back of everyone he meets is regarded as no one's friend. —Aristotle, *Nicomachean Ethics*, 4th c. B.C.

**1972.** The strong man in the world is he who stands most alone. —Henrik Ibsen, *An Enemy of the People*, 1882

**1973.** Leadership is not manifested by coercion, even against the resented. —Margaret Chase Smith, speech, April 16, 1962

**1974.** Leadership is demonstrated when the ability to inflict pain is confirmed. —Robert Malott, in *Fortune*, August 6, 1984

**1975.** Grace under pressure. —Ernest Hemingway, defining "guts" during an interview, November 30, 1929

**1976.** The great art of governing consists in not letting men grow old in their jobs. —Napoleon I, letter, August 9, 1796

**1977.** Some see leadership as high drama, and the sound of trumpets calling. But I see history as a book with many pages and each day we fill a page with acts of hopefulness and meaning. —George Bush, inaugural address, January 20, 1989

## *Legislatures*

### *See also* Political Action; Politicians

**1978.** Now any member of the assembly, taken separately, is certainly inferior to the wise man. But the state is made up of many individuals. And as a feast to which all the guests contribute is better than a banquet by a single man, as a multitude is a better judge of many things than any one individual. —Aristotle, *Politics*, 4th c. B.C.

**1979.** Instead of the function of

governing, for which it is radically unfit, the proper office of a representative assembly is to watch and control the government. — John Stuart Mill, *Dissertations and Discussions,* 1859

**1980.** England is the mother of parliaments. — John Bright, speech, January 18, 1865

**1981.** Discordant harmony. — Horace, *Epistles,* 1st c. B.C.

**1982.** Exhaustion and exasperation are frequently the handmaidens of legislative decisions. — Barber B. Conable Jr., in *Time,* October 22, 1984

**1983.** Though we cannot out-vote them we will out-argue them. — Samuel Johnson, in James Boswell, *Life of Samuel Johnson,* 1791

**1984.** Parliament can compel people to obey or submit, but it cannot compel them to agree. — Winston S. Churchill, speech, September 27, 1926

**1985.** That fatal drollery called a representative government. — Benjamin Disraeli, *Tancred,* 1847

**1986.** I don't think it's the function of Congress to function well. It should drag its heels on the way to decision. — Barber B. Conable Jr., in *Time,* October 22, 1984

**1987.** Poets and philosophers are the unacknowledged legislators of the world. — Percy Bysshe Shelley, *A Philosophical View of Reform,* 1819–20

**1988.** Creativity always dies a quick death in rooms that house conference tables. — Bruce Herschensohn, in *New York Times,* April 2, 1975

**1989.** Only people who look dull ever get into the House of Commons, and only people who are dull ever succeed there. — Oscar Wilde, *An Ideal Husband,* 1895

**1990.** Congress has become a professional legislature, where members come early, stay late, and die with their boots on. — Bill Frenzel, in *Nation's Business,* November 25, 1991

**1991.** Everybody hates Congress, but loves their Congressman. — John DiIulio Jr., in *Christian Science Monitor,* April 9, 1992

**1992.** Can any of you seriously say the Bill of Rights could get through Congress today? It wouldn't even get out of committee. — F. Lee Bailey, in *Newsweek,* April 17, 1967

**1993.** "I'll get back to you" is the moral equivalent of "The check is in the mail." — David A. Stockman, *The Triumph of Politics,* 1987

**1994.** There is good news from Washington today. Congress is deadlocked and can't act. — Will Rogers, in *Newsweek,* June 9, 1975

**1995.** All the public business in Congress now connects itself with intrigues, and there is a great danger that the whole government will degenerate into a struggle of cabals. — John Quincy Adams, *Diary,* January, 1819

**1996.** The man who is selling newspapers outside the Houses of Parliament can safely leave his papers to go for a drink and his cap beside them: anyone who takes a paper is sure to drop a copper into the cap. But the men who are inside the Houses of Parliament — they cannot trust one another like that, still less can the Government they compose trust other governments. No caps upon the pavement here. — E. M. Forster, *Two Cheers for Democracy,* 1951

**1997.** If Hitler invaded hell I would make at least a favorable reference to the devil in the House of Commons. — Winston S. Churchill, *The Grand Alliance,* 1950

**1998.** "Do you pray for the senators, Dr. Hale?" "No, I look at the senators and I pray for the country." — Edward Everett Hale, in Van Wyck Brooks, *New England Indian Summer,* 1940

**1999.** My greatest disappointment in Washington was the caliber of the Congress. Most of the people I've seen we wouldn't hire as a warehouse manager. — Drew Lewis, in *USA Today,* June 7, 1989

**2000.** People are angry at Congress. They see this body as out of touch, as incompetent, and I tell them, "If you are not angry now, democracy is brain dead." — Nancy L. Johnson, in *New York Times,* February 28, 1992

**2001.** It's a terribly hard job to spend a billion dollars and get your money's worth. — George M. Humphrey, in *Look,* February 23, 1954

**2002.** It could probably be shown by facts and figures that there is no distinctly native American criminal class except Congress. — Mark Twain, *Following the Equator,* 1897

**2003.** The House of Lords is the British Outer Mongolia. — Anthony Wedgwood Benn, in *New York Times,* February 11, 1962

**2004.** I will retort the question of the leader of the Opposition by another question. Has the House of Lords ever been right? — Winston S. Churchill, speech, June 29, 1907

**2005.** A severe though not unfriendly critic of our institutions said that "the cure for admiring the House of Lords was to go and look at it." — Walter Bagehot, *The English Constitution,* "The House of Lords," 1867

**2006.** The House of Lords, an illusion to which I have never been able to subscribe — responsibility without power, the prerogative of the eunuch throughout the ages. — Tom Stoppard, *Lord Malquist and Mr. Moon,* 1966

**2007.** People must not do things for fun. We are not here for fun. There is no reference to fun in any Act of Parliament. — A. P. Herbert, *Uncommon Law,* 1935

**2008.** Give a member of Congress a junket and a mimeograph machine and he thinks he is secretary of state. — Dean Rusk, in *Time,* May 6, 1985

# Liberals

## See also Conservatives

**2009.** The essence of the Liberal outlook lies not in *what* opinions are held, but in *how* they are held: instead of being held dogmatically, they are held tentatively, and with a consciousness that new evidence may at any moment lead to their abandonment. — Bertrand Russell, *Unpopular Essays,* 1950

**2010.** Politics without ideology, and with a strong tendency towards autobiography, equals Liberalism. — Stephen Stender, *The Thirties and After,* 1978

**2011.** Lady Bracknell: What are your politics? Jack: Well, I am afraid I really have none. I am a liberal . . . — Oscar Wilde, *The Importance of Being Earnest,* 1895

**2012.** The liberal, emphasizing the civil and property rights of the individual, insists that the individual must remain so supreme as to make the state his servant. — Wayne Morse, in *New Republic,* July 22, 1946

**2013.** The liberal philosophy holds that enduring governments must be accountable to someone beside themselves; that a government responsible only to its own conscience is not for long tolerable. — Walter Lippmann, in *Vanity Fair,* November, 1934

**2014.** The definition of liberalism, as I see it, is the expansion of the economic pie. If Democrats don't understand how to create jobs, and the pie shrinks . . . there is nothing liberal about that. — Paul Tsongas, in *Christian Science Monitor,* September 17, 1991

**2015.** It is the duty of the liberal to protect and to extend the basic democratic freedoms. — Chester Bowles, in *New Republic,* July 22, 1946

**2016.** Interest group liberalism . . . transforms logrolling from necessary evil to greater good . . . and conflict of interest a principle of government rather than a criminal act. — Theodore Lowi, in *American Political Science Review,* March, 1967

**2017.** A liberal mind is a mind that is able to imagine itself believing anything. — Max Eastman, in *Masses,* September, 1917

**2018.** Somehow liberals have been able to acquire from life what conservatives seem to be endowed with at birth: namely, a healthy skepticism of the powers of government agencies to do good. — Daniel P. Moynihan, in *New York Post,* May 14, 1969

**2019.** Liberalism is trust of the people tempered by prudence. — William E. Gladstone, speech, 1878

**2020.** I am a Liberal, yet I am a Liberal tempered by experience, reflection, and renouncement, and I am, above all, a believer in culture. — Matthew Arnold, *Culture and Anarchy,* 1869

**2021.** A liberal is a man who tells other people what to do with their money. — LeRoi Jones, *Home,* 1966

**2022.** Just as the left is benefited when class differences are recognized as the principal basis of political division, the right often gains the advantage when nonclass issues — foreign policy, morality, administrative efficiency, the personality of the candidates — are of central concern to voters. — Seymour Martin Lipset, *Political Man,* 1981

**2023.** Don't listen to that tired, liberal, divide, class-warfare rhetoric about soaking the rich. Hold on to your wallets. — George Bush, speech, November 5, 1990

**2024.** What liberals have never been able to bring themselves to admit is that capitalism is the product of capitalists. — David A. Stockman, *The Triumph of Politics,* 1987

**2025.** The liberals in the House strongly resemble liberals I have known through the last two decades in the civil rights conflict. When it comes time to show on which side they will be counted, they suddenly excuse themselves. — Shirley Chisholm, *Unbought and Unbossed,* 1970

**2026.** The definition of the Left is a group of people who will never be happy unless they can convince themselves that they are about to be betrayed by their leaders. — R. H. S. Crossman, *Diary,* July 3, 1959

**2027.** Liberal institutions immediately cease from being liberal the moment they are soundly established. — Friedrich Wilhelm Nietzsche, *Twilight of the Idols,* 1888

**2028.** A liberal is a conservative who's been mugged by reality. — Anonymous

**2029.** There are no more liberals. . . . They've all been mugged. — James Q. Wilson, in *Time,* January 21, 1985

**2030.** The Liberals talk about a stable government but we don't know how bad the stable is going to smell. — T. C. Douglas, news summaries, October 30, 1965

**2031.** The politics of the left and center of this country are frozen in an out-of-date mold which is bad for the political and economic health of Britain and increasingly inhibiting for those who live within the mold. Can it be broken? — Roy Jenkins, speech, June 9, 1980

**2032.** The Liberals are the flying saucers of politics. No one can make head nor tail of them, and they never are seen twice in the same place. — John G. Diefenbaker, speech, May 5, 1962

**2033.** The most important difference between liberals and conservatives . . . is to be found in the interest groups they identify with. Congressmen are guided in their votes, Presidents in their programs, and administrators in their discretion, by whatever organized interests they have taken for themselves as the most legitimate; and that is the measure of the legitimacy of demands. — Theodore Lowi, in *American Political Science Review,* March, 1967

**2034.** *Liberal* The term generally applied to those in American politics who advocate a rather advanced position on both foreign and domestic issues. . . . The American liberal is generally optimistic and progressive in politics, concerned over the protection of individual liberties and civil rights, tolerant of the views of others, and is somewhat more willing to use government as an agency for advancing the common good than are those who oppose him. Eugene J. McCarthy, *Dictionary of American Politics,* 1968

**2035.** *Progressive* In American politics, one who advocates change. The word is sometimes used as being synonymous with the word *liberalism,* although in a somewhat stricter sense the word *progressive* applied primarily to a program of action, and the word *liberalism,* in modern usage, applies to an attitude and general approach to political problems. —Eugene J. McCarthy, *Dictionary of American Politics,* 1968

**2036.** *Conservative* One who generally supports the status quo. He is slow to accept change and is generally considered to be opposed to *liberals* and *progressives.* —Eugene J. McCarthy, *Dictionary of American Politics,* 1968

## Liberty

### See also Freedom

**2037.** The true aim of government is liberty. —Baruch Spinoza, *Tractatus Theologico-Politicus,* 1670

**2038.** The more liberty is given to everything which is in a state of growth, the more perfect it will become. —Joseph Priestley, *Essay on Government,* 1768

**2039.** I love the Americans because they love liberty. —William Pitt (I), speech, March 2, 1770

**2040.** We do not profess to be the champions of liberty, and then consent to see liberty destroyed. —Woodrow Wilson, speech, September 4, 1919

**2041.** The God who gave us life, gave us liberty at the same time. —Thomas Jefferson, *Summary View of the Rights of British America,* 1774

**2042.** Abstract liberty, like other mere abstractions, is not to be found. —Edmund Burke, speech, March 22, 1775

**2043.** Is life so dear or peace so sweet, as to be purchased at the price of chains and slavery? Forbid it, Almighty God! I know not what course others may take, but as for me, give me liberty or give me death. —Patrick Henry, speech, March 23, 1775

**2044.** What country can preserve its liberties, if its rulers are not warned from time to time that this people preserve the spirit of resistance? —Thomas Jefferson, letter, November 13, 1787

**2045.** Liberty has never come from government. Liberty has always come from the subjects of government. The history of liberty is the history of resistance. —Woodrow Wilson, speech, May 9, 1912

**2046.** The preservation of the sacred fire of liberty, and the destiny of the republican model of government, are justly considered as deeply, perhaps as finally staked, on the experiment entrusted to the hands of the American people. —George Washington, inaugural address, April 30, 1789

**2047.** The ground of liberty is to be gained in inches. —Thomas Jefferson, letter, January 27, 1790

**2048.** Now, methinks, I see the ardor for liberty catching and spreading; a general amendment beginning in human affairs; the dominion of kings changed for the dominion of laws, and the dominion of priests giving way to the dominion of reason and conscience. —Richard Price, *A Discourse on the Love of Our Country,* 1790

**2049.** The condition upon which God hath given liberty to men is eternal vigilance. —John Philpot Curran, speech, July 10, 1790

**2050.** Oh liberty! Oh liberty! What

crimes are committed in thy name! —Jeanne Manon Roland, words upon the guillotine, 1793

**2051.** The contest, for ages, has been to rescue liberty from the grasp of executive power. —Daniel Webster, speech, May 27, 1834

**2052.** God grants liberty only to those who love it, and are always ready to guard and defend it. —Daniel Webster, speech, June 3, 1834

**2053.** The word *liberty* in the mouth of Mr. Webster sounds like the word *love* in the mouth of a courtesan. —Ralph Waldo Emerson, *Journals,* February, 1851

**2054.** The blessings of liberty which our constitution secures may be enjoyed alike by minorities and majorities. —James K. Polk, inaugural address, March 4, 1845

**2055.** Liberty relies upon itself, invites no one, promises nothing, sits in calmness and light, is positive and composed, and knows no discouragement. —Walt Whitman, *Leaves of Grass,* 1855

**2056.** Liberty consists in doing what one desires. —John Stuart Mill, *On Liberty,* 1859

**2057.** Whether in chains or in laurels, Liberty knows nothing but victories. —Wendell Phillips, speech, November 1, 1859

**2058.** One of the qualities of liberty is that, as long as it is being striven after, it goes on expanding. Therefore, the man who stands in the midst of the struggle and says, "I have it," merely shows by doing so that he has just lost it. —Henrik Ibsen, letter, February 17, 1871

**2059.** The tree of liberty must be refreshed from time to time, with the blood of patriots and tyrants. It is its natural manure. —Thomas Jefferson, letter, November 13, 1787

**2060.** Liberty trains for liberty. Responsibility is the first step in responsibility. —W. E. B. DuBois, *John Brown,* 1909

**2061.** You cannot tear up ancient rootages and safely plant the tree of liberty in soil that is not native to it. —Woodrow Wilson, speech, September 25, 1912

**2062.** Liberty, like charity, must begin at home. —James Bryant Conant, speech, June 30, 1942

**2063.** Liberty lies in the hearts of men and women; when it dies there, no constitution, no law, no court can save it. —Learned Hand, *The Spirit of Liberty,* 1944

**2064.** We can afford no liberties with liberty itself. —Robert H. Jackson, *Zorach v. Clausor,* April 7, 1952

**2065.** Let every nation know, whether it wishes us well or ill, that we shall pay any price, bear any burden, meet any hardship, to assure the survival and the success of liberty. —John F. Kennedy, inaugural address, January 20, 1961

**2066.** What to some is called liberty is called license in others. —Quintilian, *Institutio Oratoria,* 1st c.

**2067.** When liberty becomes license, some form of one-man power is not far distant. —Theodore Roosevelt, *Works,* 1887

**2068.** Of course liberty is not license. Liberty in my view is conforming to majority opinion. —Hugh Scanlon, interview, August 9, 1977

**2069.** They that can give up essential liberty to obtain a little temporary safety deserve neither liberty nor safety. —Benjamin Franklin, *Historical Review of Pennsylvania,* 1759

**2070.** Liberty too must be limited in order to be possessed. —Edmund Burke, *Letter to the Sheriffs of Bristol,* 1777

**2071.** Liberty exists in proportion to wholesome restraint. —Daniel Webster, speech, May 10, 1847

**2072.** The sole end for which mankind are warranted, individually or collectively, in interfering with the liberty of action of any of their number is self-protection. —John Stuart Mill, *On Liberty,* 1859

**2073.** It is harder to preserve than to obtain liberty. —John C. Calhoun, speech, January, 1848

2074. Liberty of each, limited by the like liberties of all, is the rule of conformity with which society must be organized. — Herbert Spencer, *Social Statics, Part II*, 1851

2075. The liberty of the individual must be thus far limited; he must not make himself a nuisance to other people. — John Stuart Mill, *On Liberty*, 1859

2076. The shepherd drives the wolf from the sheep's throat, for which the sheep thanks the shepherd as his liberator, while the wolf denounces him for the same act.... Plainly, the sheep and the wolf are not agreed upon a definition of liberty. — Abraham Lincoln, speech, April 18, 1864

2077. The shallow consider liberty a release from all law, from every constraint. The wise see in it, on the contrary, the potent Law of Laws. — Walt Whitman, *Notes Left Over*, 1881

2078. But little do or can the best of us: That little is achieved through Liberty. — Robert Browning, *Why I Am a Liberal*, 1885

2079. Liberty means responsibility. That is why most men dread it. — George Bernard Shaw, *Man and Superman*, 1903

2080. It is true that liberty is precious — so precious that it must be rationed. — Lenin, in Sidney and Beatrice Webb, *Soviet Communism*, 1936

2081. The spirit of liberty is the spirit which is not too sure it is right. — Learned Hand, speech, May 21, 1944

2082. Too little liberty brings stagnation, and too much brings chaos. — Bertrand Russell, *Authority and the Individual*, 1949

2083. Liberty is never out of bounds or off limits; it spreads wherever it can capture the imagination of men. — E. B. White, *The Points of My Compass*, 1960

2084. I flatter myself that I love a manly, moral, regulated liberty as well as any gentleman. — Edmund Burke, *Reflections on the Revolution in France*, 1790

2085. Liberty without learning is always in peril and learning without liberty is always in vain. — John F. Kennedy, remark, March 18, 1963

2086. There is no "slippery slope" toward loss of liberties, only a long staircase where each step downward must first be tolerated by the American people and their leaders. — Alan K. Simpson, in *New York Times*, September 26, 1982

2087. The basis of a democratic state is liberty. — Aristotle, *Politics*, 4th c. B.C.

2088. Liberty is the right of doing whatever the law permits. — Charles-Lewis de Secondat, *De l'Esprit des Lois*, 1748

2089. Liberty is, to the lowest rank of every nation, little more than the choice of working or starving. — Samuel Johnson, in *The British Magazine*, "The Bravery of the English Common Soldier," January, 1760

2090. The true character of liberty is independence, maintained by force. — Voltaire, *Philosophical Dictionary*, "Venice and Incidentally, of Liberty," 1764

2091. Liberty is to faction what air is to fire, an ailment without which it instantly expires. — James Madison, *The Federalist*, 1787

2092. Liberty is the only true riches; of all the rest we are at once the masters and the slaves. — William Hazlitt, *The Round Table*, "Commonplaces," 1817

2093. Individual liberty is individual power, and as the power of a community is a mass compounded of individual powers, the nation which enjoys the most freedom must necessarily be in proportion to its numbers the most powerful nation. — John Quincy Adams, letter, October 1, 1822

2094. Liberation is not deliverance. — Victor Hugo, *Les Misérables*, 1862

2095. Liberty is not a means to a higher political end. It is itself the highest political end. — John E. E. Dalberg, speech, February 26, 1877

2096. Liberty is the soul's right to breathe, and, when it cannot take a long breath, laws are girded too tight. — Henry

Ward Beecher, *Proverbs from Plymouth Pulpit*, 1887

**2097.** Liberty is the most jealous and exacting mistress that can beguile the brain and soul of man. — Clarence Darrow, speech, March 14, 1902

**2098.** The love of liberty is the love of others; the love of power is the love of ourselves. — William Hazlitt, *Political Essays*, 1819

**2099.** Liberty, *n.* One of Imagination's most precious possessions. — Ambrose Bierce, *The Devil's Dictionary*, 1906

**2100.** Liberty is the means in the pursuit of happiness. — William H. Taft, speech, October 10, 1909

**2101.** Liberty is its own reward. — Woodrow Wilson, speech, September 12, 1912

**2102.** Liberty is not collective, it is personal. All liberty is individual liberty. — Calvin Coolidge, speech, September 21, 1924

**2103.** Liberty is so much latitude as the powerful choose to accord to the weak. — Learned Hand, speech, June, 1930

**2104.** Liberty is the hardest test that one can inflict on a people. To know how to be free is not given equally to all men and all nations. — Paul Valéry, *Reflections on the World Today*, "On the Subject of Dictatorship," 1931

**2105.** Liberty is a different kind of pain from prison. — T. S. Eliot, *The Family Reunion*, 1939

**2106.** If liberty has any meaning it means freedom to improve. — Philip Wylie, *Generation of Vipers*, 1942

**2107.** If liberty means anything at all, it means the right to tell people what they do not want to hear. — George Orwell, *Animal Farm*, 1945

**2108.** Liberty is a beloved discipline. — George C. Homans, *The Human Group*, 1950

**2109.** Liberty is the possibility of doubting, the possibility of making a mistake, the possibility of searching and experimenting, the possibility of saying "No" to any authority — literary, artistic, philosophic, religious, social, and even political. — Ignazio Silone, *The God That Failed*, 1950

**2110.** Liberty is liberty, not equality or fairness or justice or human happiness or a quiet conscience. — Isaiah Berlin, *Two Concepts of Liberty*, 1958

**2111.** Liberty is the bread of man's spirit. — Salvador de Madariaga, in *Saturday Review*, April 4, 1967

---

# Lies

## See also Facts; Gossip and Publicity; Opinion, Difference of; Truth

**2112.** The rulers of the state are the only ones who should have the privilege of lying, either at home or abroad; they may be allowed to lie for the good of the state. — Plato, *The Republic*, ca. 370 B.C.

**2113.** That politician tops his part Who readily can lie with art. — John Gay, *Fables*, "The Squire and his Cur," 1738

**2114.** Take the life-lie away from the average man, and immediately you take away his happiness. — Henrik Ibsen, *The Wild Duck*, 1884

**2115.** Lies are essential to humanity. They are perhaps as important as the pursuit of pleasure and moreover are dictated by that pursuit. — Marcel Proust, *Remembrance of Things Past*, 1913–26

**2116.** In human relations kindness and lies are worth a thousand truths. — Graham Greene, *The Heart of the Matter*, 1948

**2117.** A little inaccuracy sometimes saves tons of explanation. — Saki, *The Square Egg*, 1924

2118. The great masses of the people...will more easily fall victim to a big lie than to a small one. — Adolf Hitler, *Mein Kampf*, 1933

2119. It is not in human nature to deceive others, for any long time, without, in a measure, deceiving ourselves. —J. H. Newman, *Parochial and Plain Sermons*, 1837–42

2120. Freedom is a very great reality. But it means, above all things, freedom from lies. —D. H. Lawrence, *Pornography and Obscenity*, 1930

2121. Lies—there you have the religion of slaves and taskmasters. — Maksim Gorki, *The Lower Depths*, 1903

2122. The best liar is he who makes the smallest amount of lying go the longest way. — Samuel Butler (II), *The Way of All Flesh*, 1903

2123. It often happens that if a lie be believed only for an hour, it has done its work, and there is no further occasion for it. —Jonathan Swift, *The Examiner*, 1715

2124. The fact of a man's having proclaimed (as leader of a political party, or in any other capacity) that it is wicked to lie obliges him as a rule to lie more than other people. — Marcel Proust, *Remembrance of Things Past*, 1913–26

2125. Once to every man and nation comes the moment to decide. In the strife of Truth with Falsehood, for the good or evil side. — James Russell Lowell, "The Present Crisis," 1845

2126. In the war between falsehood and truth, falsehood wins the first battle and truth the last. — Majubur Rahman, in *Newsweek*, January 24, 1972

2127. He who does not bellow the truth when he knows the truth makes himself the accomplice of liars and forgers. — Charles Péguy, *Basic Verities*, 1943

2128. Lord, lord, how this world is given to lying! — William Shakespeare, *Henry IV, Part I*, 1597

2129. There is no worse lie than a truth misunderstood by those who hear it. — William James, *The Varieties of Religious Experience*, 1902

2130. Sometimes we have to change the truth in order to remember it.

— George Santayana, in *Time*, July 28, 1975

2131. Anyone who does not feel sufficiently strong in memory should not meddle with lying. — Michel Eyquem de Montaigne, *Essays*, 1580

2132. A liar should have a good memory. — Quintilian, *Institutio Oratorio*, 1st c.

2133. I hate deception, even where the imagination only is concerned. — George Washington, letter, August 16, 1779

2134. Truths may clash without contradicting each other. — Antoine de Saint-Exupéry, *The Wisdom of the Sands*, 1950

2135. There are infinite possibilities of error, and more cranks take up unfashionable untruths than unfashionable truths. — Bertrand Russell, *Unpopular Essays*, 1950

2136. Convictions are more dangerous to truth than lies. — Friedrich Wilhelm Nietzsche, *Human, All Too Human*, 1878

2137. The best time to listen to a politician is when he's on a stump on a street corner in the rain late at night when he's exhausted. Then he doesn't lie. — Theodore H. White, in *New York Times*, January 5, 1969

2138. The cruelest lies are often told in silence. — Robert Louis Stevenson, *Virginibus Puerisque*, "The Truth of Intercourse," 1881

2139. Secrecy in government has become synonymous in the public mind, with deception by the government. — Lawton M. Chiles Jr., in *Christian Science Monitor*, November 4, 1975

2140. [Lyndon] Johnson's manners, his training and his conduct as a war leader added up to something genuinely alarming as President-politician: people doubted his word...there emerged one of the operative clichés of political discussion: the credibility gap. — Theodore H. White, *The Making of the President 1968*, 1969

2141. History, sir, will tell lies as usual. — George Bernard Shaw, *The Devil's Disciple*, 1901

# Lobbyists *see* Politicians

─────────── *Majority and Minority* ───────────

**See also** Common Interests; Party; Prejudice; Rights;
Voting and Elections; Winners and Losers

2142. That action is best which procures the greatest happiness for the greatest numbers. — Francis Hutcheson, *Inquiry concerning Moral Good and Evil,* 1720

2143. A majority is always the best repartee. — Benjamin Disraeli, *Tancred,* 1847

2144. The whole business of government is building majorities. — David Roberti, in *Los Angeles Times,* November 29, 1991

2145. The smaller the number of individuals composing a majority, and the smaller the compass within which they are placed, the more easily will they concert and execute their plans of oppression. Extend the sphere, and you will take in a greater variety of parties and interests; you make it less probable that a majority of the whole will have a common motive to invade the rights of other citizens. — James Madison, *The Federalist Papers,* "The Advantages of Union," 1787

2146. All politics are based on the indifference of the majority. — James Reston, in *New York Times,* June 12, 1968

2147. In a democracy the general good is furthered only when the special interests of competing minorities accidentally coincide — or cancel each other out. — Alexander Chase, *Perspectives,* 1966

2148. All, too, will bear in mind this sacred principle, that though the will of the majority is in all cases to prevail, that will to be rightful must be reasonable; that the minority possess their equal rights, which equal law must protect, and to violate would be oppression.

— Thomas Jefferson, inaugural address, March 4, 1801

2149. When were the good and the brave ever in a majority? — Henry David Thoreau, *A Plea for Captain John Brown,* 1859

2150. Hain't we got all the fools in town on our side? And ain't that a big enough majority in any town? — Mark Twain, *Adventures of Huckleberry Finn,* 1884

2151. A majority can do anything. — Joseph G. Cannon, in *Baltimore Sun,* March 4, 1923

2152. For who can be secure of private right. If sovereign sway may be dissolved by might? Nor is the people's judgment always true: The most may err as grossly as the few. — John Dryden, *Absalom and Achitophel,* 1681

2153. In a democracy the majority of the citizens is capable of exercising the most cruel oppressions upon the minority. — Edmund Burke, *Reflections on the Revolution in France,* 1790

2154. The tyranny of the majority. — Alexis de Tocqueville, *Democracy in America,* 1835

2155. In political speculations "the tyranny of the majority" is now generally included among the evils against which society requires to be on its guard. — John Stuart Mill, *On Liberty,* 1859

2156. The one pervading evil of democracy is the tyranny of the majority, or rather of that party, not always the majority, that succeeds by force or fraud, in carrying elections. — John E. E. Dalberg, *The History of Freedom and Other Essays,* 1907

2157. The majority rules. If they want anything, they get it. If they want

anything not right, they get it, too.
— Sojourner Truth, speech, 1871

**2158.** You cannot have a decent, popular government unless the majority exercise the self-restraint that men with great power ought to exercise. — William H. Taft, speech, October 10, 1909

**2159.** In the majority beat many hearts, but it has no heart. — Otto von Bismarck, speech, June 12, 1882

**2160.** If by the mere force of numbers a majority should deprive a minority of any clearly written constitutional right, it might, in a moral point of view, justify revolution — certainly would if such a right were a vital one. — Abraham Lincoln, inaugural address, March 4, 1861

**2161.** A government is free in proportion to the rights it guarantees to the minority. — Alf Landon, speech, October, 1936

**2162.** It is hell to belong to a suppressed minority. — Claude McKay, *A Long Way from Home,* 1937

**2163.** Governments exist to protect the rights of minorities. The loved and the rich need no protection: they have many friends and few enemies. — Wendell Phillips, speech, December 21, 1860

**2164.** A respectable minority is useful as censors. — Thomas Jefferson, letter, May 3, 1802

**2165.** The minority is always right. — Henrik Ibsen, *An Enemy of the People,* 1882

**2166.** When great change occurs in history, when great principles are involved, as a rule the majority are wrong. The minority are right. — Eugene V. Debs, speech, September 11, 1918

**2167.** Minorities ... are almost always in the right. — Sydney Smith, in H. Pearson, *The Smith of Smiths,* 1934

**2168.** Any man more right than his neighbors constitutes a majority of one. — Henry David Thoreau, *Civil Disobedience,* 1849

**2169.** Desperate courage makes One a majority. — Andrew Jackson, in James Parton, *The Life of Andrew Jackson,* 1888

**2170.** A majority can never replace the man.... Just as a hundred fools do not make one wise man, an heroic decision is not likely to come from a hundred cowards. — Adolf Hitler, *Mein Kampf,* 1933

**2171.** A man with God is always in the majority. — John Knox, inscription in the Reformation Monument, 16th c.

**2172.** One with the law is a majority. — Calvin Coolidge, speech, July 27, 1920

**2173.** If a man is in a minority of one, we lock him up. — Oliver Wendell Holmes Jr., speech, February 15, 1913

**2174.** What's a cult? It just means not enough people to make a minority. — Robert Altman, in *Guardian,* April 11, 1981

--------- *Masses and Elites* ---------

## *See also* Class; Fools; Haves and Have Nots; Leaders; the People; Poverty

**2175.** I can't help feeling wary when I hear anything said about the masses. First you take their faces from 'em by calling 'em the masses and then you accuse 'em of not having any faces. — J. B. Priestley, *Saturn Over the Water,* 1961

**2176.** This is one of the paradoxes of the democratic movement — that it loves a crowd and fears the individuals who compose it — that the religion of humanity should have no faith in human beings. — Walter Lippmann, *A Preface to Politics,* 1914

2177. All the world over, I will back the masses against the classes. — William E. Gladstone, speech, June 28, 1886

2178. Minorities are individuals or groups of individuals especially qualified. The masses are the collection of people not specially qualified. — José Ortega y Gasset, *The Revolt of the Masses*, 1930

2179. I was told that the Privileged and the People formed Two Nations. — Benjamin Disraeli, *Sybil*, 1845

2180. Since the campaign of 1894 *mugwump* has been in general use to indicate a political bolter, but it still carries the special significance of one professing to a certain undemocratic superiority. Soon after it came in General Horace Porter defined it as meaning "a person educated beyond his intellect." — H. L. Mencken, *The American Language, Supplement I*, 1945

2181. Government is everywhere to a great extent controlled by powerful minorities, with an interest distinct from that of the mass of the people. — G. Lowes Dickinson, *The Choice Before Us*, 1917

2182. We cannot have our cake and eat it too. We cannot have the advantages of an aristocratic *and* a democratic society; we cannot have segregated elite schools in a society that stresses equality; we cannot have a cultured elite which produces without regard to mass taste in a society which emphasizes the value of popular judgment. — Seymour Martin Lipset, *Political Man*, 1981

2183. By the use of sanctioned words and gestures the elite elicits blood, work, taxes, applause, from the masses. — Harold Laswell, *Politics, Who Gets What, When, How*, 1951

2184. Nothing appears more surprising to those who consider human affairs with a philosophical eye, than the easiness with which the many are governed by the few. — David Hume, *Essays*, "First Principles of Government," 1742

2185. People, like sheep, tend to follow a leader — occasionally in the right direction. — Alexander Chase, *Perspectives*, 1966

2186. The great masses of people (of all classes) cannot think at all. That is why the majority never rule. They are led like sheep by the few who know what they cannot think. — Robert Blatchford, *God and My Neighbor*, 1903

2187. Ours is not yet a totalitarian government, but it is an elitist democracy — and becoming more so every year. — Victor L. Marchetti, in *Inquiry*, February 6, 1978

2188. The way in which the man of genius rules is by persuading an efficient minority to coerce an indifferent and self-indulgent majority. — James F. Stephen, *Liberty, Equality and Fraternity*, 1873

2189. The masses are the material of democracy, but its form . . . can only be rightly shaped by wisdom, which is by no means a universal property. — Henri Frédéric Amiel, *Journal*, February 16, 1874

2190. All the civilizations we know have been created and directed by small intellectual aristocracies, never by people in the mass. The power of crowds is only to destroy. — Gustave Lebon, *Psychologie des foules*, 1895

2191. The multitude is always in the wrong. — Wentworth Dillon, *Essay on Translated Verse*, 1684

2192. In the republic of mediocrity genius is dangerous. — Robert G. Ingersoll, *Liberty in Literature*, 1890

2193. Mobs will never do to govern states or command armies. — John Adams, letter, January 27, 1787

2194. Who builds on the mob builds on sand. — Italian proverb

2195. The populace drag down the gods to their own level. — Ralph Waldo Emerson, *Journals*, 1858

2196. The masses are cowardly, fickle, and ever ready to be deceived. — Niccolò Machiavelli, *The Prince*, 1513

2197. The better I get to know men, the more I find myself loving dogs. — Charles de Gaulle, in *Time*, December 8, 1967

2198. Our supreme governors, the mob. — Horace Walpole, letter, September 7, 1943

**2199.** Everyone has observed how much more dogs are animated when they hunt in a pack, than when they pursue their game apart. We might, perhaps, be at a loss to explain this phenomenon, if we had not experience of a similar in ourselves. — David Hume, *A Treatise of Human Nature*, 1739

**2200.** Everyone in a crowd has the power to throw dirt: nine out of ten have the inclination. — William Hazlitt, "On Reading Old Books," 1821

**2201.** The public! The public! How many fools does it take to make up a public? — Sébastien Roch Nicholas Chamfort, *Caractères et anecdotes*, 1771

**2202.** Fools invent fashions and wise men are fain to follow them. — Samuel Butler (I), *Prose Observations*, 1660–80

**2203.** "It's always best on these occasions to do what the mob do." "But suppose there are two mobs?" suggested Mr. Snodgrass. "Shout with the largest," replied Mr. Pickwick. — Charles Dickens, *Pickwick Papers*, 1837

**2204.** To most people nothing is more troublesome than the effort of thinking. — James Bryce, *Studies in History and Jurisprudence*, 1901

**2205.** Men credit most easily the things which they do not understand. They believe most easily things which are obscure. — Cornelius Tacitus, *Histories*, ca. 95

**2206.** For the crowd, the incredible has sometimes more power and is more credible than the truth. — Menander, *Fragment 622*, 3rd c. B.C.

**2207.** All that is necessary to raise imbecility into what the mob regards as profundity is to lift it off the floor and put it on a platform. — George Jean Nathan, in *American Mercury*, "Profundity," September, 1929

**2208.** The masses feel that it is easy to flee from reality, when it is the most difficult thing in the world. — José Ortega y Gasset, *The Dehumanization of Art*, 1948

**2209.** And, quite often, both reformers and traditionalists dislike the same features of the present, like the nature of popular culture, which the leftist blames on the institutions of a business society, and the conservative sees as the necessary outcome of democracy's giving the masses power over taste. — Seymour Martin Lipset, *Political Man*, 1981

**2210.** When I hear the word culture...I release the safety-catch on my Browning. — Hanns Johst, *Schlageter*, 1933

**2211.** Commonplace people have an answer for everything and nothing ever surprises them. — Ferdinand Delacroix, *Journal*, 1852

**2212.** Prince I am not, yet I am nobly born. — Thomas Dekker, *The Shoemaker's Holiday*, 1600

**2213.** Insignificant people are a necessary relief in society. Such characters are extremely agreeable, and ever favorites, if they appear satisfied with the part they have to perform. — William Hazlitt, *Characteristics*, 1823

**2214.** As long as the great majority of men are not deprived of either property or honor, they are satisfied. — Niccolò Machiavelli, *The Prince*, 1513

**2215.** The mass of men lead lives of quiet desperation. — Henry David Thoreau, *Walden*, "Economy," 1854

**2216.** Society is a more level surface than we imagine. Wise men or absolute fools are hard to be met with, as there are few giants or dwarfs. — William Hazlitt, *Characteristics*, 1823

**2217.** Really, if the lower orders don't set us a good example, what on earth is the use of them? — Oscar Wilde, *The Importance of Being Earnest*, 1895

# Minority *see* Majority and Minority

# Moderation

## See also Extremism

2218. Real liberty is neither found in despotism or the extremes of democracy, but in moderate governments. — Alexander Hamilton, *Debates of the Federal Convention,* June 26, 1787

2219. In politics the middle way is none at all. — John Adams, letter, March 23, 1776

2220. Men generally decide upon a middle course...for they know neither how to be extremely good nor extremely bad. — Niccolò Machiavelli, *Discourses on the First Ten Books of Titus Livius,* 1513–17

2221. The field of politics always presents the same struggle. There are the Right and the Left, and in the middle is the Swamp. — August Bebel, speech, 1906

2222. We know what happens to people who stay in the middle of the road. They get run down. — Aneurin Bevan, in *Observer,* December 6, 1953

2223. A playful moderation in politics is just as absurd as a remonstrative whisper to a mob. — Leigh Hunt, in *Examiner,* March 6, 1808

2224. There is moderation in everything. — Horace, *Satires,* 1st c. B.C.

2225. There is moderation even in excess. — Benjamin Disraeli, *Vivian Grey,* 1826

2226. A thing moderately good is not so good as it ought to be. Moderation in temper is always a virtue; but moderation in principle is always a vice. — Thomas

Paine, *The Rights of Man, Part II,* 1792

2227. I would remind you that extremism in the defense of liberty is no vice. And let me remind you also that moderation in the pursuit of justice is no virtue. — Barry Goldwater, speech, July 16, 1964

2228. Extremism in the pursuit of the presidency is an unpardonable vice. Moderation in the affairs of the nation is the highest virtue. — Lyndon B. Johnson, speech, October 31, 1964

2229. Sudden power is apt to be insolent, sudden liberty saucy; that behaves best which has grown gradually. — Benjamin Franklin, *Poor Richard's Almanac,* 1733–58

2230. Because free institutions are maintained by moderate policies and acquired and protected by immoderate ones, they depend on politicians who have a preference for moderate over immoderate policies but the capacity and willingness to use either when needed. — Stimson Bullitt, *To Be a Politician,* 1977

2231. The characteristic pattern of stable Western democracies in the mid-twentieth century is that they are in a "post politics" phase — that is, there is relatively little difference between the democratic left and right, the socialists and moderates, and the conservatives accept the welfare state. — Seymour Martin Lipset, *Political Man,* 1981

# Modern Times

## See also Future; History

2232. The golden age never was the present age. — Benjamin Franklin, *Poor Richard's Almanac,* 1733–58

2233. The age of chivalry is gone. — That of sophisters, economists, and calculators, has succeeded; and the glory of Europe is extinguished for ever. —Edmund Burke, *Reflections on the Revolution in France,* 1790

**2234.** I hold that the characteristic of the present age is craving credulity. —Benjamin Disraeli, speech, November 25, 1864

**2235.** Dissatisfaction with the world in which we live and determination to realize one that shall be better, are the prevailing characteristics of the modern spirit. —G. Lowes Dickinson, *The Greek View of Life,* 1898

**2236.** Th' modhren idee iv govern-mint is "Snub th' people, buy th' people, jaw th' people." —Finley Peter Dunne, *Mr. Dooley's Philosophy,* "Casual Observations," 1900

**2237.** The world is disgracefully managed, one hardly knows to whom to complain. —Ronald Firbank, *Vainglory,* 1915

**2238.** The lamps are going out all over Europe; we shall not see them lit again in our lifetime. —Edward Grey, *25 Years,* 1925

**2239.** As society is now constituted a literal adherence to the moral precepts scattered throughout the Gospels would

mean sudden death. —Alfred North Whitehead, *Adventures of Ideas,* 1933

**2240.** The world is becoming like a lunatic asylum run by lunatics. —David Lloyd George, in *Observer,* January 8, 1933

**2241.** The trouble with our age is all signposts and no destination. —Louis Kronenberger, in *Look,* May 17, 1954

**2242.** These are the days when men of all social disciplines and all political faiths seek the comfortable and the accepted; when the man of controversy is looked upon as a disturbing influence; when originality is taken to be a mark of instability; and when, in minor modification of the scriptural parable, the bland lead the bland. —John Kenneth Galbraith, *The Affluent Society,* 1958

**2243.** The rising generation cannot spell...its English is slipshod...veteran teachers are saying that never in their experience were young people so thirstily avid of pleasure as now...so selfish, and so hard! —Cornelia A. P. Comer, 1991 article, in Neil Howe and William Strauss, *Atlantic,* "The New Generation Gap," December, 1992

---

# *Monarchy*

## *See also* Rulers and Ruling

**2244.** The rising generation has a very real feeling of coming straight up against a wall of diminishing opportunity. I do not see how it can be denied that practical opportunity is less for this generation than it has been for those preceding it. —Randolph Burne, in Neil Howe and William Strauss, *Atlantic,* "The New Generation Gap," December, 1992

**2245.** The best reason why Monarchy is a strong government is that it is an intelligible government. The mass of mankind understand it, and they hardly anywhere in the world understand any other. —Walter Bagehot, *The English Constitution,* "The Monarchy," 1867

**2246.** A multitude of rulers is not a

good thing. Let there be one ruler, one king. —Homer, *Iliad,* ca. 700 B.C.

**2247.** There's such divinity doth hedge a king, That treason can but peep to what it would. —William Shakespeare, *Hamlet,* 1601

**2248.** The king never dies. —William Blackstone, *Commentaries on the Laws of England,* 1765

**2249.** The Right Divine of Kings to govern wrong. —Alexander Pope, *The Dunciad,* 1743

**2250.** Not all the water in the rough rude sea Can wash the balm from an anointed king. —William Shakespeare, *Richard II,* 1595

**2251.** The saddest of all Kings

Crowned, and again discrowned. — Lionel Johnson, "By the Statue of King Charles I at Charing Cross," 1895

**2252.** The man who would be king. — Rudyard Kipling, story title, 1888

**2253.** The king's name is a tower of strength. — William Shakespeare, *Richard III*, 1591

**2254.** The heart of kings is unsearchable. — Bible, *Proverbs 25:3*

**2255.** But methought it lessened my esteem of a king, that he should not be able to command the rain. — Samuel Pepys, *Diary*, July 19, 1662

**2256.** You're still the king — even in your underwear. — Ludwig Fulda, *Der Talisman*, 1893

**2257.** The characteristic of the English Monarchy is that it retains the feelings by which the heroic kings governed their rude age, and has added the feelings by which the constitutions of later Greece ruled in more refined ages. — Walter Bagehot, *The English Constitution*, "The Monarchy," 1867

**2258.** If... the status of major conservative groups and symbols is not threatened... even though they lose most of their power, democracy seems to be much more secure. And thus we have the absurd fact that ten out of the twelve stable European and English-speaking democracies are monarchies. — Seymour Martin Lipset, *Political Man*, 1981

**2259.** Monarchy alone tends to bring men together, to unite them in compact, efficient masses, and to make them capable by their combined efforts of the highest degree of culture and civilization. — Clemens von Metternich, remark, 1835

**2260.** Royalty is a government in which the attention of the nation is concentrated on one person doing interesting actions. A Republic is a government in which that attention is divided between many, who are all doing uninteresting actions. Accordingly, so long as the human heart is strong and the human reason weak, Royalty will be strong because it appeals to diffused feelings, and Republics weak because they appeal to the understanding. — Walter Bagehot, *The English Constitution*, "The Monarchy," 1867

**2261.** That the king can do no wrong, is a necessary and fundamental principle of the English constitution. — William Blackstone, *Commentaries on the Laws of England*, 1765

**2262.** It is the misfortune of kings that they will not listen to the truth. — Johann Jacoby, letter, November 2, 1848

**2263.** The Sovereign has, under a constitutional monarchy such as ours, three rights — the right to be consulted, the right to encourage, the right to warn. — Walter Bagehot, *The English Constitution*, "The Monarchy (continued)," 1867

**2264.** All hereditary government is in its nature tyranny.... To inherit a government, is to inherit the people, as if they were flocks and herds. — Thomas Paine, *The Rights of Man, Part II*, 1792

**2265.** Monarchy is the gold filling in the mouth of decay. — John Osborne, in Bernard Levin, *The Pendulum Years*, 1976

**2266.** Plots, true or false, are necessary things To raise up commonwealths and ruin kings. — John Dryden, *Absalom and Achitophel*, 1681

**2267.** Anything done against kings was to be applauded — unless, indeed, it were done by priests, like Becket, in which case one sided with the king. — Bertrand Russell, *Portraits from Memories*, 1956

**2268.** All kings is mostly rapscallions. — Mark Twain, *Adventures of Huckleberry Finn*, 1884

# *Morality*

## See also Virtue and Vice

2269. Finally, there is an imperative which commands a certain conduct immediately, without having as its condition any other purpose to be attained by it. This imperative is Categorical.... This imperative may be called that of Morality. — Immanuel Kant, *Fundamental Principles of the Metaphysics of Ethics,* 1785

2270. He who is as faithful to his principles as he is to himself is the true partisan. — William Hazlitt, *Sketches and Essays,* "On the Spirit of Partisanship," 1839

2271. The time has come for all good men to rise above principle. — Huey Long, attributed

2272. Righteousness exalteth a nation. — Bible, *Proverbs 14:34*

2273. When there is a lack of honor in government, the morals of the whole people are poisoned. — Herbert Hoover, in *New York Times,* August 9, 1964

2274. The humblest citizen of all the land, when clad in the armor of a righteous cause, is stronger than all the hosts of error. — William Jennings Bryan, speech, July 8, 1896

2275. A man who wants to act virtuously in every way necessarily comes to grief among so many who are not virtuous. — Niccolò Machiavelli, *The Prince,* 1513

2276. The just upright man is laughed to scorn. — Bible, *Job 12:4*

2277. What is morality in any given time or place? It is what the majority then and there happen to like, and immorality is what they dislike. — Alfred North Whitehead, *Dialogues,* 1954

2278. Morality is simply the attitude we adopt toward people we personally dislike. — Oscar Wilde, *An Ideal Husband,* 1895

2279. Moral indignation is jealousy with a halo. — H. G. Wells, *The Wife of Sir Isaac Harman,* 1914

2280. The defense of morals is the battle-cry which best rallies stupidity against change. — Alfred North Whitehead, *Adventures of Ideas,* 1933

2281. There is much cant in American moralism and not a little inconsistency. — J. William Fulbright, speech, March 27, 1964

2282. The more cant there is in politics the better. Cant is nothing in itself; but attached to even the smallest quantity of sincerity, it serves like a nought after a numeral, to multiply whatever of genuine good-will may exist. — Aldous Huxley, *Jesting Pilate,* 1926

2283. Morality is the best of all devices for leading mankind by the nose. — Friedrich Wilhelm Nietzsche, *The Anti-Christ,* 1888

2284. What we call "Morals" is simply blind obedience to words of command. — Havelock Ellis, *The Dance of Life,* 1923

2285. Obedience is the primary and irremissible motive and the foundation of all morality. — Friedrich Julius Stahl, *Die Philosophie des Rechts,* 1830–37

2286. Obedience stimulates subordination as fear of the police stimulates honesty. — George Bernard Shaw, *Man and Superman,* 1903

2287. The oppressed are always morally in the right. — Robert Briffault, *Rational Evolution,* 1930

2288. One becomes moral as soon as one is unhappy. — Marcel Proust, *A l'ombre des jeunes filles en fleurs,* 1918

2289. Whoever fights monsters should see to it that in the process he does not become a monster. — Friedrich Wilhelm Nietzsche, *Beyond Good and Evil,* 1886

2290. Ethics is not a branch of economics. — Yerachmiel Kugel, in *St. Louis Post-Dispatch,* July 24, 1977

2291. Government is essentially immoral. — Herbert Spencer, *Social Statics, Part II*, 1851

2292. Nothing is more foreign to us Christians than politics. — Tertullian, *The Christian's Defense*, ca. 215

2293. The highest possible stage in moral culture is when we recognize that we ought to control our thoughts. — Charles Darwin, *The Descent of Man*, 1871

2294. Be a good animal, true to your instincts. — D. H. Lawrence, *The White Peacock*, 1911

2295. Education is the art of making men ethical. — Georg Wilhelm Friedrich Hegel, *The Philosophy of Right*, 1821

# Mottoes and Slogans

## See also Adages and Maxims

2296. *Veni, vidi, vici.* (I came, I saw, I conquered.) — Julius Caesar, announcement of the victory of Zela, 1st c. B.C.

2297. Caesar or nothing. — Cesare Borgia, motto, 15th c.

2298. I have not yet begun to fight. — John Paul Jones, statement, September 23, 1779

2299. Freedom! Equality! Brotherhood! — Anonymous, motto of the French Revolution

2300. Peace, commerce, and honest friendship with all nations — entangling alliances with none. — Thomas Jefferson, inaugural address, March 4, 1801

2301. Tranquility at home and peaceful relations abroad constitute the true permanent policy of our country. — James K. Polk, message to Congress, December 5, 1848

2302. With malice toward none; with charity for all; with firmness in the right, as God gives us to see the right, let us strive on to finish the work we are in: to bind up the nation's wounds; to care for him who shall have borne the battle, and for his widow and his orphan, to do all which may achieve and cherish a just and lasting peace among ourselves, and with all nations. — Abraham Lincoln, inaugural address, March 4, 1865

2303. Proletarians of all lands, unite! You have nothing to lose but your chains. You have a world to win. — Karl Marx and Friedrich Engels, *Communist Manifesto*, 1848

2304. Defense, not defiance. — Anonymous, motto of the Volunteers Movement, 1859

2305. Fourscore and seven years ago our fathers brought forth on this continent, a new nation, conceived in Liberty, and dedicated to the proposition that all men are created equal. — Abraham Lincoln, Gettysburg Address, November 19, 1863

2306. From each according to his abilities, to each according to his needs. — Karl Marx, *Critique of the Gotha Programme*, 1875

2307. Give me your tired, your poor, Your huddled masses yearning to breathe free, The wretched refuse of your teeming shore, Send these, the homeless, tempest-tossed to me: I lift my lamp beside the golden door. — Emma Lazarus, "The New Colossus," inscription on the Statue of Liberty, 1883

2308. I am as strong as a bull moose and you can use me to the limit. — Theodore Roosevelt, letter, June 27, 1900

2309. We have ... fought for our place in the sun and we have won it. — Wilhelm II, speech, June 18, 1901

2310. A man who is good enough to shed his blood for the country is good enough to be given a square deal afterwards. — Theodore Roosevelt, speech, June 4, 1903

**2311.** America's present need is not heroics, but healing; not nostrums but normalcy; not revolution, but restoration. — Warren G. Harding, speech, May 14, 1920

**2312.** I pledge you, I pledge myself, to a new deal for the American people. — Franklin D. Roosevelt, speech, July 2, 1932

**2313.** Strength through joy. — Robert Ley, slogan, 1933

**2314.** Here we are the way politics ought to be in America, the politics of happiness, the politics of purpose and the politics of joy. — Hubert H. Humphrey, speech, April 27, 1968

**2315.** Let "Dig for Victory" be the motto of everyone with a garden and of every able-bodied man and woman capable of digging an allotment in their spare time. — Reginald Dorman-Smith, radio broadcast, October 3, 1939

**2316.** The century on which we are entering...can be and must be the century of the common man. — Henry Wallace, speech, May 8, 1942

**2317.** A brilliant diversity spread like stars, like a thousand points of light in a broad and peaceful sky. — George Bush, speech, August 18, 1988

**2318.** Let us never negotiate out of fear. But let us never fear to negotiate. — John F. Kennedy, inaugural address, January 20, 1961

**2319.** The buck stops here. — Harry S Truman, motto

**2320.** Better red than dead. — Anonymous, 1950's

**2321.** Rather dead than red!

— Thomas S. Power, *Design for Survival,* 1964

**2322.** We stand today on the edge of a new frontier.... But the new frontier of which I speak is not a set of promises — it is a set of challenges. It sums up not what I intend to offer the American people, but what I intend to ask of them. — John F. Kennedy, speech, July 15, 1960

**2323.** In your heart, you know he's right. — Barry Goldwater, campaign slogan, 1964

**2324.** And so, my fellow Americans, ask not what your country can do for you; ask what you can do for your country. — John F. Kennedy, inaugural address, January 20, 1961

**2325.** It is time to break the habit of expecting something for nothing, from our government or from each other. Let us all take more responsibility...for our communities and our country. — Bill Clinton, inaugural address, January 20, 1993

**2326.** The great silent majority. — Richard M. Nixon, broadcast, November 3, 1969

**2327.** I never give them hell. I just tell the truth, and they think it is hell. — Harry S Truman, in *Look,* April 3, 1956

**2328.** Nearly all the campaign slogans in American history, from the pledges to the veterans of the Revolution down through the "Vote yourself a farm" of 1846 and the "Share the wealth" of Huey Long to the grandiose promises of the New Deal have voiced engagements to loot A for the use and benefit of B. — H. L. Mencken, *The American Language, Supplement I,* 1945

## Nationalism

### See also International Relations; Patriotism

**2329.** Size is not grandeur, and territory does not make a nation. — T. H. Huxley, *On University Education,* 1876

**2330.** That country is the richest

which nourishes the greatest number of noble and happy human beings. — John Ruskin, *Unto This Last,* 1862

**2331.** Energy in a nation is like sap

in a tree; it rises from bottom up. — Woodrow Wilson, speech, October 28, 1912

**2332.** The spirit of a nation is what counts — the look in its eyes. — Jean Giraudoux, *Electra,* 1937

**2333.** When an American says that he loves his country, he . . . means that he loves an inner air, an inner light in which freedom lives and in which a man can draw the breath of self-respect. — Adlai Stevenson, speech, August 27, 1952

**2334.** You in America should trust to that volcanic political instinct which I have divined in you. — George Bernard Shaw, speech, April 11, 1933

**2335.** You cannot conquer America. — William Pitt (I), speech, November 18, 1777

**2336.** A nation will not count the sacrifices it makes, if it supposes it is engaged in a struggle for its fame, its influence and its existence. — Benjamin Disraeli, speech, May 24, 1855

**2337.** A major test of legitimacy is the extent to which given nations have developed a common "secular political culture," mainly national rituals and holidays. — Seymour Martin Lipset, *Political Man,* 1981

**2338.** It is far more difficult to change the mentality of the people than it is to change a country's political order or even its economy. — Ilya Ehrenburg, in *Saturday Review,* "What I Have Learned," September 30, 1967

**2339.** Physical strength can never permanently withstand the impact of a spiritual force. — Franklin D. Roosevelt, speech, May 4, 1941

**2340.** Soft countries give birth to soft men. — Herodotus, *The History,* ca. 450 B.C.

**2341.** The workers have no fatherland. . .one cannot take from them that which they do not possess. — Karl Marx and Friedrich Engels, *Communist Manifesto,* 1848

**2342.** That kind of patriotism which consists in hating all other nations. — Elizabeth Gaskell, *Sylvia's Lovers,* 1863

**2343.** The nationalist has a broad hatred and a narrow love. He cannot stifle a predilection for dead cities. — André Gide, *Journals,* 1918

**2344.** Nations, like men, die by imperceptible disorders. We recognize a doomed people by the way they sneeze or pare their nails. — Jean Giraudoux, *Tiger at the Gates,* 1935

**2345.** Nationalism is our form of incest, is our idolatry, is our insanity. "Patriotism" is its cult. — Eric Fromm, *The Sane Society,* 1955

**2346.** Nationalism is an infantile sickness. It is the measles of the human race. — Albert Einstein, in Helen Dukas and Banesh Hoffman, *Albert Einstein, the Human Side,* 1979

**2347.** There is no longer division between what is foreign and what is domestic — the world economy, the world environment, the world AIDS crisis, the world arms race — they affect us all. — Bill Clinton, inaugural address, January 20, 1993

**2348.** Our true nationality is mankind. — H. G. Wells, *The Outline of History,* 1920

# Natural Law

## See also Equality; Law; the People; Rights

**2349.** The natural liberty of man is to be free from any superior power on earth, and not to be under the will or legislative authority of man, but to have

only the law of nature for his rule. — John Locke, *The Second Treatise of Government,* 1690

**2350.** No man who knows aught,

can be so stupid to deny that all men naturally were born free. — John Milton, *Tenure of Kings and Magistrates,* 1649

**2351.** That all men are by nature equally free and independent, and have certain inherent rights, of which, when they enter into a state of society, they cannot by any compact deprive or divest their posterity; namely, the enjoyment of life and liberty, with the means of acquiring and possessing property, and pursuing and obtaining happiness and safety. — George Mason, *Virginia Bill of Rights,* June 12, 1776

**2352.** We hold these truths to be self-evident; that all men are created equal; that they are endowed by their creator with certain unalienable rights; that among these are life, liberty, and the pursuit of happiness. — Thomas Jefferson, *Declaration of Independence,* July 4, 1776

**2353.** Nature has never read the Declaration of Independence. It continues to make us unequal. — Will Durant, in *New York Daily News,* May 3, 1970

**2354.** Inequalities of mind and body are so established by God Almighty, in his constitution of human nature, that no art or policy can ever plane them down to a level. — John Adams, letter, July 13, 1813

**2355.** Every man, when he comes to be sensible of his natural rights, and to feel his own importance, will consider himself as fully equal to any other person whatever. — Joseph Priestley, *An Essay on Government,* 1768

**2356.** Men are made by nature unequal. It is vain, therefore, to treat them as if they were equal. — James Anthony Froude, *Short Studies on Great Subjects, Third Series,* "Party Politics," 1877

**2357.** Men are born equal but they are also born different. — Erich Fromm, *Escape from Freedom,* 1941

**2358.** It is human nature that rules the world, not governments and regimes. — Svetlana Alliluyeva, in *New York Times,* November 3, 1984

**2359.** Natural rights is simple nonsense: natural and imprescriptible rights, rhetorical nonsense — nonsense upon stilts. — Jeremy Bentham, "Anarchical Fallacies," in J. Bowring, ed., *Works, Vol. 2,* 1843

---
# *Necessity*
---

## *See also* Crisis

**2360.** Cruel necessity. — Oliver Cromwell, in Joseph Spence, *Anecdotes,* 1820

**2361.** Necessity makes an honest man a knave. — Daniel Defoe, *The Serious Reflections of Robinson Crusoe,* 1720

**2362.** Necessity never made a good bargain. — Benjamin Franklin, *Poor Richard's Almanac,* 1733–58

**2363.** Political necessities sometimes turn out to be political mistakes. — George Bernard Shaw, *Saint Joan,* 1924

**2364.** Necessity is the plea of every infringement of human freedom. It is the argument of tyrants; it is the creed of slaves. — William Pitt (II), speech, November 18, 1783

**2365.** There are things a man must not do even to save a nation. — Murray Kempton, *America Comes of Middle Age,* 1963

**2366.** Why has government been instituted at all? Because the passions of men will not conform to the dictates of reason and justice, without constraint. — Alexander Hamilton, *The Federalist,* 1787–88

**2367.** One's choice, liberal or conservative, depends on the shape of one's outlook and the needs of the time. — Stimson Bullitt, *To Be a Politician,* 1977

# Office

## See also Bureaucracy; Politicians; U.S. Presidency

2368. High office teaches decision making, not substance. It consumes intellectual capital; it does not create it. — Henry Kissinger, in *Time,* October 15, 1979

2369. Government is a trust, and the officers of the government are trustees; and both the trust and the trustees are created for the benefit of the people. — Henry Clay, speech, May 16, 1829

2370. The very essence of a free government consists in considering offices as public trusts, bestowed for the good of the country, and not for the benefit of an individual or a party. — John C. Calhoun, speech, February 13, 1835

2371. The phrase, "public office is a public trust," has of late become public property. — Charles Sumner, speech, May 31, 1872

2372. Public officers are the servants and agents of the people, to execute the laws which the people have made. — Grover Cleveland, letter, October, 1882

2373. Your every voter, as surely as your chief magistrate, exercises a public trust. — Grover Cleveland, inaugural address, March 4, 1885

2374. Public office is a public trust. — Grover Cleveland, administration motto and phrase used in the Democratic national platform of 1892

2375. Are you a politician who says to himself: "I will use my country for my own benefit"?...Or are you a devoted patriot, who whispers in the ear of his inner self: "I love to serve my country as a faithful servant." — Kahlil Gibran, *The New Frontier,* 1931

2376. In our democracy officers of the government are the servants, and never the masters of the people. — Franklin D. Roosevelt, speech, February 27, 1941

2377. If we do not lay out ourselves in the service of mankind whom should we serve? — Abigail Adams, letter, September 29, 1778

2378. The public official must pick his way nicely, must learn to placate though not to yield too much, to have the art of honeyed words but not to seem neutral, and above all to keep constantly audible, visibly likable, even kissable. — Learned Hand, speech, March 8, 1932

2379. Public life is a situation of power and energy; he trespasses against his duty who sleeps upon his watch, as well as he that goes over to the enemy. — Edmund Burke, *Thoughts on the Cause of the Present Discontents,* 1770

2380. No personal consideration should stand in the way of performing a public duty. — Ulysses S. Grant, in E. P. Oberholtzer, *History of the United States Since the Civil War,* 1937

2381. Men forget that high office is a tool and not a prize. — Stimson Bullitt, *To Be a Politician,* 1977

2382. Nowadays, for the sake of the advantage which is to be gained from the public revenues and from office, men want to be always in office. — Aristotle, *Politics,* 4th c. B.C.

2383. Few die and none resign. — Thomas Jefferson, letter, July 12, 1801

2384. The passion for office among members of Congress is very great, if not absolutely disreputable, and greatly embarrasses the operations of the Government. — James K. Polk, *Diary,* June 22, 1846

2385. *Pension.* Pay given to a state hireling for treason to his country. — Samuel Johnson, *A Dictionary of the English Language,* 1755

2386. In public life, instead of modesty, incorruptibility and honesty — shamefulness, bribery and rapacity hold sway. — Sallust, *The War with Citiline,* ca. 40 B.C.

2387. Whenever a man has cast a longing eye on them [official positions], a rottenness begins in his conduct. — Thomas Jefferson, letter, May 21, 1799

2388. Every public official should be recycled occasionally. — John Lindsay, in *Chicago Tribune*, January 22, 1978

2389. I will undoubtedly have to seek what is happily known as gainful employment, which I am glad to say does not describe holding public office. — Dean Acheson, in *Time*, December 22, 1952

2390. Public office is the last refuge of the scoundrel. — Boies Penrose, in *Collier's Weekly*, February 14, 1931

2391. Issues are the last refuge of scoundrels. — Edmund G. Brown Jr., in *Washingtonian*, November, 1979

2392. A technical objection is the first refuge of a scoundrel. — Heywood Broun, in *New Republic*, December 15, 1937

2393. It is not the least praise to have pleased leading men. Not everyone is lucky enough to get to Corinth. — Horace, *Epistles*, 1st c. B.C.

2394. To enjoy a prince's favor does not rule out the possibility of merit, but neither does it argue for its existence. — John La Bruyère, *Characters*, "Of Opinions," 1688

2395. Every time I create an appointment, I create a hundred malcontents and one ingrate. — Louis XIV, in Voltaire, *The Century of Louis XIV*, 1768

2396. It is the nature of men to be bound by the benefits they confer as much as by those they receive. — Niccolò Machiavelli, *The Prince*, 1513

2397. We are the President's men. — Henry Kissinger, in M. and B. Kalb, *Kissinger*, 1974

2398. The amount of effort put into a campaign by a worker expands in proportion to the personal benefits that he will derive from his party's victory. — Milton Rakove, in *Virginia Quarterly Review*, Summer, 1965

2399. Civil service has made campaign activity unnecessary to keep a job and unavailing to get one. For those who work for Uncle Sam, the Hatch Act has converted campaign work from insurance to a risk. — Stimson Bullitt, *To Be a Politician*, 1977

2400. Those who insist on the dignity of their office, show they have not deserved it. — Balthasar Gracián, *The Art of Worldly Wisdom*, 1647

2401. Official dignity tends to increase in inverse ratio to the importance of the country in which the office is held. — Aldous Huxley, *Beyond the Mexique Bay*, 1934

2402. My only great qualification for being put at the head of the Navy is that I am very much at sea. — Edward Carson, in Ian Colvin, *Life of Lord Carson*, 1936

--- *Opinion, Difference of* ---

See also Belief; Facts; Freedom of Speech; Gossip and Publicity; Leadership; Lies; Press and Media; Opinion, Public; Truth

2403. So many men, so many opinions. — Terence, *Phormio*, 161 B.C.

2404. Opinion is darker than knowledge and brighter than ignorance. — Plato, *The Republic*, ca. 370 B.C.

2405. What you *see* is news, what you *know* is background, what you *feel* is

opinion. — Lester Markel, *While You Were Gone*, 1946

2406. It were not best that we should all think alike; it is difference of opinion that makes horse races. — Mark Twain, *Pudd'nhead Wilson*, 1894

2407. Men's features are not alike;

nor are their opinions. — Maimonides, *Second Law*, 1180

**2408.** It is probable that a given opinion, as held by several individuals, even when of the most congenial views, is as distinct from itself as are their faces. — J. H. Newman, *Oxford University Sermons*, 1843

**2409.** Diversity of opinion within the framework of loyalty to our free society is not only basic to a university but to the entire nation. — James Bryant Conant, *Education in a Divided World*, 1948

**2410.** It takes in reality only one to make a quarrel. It is useless for the sheep to pass resolutions in favor of vegetarianism, while the wolf remains of a different opinion. — William Ralph Inge, *Outspoken Essays: First Series*, "Patriotism," 1919

**2411.** The lion and the calf shall lie down together, but the calf won't get much sleep. — Woody Allen, in *Time*, February 26, 1979

**2412.** I think we Americans tend to put too high a price on unanimity...as if there were something dangerous and illegitimate about honest differences of opinion honestly expressed by honest men. — J. William Fulbright, speech, October 22, 1965

**2413.** Never did two men judge alike about the same thing, and it is impossible to find two opinions exactly alike, not only in different men, but in the same man at different times. — Michel Eyquem de Montaigne, *Essays*, 1580

**2414.** Every difference of opinion is not a difference of principle. — Thomas Jefferson, inaugural address, March 4, 1801

**2415.** Nothing that is not a real crime makes a man appear so contemptible and little in the eyes of the world as inconsistency. — Joseph Addison, in *The Spectator*, September 5, 1711

**2416.** Inconsistencies of opinion, arising from changes of circumstances, are often justifiable. — Daniel Webster, speech, July 25, 1846

**2417.** Those who never retract their opinions love themselves more than they love the truth. — Joseph Joubert, *Pensées*, 1842

**2418.** The miseries of life would be increased beyond all human power of endurance, if we were to enter the world with the same opinions we carry from it. — Samuel Johnson, *The Rambler*, 1750–52

**2419.** We do not know, nor can we know, with absolute certainty that those who disagree with us are wrong. We are human and therefore fallible, and being fallible, we cannot escape the element of doubt as to our own opinions and convictions. — J. William Fulbright, speech, December 5, 1963

**2420.** The recipe for perpetual ignorance is: be satisfied with your opinions and content with your knowledge. — Elbert Hubbard, *The Philistine*, 1897

**2421.** Persistence in one opinion has never been considered a merit in political leaders. — Cicero, *Epistulae ad Damiliares*, ca. 50 B.C.

**2422.** The man who never alters his opinion is like standing water, and breeds reptiles of the mind. — William Blake, *The Marriage of Heaven and Hell*, "A Memorable Fancy," 1790

**2423.** If in the last few years you hadn't discarded a major opinion or acquired a new one, check your pulse. You may be dead. — Galett Burgess, in *Forbes*, August 1, 1977

**2424.** The foolish and the dead alone never change their opinion. — James Russell Lowell, *My Study Windows*, "Abraham Lincoln," 1871

**2425.** Nothing is more conducive to peace of mind than not having any opinion at all. — Georg Christoph Lictenberg, *Aphorisms*, 1764–99

**2426.** They that approve a private opinion, call it opinion; but they that mislike it, heresy; and heresy signifies no more than private opinion. — Thomas Hobbes, *Leviathan*, 1651

**2427.** New opinions are always suspected, and usually opposed, without any other reason but because they are not already common. —John Locke, *An Essay concerning Human Understanding,* 1690

**2428.** Custom, then, is the great guide of human life. —David Hume, *An Enquiry concerning Human Understanding,* 1748

**2429.** The dissenting opinions of one generation become the prevailing interpretation of the next. —Burton J. Hendrik, *Bulwarks of the Republic,* 1937

**2430.** New opinions often appear first as jokes and fancies, then as blasphemies and treason, then as questions open to discussion, and finally as established truths. —George Bernard Shaw, *Everybody's Political What's What?,* 1944

**2431.** Opinion is something wherein I go about to give Reason why all the World should think as I think. —John Selden, *Table Talk,* "Opinion," 1689

**2432.** I am always of the opinion with the learned, if they speak first. —William Congreve, *Incognita,* 1692

**2433.** Opinion in good men is but knowledge in the making. —John Milton, *Areopagitica,* 1644

**2434.** Honest difference of views and honest debate are not disunity. They are the vital process of policy among free men. —Herbert Hoover, speech, December 20, 1950

**2435.** An illogical opinion only requires rope enough to hang itself. —Augustine Birrell, *Obiter Dicta,* "The Via Media," 1884

**2436.** Opinions cannot survive if one has no chance to fight for them. —Thomas Mann, *The Magic Mountain,* 1924

**2437.** Thought is not free if the profession of certain opinions make it impossible to earn a living. —Bertrand Russell, *Sceptical Essays,* 1928

**2438.** It is setting a high value upon our opinions to roast men and women alive on account of them. —Michel Eyquem de Montaigne, *Essays,* 1580

**2439.** All empty souls tend to extreme opinion. —William Butler Yeats, *Dramatis Personae,* 1936

**2440.** Opinion is ultimately determined by the feelings, and not by the intellect. —Herbert Spencer, *Social Statics, Part IV,* 1851

**2441.** A man's opinions, look you, are generally of much more value than his arguments. —Oliver Wendell Holmes Sr., *The Professor at the Breakfast-Table,* 1860

**2442.** "That was excellently observed," say I when I read a passage in another where his opinion agrees with mine. When we differ, then I pronounce him to be mistaken. —Jonathan Swift, *Thoughts on Various Subjects,* 1711

**2443.** Men are never so good or so bad as their opinions. —James Mackintosh, *Dissertation on the Progress of Ethical Philosophy,* 1830

**2444.** The only sin in which we never forgive each other is difference of opinion. —Ralph Waldo Emerson, *Society and Solitude,* "Clubs," 1870

————————— *Opinion, Public* —————————

### *See also* Character; Gossip and Publicity; Leaders; Opinion, Difference of; Press and Media

**2445.** A government is based on public opinion and must keep in step with what public opinion decides, which considers and calculates everything. —Napoleon I, letter, November 25, 1803

**2446.** [Democratic politicians] advance politically only as they placate, appease, bribe, seduce, bamboozle, or otherwise manage to manipulate the demanding and threatening elements in their constituencies. The decisive consideration is not whether the proposition is good but whether it is popular—not whether it will work well and prove itself but whether the active talking constituents like it immediately. Politicians rationalize this servitude by saying that in a democracy public men are servants of the people.—Walter Lippmann, *The Public Philosophy,* 1983

**2447.** The idea of what the public will think prevents the public from ever thinking at all, and acts like a spell on the exercise of private judgment.—William Hazlitt, *Table Talk,* "On Living to One's-self," 1821–22

**2448.** That mysterious independent variable of political calculation, Public Opinion.—T. H. Huxley, *Universities, Actual and Ideal,* 1874

**2449.** In the modern world the intelligence of public opinion is the one indispensable condition of social progress.—Charles W. Eliot, speech, 1869

**2450.** A government can be no better than the public opinion which sustains it.—Franklin D. Roosevelt, speech, January 8, 1936

**2451.** Its name is Public Opinion. It is held in reverence. It settles everything. Some think it is the voice of God.—Mark Twain, *Europe and Elsewhere,* "Corn Pone Opinions," 1925

**2452.** Public opinion is the most potent monarch this world knows.—Benjamin Harrison, speech, February 22, 1888

**2453.** Public opinion in this country is everything.—Abraham Lincoln, speech, September 16, 1859

**2454.** A man ain't got no right to be a public man, unless he meets the public views.—Charles Dickens, *Martin Chuzzlewit,* 1844

**2455.** No written law has ever been more binding than unwritten custom supported by popular opinion.—Carrie Chapman Catt, testimony, February 13, 1900

**2456.** There must be public opinion back of the laws or the laws themselves will be of no avail.—Theodore Roosevelt, message to Congress, December 3, 1907

**2457.** We are ruled by Public Opinion, not by Statute-law.—Elbert Hubbard, *The Note Book,* 1927

**2458.** Public opinion's always in advance of the law.—John Galsworthy, *Windows,* 1922

**2459.** It is the besetting vice of democracies to substitute public opinion for law. This is the usual form in which the masses of men exhibit their tyranny.—James Fenimore Cooper, *The American Democrat,* 1838

**2460.** Government, in the last analysis, is organized opinion. Where there is little or no public opinion, there is likely to be bad government, which sooner or later becomes autocratic government.—W. L. Mackenzie King, *Message of the Carillon,* 1927

**2461.** One should respect public opinion insofar as is necessary to avoid starvation and to keep out of prison, but anything that goes beyond this is voluntary submission to an unnecessary tyranny.—Bertrand Russell, *The Conquest of Happiness,* 1930

**2462.** There is nothing that makes more cowards and feeble men than public opinion.—Henry Ward Beecher, *Proverbs from Plymouth Pulpit,* 1887

**2463.** You may talk of the tyranny of Nero and Tiberius; but the real tyranny is the tyranny of your—next-door neighbor. . . . Public opinion is a permeating influence, and it exacts obedience to itself; it requires us to think other men's thoughts, to speak other men's words, to follow other men's habits. —Walter Bagehot, *Biographical Studies,* "Sir Robert Peel," 1907

**2464.** A menace now is not a dark, unrelenting oppressor but a decisive weather vane, who measures the wind's direction, then bolts headlong that way to run interference for his constituents; he is a warm and shiny salesman who rehearses his sincerity before a mirror every morning and burns a candle to opinion polls each night.—Stimson Bullitt, *To Be a Politician,* 1977

**2465.** Public opinion exists only where there are no ideas.—Oscar Wilde, in *Saturday Review,* November 17, 1894

**2466.** What we call public opinion is generally public sentiment. — Benjamin Disraeli, speech, August 3, 1880

**2467.** Opinion is that exercise of the human will which helps us to make a decision without information. — John Erskine, *The Complete Life,* 1943

**2468.** Of the opinions which people hold, we ought to value some highly, but not all. — Plato, *Crito,* ca. 370 B.C.

**2469.** Most people's opinions are of no value at all. — A. L. Rowse, in *Observer,* August 26, 1979

**2470.** Public opinion, a vulgar, anonymous tyrant who deliberately makes life unpleasant for anyone who is not content to be the average man. — William Ralph Inge, *Outspoken Essays: First Series,* "Our Present Discontents," 1919

**2471.** Public opinion is a weak tyrant compared with our own private opinion. What a man thinks of himself, that it is which determines, or rather indicates, his fate. — Henry David Thoreau, *Walden,* "Economy," 1854

**2472.** Thus to be independent of public opinion is the first formal condition of achieving anything great or rational, whether in life or in science. — Georg Wilhelm Friedrich Hegel, *Philosophy of Right,* 1821

**2473.** In a democracy such as ours military policy is dependent on public opinion. — George C. Marshall, in *Yank,* January 28, 1943

**2474.** You cannot stay at 91 per cent in the polls by cheering yesterday's war. — Mario Cuomo, in *Washington Post,* March 8, 1991

**2475.** War makes rattling good history; but Peace is poor reading. — Thomas Hardy, *The Dynasts,* 1904

**2476.** No minister ever stood, or could stand, against public opinion. — John Wilson Croker, in *Quarterly Review,* February, 1835

**2477.** The public seldom forgives twice. — Johann Kaspar Lavater, *Aphorisms on Man,* 1788

**2478.** Even though counting heads is not an ideal way to govern, at least it is better than breaking them. — Learned Hand, speech, March 8, 1932

**2479.** The sound of tireless voices is the price we pay for the right to hear the music of our own opinions. — Adlai Stevenson, speech, August 28, 1952

**2480.** Politicians, after all, are not over a year behind Public Opinion. — Will Rogers, *The Autobiography of Will Rogers,* 1949

**2481.** Public sentiment is to public officers what water is to the wheel of the mill. — Henry Ward Beecher, *Proverbs from Plymouth Pulpit,* 1887

**2482.** As the master politician navigates the ship of state, he both creates and responds to public opinion. Adept at tacking with the wind, he also succeeds, at times, in generating breezes of his own. — Stewart L. Udall, *The Quiet Crisis,* 1963

**2483.** With public sentiment nothing can fail; without it, nothing can succeed. Consequently he who molds public sentiment goes deeper than he who enacts statutes or pronounces decisions. — Abraham Lincoln, speech, July 31, 1858

---

# *Order*

## See also **Anarchy; Law**

**2484.** Good order is the foundation of all good things. — Edmund Burke, *Reflections on the Revolution in France,* 1790

**2485.** All religions, laws, moral and political systems are but necessary means to preserve social order. — Ch'en Tu-hsiu, in *The New Youth,* February, 1918

2486. Order is not pressure which is imposed on society from without, but an equilibrium which is set up from within. —José Ortega y Gasset, *Mirabeau and Politics*, 1927

2487. The magistrate should obey the laws, the people should obey the magistrate. —Benjamin Franklin, *Poor Richard's Almanac*, 1733–58

2488. Good laws, if not obeyed, do not constitute good government. —Aristotle, *Politics*, 4th c. B.C.

2489. As for rioting, the old Roman way of dealing with that is always the right one; flog the rank and file, and fling the ringleaders from the Tarpeian rock. —Thomas Arnold, unpublished letter, 1820's

2490. We do not want a police state, but we need a state of law and order, and neither mob violence nor police brutality have any place in America. —Hubert H. Humphrey, in Theodore H. White, *The Making of the President 1968*, 1969

2491. It's the orders you disobey that make you famous. —Douglas MacArthur, in *Time*, September 11, 1978

2492. In my youth I stressed freedom, and in my old age I stress order. I have made the great discovery that liberty is a product of order. —Will Durant, in *Time*, August 13, 1965

2493. I hold that the only discipline important for its own sake, is self-discipline, and that this can only be acquired by a wide use of freedom. —Alfred North Whitehead, *The Aims of Education*, 1929

2494. Discipline means power at command; mastery of the resources available for carrying through the actions undertaken. To know what one is to do and to move to do it promptly and by the use of the requisite means is to be disciplined, whether we are thinking of an army or the mind. —John Dewey, *Democracy and Education*, 1916

2495. Civilization advances by extending the number of important operations which we can perform without thinking about them. —Alfred North Whitehead, *An Introduction to Mathematics*, 1911

2496. The graveyard is completely ordered because absolutely nothing happens there. —C. J. Friedrich, *An Introduction to Political Theory*, 1967

# Parties

## See also Campaigns; Party System

2497. Government has become a Stop and Shop for every conceivable greedy and narrow interest. There are no new ideas and no real debate. We're down to a single political party: the incumbent party. —Edmund G. Brown Jr., in *New York Times*, December 28, 1991

2498. An independent is the guy who wants to take the politics out of politics. —Adlai Stevenson, in Bill Adler, ed., *The Stevenson Wit*, "The Art of Politics," 1966

2499. I am driving to grudging toleration of the Conservative Party because it is the party of non-politics, of resistance to politics. —Kingsley Amis, in *Sunday Telegraph*, July 2, 1967

2500. A wise Tory and a wise Whig, I believe, will agree. Their principles are the same, though their modes of thinking are different. —Samuel Johnson, in James Boswell, *Life of Samuel Johnson*, 1791

2501. Tories, in short, are atrophied Englishmen, lacking certain moral and intellectual reflexes. They are recognizable, homely—even, on occasions, endearing—but liable to turn very nasty at short notice. —Paul Johnson, *New Statesman*, "Rule Like Pigs," 1958

**2502.** The Labor Party owes more to Methodism than to Marxism. — Morgan Phillips, in James Callaghan, *Time and Chance,* 1987

**2503.** Studies of the social bases of the Federalists, America's first conservative party, and the Jeffersonian Democrats in the late eighteenth and early nineteenth centuries indicate that they corresponded closely to the bases of the modern Republicans and Democrats, respectively. — Seymour Martin Lipset, *Political Man,* 1981

**2504.** The deeper we penetrate into the inmost thought of these parties, the more we perceive that the object of the one is to limit and that of the other to extend the authority of the people. — Alexis de Tocqueville, *Democracy in America,* 1835

**2505.** A party of order or stability, and a party of progress or reform, are both necessary elements of a healthy state of political life. — John Stuart Mill, *On Liberty,* 1859

**2506.** For a working man or woman to vote Republican this year is the same as a chicken voting for Colonel Sanders. — Walter Mondale, in *Rolling Stone,* November 4, 1976

**2507.** Every Harvard class should have one Democrat to rescue it from oblivion. — Will Rogers, *The Autobiography of Will Rogers,* 1949

**2508.** Any well-established village in New England or the northern Middle West could afford a town drunkard, a town atheist, and a few Democrats. — D. W. Brogan, *The American Character,* 1944

**2509.** Tell me thy company, and I'll tell thee what thou art. — Miguel de Cervantes, *Don Quixote,* 1615

**2510.** Southern Democrats always had a special brand of intra-party politics. They enjoyed bare-knuckles politics, and if they didn't invent it, they sure perfected the art. They truly enjoy the game. — Stephen Hess, in *Christian Science Monitor,* May 15, 1990

**2511.** Th' dimmycratic party ain't on speakin' terms with itsilf. — Finley Peter Dunne, *Mr. Dooley's Opinions,* "Mr. Dooley Discusses Party Politics," 1900

**2512.** I am not a member of any organized party. I am a Democrat. — Will Rogers, in P. J. O'Brien, *Will Rogers, Ambassador of Good Will, Prince of Wit and Wisdom,* 1935

**2513.** The Democratic Party is like a mule. It has neither pride of ancestry nor hope of posterity. — Ignatius Donnelly, speech, September 13, 1860

**2514.** [Democrats] can't get elected unless things get worse — and things won't get worse unless they get elected. — Jeane J. Kirkpatrick, in *Time,* June 17, 1985

**2515.** Th' raypublican party broke ye, but now that ye're down we'll not turn a cold shoulder to ye. Come in an' we'll keep ye — broke. — Finley Peter Dunne, *Mr. Dooley's Opinions,* "Mr. Dooley Discusses Party Politics," 1900

**2516.** Democrats have been famous for dividing the pie fairly. Now there's no pie left. So Democrats must learn how to produce wealth. — Paul Tsongas, in *Time,* June 24, 1991

**2517.** Histhry always vindicates th' Dimmycrats, but niver in their lifetime. The see th' thruth first, but th' trouble is that nawthin' is iver officially thrue till a Raypublican sees it. — Finley Peter Dunne, in *New York Times Magazine,* December 9, 1962

**2518.** The problem with Democrats is we promise more than we can deliver, and then we don't deliver on the promises we make, and people view us as irresponsible. — Dan Rostenkowski, in *New York Times,* August 5, 1991

**2519.** Democrats are . . . the party that says government can make you richer, smarter, taller and get the chickweed out of your lawn. — P. J. O'Rourke, *Parliament of Whores,* 1991

**2520.** Republicans believe every day is the Fourth of July, but Democrats believe every day is April 15. — Ronald Reagan, in *New York Times,* October 10, 1984

**2521.** We are Republicans and don't propose to leave our party and identify ourselves with the party whose antecedents are rum, Romanism and rebellion. — Samuel D. Burchard, speech, October 29, 1884

**2522.** The elephant has a thick skin, a head full of ivory, and as everyone who has seen a circus parade knows, proceeds best by grasping the tail of his predecessor. — Adlai Stevenson, in Bill Adler, ed., *The Stevenson Wit,* "The Art of Politics," 1966

**2523.** Republicans are the party that says government doesn't work, and then they get elected and prove it. — P. J. O'Rourke, *Parliament of Whores,* 1991

**2524.** Since its centers of electoral strength, particularly during periods of Democratic dominance, are in the "provinces" rather than the large metropolitan cities, the Republican party can be more properly accused of being the agent of the small-town *bourgeoisie* than of big business. — Seymour Martin Lipset, *Political Man,* 1981

**2525.** Within the Republican Party are combined a stream of the loftiest American idealism and a stream of the coarsest American greed. — Theodore H. White, *The Making of the President 1960,* 1961

**2526.** Republicans have found a way to sell the interests of the wealthiest as the national good so that people think, This is good for me too. — Benjamin R. Barber, in *Harper's Magazine,* January, 1990

**2527.** The Republican quarrel with the American welfare state is over. The half-trillion-dollar budget which remains in 1986 after five years of sustained ideological challenge is there because the rank and file of GOP politicians want it for their constituents no less than the Democrats do. — David A. Stockman, *The Triumph of Politics,* 1987

**2528.** There's nothing wrong with the Republican Party that double-digit inflation won't cure. — Richard Scammon, in *Guardian Weekly,* November 12, 1978

**2529.** The trouble with the Republican Party is that it has not had a new idea in thirty years. — Woodrow Wilson, speech, January 8, 1915

**2530.** I am for "Peace, retrenchment, and reform," the watchword of the great Liberal party thirty years ago. — John Bright, speech, April 28, 1859

**2531.** It is getting so that a Republican promise is not much more to be depended on than a Democratic one. And that has always been considered the lowest form of collateral in the world. — Will Rogers, in William R. Brown, *Imagemaker: Will Rogers and the American Dream,* 1970

# Party System

## See also Campaigns; Parties

**2532.** A party spirit betrays the greatest man to act as meanly as the vulgar herd. — Jean La Bruyère, *Characters,* "Of Mankind," 1688

**2533.** Party is the madness of many for the gain of a few. — Jonathan Swift, *Thoughts on Various Subjects,* 1711

**2534.** Party-spirit, which at best is but the madness of many for the gain of a few. — Alexander Pope, letter, August 27, 1714

**2535.** Parties must ever exist in a free country. — Edmund Burke, *On Conciliation with America,* 1775

**2536.** A sect or party is an elegant incognito devised to save a man from the vexation of thinking. — Ralph Waldo Emerson, *Journals,* 1831

**2537.** The duty of an Opposition [is] to oppose everything, and propose nothing. — Edward Stanley, speech, June 4, 1841

**2538.** No government can be long secure without a formidable Opposition. — Benjamin Disraeli, *Coningsby*, 1844

**2539.** All parties, without exception, insofar as they seek power, are varieties of absolutism. — Pierre Joseph Proudhon, *Confessions of a Revolutionary*, 1849

**2540.** I believe that without party Parliamentary government is impossible. — Benjamin Disraeli, speech, April 3, 1872

**2541.** All free governments are party governments. — James A. Garfield, speech, January 18, 1878

**2542.** There is no greater hindrance to the progress of thought than an attitude of irritated party-spirit. — Alfred North Whitehead, *Adventures of Ideas*, 1933

**2543.** There can be but two great political parties in this country. — Stephen A. Douglas, speech, July 16, 1858

**2544.** Saying we should keep the two-party system simply because it is working is like saying the *Titanic* voyage was a success because a few people survived on life rafts. — Eugene J. McCarthy, in *Chicago Tribune*, September 10, 1978

**2545.** There is a dirty little secret that sophisticates have been hiding from the masses for three or four decades. The secret is that the two-party system is dying. [It] has failed to make the adjustment to the requirements of modern 20th century democratic government. — Theodore Lowi, in *Christian Science Monitor*, July 13, 1992

**2546.** The most dangerous follower is he whose defection would destroy the whole party: that is to say, the best follower. — Friedrich Wilhelm Nietzsche, *The Wanderer and His Shadow*, 1880

**2547.** This party is a moral crusade or it is nothing. — Harold Wilson, speech, October 1, 1962

**2548.** Party is organized opinion. — Benjamin Disraeli, speech, November 25, 1864

**2549.** In the hard life of politics it is well known that no platform nor any program advanced by either major American party has any purpose beyond expressing emotion. Platforms are a ritual with a history of their own and after being written, they are useful chiefly to scholars who dissect them as archeological political remains. — Theodore H. White, *The Making of the President 1960*, 1961

**2550.** To me, party platforms are contracts with the people. — Harry S Truman, *Memoirs*, 1955

**2551.** All forms of political organization have a bias in favor of the exploitation of some kinds of conflict and the suppression of others because organization is the mobilization of bias. Some issues are organized into politics while others are organized out. — E. E. Schattschneider, *The Semi-Sovereign People*, 1960

**2552.** Where parties are cut off from gaining support among a major stratum, they lose a major reason for compromise. — Seymour Martin Lipset, *Political Man*, 1981

**2553.** No political party can be a friend of the American people which is not a friend of American business. — Lyndon B. Johnson, speech, August 12, 1963

**2554.** A democratic party can very rarely be persuaded to give up one of its central principles, and can never afford to scrap its central myth. Conservatives must defend free enterprise even when they are actually introducing state planning. — R. H. S. Crossman, in *Encounter*, "On Political Neurosis," May, 1954

**2555.** Damn your principles! Stick to your party. — Benjamin Disraeli, attributed

**2556.** All political parties die at last of swallowing their own lies. — John Arbuthnot, epigram, ca. 1735

**2557.** The American people are quite competent to judge a political party that works both sides of a street. — Franklin D. Roosevelt, speech, November 4, 1944

**2558.** We have a country as well as a party to obey. — James K. Polk, *Diary*, December 12, 1848

2559. Honor is not the exclusive property of any political party. — Herbert Hoover, in *Christian Science Monitor*, May 21, 1964

2560. It is impossible that the whisper of a faction should prevail against the voice of a nation. — John Russell, statement, October, 1831

2561. He serves his party best who serves his country best. — Rutherford B. Hayes, inaugural address, March 5, 1877

2562. More important than winning the election, is governing the nation. That is the test of a political party — the acid, final test. — Adlai Stevenson, speech, July 26, 1952

2563. Now who is responsible for this work of development on which so much depends? To whom must the praise be given? To the boys in the back rooms. They do not sit in the limelight. But they are the men who do the work. — Max Aitken, in *Listener*, March 27, 1941

2564. Where a party is weak and small a new arrival may be welcomed with hospitality. His recognition will be quicker and his apprenticeship shorter than where the ranks are crowded and places of responsibility are more sought after and more tightly held. — Stimson Bullitt, *To Be a Politician*, 1977

2565. There is a hundred things to single you out for promotion in party politics besides ability. — Will Rogers, *The Autobiography of Will Rogers*, 1949

2566. In a democratic system which has a turnover of its officers, members and citizens can blame any particular evil on the incumbents and remain completely loyal to the organization. — Seymour Martin Lipset, *Political Man*, 1981

2567. A great party is not to be brought down because of a scandal by a woman of easy virtue and a proved liar. — Quinton Hogg, in *The Times*, June 14, 1963

2568. Any political party whose leaders knew a little psychology could sweep the country. — Bertrand Russell, *Sceptical Essays*, 1928

2569. The more you read and observe about this Politics thing, you got to admit that each party is worse than the other. The one that's out always looks the best. — Will Rogers, *The Illiterate Digest*, 1924

---

## *Patriotism*

### *See also* Duty; Liberty; Nationalism

2570. Lovely and honorable it is to die for one's country. — Horace, *Odes*, 1st c. B.C.

2571. What pity it is That we can die but once to serve our country! — Joseph Addison, *Cato*, 1713

2572. I only regret that I have but one life to lose for my country. — Nathan Hale, last words, September 22, 1776

2573. Everything belongs to the fatherland when the fatherland is in danger. — Georges Jacques Danton, speech, August 28, 1792

2574. Martyred many times must be Who would keep his country free. — Edna St. Vincent Millay, *Make Bright the Arrows*, 1940

2575. War service has always been regarded as proof of national loyalty; it was the custom in the Roman Republic that a candidate for consul would expose his wound scars to the citizens. — Stimson Bullitt, *To Be a Politician*, 1977

2576. Protection and patriotism are reciprocal. — John C. Calhoun, speech, December 12, 1811

2577. The love of country is the first virtue in a civilized man. — Napoleon I, speech, July 14, 1812

2578. Love of our country is another of those specious illusions, which have been invented by imposters in order to render the multitude the blind instruments of their crooked designs. — William Godwin, *An Enquiry concerning the Principles of Political Justice*, 1793

2579. Patriotism is the willingness to kill and be killed for trivial reasons. — Bertrand Russell, attributed

2580. Patriotism is the last refuge of a scoundrel. — Samuel Johnson, in James Boswell, *Life of Samuel Johnson*, 1791

2581. Patriotism is the last refuge of a party without any other ideas. — Robert Shrum, in *New York Times*, March 8, 1991

2582. To strike freedom of the mind with the fist of patriotism is an old and ugly subtlety. — Adlai Stevenson, speech, August 27, 1952

2583. When a whole nation is roaring Patriotism at the top of its voice, I am fain to explore the cleanness of its hands and purity of its heart. — Ralph Waldo Emerson, *Journals*, 1824

2584. A politician will do anything to keep his job — even become a patriot. — William Randolph Hearst, in *San Francisco Examiner*, August 28, 1933

2585. I think patriotism is like charity — it begins at home. — Henry James, *The Portrait of a Lady*, 1881

2586. My kind of loyalty was loyalty to one's country, not to its institutions or its officeholders. — Mark Twain, *A Connecticut Yankee in King Arthur's Court*, 1889

2587. The love of Americans for their country is not an indulgent, it is an exacting and chastising love; they cannot tolerate its defects. — Jacques Maritain, *Reflections on America*, 1958

2588. Our country! In her intercourse with foreign nations, may she always be in the right; but our country, right or wrong. — Stephen Decatur, toast, April, 1816

2589. "My country right or wrong" is like saying "My mother, drunk or sober." — Gilbert K. Chesterton, *The Defendant*, 1901

2590. My country, right or wrong; if right, to be kept right; and if wrong, to be set right. — Carl Schurz, speech, February 29, 1872

2591. Would the honest patriot, in the full tide of successful experiment, abandon a government which has so far kept us free and firm? — Thomas Jefferson, inaugural address, March 4, 1801

2592. Patriotism is when love of your own people comes first; nationalism, when the hate for people other than your own comes first. — Charles de Gaulle, in *Life*, May 9, 1969

2593. Patriotism is a lively sense of responsibility. Nationalism is a silly cock crowing on its own dunghill. — Richard Aldington, *The Colonel's Daughter*, 1931

2594. It is a most mistaken way of teaching men to feel they are brothers, by imbuing their mind with perpetual hatred. — William Godwin, *An Enquiry concerning the Principles of Political Justice*, 1793

2595. I realize that patriotism is not enough. I must have no hatred or bitterness towards anyone. — Edith Cavell, last words, October 12, 1915

2596. It is sad that being a good patriot often means being the enemy of the rest of mankind. — Voltaire, *Philosophical Dictionary*, "Patrie," 1764

2597. There is something worse than the cant of patriotism; that is the recant of patriotism. — John Russell, attributed

2598. In the beginning of a change, the patriot is a scarce man, and brave, and hated and scorned. When his cause succeeds, the timid join him, for then it costs nothing to be a patriot. — Mark Twain, *Notebook*, 1935

2599. Imperialism, sane Imperialism, as distinguished from what I may call wild-cat Imperialism, is nothing but this — a larger patriotism. — Archibald P. Primrose, speech, May 5, 1899

2600. Patriotism, as I see it, is often an arbitrary veneration of real estate above principles. — George Jean Nathan, *Living Philosophies*, 1931

2601. Never was patriot yet, but was a fool. —John Dryden, *Absalom and Achitophel,* 1681

2602. A patriot is a fool in ev'ry age. —Alexander Pope, *Imitations of Horace,* 1733–38

2603. Patriotism is in political life what faith is in religion. —John E. E. Dalberg, in *The Home and Foreign Review,* "Nationality," July, 1862

2604. Priests are no more necessary to religion than politicians to patriotism. —John Haynes Holmes, *The Sensible Man's View of Religion,* 1933

2605. Patriotism is easy to understand in America. It means looking out for yourself by looking out for your country. —Calvin Coolidge, speech, May 30, 1923

2606. In time of war the loudest patriots are the greatest profiteers. —August Bebel, speech, November, 1870

2607. You'll never have a quiet world till you knock the patriotism out of the human race. —George Bernard Shaw, *O'Flaherty V. C.,* 1919

2608. Patriotism is not a short and frenzied outburst of emotion, but the tranquil and steady dedication of a lifetime. —Adlai Stevenson, speech, August 30, 1952

# Peace

## See also Diplomacy; International Relations; War

2609. Peace, *n.* In international affairs, a period of cheating between two periods of fighting. —Ambrose Bierce, *The Devil's Dictionary,* 1906

2610. It is easier to make war than to make peace. —Georges Clemenceau, speech, July 20, 1919

2611. He that makes a good war makes a good peace. —George Herbert, *Outlandish Proverbs,* 1940

2612. Happy is the city which in times of peace thinks of war. —Anonymous, 17th c.

2613. The legitimate object of war is a more perfect peace. —William Sherman, speech, July 20, 1865

2614. Nobody ever forgets where he buried the hatchet. —Frank McKinney Hubbard, in *Indianapolis News,* January 4, 1925

2615. We do not admire a man of timid peace. —Theodore Roosevelt, speech, April 10, 1899

2616. We love peace, as we abhor pusillanimity; but not peace at any price. There is a peace more destructive of the manhood of living man than war is destructive of his material body. Chains are worse than bayonets. —Douglas Jerrold, *The Wit and Opinions of Douglas Jerrold,* "Peace," 1859

2617. If peace cannot be maintained with honor, it is no longer peace. —John Russell, speech, September 19, 1853

2618. Lord Salisbury and myself have brought you back peace—but a peace, I hope, with honor. —Benjamin Disraeli, speech, July 16, 1878

2619. This is the second time in our history that there has come back from Germany to Downing Street peace with honor. I believe it is peace for our time. —Neville Chamberlain, speech, September 30, 1938

2620. Anything for a quiet life. —Thomas Middleton, play title, ca. 1620

2621. There never was a good war or a bad peace. —Benjamin Franklin, letter, September 11, 1773

2622. I have many times asked myself whether there can be more potent advocates of peace upon earth through the years to come than this massed multitude of silent witnesses to the desolation of war. —George V, message, May 13, 1922

2623. It's a maxim not to be despised, "Though peace be made, yet it's interest that keeps peace." — Oliver Cromwell, speech, September 4, 1654

2624. It must be a peace without victory.... Only a peace between equals can last. — Woodrow Wilson, speech, January 22, 1917

2625. Our foreign policy has one primary object, and that is peace. — Herbert Hoover, speech, August 11, 1928

2626. You don't promote the cause of peace by talking only to people with whom you agree. — Dwight D. Eisenhower, news conference, January 30, 1957

2627. Can two walk together, except they be agreed? — Bible, *Amos 3:3*

2628. You cannot shake hands with a clenched fist. — Indira Gandhi, in *Christian Science Monitor,* May 17, 1982

2629. As long as there are sovereign nations possessing great power, war is inevitable. — Albert Einstein, in *Atlantic,* "Einstein on the Atomic Bomb," November, 1945

2630. Mankind must put an end to war, or war will put an end to mankind. — John F. Kennedy, speech, September 25, 1961

2631. Either war is obsolete or men are. — R. Buckminister Fuller, in *New Yorker,* January 8, 1966

2632. Every gun that is made, every warship launched, every rocket fired signifies, in the final sense, a theft from those who hunger and are not fed, those who are cold and are not clothed. The world in arms is not spending money alone. It is spending the sweat of its laborers, the genius of its scientists, the hopes of its children. — Dwight D. Eisenhower, speech, April 16, 1953

2633. The world has achieved brilliance without wisdom, power without conscience. Ours is a world of nuclear giants and ethical infants. — Omar Bradley, speech, 1948

2634. The more bombers, the less room for doves of peace. — Nikita S. Khrushchev, on *Moscow Radio,* March 14, 1958

2635. The work, my friend, is peace. More than an end of this war — an end to the beginnings of all wars. — Franklin D. Roosevelt, undelivered speech scheduled for April 13, 1945

2636. Now this is not the end. It is not even the beginning of the end. But it is, perhaps, the end of the beginning. — Winston S. Churchill, speech, November 10, 1942

2637. I think that people want peace so much that one of these days governments had better get out of the way and let them have it. — Dwight D. Eisenhower, broadcast, August 31, 1959

2638. God and the politicians willing, the United States can declare peace upon the world, and win it. — Ely Culbertson, *Must We Fight Russia?,* 1946

2639. Don't tell me peace has broken out, when I've just bought some new supplies. — Bertolt Brecht, *Mutter Courage,* 1939

2640. All quiet along the Potomac. — George B. McClellan, attributed

2641. Peace is much more precious than a piece of land. — Anwar al-Sadat, speech, March 8, 1978

2642. Non-violence is the first article of my faith. It is also the last article of my creed. — Mohandas K. Gandhi, speech, March 18, 1922

2643. War will cease when men refuse to fight. — Anonymous, 1930's

2644. A peace above all earthly dignities, A still and quiet conscience. — William Shakespeare, *Henry VIII,* 1613

# *The People*

## See also Citizenship; Democracy

2645. Whatever madness their kings commit, the Greeks take the beating. — Horace, *Epistles,* 1st c. B.C.

2646. There is nothing, absolutely nothing, which needs to be more carefully guarded against than that one man should be allowed to become more powerful than the people. — Demosthenes, *Philippic 2*, 344 B.C.

2647. Let no one oppose this belief of mine with that well-worn proverb: "He who builds on the people builds on mud." — Niccolò Machiavelli, *The Prince*, 1513

2648. What is the city but the people? — William Shakespeare, *Coriolanus*, 1608

2649. To worship the people is to be worshipped. — Francis Bacon, *De Augmentis Scientiarum*, 1623

2650. The worst of all states is the people's state. — Pierre Corneille, *Cinna*, 1640

2651. Any government is free to the people, under it where the laws rule and the people are a party to the laws. — William Penn, *Frame of Government*, 1682

2652. When the people contend for their liberty, they seldom get anything by their victory but new masters. — George Savile, *Political, Moral, and Miscellaneous Thoughts and Reflections*, 1750

2653. Let the people think they govern and they will be governed. — William Penn, *Some Fruits of Solitude*, 1693

2654. The people are the masters. — Edmund Burke, speech, February 11, 1780

2655. Every government degenerates when trusted to the rules of the people alone. The people themselves therefore are its only safe depositories. — Thomas Jefferson, *Notes on the State of Virginia*, 1781–85

2656. The idea of a people is the idea of a corporation. It is wholly artificial and made, like all other fiction, by common agreement. — Edmund Burke, *Reflections on the Revolution in France*, 1790

2657. Any institution which does not suppose the people good, and the magistrate corruptible, is evil. — Maximilien Robespierre, *Déclaration des droits de l'homme*, April 24, 1793

2658. Man being . . . all free, equal, and independent, no one can be put out of this estate, and subjected to the political power of another, without his own consent. — John Locke, *Second Treatise of Civil Government*, 1690

2659. No man is good enough to govern another man without that other's consent. — Abraham Lincoln, speech, October 16, 1854

2660. If government is founded in the consent of the people, it can have no power over any individual by whom that consent is refused. — William Godwin, *An Enquiry concerning Political Justice*, 1793

2661. The basis of our political system is the right of the people to make and to alter their constitutions of government. — George Washington, farewell address, September 17, 1796

2662. The people are always in the wrong when they are faced by the armed forces. — Napoleon I, letter, October 2, 1810

2663. In all forms of Government the people is the true legislator. — Edmund Burke, *A Tract on the Popery Laws*, 1812

2664. I know no safe depository of the ultimate powers of the society but the people themselves. — Thomas Jefferson, letter, September 28, 1820

2665. No government has ever been beneficent when the attitude of government was that it was taking care of the people. The only freedom consists in the people taking care of the government. — Woodrow Wilson, speech, September 4, 1912

2666. The king reigns, and the people govern themselves. — Louis Adolphe Thiers, in *Le National*, January 20, 1830

2667. The people is that part of the State that does not know what it wants. — Georg Wilhelm Friedrich Hegel, *The Philosophy of History*, 1832

2668. Among democratic nations, each new generation is a new people. — Alexis de Tocqueville, *Democracy in America*, 1835

2669. Each generation of Americans

must define what it means to be an American. — Bill Clinton, inaugural address, January 20, 1993

2670. The people are the safest, the best, and the most reliable lodgement of power. — Andrew Johnson, speech, May 20, 1858

2671. The instinct of the people is right. — Ralph Waldo Emerson, *The Conduct of Life*, "Power," 1860

2672. Why should there not be a patient confidence in the ultimate justice of the people? Is there any better or equal hope in the world? — Abraham Lincoln, inaugural address, March 4, 1861

2673. The "people" who exercise the power are not always the same people over whom it is exercised. — John Stuart Mill, *On Liberty*, 1859

2674. Everyone is really responsible to all men for all men and for everything. — Fyodor Dostoyevski, *The Brothers Karamazov*, 1880

2675. We cannot safely leave politics to politicians, or political economy to college professors. The people themselves must think, because the people alone can act. — Henry George, *Social Problems*, 1884

2676. Politics and laws are (or rather, should be) — merely results, merely the expression of what the people wish. — Rutherford B. Hayes, letter, November 25, 1885

2677. He mocks the people who proposes that the Government shall protect the rich and that they in turn will care for the laboring poor. — Grover Cleveland, message to Congress, December 3, 1888

2678. When the people rule, they must be rendered happy, or they will overturn the state. — Alexis de Tocqueville, *Democracy in America*, 1835

2679. Where the people rule, discussion is necessary. — William H. Taft, speech, September 21, 1909

2680. Government is less progressive than the people. — Charles A. Lindburgh Sr., *Why Is Our Country at War?*, 1917

2681. Government cannot be stronger or more tough-minded than its people. It cannot be more inflexibly committed to the task than they. — Adlai Stevenson, speech, September 29, 1952

2682. This Bible is for the government of the People, by the People, and for the People. — John Wycliffe, attributed, 1382

2683. The people's government, made for the people, made by the people, and answerable to the people. — Daniel Webster, speech, January 26, 1830

2684. The American idea . . . is a democracy, that is a government of all the people, by all the people, and for all the people. — Theodore Parker, speech, May 29, 1850

2685. Government of the people, by the people and for the people. — Abraham Lincoln, Gettysburg Address, November 19, 1863 (with earlier American origins, e.g. Thomas Cooper, "Some Information Respecting America," Dublin, 1794)

2686. High hopes were once formed of democracy; but democracy means simply the bludgeoning of the people by the people for the people. — Oscar Wilde, *The Soul of Man under Socialism*, 1895

2687. You may fool all of the people some of the time; you can even fool some of the people all of the time; but you can't fool all of the people all the time. — Abraham Lincoln, in Alexander K. McClure, *Lincoln's Yarns and Stories*, 1904

2688. You can fool too many of the people too much of the time. — James Thurber, *Fables for Our Time*, 1940

2689. Ninety-nine percent of the people in the world are fools and the rest of us are in great danger of contagion. — Thornton Wilder, *The Matchmaker*, 1954

## Place

2690. Canada could have enjoyed: English government, French culture, and American know-how. Instead it ended up with: English know-how, French government, and American culture. —John Robert Colombo, "Oh Canada," 1965

2691. Most agreed that [Joe] Clark was a better human being.... But Trudeau was what Canadians really wanted to be—intellectual, suave, worldly, independent, and unpredictable—while Clark was what they feared they were—earnest, nice, competent, unimaginative, honest and rather dull. —Ron Graham, *Saturday Night*, "The Legacy of Joe Clark," September, 1983

2692. In Pierre Elliott Trudeau Canada has at last produced a political leader worthy of assassination. —Irving Layton, *The Whole Bloody Bird*, 1969

2693. The only reason hockey exists is so that Canadian politicians can make analogies. —Michael C. Thomsett, *A Treasury of Political Quotations*, 1994

2694. England does not love coalitions. —Benjamin Disraeli, speech, December 16, 1852

2695. We [the English] seem, as it were, to have conquered and peopled half the world in a fit of absence of mind. —John Seeley, *The Expansion of England*, 1883

2696. To succeed pre-eminently in English public life it is necessary to conform either to the popular image of a bookie or of a clergyman. —Malcolm Muggeridge, *The Infernal Grove*, 1973

2697. Other nations use "force"; we Britons alone use "Might." —Evelyn Waugh, *Scoop*, 1938

2698. The Englishman, be it noted, seldom resorts to violence; when he is sufficiently goaded he simply opens up, like the oyster, and devours his adversary. —Henry Miller, *The Wisdom of the Heart*, 1941

2699. This island is made mainly of coal and surrounded by fish. Only an organizing genius could produce a shortage of coal and fish at the same time. —Aneurin Bevan, speech, May 24, 1945

2700. An Englishman, even if he is alone, forms an orderly queue of one. —George Mikes, *How to Be an Alien*, 1946

2701. I think the British have the distinction above all other nations of being able to put new wine into old bottles without bursting them. —Clement Attlee, in *Time*, November 6, 1950

2702. In the end it may well be that Britain will be honored by the historians more for the way she disposed of an empire than for the way in which she acquired it. —David Ormsby Gore, in *New York Times*, October 28, 1962

2703. France, mother of arts, of warfare, and of laws. —Joachim Du Bellay, *Les Regrets*, 1558

2704. France was long a despotism tempered by epigrams. —Thomas Carlyle, *History of the French Revolution*, 1837

2705. The simple thing is to consider the French as an erratic and brilliant people...who have all the gifts except that of running their country. —James Cameron, *News Chronicle*, 1954

2706. Political thought in France is either nostalgic or utopian. —Raymond Aron, *The Opium of the Intellectual*, 1957

2707. How can you be expected to govern a country that has two hundred and forty-six kinds of cheese? —Charles de Gaulle, in *Newsweek*, October 1, 1962

2708. The French at heart are monarchists. They like to prostrate themselves in front of the monarch, whom they now call president, and every seven years or so they guillotine him. —Hervé de Charette, in *New York Times*, November 26, 1987

2709. I have tried to lift France out of the mud. But she will return to her errors and vomiting. I cannot prevent the French from being French. —Charles de Gaulle, in *Time*, December 8, 1967

**2710.** The French are wiser than they seem, and the Spaniards seem wiser than they are. — Francis Bacon, *Essays,* "Of Seeming Wise," 1625

**2711.** Thus you have a starving population, an absentee aristocracy, and an alien Church, and in addition the weakest executive in the world. That is the Irish Question. — Benjamin Disraeli, speech, February 16, 1844

**2712.** Politics is the chloroform of the Irish people, or, rather, the hashish. — Oliver St. John Gogarty, *As I Was Going Down Sackville Street,* 1937

**2713.** The German soul is opposed to the pacifist ideal of civilization, for is not peace an element of civil corruption. — Thomas Mann, *Reflections of a Non-Political Man,* 1917

**2714.** All free men, wherever they may live, are citizens of Berlin. And therefore, as a free man, I take pride in the words, *"Ich bin ein Berliner."* — John F. Kennedy, speech, June 26, 1963 *(Ein Berliner* is a type of doughnut in Berlin, which led to a humorous Berlin response to the statement.)

**2715.** We have always said that in our war with the Arabs we had a secret weapon — no alternative. — Golda Meir, in *Life,* October 3, 1969

**2716.** Let me tell you something that we Israelis have against Moses. He took us 40 years through the desert in order to bring us to the one spot in the Middle East that has no oil. — Golda Meir, in *New York Times,* June 10, 1973

**2717.** Very little counts for less in Italy than the state. — Peter Nichols, *Italia, Italia,* 1973

**2718.** The smoke and wealth and din of Rome. — Horace, *Odes,* 1st c. B.C.

**2719.** In Italy for thirty years under the Borgias they had warfare, terror, murder, bloodshed — they produced Michelangelo, Leonardo da Vinci and the Renaissance. In Switzerland they had brotherly love, five hundred years of democracy and peace and what did they produce...? The cuckoo clock. — Orson Welles, *The Third Man,* 1949

**2720.** Every country has its own constitution; ours is absolutism moderated by assassination. — Anonymous, Russia, 19th c.

**2721.** I cannot forecast to you the action of Russia. It is a riddle wrapped in a mystery inside an enigma. — Winston S. Churchill, radio broadcast, October 1, 1939

**2722.** [Russian Communism is] the illegitimate child of Karl Marx and Catherine the Great. — Clement Attlee, speech, April 11, 1956

**2723.** Certain people in the United States are driving nails into this structure of our relationship, then cutting off the heads. So the Soviets must use their teeth to pull them out. — Mikhail S. Gorbachev, in *Time,* September 9, 1985

**2724.** Russia is a matriarchy ruled by men. — Suzanne Massey, in *Atlantic,* February, 1992

**2725.** The people of Crete unfortunately make more history than they can consume locally. — Saki, *Chronicles of Clovis,* 1911

**2726.** Holland...lies so low they're only saved by being dammed. — Thomas Hood, *Up the Rhine,* 1840

**2727.** Poor Mexico, so far from God and so close to the United States. — Porfirio Diaz, attributed

**2728.** If ever there is another war in Europe, it will come out of some damned silly thing in the Balkans. — Otto von Bismarck, in *Hansard,* August 16, 1945

**2729.** Purity of race does not exist. Europe is a continent of energetic mongrels. — H. A. L. Fisher, *A History of Europe,* 1934

**2730.** As the editor of one of the leading Swedish newspapers once said to me, "Politics is now boring. The only issues are whether the metal workers should get a nickel more an hour, the price of milk should be raised, or old-age pensions extended." — Seymour Martin Lipset, *Political Man,* 1981

**2731.** Americans are so enamored of equality that they would rather be equal in slavery than unequal in freedom. — Alexis de Tocqueville, *Democracy in America,* 1835

**2732.** Max Weber, who visited the

United States in the early 1900's, noted the high degree of "submission to fashion in America, to a degree unknown in Germany," and explained it as a natural attribute of a democratic society without inherited class status. — Seymour Martin Lipset, *Political Man*, 1981

2733. I could come back to America...to die — but never, never to live. — Henry James, letter, April 1, 1913

2734. America is a country of young men. — Ralph Waldo Emerson, *Society and Solitude*, "Old Age," 1870

2735. On my arrival in the United States, I was struck by the degree of ability among the governed and the lack of it among the governing. — Alexis de Tocqueville, *Democracy in America*, 1835

2736. The more I observed Washington, the more frequently I visited it, and the more people I interviewed there, the more I understood how prophetic L'Enfant was when he laid it out as a city that goes around in circles. — John Mason Brown, *Through These Men*, 1956

2737. You may be sure that the Americans will commit all the stupidities they can think of, plus some that are beyond imagination. — Charles de Gaulle, in *Time*, December 17, 1965

2738. My question is whether America can overcome the fatal arrogance of power. — J. William Fulbright, *The Arrogance of Power*, 1966

2739. America's dissidents are not committed to mental hospitals and sent into exile; they thrive and prosper and buy a house in Nantucket and take flyers in the commodities market. — Ted Morgan, *On Becoming American*, 1978

2740. America is never wholly herself unless she is engaged in high moral principle. We as a people have such a purpose today. It is to make kinder the face of the nation and gentler the face of the world. — George Bush, inaugural address, January 20, 1989

2741. [The U.S.] will continue to be what we would call the nation of last resort, the nation whom you can always rely on to be free [and] enterprising. — Margaret Thatcher, in *Newsweek*, October 8, 1990

# Planning *see* Future

# Political Action

## See also Legislatures

2742. Talkers are no good doers. — William Shakespeare, *Richard III*, 1591

2743. He who is too busy doing good finds no time to be good. — Rabindranath Tagore, *Stray Birds*, 1916

2744. Political action is not moral action, any more than a box on the ear is an argument. — William Lloyd Garrison, in *The Liberator*, March 13, 1846

2745. Every cook has to learn how to govern the state. — Lenin, *Will the Bolsheviks Retain Government Power?*, 1917

2746. Action is consolatory. It is the enemy of thought and the friend of flattering illusions. — Joseph Conrad, *Nostromo*, 1904

2747. It is indeed a law of politicks as well as of physicks, that a body in action must overcome an equal body at rest. — Fisher Ames, *The Dangers of American Liberty*, 1805

2748. For every action there is an equal and opposite government program. — Michael Main, in *Omni*, May, 1979

2749. One thing our government is doing is vigorously agreeing with us that it should be doing something. — P. J. O'Rourke, *Parliament of Whores*, 1991

**2750.** Delays have dangerous ends. — William Shakespeare, *Henry VI, Part I*, 1592

**2751.** The world is divided into those who want to become someone and those who want to accomplish something. — Jean Monnet, in *Time*, March 26, 1979

**2752.** In nature there are neither rewards nor punishments — there are consequences. — Robert G. Ingersoll, *Some Reasons Why*, 1881

**2753.** Conviction, were it never so excellent, is worthless till it convert itself into Conduct. — Thomas Carlyle, *Sartor Resartus*, 1833

**2754.** Look with favor upon a bold beginning. — Virgil, *Georgics*, ca. 30 B.C.

**2755.** Liberty does not consist in mere general declarations of the rights of men. In consists in the translation of those declarations into definite action. — Woodrow Wilson, speech, July 4, 1914

**2756.** If you begin by saying, "Thou shalt not lie," there is no longer any possibility of political action. — Jean-Paul Sartre, in *Time*, April 28, 1980

**2757.** The man who makes no mistakes does not usually make anything. — William Connor Magee, speech, January 24, 1889

**2758.** Methods and means cannot be separated from the ultimate aim. — Emma Goldman, *My Further Disillusionment*, 1924

**2759.** Life is made up of constant calls to action, and we seldom have time for more than hastily contrived answers. — Learned Hand, speech, January 27, 1952

**2760.** The tragedy of all political action is that some problems have no solution; none of the alternatives are intellectually consistent or morally uncompromising; and whatever decision is taken will harm somebody. — James Joll, *Three Intellectuals in Politics*, 1960

**2761.** Now the trumpet summons us again — not as a call to bear arms, though arms we need — not as a call to battle, though embattled we are — but as a call to bear the burden of a long twilight struggle, year in and year out "rejoicing in hope, patient in tribulation" — a struggle against the common enemies of man: tyranny, poverty, disease and war itself. — John F. Kennedy, inaugural address, January 20, 1961

**2762.** We have heard the trumpets. We have changed the guard. And now, each in our way, and with God's help, we must answer the call. — Bill Clinton, inaugural address, January 20, 1993

**2763.** The beginning is the most important part of any work. — Plato, *The Republic*, ca. 370 B.C.

**2764.** This power to act according to discretion for the public good, without the prescription of the law, and sometimes even against it, is that which is called prerogative. — John Locke, *Some Thoughts of Civil Government*, 1690

**2765.** Just as the meanest and most vicious deed require spirit and talent, so even the greatest deeds require a certain insensitiveness which on other occasions is called stupidity. — Georg Christoph Lichtenberg, *Aphorisms*, 1764–99

**2766.** Who reflects too much will accomplish little. — Friedrich von Schiller, *William Tell*, 1804

**2767.** All this will not be finished in the first one hundred days. Nor will it be finished in the first one thousand days, nor in the life of this administration, nor even perhaps in our lifetime on this planet. But let us begin. — John F. Kennedy, inaugural address, January 20, 1961

**2768.** Let us begin with energy and hope, with faith and discipline, and let us work until our work is done. — Bill Clinton, inaugural address, January 20, 1993

**2769.** In accomplishing anything definite a man renounces everything else. — George Santayana, *The Life of Reason*, 1905–06

## The Political Animal

2770. It is evident that the state is a creation of nature, and that man is by nature a political animal. — Aristotle, *Politics*, 4th c. B.C.

2771. Man is a social rather than a political animal; he can exist without a government. — George Santayana, *Obiter Scripta*, 1936

2772. We first throw away the tales along with the rattles of our nurses; those of the priest keep their hold a little longer; those of the government the longest of all. — Edmund Burke, *A Vindication of Natural Society*, 1756

2773. As soon as any man says of the affairs of State, "What does it matter to me?" the State may be given up as lost. — Jean-Jacques Rousseau, *The Social Contract*, 1762

2774. There is no private life which has not been determined by a wider public life. — George Eliot, *Felix Holt*, 1866

2775. Men are to a great extent products of their institutional environment. — M. Judd Harmon, *Political Thought*, 1964

2776. The friend of humanity cannot recognize a distinction between what is political and what is not. There is nothing that is not political. — Thomas Mann, *The Magic Mountain*, 1924

2777. What is right must unavoidably be politic. — Robert Peel, letter, September 23, 1822

2778. During the time men live without a common power to keep them all in awe, they are in that condition which is called war; and such a war is as of every man against every man. — Thomas Hobbes, *Leviathan*, 1651

2779. Knowledge of human nature is the beginning and end of political education. — Henry Brooks Adams, *The Education of Henry Adams*, 1907

2780. Man... is simply the most formidable of all the beasts of prey, and, indeed, the only one that preys system-atically on its own species. — William James, in *Atlantic*, December, 1904

2781. [In a state of nature] no arts; no letters; no society; and which is worst of all, continual fear and danger of violent death; and the life of man, solitary, poor, nasty, brutish, and short. — Thomas Hobbes, *Leviathan*, 1651

2782. I could not be leading a religious life unless I identified myself with the whole of mankind, and that I could not do unless I took part in politics. — Mohandas K. Gandhi, *Non-Violence in Peace and War*, 1948

2783. I am a free man, an American, a United States Senator, and a Democrat, in that order. — Lyndon B. Johnson, in *Texas Quarterly*, Winter, 1958

2784. Those who would treat politics and morality apart will never understand the one or the other. — John Morley, *Rousseau*, 1876

2785. If we accept the Greeks' definition of the idiot as an altogether private man, then we must conclude that many American citizens are now idiots. — C. Wright Mills, *The Power Elite*, 1956

2786. It is necessary that one who fights for the right, if he is to survive even for a short time, shall act as a private man, not as a public man. — Plato, *Apology*, ca. 370 B.C.

2787. What Englishman will give his mind to politics as long as he can afford to keep a motor car? — George Bernard Shaw, *The Apple Cart*, 1930

2788. How small, of all that human hearts endure, That part which laws or kings can cause or cure! — Oliver Goldsmith, *The Traveler*, 1765

2789. Many who have lost faith in prevailing loyalties have not acquired new ones, and so pay no attention to politics of any kind. They are not radical, not liberal, not conservative, not reactionary. They are inactionary. They are out of it. — C. Wright Mills, *The Power Elite*, 1956

2790. If you take the game of life seriously, if you take your nervous system seriously, if you take your sense organs seriously, if you take the energy process seriously, you must turn on, tune in, and drop out. — Timothy Leary, lecture, June, 1966

# Politicians

*See also* Adages and Maxims; Character; Gossip and Publicity; Legislatures; Office; Opinion, Public; Speech

2791. I do not admire politicians; but when they are excellent in their way, one cannot help allowing them their due. — Horace Walpole, letter, November 17, 1763

2792. What you see done in the halls of the politicians may not be wise, but it is the only real and viable definition of what the electorate wants. — David A. Stockman, *The Triumph of Politics,* 1987

2793. Some stay in politics because they like the work. Gregarious, energetic, internally secure, they enjoy the attention and acclaim and do not mind the knocks. Children, debts, and other hostages to fortune do not trouble those to whom the stony road of politics is like the brier patch to Br'er Rabbit. — Stimson Bullitt, *To Be a Politician,* 1977

2794. I seldom think of politics more than 18 hours a day. — Lyndon B. Johnson, in *A Guide to the 99th Congress,* 1985

2795. It's a piece of cake until you get to the top. You find you can't stop playing the game the way you've always played it. — Richard M. Nixon, in *Washington Post,* August 9, 1979

2796. The kind of thing I'm good at is knowing every politician in the state and remembering where he itches. — Earl Long, in *New Yorker,* June 4, 1960

2797. A man to be a sound politician and in any degree useful to his country must be governed by higher and steadier considerations than those of personal sympathy and private regard. — Martin Van Buren, letter, April 22, 1819

2798. When these two [the just man and the unjust man] hold public office, the just man gets his private affairs, by neglecting them, into a bad state...and he has no profits from the treasury because he is just; besides, he is unpopular with friends and acquaintances if he will not serve them contrary to justice; but it is quite the opposite with the unjust man. — Plato, *The Republic,* ca. 370 B.C.

2799. Most politicians have a right to feel morally superior to their constituencies. — Daniel P. Moynihan, in *Rolling Stone,* August 12, 1976

2800. Most politicians are disposed to lean toward judging issues and understanding men. — Stimson Bullitt, *To Be a Politician,* 1977

2801. To get involved in politics, it is not enough to have a clean criminal record. One's dealings must be transparent. — Oscar Luigi Scalfaro, speech, May 28, 1992

2802. It is as hard and severe a thing to be a true politician as to be truly moral. — Francis Bacon, *The Advancement of Learning,* 1605

2803. No man can be a politician, except he be first a historian or a traveler; for except he can see what must be, or what may be, he is no politician. — James Harrington, *Oceana,* 1656

2804. A man known to us only as a celebrity in politics or in trade, gains largely in our esteem if we discover that he has some intellectual taste or skill. — Ralph Waldo Emerson, *The Conduct of Life,* "Culture," 1860

2805. For a man of active intellect the most severe condition of politics is to abstain from the full and constant use of his powers. He must be willing to submit to boredom and make the effort to conceal it. — Stimson Bullitt, *To Be a Politician*, 1977

2806. Coffee, which makes the politician wise. — Alexander Pope, *The Rape of the Lock*, 1712

2807. The effective [lobbyists] are those who marshall the things which influence politicians: vocal constituents, campaign contributors, and persuasive information about the matter to be decided. — Stimson Bullitt, *To Be a Politician*, 1977

2808. Get thee glass eyes; And, like a scurvy politician, seem To see the things thou dost not. — William Shakespeare, *King Lear*, 1605–06

2809. Under every stone lurks a politician. — Aristophanes, *Thesmophoriazusae*, 410 B.C.

2810. If people want a sense of purpose they should get it from their archbishop. They should certainly not get it from their politicians. — Harold Macmillan, in Henry Fairlie, *The Life of Politics*, 1969

2811. A statesman is a politician who places himself at the service of the nation. A politician is a statesman who places the nation at his service. — Georges Pompidou, in *Observer*, December 30, 1973

2812. A politician becomes a statesman after he is elected. — Edgar Watson Howe, *Country Town Sayings*, 1911

2813. There are some whom the applause of the multitude has deluded into the belief that they are really statesmen. — Plato, *The Republic*, ca. 370 B.C.

2814. The world is weary of statesmen whom democracy has degraded into politicians. — Benjamin Disraeli, *The Infernal Marriage*, 1834

2815. At home, you always have to be a politician; when you're abroad, you almost feel yourself a statesman. — Harold Macmillan, in *Look*, April 15, 1958

2816. I attribute the small number of distinguished men in political life to the ever increasing despotism of the majority in the United States. — Alexis de Tocqueville, *Democracy in America*, 1835

2817. Young people see politics as a dirty business.... In a democratic nation, when there is a big gulf between politics and ordinary citizens, there is a real danger. It discourages talented people from going in and out of politics. — Paul Allen Beck, in *Christian Science Monitor*, August 11, 1989

2818. If they had lived a hundred years ago probably a number of the best contemporary entertainers would have entered politics or the ministry instead. — Stimson Bullitt, *To Be a Politician*, 1977

2819. A passion for politics stems usually from an insatiable need, either for power, or for friendship and adulation, or a combination of both. — Fawn M. Brodie, *Thomas Jefferson*, 1974

2820. The politician in my country seeks votes, affection and respect, in that order.... With few notable exceptions, they are simply men who want to be loved. — Edward R. Murrow, speech, October 19, 1959

2821. It is now known that men enter local politics solely as a result of being unhappily married. — C. Northcote Parkinson, *Parkinson's Law*, 1958

2822. A politician...one that would circumvent God. — William Shakespeare, *Hamlet*, 1601

2823. Politicians neither love nor hate. Interest, not sentiment, directs them. — Philip D. Stanhope, *Letters*, 1748

2824. Patience. Patience. Patience! the first, the last, and the middle virtue of a politician. — John Adams, letter, February 8, 1778

2825. Here is an animal [the rhinoceros] with a hide two feet thick, and no apparent interest in politics. What a waste. — James Wright, in *New York Times*, December 9, 1986

2826. Politicians trim and tack in

their quest for power, but they do so in order to get the wind of votes in their sails. — Ian Gilmour, *The Body Politic,* 1969

**2827.** Politicians are ambitious not to make important decisions but to say important things. — R. H. S. Crossman, in *New Statesman,* 1947

**2828.** A politician is a man who understands government, and it takes a politician to run a government. A statesman is a politician who's been dead 10 or 15 years. — Harry S Truman, in *New York World Telegram and Sun,* April 12, 1958

**2829.** The distinction between a statesman and a politician is that the former imposes his will and his ideas on his environment while the latter adapts himself to it. — R. H. S. Crossman, in *New Statesman,* 1957

**2830.** A politician was a person with whose politics you did not agree. When you did agree, he was a statesman. — David Lloyd George, speech, July 2, 1935

**2831.** Politicians fascinate because they constitute such a paradox: they are an elite that accomplishes mediocrity for the public good. — Garry Wills, in *Time,* April 23, 1979

**2832.** Old politicians chew on wisdom past, And totter on in business to the last. — Alexander Pope, *Epistles to Several Persons,* 1734

**2833.** Politicians are like the bones of a horse's foreshoulder — not a straight one in it. — Wendell Phillips, speech, July, 1864

**2834.** The trouble with practical jokes is that very often they get elected. — Will Rogers, in *Rocky Mountain News,* May 28, 1980

**2835.** An honest politician is one who, when he is bought, stays bought. — Simon Cameron, attributed

**2836.** The politician is an acrobat. He keeps his balance by saying the opposite of what he does. — Maurice Barrès, *Mes cahiers,* 1923

**2837.** Probably the most distinctive characteristic of the successful politician is selective cowardice. — Richard Harris, in *New Yorker,* December 14, 1968

**2838.** You have all the characteristics of a popular politician: a horrible voice, bad breeding, and a vulgar manner. — Aristophanes, *Knights,* 424 B.C.

**2839.** He knows nothing and he thinks he knows everything. That points clearly to a political career. — George Bernard Shaw, *Major Barbara,* 1905

## Politicians, Ambitions of *see* Ambition

## Politicians, Honesty of *see* Honesty

# ——————— *Politics* ———————

### See also Change; Dirty Politics; Language; the Political Animal

**2840.** The good of man must be the end of the science of politics. — Aristotle, *Nicomachean Ethics,* ca. 340 B.C.

**2841.** I refuse to believe that politics and wisdom are definitely irreconcilable. — Michel Rocard, in *Washington Post,* May 23, 1990

**2842.** I must study politics and war that my sons may have liberty to study mathematics and philosophy. — John Adams, letter, May 12, 1780

**2843.** He [Jim Baker] was a decent student of policy, but he was an awesome student of politics. — David A. Stockman, *The Triumph of Politics,* 1987

2844. Politics are too serious a matter to be left to the politicians. — Charles de Gaulle, in Clement Attlee, *A Prime Minister Remembers,* 1961

2845. The older you get the more you realize that gray isn't such a bad color. And in politics you work with it or you don't work at all. — Agnes Sligh Turnbull, *The Golden Journey,* 1955

2846. In politics experiments mean revolutions. — Benjamin Disraeli, *Popanilla,* 1827

2847. In politics, what begins in fear usually ends in folly. — Samuel Taylor Coleridge, *Table Talk,* "October 5, 1830," 1835

2848. The laws of libel, the decencies of political reportage, the conventions of friendship and custom, the obstacles of distance and parochialism, all effectively conceal the ever-changing topography of American politics. — Theodore H. White, *The Making of the President 1960,* 1961

2849. There is one thing solid and fundamental in politics — the law of change. What's up today is down tomorrow. — Richard M. Nixon, in *Time,* August 19, 1974

2850. Nothing is so admirable in politics as a short memory. — John Kenneth Galbraith, in *A Guide to the 99th Congress,* 1985

2851. Nothing is so dull as political agitation. — William E. Gladstone, speech, December 5, 1879

2852. [Boswell:] So, Sir, you laugh at schemes of political improvement. [Johnson:] Why, Sir, most schemes of political improvement are very laughable things. — Samuel Johnson, in James Boswell, *Life of Samuel Johnson,* 1791

2853. [The English] do not regard *politics* as an opprobrious word. They know nothing of *office politics,* or *campus politics,* or *church politics,* nor do they *play politics.* — H. L. Mencken, *The American Language, Supplement I,* 1945

2854. The best politics is no politics. — Henry M. Jackson, speech, February 3, 1980

2855. Half a truth is better than no politics. — Gilbert K. Chesterton, *All Things Considered,* "The Boy," 1908

2856. The political spirit is the great force in throwing love of truth and accurate reasoning into a secondary place. — John Morley, *On Compromise,* 1874

2857. Everything begins in mysticism and ends in politics. — Charles Péguy, *Basic Verities,* 1943

2858. The political is replacing the metaphysical as the characteristic mode of grasping reality. — Harvey Cox, *The Secular City,* 1966

2859. Politics, like religion, hold up the torches of martyrdom to the reformers of error. — Thomas Jefferson, letter, August 4, 1811

2860. There is a holy mistaken zeal in politics as well as in religion. By persuading others, we convince ourselves. — Junius, in *Public Advertiser,* December 19, 1769

2861. Difference of religion breeds more quarrels than difference of politics. — Wendell Phillips, speech, November 7, 1860

2862. The first mistake in public business is going into it. — Benjamin Franklin, *Poor Richard's Almanac,* 1733–58

2863. If you do nothing but politics, you drive yourself into the ground, and then you're no good for the constituents you represent, because you come to wrong conclusions and support the wrong things. Balance is all-important to life. — Edward Heath, in *Wall Street Journal,* July 3, 1989

2864. I find the remark "Tis distance lends enchantment to the view" is no less true of the political than of the natural world. — Franklin Pierce, letter, 1832

2865. Being in politics is like being in a football game. You have to be smart enough to know the game and stupid enough to think it is important. — Eugene J. McCarthy, in *Los Angeles Times,* October 7, 1991

2866. In politics, as in womanizing, failure is decisive. It sheds its retrospective gloom on earlier endeavor which at the time seemed full of promise. — Malcolm Muggeridge, *The Most of Malcolm Muggeridge*, "Boring for England," 1966

**2867.** Next to knowing when to seize an opportunity, the most important thing in life is to know when to forego an advantage. — Benjamin Disraeli, *The Infernal Marriage*, 1834

**2868.** In politics one must take nothing tragically and everything seriously. — Louis Adolphe Thiers, speech, May 24, 1873

**2869.** In writing and politicking, it's best not to think about it, just do it. — Gore Vidal, in *A Guide to the 99th Congress*, 1985

**2870.** Politics are almost as exciting as war, and quite as dangerous. In war, you can only be killed once, but in politics, many times. — Winston S. Churchill, *The Churchill Wit*, "Politics," 1965

**2871.** The root question of American politics is always: Who's the Man to See? To understand American politics is, simply, to know people, to know the relative weight of names — who are heroes, who are straw men, who controls, who does not. — Theodore H. White, *The Making of the President 1960*, 1961

**2872.** Finality is not the language of politics. — Benjamin Disraeli, speech, February 28, 1859

**2873.** In politics, as in other things, there is no such thing as one getting something for nothing. The payoff may involve compromises of various types that may strike at the ideals and principles one has held dear all his life. — A. Philip Randolph, in *The Call*, April 28, 1944

**2874.** The practice of politics in the East may be defined by one word — dissimulation. — Benjamin Disraeli, *Contarini Fleming*, 1832

**2875.** What matters most about political ideas is the underlying emotions, the music, to which ideas are a mere libretto, often of very inferior quality. — Lewis Namier, *Personalities and Power*, 1955

**2876.** Washington has no memory. — James Reston, in *Observer*, September 9, 1979

**2877.** Practical politics consists in ignoring facts. — Henry Brooks Adams, *The Education of Henry Adams*, 1907

**2878.** I have never found, in a long experience of politics, that criticism is ever inhibited by ignorance. — Harold Macmillan, in *Wall Street Journal*, August 13, 1963

**2879.** Politicians have the same occupational hazard as generals — focusing on the last battle and overreacting to that. — Ann F. Lewis, in *New York Times*, September 24, 1986

**2880.** Political principles resemble military tactics; they are usually designed for a war which is over. — R. H. Tawney, *Equality*, 1931

**2881.** In politics, guts is all. — Barbara Castle, *Castle Diaries*, April 18, 1975

**2882.** When I make a mistake, it's a beaut! — Fiorello La Guardia, in William Manngers, *Patience and Fortitude*, 1976

**2883.** Politics is not an exact science. — Otto von Bismarck, speech, December 13, 1863

**2884.** Politics is the science of liberty. — Pierre Joseph Proudhon, *What Is Property?*, 1840

**2885.** Politics is the art of the possible. — Otto von Bismarck, conversation, August 11, 1867

**2886.** Politics is not the art of the possible. It consists in choosing between the disastrous and the unpalatable. — John Kenneth Galbraith, *Ambassador's Journal*, 1969

**2887.** Exploitation and government are two inseparable expressions of what is called politics. — Michael Bakunin, *The Knouto-Germanic Empire and the Social Revolution*, 1871

**2888.** Modern politics is, at bottom, a struggle not of men but of forces. — Henry Brooks Adams, *The Education of Henry Adams*, 1907

**2889.** Politics is perhaps the only profession for which no preparation is thought necessary. — Robert Louis Stevenson, *Familiar Studies of Men and Books,* 1882

**2890.** Politics is not a science, as many professors imagine, but an art. — Otto von Bismarck, speech, March 15, 1884

**2891.** Politics is the art of human happiness. — H. A. L. Fisher, *A History of Europe,* 1934

**2892.** Politics is the art of preventing people from taking part in affairs which properly concern them. — Paul Valéry, *Tel Quel,* 1943

**2893.** Politics is the art of postponing decisions until they are no longer relevant. — Henri Queville, in *The Bureaucrat,* Winter, 1985–86

**2894.** The whole art of politics consists in directing rationally the irrationalities of men. — Reinhold Niebuhr, in *New York Times,* June 2, 1971

**2895.** Politics is an art and it is played by ear, though politicians often wish that they could use with profit more scientific method in the conduct of their work. — Stimson Bullitt, *To Be a Politician,* 1977

**2896.** Politics is not an art, but a means. It is not a product, but a process. — Calvin Coolidge, in Edward E. Whiting, *Calvin Coolidge: His Ideals of Citizenship,* 1924

**2897.** History is past politics, and politics is present history. — E. A. Freeman, *Methods of Historical Study,* 1886

**2898.** Politics, *n.* A strife of interests masquerading as a contest of principles. — Ambrose Bierce, *The Devil's Dictionary,* 1906

**2899.** Politics, as a practice, whatever its professions, has always been the systematic organization of hatreds. — Henry Brooks Adams, *The Education of Henry Adams,* 1907

**2900.** Politics is the reflex of the business and industrial world. — Emma Goldman, *Anarchism and Other Essays,* 1911

**2901.** I tell you folks, all politics is applesauce. — Will Rogers, *The Illiterate Digest,* 1924

**2902.** Politics, as hopeful men practice it in the world, consists mainly of the delusion that a change in form is a change in substance. — H. L. Mencken, *Prejudices: Fourth Series,* 1924

**2903.** Politics: Who Gets What, When, How. — Harold Laswell, book title, 1936

**2904.** The public attitude reveals itself in a common definition of *politics,* to wit, "Who gets what, when, how?" — H. L. Mencken, *The American Language, Supplement I,* 1945

**2905.** Politics is war without bloodshed, while war is politics with bloodshed. — Mao Zedong, lecture, 1938

**2906.** All politics seems like provincial struggles for booty between dusky tribes. — Stephen Spender, in *Horizon,* September, 1940

**2907.** Power politics is the diplomatic name for the law of the jungle. — Ely Culbertson, *Must We Fight Russia?,* 1946

**2908.** What is politics but persuading the public to vote for this and support that and endure these for the promise of those? — Gilbert Highet, in *Vogue,* January, 1951

**2909.** Politics is a systematic effort to move other men in the pursuit of some design. — Bertrand de Jouvenel, *The Pure Theory of Politics,* 1963

**2910.** Ideas are great arrows, but there has to be a bow. And politics is the bow of idealism. — Bill Moyers, in *Time,* October 29, 1965

**2911.** Politics is the skilled use of blunt objects. — Lester B. Pearson, on CBC-TV, "The Tenth Decade," 1972

**2912.** Politics is the greatest sport there is. It's competitive. People win, people lose, people come back. — Richard M. Nixon, on C-SPAN interview, February 23, 1992

**2913.** Politics, like music and golf, is best learned at an early age. — Lawrence Welk, in *Time,* April 14, 1975

**2914.** The sad duty of politics is to establish justice in a sinful world. — Reinhold Niebuhr, in Jimmy Carter, *Why Not the Best?,* 1975

**2915.** Politics is motion and excitement. — John Sears, in *Time,* November 12, 1979

**2916.** Politics in America is the binding secular religion. — Theodore H. White, in *Time,* December 29, 1986

**2917.** Politics is truly the art of indicting the innocent and rewarding the guilty. — David A. Stockman, *The Triumph of Politics,* 1987

**2918.** The public gets the kind of politician it deserves. Politics is an act of faith; you have to show some confidence in the intellectual and moral capacity of the public. Sometimes that faith is rewarded, and sometimes it isn't. — George McGovern, in *USA Today,* January 25, 1989

**2919.** Politics is part reality and part fiction. I even believe that literature, by its humanistic and universal vision of the world, leads one to politics. — Jose Sarney, in *World Press Review,* March, 1989

**2920.** Politics is the process of getting along with the querulous, the garrulous and the congenitally unlovable. — Marilyn Moats Kennedy, in *Newsweek,* September 16, 1985

# Politics, Dirty *see* Dirty Politics
# Posterity *see* Future

# ———— *Poverty* ————
## *See also* Haves and Have Nots; Revolution; Welfare

**2921.** It is not easy for men to rise whose qualities are thwarted by poverty. — Juvenal, *Satires,* ca. 110

**2922.** Any man may be in good spirits and good temper when he's well dressed. There ain't much credit in that. — Charles Dickens, *Martin Chuzzlewit,* 1844

**2923.** For every talent that poverty has stimulated it has blighted a hundred. — John W. Gardner, *Excellence,* 1961

**2924.** There is no scandal like rags, nor any crime so shameful as poverty. — George Farquhar, *The Beaux' Stratagem,* 1707

**2925.** As covetousness is the root of all evil, so poverty is the worst of all snares. — Daniel Defoe, *Moll Flanders,* 1721

**2926.** Poverty is a great enemy to human happiness; it certainly destroys liberty, and it makes some virtues unpracticable, and others extremely difficult. — Samuel Johnson, in James Boswell, *Life of Samuel Johnson,* 1791

**2927.** To understand another human being you must gain some insight into the conditions which made him what he is. — Margaret Bourke-White, in Anne Tucker, *The Woman's Eye,* 1973

**2928.** Hungry men have no respect for law, authority or human life. — Marcus M. Garvey, *Philosophy and Opinions,* 1923

**2929.** A hungry man is more interested in four sandwiches than four freedoms. — Henry Cabot Lodge Jr., in *New York Times,* March 29, 1955

**2930.** The hungry and the homeless don't care about liberty any more than they care about cultural heritage. To pretend that they do care is cant. — E. M. Forster, *Alinger Harvest,* 1936

**2931.** A hungry man is not a free man. — Adlai Stevenson, speech, September 6, 1952

**2932.** Come away; poverty's catching. — Aphra Behn, *The Rover,* 1681

**2933.** We hand folks over to God's mercy, and show none ourselves. — George Eliot, *Adam Bede,* 1859

**2934.** It's no disgrace t'be poor, but

it might as well be. — Frank McKinney Hubbard, *Short Furrows,* 1911

2935. As for the virtuous poor, one can pity them, of course, but one cannot possibly admire them. — Oscar Wilde, *Sebastian Melmoth,* 1891

2936. The misfortunes of poverty carry with them nothing harder to bear than that they make man ridiculous. — Juvenal, *Satires,* ca. 110

2937. People don't resent having nothing nearly as much as having too little. — Ivy Compton-Burnett, *A Family and a Fortune,* 1939

2938. Please, sir, I want some more. — Charles Dickens, *Oliver Twist,* 1838

2939. "Take some more tea," the March Hare said to Alice, very earnestly. "I've had nothing yet," Alice replied in an offended tone. "So I can't take more." "You mean you can't take *less*," said the Hatter. "It's very easy to take *more* than nothing." — Lewis Carroll, *Alice's Adventures in Wonderland,* 1865

2940. We all live in a state of ambitious poverty. — Juvenal, *Satires,* ca. 110

2941. The greatest of evils and the worst of crimes is poverty...our first duty — a duty to which every other consideration should be sacrificed — is not to be poor. — George Bernard Shaw, *Major Barbara,* 1905

2942. The greatest redeeming feature of poverty: the fact that it annihilates the future. — George Orwell, *Down and Out in Paris and London,* 1933

2943. Stable poverty in which individuals are not exposed to the possibilities of change breeds, if anything, conservatism. — Seymour Martin Lipset, *Political Man,* 1981

2944. O world! how apt the poor are to be proud. — William Shakespeare, *Twelfth Night,* 1601

# *Power*

## *See also* Ambition; Character; Fame; Government; Honesty

2945. All empire is no more than power in trust. — John Dryden, *Absalom and Achitophel,* 1681

2946. The first principle of a civilized state is that power is legitimate only when it is under contract. — Walter Lippmann, *The Public Philosophy,* 1955

2947. Power must never be trusted without a check. — John Adams, letter, February 2, 1816

2948. Power invariably means both responsibility and danger. — Theodore Roosevelt, in *New York Times Magazine,* October 27, 1957

2949. A certain *quantum* of power must always exist in the community, in some hands, and under some appellation. — Edmund Burke, *Reflections on the Revolution in France,* 1790

2950. The essence of government is power; and power, lodged as it must be in human hands, will ever be liable to abuse. — James Madison, speech, December 2, 1829

2951. Those that make things happen are politically skilled and understand the use of power. — Robert H. Waterman, *The Renewal Factor,* 1987

2952. All political structures are based on power. — Max Weber, *Wirtschaft und Gesellschaft,* 1922

2953. Closeness to power heightens the dignity of all men. — Theodore H. White, *The Making of the President 1960,* 1961

2954. The new source of power is not money in the hands of a few but information in the hands of many. — John Naisbitt, *Megatrends,* 1984

2955. Talent is that which is in a man's power; genius is that in whose power a man is. — James Russell Lowell, *Among My Books*, 1870

2956. When the will to power is wanting, there is decline. — Friedrich Wilhelm Nietzsche, *The Anti-Christ*, 1888

2957. The secret of power is the will. — Giuseppe Mazzini, letter, 1831

2958. Power is given only to him who dares to stoop and take it...one must have the courage to dare. — Fyodor Dostoyevski, *Crime and Punishment*, 1866

2959. The depository of power is always unpopular. — Benjamin Disraeli, *Coningsby*, 1844

2960. You can have power over people as long as you don't take *every-thing* away from them. But when you've robbed a man of *everything* he's no longer in your power — he's free again. — Alexander Solzhenitsyn, *The First Circle*, 1968

2961. People demand freedom only when they have no power. — Friedrich Wilhelm Nietzsche, *The Will to Power*, 1888

2962. In power I look only at one thing, what does it belong to and what does it effect. — Plato, *The Republic*, ca. 370 B.C.

2963. Knowledge — Zzzzzp! Money — Zzzzzp! — Power! That's the cycle democracy is built on! — Tennessee Williams, *The Glass Menagerie*, 1945

2964. The official world, the corridors of power. — C. P. Snow, *Homecomings*, 1956

2965. A friend in power is a friend lost. — Henry Brooks Adams, *The Education of Henry Adams*, 1907

2966. As wealth is power, so all power will infallibly draw wealth to itself by some means or other. — Edmund Burke, speech, February 11, 1780

2967. The purpose of getting power is to be able to give it away. — Aneurin Bevan, in Michael Foot, *Aneurin Bevan 1945–1960*, 1962

2968. In all supremacy of power, there is inherent a prerogative to pardon. — Benjamin Whichcote, *Moral and Religious Aphorisms*, 1703

2969. Omnipotence cannot work contradictions; it can only effect all possible things. — Soame Jenyns, *A Free Enquiry into the Nature and Origin of Evil*, 1757

2970. We have the power to do any damn fool thing we want to do, and we seem to do it about every ten minutes. — J. William Fulbright, in *Time*, February 4, 1952

2971. Power without responsibility: the prerogative of the harlot throughout the ages. — Rudyard Kipling, *Kipling Journal*, December, 1971

2972. Power is the great aphrodisiac. — Henry Kissinger, in *New York Times*, January 19, 1971

2973. Power makes you attractive; it even makes women love old men. — Joseph Joubert, *Pensées*, 1842

2974. Power tends to corrupt and absolute power corrupts absolutely. — John E. E. Dalberg, letter, April 5, 1887

2975. If power corrupts, being out of power corrupts absolutely. — Douglass Cater, in *Book Digest*, December, 1979

2976. Power corrupts the few, while weakness corrupts the many. — Eric Hoffer, *The Passionate State of Mind*, 1954

2977. Powerlessness frustrates; absolute powerlessness frustrates absolutely. — Russell Baker, in *New York Times*, May 1, 1969

2978. It is not power itself, but the legitimation of the lust for power, which corrupts absolutely. — R. H. S. Crossman, in *New Statesman*, April 21, 1951

2979. Liberals have learned at a fearful cost, the lesson that absolute power corrupts absolutely. They have yet to learn that absolute liberality corrupts absolutely. — Gertrude Himmelfarb, *On Liberty and Liberalism*, 1974

2980. The greater the power, the more dangerous the abuse. — Edmund Burke, speech, February 7, 1771

2981. Power will intoxicate the best

hearts, as wine the strongest heads. —Charles Caleb Colton, *Lacon,* 1820–22

**2982.** Those who have been once intoxicated with power, and have desired any kind of emolument from it, even though for but one year, can never willingly abandon it. —Edmund Burke, *Letter to a Member of the National Assembly,* 1791

**2983.** Few men are satisfied with less power than they are able to procure. —William Henry Harrison, speech, 1840

**2984.** He who has the greatest power put into his hands will only become the more impatient of any restraint in the use of it. —William Hazlitt, "On the Spirit of Monarchy," 1823

**2985.** The only prize much cared for by the powerful is power. The prize of the general is not a bigger tent, but command. —Oliver Wendell Holmes Jr., *Law and the Court,* 1913

**2986.** Power, like a desolating pestilence, Pollutes whate'er it touches, and obedience, Bane of all genius, virtue, freedom, truth, Makes slaves of men, and, of the human frame, A mechanized automation. —Percy Bysshe Shelley, *Queen Mab,* 1813

**2987.** I am more and more convinced that man is a dangerous creature; and that power, whether vested in many or a few, is ever grasping, and, like the grave, cries, "Give, give!" —Abigail Adams, letter, November 27, 1775

**2988.** The arts of power and its minions are the same in all countries and in all ages. It marks its victim, denounces it, and excites the public odium and the public hatred, to conceal its own abuses and encroachments. —Henry Clay, speech, March 14, 1834

**2989.** The effect of power and publicity on all men is the aggravation of self, a sort of tumor that ends by killing the victim's sympathies. —Henry Brooks Adams, *The Education of Henry Adams,* 1907

**2990.** To know the pains of power, we must go to those who have it; to know

its pleasure, we must go to those who are seeking it. —Charles Caleb Colton, *Lacon,* 1820–22

**2991.** You shall have joy, or you shall have power, said God; you shall not have both. —Ralph Waldo Emerson, *Journals,* October, 1842

**2992.** Power is not happiness. —William Godwin, *An Enquiry concerning Political Justice,* 1793

**2993.** The monuments of wit survive the monuments of power. —Francis Bacon, *Essex's Device,* 1595

**2994.** Next to enjoying ourselves, the next greatest pleasure consists in preventing others from enjoying themselves, or, more generally, in the acquisition of power. —Bertrand Russell, *Sceptical Essays,* 1928

**2995.** Our sense of power is more vivid when we break a man's spirit than when we win his heart. —Eric Hoffer, *The Passionate State of Mind,* 1954

**2996.** Power is in inflicting pain and humiliation. Power is in tearing human minds to pieces and putting them together again in new shapes of our own choosing. —George Orwell, *1984,* 1949

**2997.** Political power, properly so called, is merely the organized power of one class for oppressing another. —Karl Marx and Friedrich Engels, *Communist Manifesto,* 1848

**2998.** Concentrated power has always been the enemy of liberty. —Ronald Reagan, in *New Republic,* December 16, 1981

**2999.** It is a strange desire to seek power and to lose liberty. —Francis Bacon, *Essays,* "Of Great Place," 1625

**3000.** What a perversion of the normal order of things! . . . to make power the primary and central object of the social system, and Liberty but its satellite. —James Madison, in *National Gazette,* December 20, 1792

**3001.** See to the government. See that the government does not acquire too much power. Keep a check upon your rulers. Do this, and liberty is safe. —William Henry Harrison, speech, 1840

3002. Political liberty is nothing else but the diffusion of power. — Quinton Hogg, *The Case for Conservatism*, 1947

3003. Power is so apt to be insolent and Liberty to be saucy, that they are very seldom upon good terms. — George Savile, *Political, Moral, and Miscellaneous Thoughts and Reflections*, 1750

3004. Like power in any shape, a full stomach always holds a dose of insolence, and this dose expresses itself first of all in the well-fed lecturing the starving. — Anton Chekhov, letter, 1891

3005. The problem of power is how to achieve its responsible use rather than its irresponsible and indulgent use — of how to get men of power to live for the public rather than off the public. — Robert F. Kennedy, *The Pursuit of Justice*, 1964

3006. People who have power respond simply. They have no minds but their own. — Ivy Compton-Burnett, *The Mighty and Their Fall*, 1961

3007. I have seen the wicked in great power, and spreading himself like a green bay tree. — Bible, *Psalms 37:35*

# Prejudice

## See also Majority and Minority

3008. Prejudice is the child of ignorance. — William Hazlitt, *Sketches and Essays*, "On Prejudice," 1839

3009. Drive out prejudices through the door, and they will return through the window. — Frederick the Great, letter, March 19, 1771

3010. Common sense is the collection of prejudices acquired by age eighteen. — Albert Einstein, in *Scientific American*, February, 1976

3011. Prejudice is never easy unless it can pass itself off for reason. — William Hazlitt, *Sketches and Essays*, "On Prejudice," 1839

3012. Nowhere are prejudices more mistaken for truth, passion for reason, and invective for documentation than in politics. That is a realm, peopled only by villains or heroes, in which everything is black or white, and gray is a forbidden color. — John Mason Brown, *Through These Men*, 1956

3013. Prejudice is a raft unto which the shipwrecked mind clambers and paddles to safety. — Ben Hecht, *A Guide to the Bedevilled*, 1944

3014. One may no more live in the world without picking up the moral prejudices of the world than one will be able to go to hell without perspiring. — H. L. Mencken, *Prejudices, Second Series*, 1920

3015. It is never too late to give up our prejudices. — Henry David Thoreau, *Walden*, "Economy," 1854

3016. But I hang on to my prejudices. They are the testicles of my mind. — Eric Hoffer, *Before the Sabbath*, 1979

3017. Law is a reflection and a source of prejudice. It both enforces and suggests forms of bias. — Diane B. Schulder, in Robin Morgan, *Sisterhood Is Powerful*, 1970

3018. The absent are always in the wrong. — Philippe N. Destouches, *The Unexpected Obstacle*, 1717

3019. For nonconformity the world whips you with its displeasure. — Ralph Waldo Emerson, *Essays, First Series*, "Self-Reliance," 1841

3020. Men hate what they cannot understand. — Moses Ibn Ezra, *Shirat Yisrael*, 12th c.

3021. You lose a lot of time hating people. — Marian Anderson, in *New York Times*, April 18, 1965

3022. The poor are Europe's blacks. — Sébastien Roch Nicholas Chamfort, *Maximes et Pensées*, 1805

3023. The world is quickly bored by the recital of misfortunes and willingly avoids the sight of distress. —W. Somerset Maugham, *The Moon and Sixpence*, 1919

3024. The suppression of civil liberties is to many less a matter of horror than the curtailment of the freedom to profit. —Marya Mannes, *But Will It Sell?*, 1964

3025. The Negro's great stumbling block in the stride toward freedom is not the White Citizens Councillor or the Ku Klux Klanner but the white moderate who is more devoted to order than to justice. —Martin Luther King Jr., letter, April 16, 1963

3026. Anti-semitism [in Germany] gave an opportunity to discharge hatred against the rich and successful without espousing the proletarian socialists. —Harold Laswell, *Politics, Who Gets What, When, How*, 1951

3027. Bigotry may be roughly defined as the anger of men who have no opinions. —Gilbert K. Chesterton, *Heretics*, 1905

3028. A bigot delights in public ridicule, for he begins to think he is a martyr. —Sydney Smith, *The Letters of Peter Plymley*, 1808

3029. Segregation now, segregation tomorrow and segregation forever. — George Wallace, speech, January, 1963

3030. The problem of the twentieth century is the problem of the color line—the relation of the darker to the lighter races of men in Asia and Africa, in America and the islands of the sea.

—W. E. B. DuBois, *The Souls of Black Folk*, 1905

3031. I have a dream that one day on the red hills of Georgia, the sons of former slaves and the sons of former slave owners will be able to sit down together at the table of brotherhood.... I have a dream that my four little children will one day live in a nation where they will not be judged by the color of their skin, but by the content of their character. —Martin Luther King Jr., speech, August 28, 1963

3032. No one has ever been barred on account of his race from fighting or dying for America. There are no "white" or "colored" signs on the foxholes or graveyards of battle. —John F. Kennedy, message to Congress, June 20, 1963

3033. None of us is infallible. I have to take responsibility for my human failures, just like everybody, black and white, does. Don't put it on racism if you screw up. —Glenn Loury, in *USA Today*, May 3, 1990

3034. The Lord so constituted everybody that no matter what color you are you require the same amount of nourishment. —Will Rogers, *The Autobiography of Will Rogers*, 1949

3035. Talented young immigrants help us advance every one of our national goals. They make us richer and not poorer, stronger and not weaker. —Julian Simon, in *Nation's Business*, August, 1990

3036. We must learn to live together as brothers or perish together as fools. —Martin Luther King Jr., speech, March 22, 1964

# Presidents *see* U.S. Presidency

# ———————— *Press and Media* ————————

## See also Freedom of Speech; Freedom of the Press; Gossip and Publicity

3037. The gallery in which the reporters sit has become a fourth estate of the realm. —Thomas Babington, *Essays Contributed to the Edinburgh Review*, 1843

**3038.** In America the president reigns for four years, and journalism governs for ever and ever. — Oscar Wilde, *The Soul of Man under Socialism,* 1895

**3039.** The men with the muck-rakes are often indispensable to the well-being of society; but only if they know when to stop raking the muck. — Theodore Roosevelt, speech, April 14, 1906

**3040.** No government ought to be without censors; and where the press is free, no one ever will. — Thomas Jefferson, letter, September 9, 1792

**3041.** Without criticism and reliable and intelligent reporting, the government cannot govern. — Walter Lippmann, speech, May 24, 1965

**3042.** We live under a government of men and morning newspapers. — Wendell Phillips, speech, January 28, 1852

**3043.** The press is no substitute for institutions. It is like the beam of a searchlight that moves restlessly about . . . men cannot do the work of the world by this light alone. They cannot govern society by episodes, incidents, and interruptions. — Walter Lippmann, *Public Opinion,* 1965

**3044.** Were it left to me to decide whether we should have a government without newspapers, or newspapers without a government, I should not hesitate for a moment to prefer the latter. — Thomas Jefferson, letter, January 16, 1787

**3045.** Nothing can now be believed which is seen in a newspaper. Truth itself becomes suspicious by being put into that polluted vehicle. — Thomas Jefferson, letter, June 11, 1807

**3046.** The abuses of the press are notorious. . . . License to the press is no proof of liberty. When a people are corrupted, the press may be made an engine to complete their ruin. — John Adams, in *Boston Gazette,* February 6, 1775

**3047.** The medium is the message. — Marshall McLuhan, *Understanding Media,* 1964

**3048.** Give me the writing of a nation's advertising and propaganda, and I care not who governs its politics. — Hugh MacLennan, in *MacLean's Magazine,* November 5, 1960

**3049.** The hand that rules the press, the radio, the screen and the far-spread magazine, rules the country. — Learned Hand, speech, December 21, 1942

**3050.** Print is the sharpest and the strongest weapon of our party. — Joseph Stalin, speech, April 19, 1923

**3051.** *The Times* has made many ministries. — Walter Bagehot, *The English Constitution,* "The Cabinet," 1867

**3052.** The press is not public opinion. — Otto von Bismarck, speech, September 30, 1862

**3053.** Well, all I know is what I read in the papers. — Will Rogers, in *New York Times,* September 30, 1923

**3054.** The man who never looks into a newspaper is better informed than he who reads them: inasmuch as he who knows nothing is nearer to the truth than he whose mind is filled with falsehood and errors. — Thomas Jefferson, letter, February 11, 1807

**3055.** One of Kennedy's techniques for dealing with the press was to say things that were so candid . . . that you knew if you printed it, you would be ending your intimate relationship; that is, the president would say, "you couldn't have thought that I would say something like that on the record." It was a way of co-opting us. — David S. Broder, in Larry J. Sabato, *Feeding Frenzy,* 1991

**3056.** It is not difficult for political journalists in America, for foreign correspondents especially, to get on familiar terms with public men. Indeed, the higher the status of a politician, the more he seems to crave a good notice abroad. — Alistair Cooke, *Six Men,* 1977

**3057.** The *press conference* is a politician's way of being informative without saying anything. Should he accidentally say something, he has at his side a *press officer* who immediately explains it away by "clarifying" it. — Emery Kelen, *Platypus at Large,* 1960

**3058.** You won't have Nixon to kick around anymore, because, gentle-

men, this is my last press conference.
—Richard M. Nixon, statement, November 7, 1962
**3059.** A politician wouldn't dream
of being allowed to call a columnist the
things a columnist is allowed to call a
politician. —Max Lerner, *Actions and
Passions,* 1949
**3060.** All newspaper and jour-
nalistic activity is an intellectual brothel
from which there is no retreat. —Leo
Tolstoy, letter, August 22, 1871
**3061.** In old days men had the rack.
Now they have the press. —Oscar Wilde,
*The Soul of Man under Socialism,* 1895
**3062.** I read the newspapers avidly.
It is my one form of continuous
fiction. —Aneurin Bevan, in *The Times,*
March 29, 1960

**3063.** If we had had the technology
back then, you would have seen Eva
Braun on the "Donahue" show and
Hitler on "Meet the Press." —Ed Turner,
in *Newsweek,* September 17, 1990
**3064.** My advice to any diplomat
who wants to have a good press is to have
two or three kids and a dog. —Carl
Rowan, in *New Yorker,* December 7,
1963
**3065.** By August 1979, if the President had been set upon by a pack of wild
dogs, a good portion of the press would
have sided with the dogs and declared
that he provoked the attack. —Jody
Powell, *The Other Side of the Story,*
1984

---

# Problems and Solutions

## See also Decisions

**3066.** What we're saying today is
that you're either part of the solution or
you're part of the problem. —Eldridge
Cleaver, speech, 1968
**3067.** I believe that government is
the problem, not the answer. —Ronald
Reagan, in *Washington Post,* April 20,
1976
**3068.** For every human problem,
there is a neat, plain solution—and it is
always wrong. —H. L. Mencken, in
*Washingtonian,* November, 1978
**3069.** I have yet to see any problem, however complicated, which, when
you looked at it in the right way, did not
become still more complicated. —Paul
Anderson, in *Washingtonian,* November, 1978
**3070.** You will be damned if you
do—And you will be damned if you
don't. —Lorenzo Dow, *Reflections on the
Love of God,* 1836
**3071.** Any solution to a problem
changes the problem. —Robert W. Johnson, in *Washingtonian,* November, 1979

**3072.** Problems reproduce themselves from generation to generation. . . .
I refer to this as a "cycle of deprivation."
—Keith Joseph, speech, June 29, 1972
**3073.** The problem isn't a shortage
of fuel, it's a surplus of government.
—Ronald Reagan, in *Newsweek,* October 1, 1979
**3074.** I have one yardstick by which
I test every major problem—and that
yardstick is: Is it good for America?
—Dwight D. Eisenhower, speech, April 16,
1956
**3075.** I am skeptical about the
ability of government to solve problems,
and I have a healthy respect for the ability of people to solve problems on their
own. —Richard B. Cheney, in *Washington Post,* November 6, 1975
**3076.** The function of genius is not
to give new answers, but to pose new
questions which time and mediocrity can
solve. —H. R. Trevor-Roper, *Men and
Events,* 1958
**3077.** Questions are never indis-

creet. Answers sometimes are. — Oscar Wilde, *An Ideal Husband,* 1895

**3078.** More trouble is caused in the world by indiscreet answers than by indiscreet questions. — Sydney J. Harris, in *Chicago Daily News,* March 27, 1958

**3079.** It is not the answer that enlightens, but the question. — Eugene Ionesco, *Decouvertes,* 1969

**3080.** Good questions outrank easy answers. — Paul A. Samuelson, in *Newsweek,* August 21, 1978

**3081.** To stir up undisputed matters seemed a great reward in itself. — Sallust, *The War with Catiline,* ca. 40 B.C.

# Progress

## See also Future; Political Action; Reform

**3082.** There must be a beginning of any great matter, but the continuing unto the end until it be thoroughly finished yields the true glory. — Francis Drake, dispatch, May 17, 1587

**3083.** Every step of progress the world has made has been from scaffold to scaffold, and from stake to stake. — Wendell Phillips, speech, October 15, 1851

**3084.** The movement of the progressive societies has hitherto been a movement *from Status to Contract.* — Henry Maine, *Ancient Law,* 1861

**3085.** The history of progress is written in the lives of infidels. — Robert G. Ingersoll, speech, May 1, 1881

**3086.** The reasonable man adapts himself to the world: the unreasonable one persists in trying to adapt the world to himself. Therefore all progress depends on the unreasonable man. — George Bernard Shaw, *Man and Superman,* 1903

**3087.** Progress is born of cooperation in the community — not from government restraints. — Herbert Hoover, inaugural address, March 4, 1929

**3088.** You can't say civilization don't advance, however, for in every war they kill you in a new way. — Will Rogers, in *New York Times,* December 23, 1929

**3089.** No progress of humanity is possible unless it shakes off the yoke of authority and tradition. — André Gide, *Journals,* March 17, 1931

**3090.** The history of the world is none other than the progress of the consciousness of freedom. — Georg Wilhelm Friedrich Hegel, *Philosophy of History,* 1832

**3091.** Is it progress if a cannibal uses knife and fork? — Stanislaw Lec, *Unkempt Thoughts,* 1962

**3092.** The concept of progress acts as a protective mechanism to shield us from the terrors of the future. — Frank Herbert, *Dune,* 1965

**3093.** Any man who thinks civilization has advanced is an egoist. — Will Rogers, in *Time,* October 7, 1974

**3094.** Progress is man's ability to complicate simplicity. — Thor Heyerdahl, *Fatu-Hira,* 1974

# Promises

## See also Diplomacy; Lies; Speech

**3095.** The rule is, jam tomorrow and jam yesterday — but never jam today. — Lewis Carroll, *Through the Looking-Glass,* 1872

**3096.** Never promise more than you can perform. — Publilius Syrus, *Maxims*, 1st c. B.C.

**3097.** If I become President we will keep a...Kosher kitchen in the White House. — Bill Clinton, speech before the Council of Jewish Organizations, March 29, 1992

**3098.** Promises may get thee friends, but non-performance will turn them into enemies. — Benjamin Franklin, *Poor Richard's Almanac*, 1733–58

**3099.** One must have a good memory to be able to keep the promises one makes. — Friedrich Wilhelm Nietzsche, *Human, All Too Human*, 1878

**3100.** Nothing so betrays the leader as reluctance to stand behind, defend and pay the price of the course of action he has chosen to follow. — Ordway Tead, *The Art of Leadership*, 1935

**3101.** When a man you like switches from what he said a year ago, or four years ago, he is a broadminded person who has courage enough to change his mind with changing conditions. When a man you don't like does it, he is a liar who has broken his promises. — Franklin P. Adams, *Nods and Becks*, 1944

**3102.** I have said this before, but I shall say it again and again and again: Your boys are not going to be sent into any foreign wars. — Franklin D. Roosevelt, speech, October 30, 1940

**3103.** We are not about to send American boys nine or ten thousand miles away from home to do what Asian boys ought to be doing for themselves. — Lyndon B. Johnson, speech, October 21, 1964

**3104.** Read my lips: no new taxes. — George Bush, in *New York Times*, August 19, 1988

**3105.** A prudent prince neither can nor ought to keep his word when to keep it is hurtful to him and the causes which led him to pledge it are removed. — Niccolò Machiavelli, *The Prince*, 1513

# Propaganda *see* Language; Press and Media

# —————— *Property* ——————

## See also Communism

**3106.** Oligarchy: A government resting on a valuation of property, in which the rich have power and the poor man is deprived of it. — Plato, *The Republic*, ca. 370 B.C.

**3107.** Man...hath by nature a power...to preserve his property—that is, his life, liberty, and estate—against the injuries and attempts of other men. — John Locke, *Second Treatise of Civil Government*, 1690

**3108.** The diversity in the faculties of men, from which the rights of property originate is not less an inseparable obstacle to a uniformity of interests. The protection of these faculties is the first object of government. — James Madison, *The Federalist*, 1787

**3109.** The poorest man may in his cottage bid defiance to all the forces of the Crown. It may be frail—its roof may shake—the wind may blow through it—the storm may enter—the rain may enter—but the King of England cannot enter. — William Pitt (I), speech, March, 1763

**3110.** As a man is said to have a right to his property, he may be equally said to have a property in his rights. — James Madison, in *National Gazette*, March 29, 1792

**3111.** The great and chief end... of men's uniting into commonwealths, and putting themselves under government, is the preservation of their property. — John Locke, *Second Treatise of Civil Government*, 1690

3112. Well! Some people talk of morality, and some of religion, but give me a little snug property. — Maria Edgeworth, *The Absentee,* 1812

3113. National honor is national property of the highest value. — James Monroe, inaugural address, March 4, 1817

3114. Private property was the original source of freedom. It still is its main bulwark. — Walter Lippmann, *The Good Society,* 1937

3115. Property is the exploitation of the weak by the strong. Communism is the exploitation of the strong by the weak. — Pierre Joseph Proudhon, *What Is Property?,* 1840

3116. The system of private property is the most important guaranty of freedom, not only for those who own property, but scarcely less for those who do not. — Friedrich A. von Hayek, *The Road to Serfdom,* 1944

3117. No man who owns his house and lot can be a Communist. He has too much to do. — William Levitt, in Frederick F. Siegel, *Troubled Journey: From Pearl Harbor to Ronald Reagan,* 1984

# Public Opinion *see* Opinion, Public

——————— *Radicals and Reactionaries* ———————

*See also* Extremism; Rebellion; Revolution; Revolutionaries

3118. A radical is one who speaks the truth. — Charles A. Lindburgh Sr., in *Labor,* June 15, 1957

3119. The liberation of the human mind has been best furthered by gay fellows who heaved dead cats into sanctuaries and then went roistering down the highways of the world, proving to all men that doubt, after all was safe — that the god in the sanctuary was a fraud. One horse-laugh is worth ten thousand syllogisms. — H. L. Mencken, in *American Mercury,* January, 1924

3120. The radical invents the views. When he has worn them out the conservative adopts them. — Mark Twain, *Notebook,* 1935

3121. A young man who is not radical about something is a pretty poor risk for education. — Jacques Barzun, *The Teacher in America,* 1944

3122. The radical of one century is the conservative of the next. — Mark Twain, *Notebook,* 1935

3123. Generally young men are regarded as radicals. This is a popular misconception. The most conservative persons I ever met are college undergraduates. — Woodrow Wilson, speech, November 19, 1905

3124. I never dared be radical when young For fear it would make me conservative when old. — Robert Frost, *A Further Range,* "Precaution," 1936

3125. No one can go on being a rebel too long without turning into an autocrat. — Lawrence Durrell, *Balthazar,* 1958

3126. A Radical is a man with both feet firmly planted — in the air. — Franklin D. Roosevelt, radio address, October 26, 1939

3127. The spirit of our American radicalism is destructive and aimless; it is not loving, it has no ulterior and divine ends; but is destructive only out of hatred and selfishness. — Ralph Waldo Emerson, *Essays: Second Series,* "Politics," 1844

3128. Radicalism itself ceases to be radical when absorbed mainly in preserving its control over a society or an economy. — Eric Hoffer, *The Passionate State of Mind,* 1954

**3129.** Radical Chic . . . is only radical in Style; in its heart it is part of Society and its tradition — Politics, like Rock, Pop, and Camp, has its uses. — Tom Wolfe, in *New York,* June 8, 1970

**3130.** By "radical," I understand one who goes too far; by "conservative," one who does not go far enough; by "reactionary," one who won't go at all. — Woodrow Wilson, speech, January 29, 1911

**3131.** In the current sense of a political conservative, *reactionary* was used by Froude in 1858. It is now used to designate any opponent of a new device to save humanity. — H. L. Mencken, *The American Language, Supplement I,* 1945

**3132.** A Reactionary is a somnambulist walking backwards. — Franklin D. Roosevelt, radio address, October 26, 1939

**3133.** All reactionaries are paper tigers. — Mao Zedong, interview, 1946

# Reason

**3134.** Since reason is given to all men by nature . . . thus a sense of what is right is common to all men. — Cicero, *De Legibus,* 1st c. B.C.

**3135.** Reason cannot be forced into belief. — Hasdai Crescas, *Or Adonai,* 1410

**3136.** Truth and reason are common to everyone, and no more belong to the man who first said them than to the man who says them later. — Michel Eyquem de Montaigne, *Essays,* 1580

**3137.** Obtruding false rules pranked in reason's garb. — John Milton, *Comus,* 1637

**3138.** People are generally better persuaded by the reasons which they have themselves discovered than by those which have come into the mind of others. — Blaise Pascal, *Pensées,* 1670

**3139.** Those who differ upon reason may come together by reason. — Benjamin Whichcote, *Moral and Religious Aphorisms,* 1703

**3140.** Time makes more converts than reason. — Thomas Paine, *Common Sense,* 1776

**3141.** Men may be convinced, but they cannot be pleased, against their will. — Samuel Johnson, *Lives of the Poets,* "Congreve," 1779

**3142.** Reason and free inquiry are the only effectual agents against error.

— Thomas Jefferson, *Notes on the State of Virginia,* 1781–85

**3143.** Every politician ought to sacrifice to the graces; and to join compliance with reason. — Edmund Burke, *Reflections on the Revolution in France,* 1790

**3144.** Consider what you think justice requires, and decide accordingly. But never give your reasons; for your judgment will probably be right, but your reasons will certainly be wrong. — William Murray, in J. Campbell, *The Lives of the Chief Justices of England,* 1849

**3145.** I'll not listen to reason. . . . Reason always means what someone else has got to say. — Elizabeth Gaskell, *Cranford,* 1853

**3146.** I can stand brute force, but brute reason is quite unbearable. There is something unfair about its use. It is hitting below the intellect. — Oscar Wilde, *The Picture of Dorian Gray,* 1891

**3147.** Government is the political representative of a natural equilibrium, of custom, of inertia; it is by no means a representative of reason. — George Santayana, *The Life of Reason,* 1905–06

**3148.** The fatal errors of life are not due to man's being unreasonable. An unreasonable moment may be one's finest. They are due to man's being logical. — Oscar Wilde, *De Profundis*, 1905

**3149.** A mind all logic is like a knife all blade. It makes the hand bleed that uses it. — Rabindranath Tagore, *Stray Birds*, 1916

**3150.** The Common Law of England has been laboriously built about a mythical figure — the figure of "The Reasonable Man." — A. P. Herbert, *Uncommon Law*, 1935

**3151.** Reason in my philosophy is only a harmony among irrational impulses. — George Santayana, *Persons and Places*, "The Middle Span," 1945

**3152.** The sign of an intelligent people is their ability to control emotions by the application of reason. — Marya Mannes, *More in Anger*, 1958

**3153.** I do not believe man possesses an avenue to truth which is superior to his reason. — Roland B. Gittelsohn, *Man's Best Hope*, 1961

**3154.** It takes a long time to realize that the rational is only a small segment of the human complex, that the spirit of reason is difficult to invoke, and that there are as many dangers in the rational as in the irrational. — Anthony Burgess, *Urgent Copy*, 1968

# *Rebellion*

## *See also* **Radicals and Reactionaries; Revolution; Revolutionaries**

**3155.** It is not rebellion itself which is noble but the demands it makes upon us. — Albert Camus, *The Plague*, 1947

**3156.** Rebellion lay in his way, and he found it. — William Shakespeare, *Henry IV, Part I*, 1597

**3157.** I hold it, that a little rebellion, now and then, is a good thing, and as necessary in the political world as storms in the physical. — Thomas Jefferson, letter, January 30, 1787

**3158.** Any people anywhere, being inclined and having the power, have the right to rise up, and shake off the existing government, and form a new one that suits them better. — Abraham Lincoln, speech, January 12, 1848

**3159.** All oppressed people are authorized, whenever they can, to rise and break their fetters. — Henry Clay, speech, March 24, 1818

**3160.** This people hath a revolting and a rebellious heart. — Bible, *Jeremiah* 5:23

**3161.** Rebellion to tyrants is obedience to God. — John Bradshaw, epitaph, 17th c.

**3162.** Treason doth never prosper, what's the reason? For if it prosper, none dare call it treason. — John Harington, *Epigrams*, 1618

**3163.** If this be treason, make the most of it. — Patrick Henry, speech, May 29, 1765

**3164.** We have counted the cost of this contest, and find nothing so dreadful as voluntary slavery.... Our cause is just, our union is perfect. — John Dickinson, declaration, July 8, 1775

**3165.** Old forms of government finally grow so oppressive that they must be thrown off even at the risk of reigns of terror. — Herbert Spencer, *Education*, 1861

**3166.** What is a rebel? A man who says no. — Albert Camus, *The Rebel*, 1951

**3167.** I will die like a true-blue rebel. Don't waste any time in mourning — organize. — Joe Hill, upon his execution, November 18, 1915

# Reform

## See also Change; Political Action; Revolution

3168. A reform is a correction of abuses; a revolution is a transfer of power. — Edward Bulwer-Lytton, speech, 1866

3169. To give up the task of reforming society is to give up one's responsibility as a free man. — Alan Paton, in *Saturday Review*, September 9, 1967

3170. The man who raises new issues has always been distasteful to politicians. He musses up what has been so tidily arranged. — Walter Lippmann, *A Preface to Politics*, 1914

3171. There is nothing more difficult to take in hand, more perilous to conduct, or more uncertain in its success, than to take the lead in the introduction of a new order of things. — Niccolò Machiavelli, *The Prince*, 1513

3172. Every man is a reformer until reform tramps on his toes. — Edgar Watson Howe, *Country Town Sayings*, 1911

3173. Every reformation must have its victims. You can't expect the fatted calf to share the enthusiasm of the angels over the prodigal's return. — Saki, *Reginald*, 1904

3174. The eager and often inconsiderate appeals of reformers and revolutionaries are indispensable to counterbalance the inertness and fossilism making so large a part of human institutions. — Walt Whitman, *Democratic Vistas*, 1871

3175. Government. . .results from contrary purposes and parties pulling against each other in a tug-of-war, for the sake of office or of some immediate reform or relief. — George Santayana, *Dialogues in Limbo*, 1925

3176. Every reform, however necessary, will by weak minds be carried to an excess, that itself will need reforming. — Samuel Taylor Coleridge, *Biographia Literaria*, 1817

3177. There is no adequate defense, except stupidity, against the impact of a new idea. — Percy W. Bridgman, *The Intelligent Individual and Society*, 1938

3178. To innovate is not to reform. — Edmund Burke, *A Letter to a Noble Lord*, 1796

3179. The urge to save humanity is almost always only a false-face for the urge to rule it. — H. L. Mencken, *Minority Report*, 1956

3180. Of all human follies there's none could be greater Than trying to render our fellow-men better. — Molière, *Le Misanthrope*, 1666

3181. All Reformers, however strict their social conscience, live in houses just as big as they can pay for. — Logan Pearsall Smith, *Afterthoughts*, 1931

3182. It is one of the consolations of middle-aged reformers that the good they inculcate must live after them if it is to live at all. — Saki, *Beasts and Super-Beasts*, 1914

3183. Nobody expects to find comfort and companionability in reformers. — Heywood Broun, in *New York World*, February 6, 1928

3184. All reformers are bachelors. — George Moore, *The Bending of the Bough*, 1900

# Revolution

## See also Haves and Have Nots; Poverty; Radicals and Reactionaries; Rebellion; Revolutionaries; State

3185. Revolution, *n*. In politics, an abrupt change in the form of misgovernment. — Ambrose Bierce, *The Devil's Dictionary*, 1906

3186. A revolution is not an easy thing to pull off. — Edmund G. Brown Jr., in *New York Times*, December 28, 1991

3187. Revolutions are as a rule not made arbitrarily. — Leon Trotsky, *Where Is Britain Going?*, 1926

3188. Revolutions are the locomotives of history. — Nikita S. Khrushchev, in *Pravda*, May 8, 1957

3189. It is easier to run a revolution than a government. — Ferdinand Marcos, in *Time*, June 6, 1977

3190. All modern revolutions have ended in a reinforcement of the State. — Albert Camus, *The Rebel*, 1951

3191. A revolution is an insurrection, an act of violence by which one class overthrows another. — Mao Zedong, *Selected Works of Mao Zedong*, 1965

3192. It is the quality of revolutions not to go by old lines or old laws; but to break up both, and make new ones. — Abraham Lincoln, speech, January 12, 1848

3193. Revolution is not the uprising against the existing order, but the setting-up of a new order contradictory to the traditional one. — José Ortega y Gasset, *The Revolt of the Masses*, 1930

3194. Revolution or dictatorship can sometimes abolish bad things, but they can never create good and lasting ones. Impatience is fatal in politics. — Thomas Masaryk, *The Foundations of Marxist Theory*, 1899

3195. A successful revolution establishes a new community. A missed revolution makes irreverent the community that persists. And a compromised revolution tends to shatter the community that was, without an adequate substitute. — Paul Goodman, *Growing Up Absurd*, 1960

3196. Who stops the revolution half way? The bourgeoisie. — Victor Hugo, *Les Misérables*, 1862

3197. Fascism was a counter-revolution against a revolution that never took place. — Ignazio Silone, *The School for Dictatorships*, 1939

3198. Every successful revolt is termed a revolution, and every unsuccessful one a rebellion. — Joseph Priestley, letter, 1791

3199. The time to stop a revolution is at the beginning, not the end. — Adlai Stevenson, speech, September 9, 1952

3200. Be not deceived. Revolutions do not go backward. — Abraham Lincoln, speech, May 19, 1856

3201. All civilization has from time to time become a thin crust over a volcano of revolution. — Havelock Ellis, *Little Essays of Love and Virtue*, 1922

3202. Revolution is not a dinner party, not an essay, nor a painting, nor a piece of embroidery. — Mao Zedong, in *Time*, December 18, 1950

3203. You cannot make a revolution with silk gloves. — Joseph Stalin, attributed

3204. The first thing we do, let's kill all the lawyers. — William Shakespeare, *Henry VI, Part II*, 1592

3205. The seed of revolution is repression. — Woodrow Wilson, message to Congress, December 2, 1919

3206. Revolutions are not made: they come. A revolution is as natural a growth as an oak. It comes out of the past. Its foundations are laid far back. — Wendell Phillips, speech, January 28, 1852

3207. The outcome of the greatest events is always determined by a trifle. — Napoleon I, letter, October 7, 1797

3208. It is impossible to arouse the people artificially. People's revolutions are born from the course of events. — Michael Bakunin, letter, 1870

3209. If there is one safe generalization in human affairs, it is that revolutions always destroy themselves. — William Ralph Inge, *Outspoken Essays: First Series*, "Our Present Discontents," 1919

3210. There was reason to fear that the Revolution, like Saturn, might devour in turn each of her children. — Pierre Vergniaud, in Alphonse de Lamartine, *Histoire des Girondins*, 1847

3211. Only those who have nothing to lose ever revolt. — Alexis de Tocqueville, *Democracy in America*, 1835

3212. There are but three ways for the populace to escape its wretched lot. The first two are by the route of the wineshop or the church; the third is by that of the social revolution. — Michael Bakunin, *God and the State*, 1882

3213. To put political power in the hands of men embittered and degraded by poverty is to tie firebrands to foxes and turn them loose amid the standing corn. — Henry George, *Progress and Poverty*, Book VI, 1879

3214. Those who make peaceful revolution impossible will make violent revolution inevitable. — John F. Kennedy, speech, March 12, 1962

3215. Better to abolish serfdom from above than to wait till it begins to abolish itself from below. — Alexander II, speech, March 30, 1856

3216. Armed insurrection stands in the same relation to revolution as revolution as a whole does to evolution. — Leon Trotsky, *The Russian Revolution*, 1933

3217. Groups which have to push their way into the body politic by force are apt to overexaggerate the possibilities which political participation affords. — Seymour M. Lipset, *Political Man*, 1981

3218. When people are oppressed by their government, it is a natural right they enjoy to relieve themselves of the oppression. — Ulysses S. Grant, *Personal Memoirs*, 1885

3219. A whole government of our own choice, managed by persons whom we love, revere, and can confide in, has charms in it for which men will fight. — John Adams, letter, May 17, 1776

3220. Not actual suffering but the hope of better things incites people to revolt. — Eric Hoffer, *The Ordeal of Change*, 1964

3221. The revolution of rising expectations. — Harlan Cleveland, 1950

3222. Beginning reform is beginning revolution. — Arthur Wellesley, letter, November 7, 1830

3223. The effect of boredom on a large scale in history is underestimated. It is the main cause of revolutions, and would soon bring to an end all the static Utopias and the farmyard civilization of the Fabians. — William Ralph Inge, *End of an Age*, 1948

3224. If we do not find anything pleasant, at least we shall find something new. — Voltaire, *Candide*, 1759

3225. A revolution only lasts fifteen years, a period which coincides with the effectiveness of a generation. — José Ortega y Gasset, *The Revolt of the Masses*, 1930

3226. Chaos often breeds life when order breeds habit. — Henry Brooks Adams, *The Education of Henry Adams*, 1907

3227. It takes a revolution to make a solution. — Bob Marley, in *To the Point International*, September 12, 1977

3228. What a glorious morning is this. — Samuel Adams, statement upon hearing gunfire at Lexington, April 19, 1775 (often quoted, "What a glorious morning for America.")

3229. It was the best of times, it was the worst of times. — Charles Dickens, *A Tale of Two Cities*, 1859

3230. Make the Revolution a parent of settlement, and not a nursery of future revolutions. — Edmund Burke, *Reflections on the Revolution in France*, 1790

3231. When smashing monuments, save the pedestals — they always come in handy. — Stanislaw Lec, *Unkempt Thoughts*, 1962

---

# *Revolutionaries*

## See also Radicals and Reactionaries; Reform; Revolution

3232. The duty of every revolutionary is to make a revolution. — Fidel Castro, in Herbert Matthews, *Castro*, 1969

3233. To be a revolutionary is to love your life enough to change it, to choose struggle instead of exile, to risk everything with only the glimmering hope of a world to win. — Andrew Kopkind, in *New York Times Magazine*, November 10, 1968

3234. The successful revolutionary is a statesman, the unsuccessful one a criminal. — Erich Fromm, *Escape from Freedom*, 1941

3235. A revolution requires of its leaders a record of unbroken infallibility; if they do not possess it, they are expected to invent it. — Murray Kempton, *Part of Our Time*, "It's Time to Go, I Heard Them Say," 1955

3236. If there were more extremists in evolutionary periods, there would be no revolutionary periods. — Benjamin R. Tucker, *Instead of a Book*, 1893

3237. A true revolutionary despises the philanthropies whereby misery is abated and revolution delayed. — John Updike, in *New Yorker*, February 26, 1966

3238. In times of disorder and stress, the fanatics play a prominent role; in times of peace, the critics. Both are shot after the revolution. — Edmund Wilson, *Memoirs of Hecate County*, 1949

3239. By a revolution in the state, the fawning sycophant of yesterday is converted into the austere critic of the present hour. — Edmund Burke, *Reflections on the Revolution in France*, 1790

3240. The scrupulous and the just, the noble, humane, and devoted natures; the unselfish and the intelligent may begin a movement — but it passes away from them. They are not the leaders of a revolution. They are its victims. — Joseph Conrad, *Under Western Eyes*, 1911

3241. Revolutionary movements attract those who are not good enough for established institutions as well as those who are too good for them. — George Bernard Shaw, *Androcles and the Lion*, 1913

3242. Thinkers prepare the revolution; bandits carry it out. — Mariano Azuela, *The Flies*, 1918

3243. All revolutions invariably encourage bad characters and potential criminals. Traitors throw off the mask; they cannot contain themselves amidst the general confusion that seems to promise easy victims. — Ferdinand Delacroix, *Journal*, 1860

3244. The revolutionary spirit is mighty convenient in this, that it frees one from all scruples as regards ideas. — Joseph Conrad, *A Personal Record*, "A Familiar Preface," 1912

3245. The true aristocracy and the true proletariat of the world are both in understanding with tragedy. To them it is the fundamental principle of God, and the key, the minor key, to existence. — Isak Dinesen, *Out of Africa*, 1937

3246. Every revolutionary ends as an oppressor or a heretic. — Albert Camus, *The Rebel*, 1951

3247. Most revolutionaries are potential Tories, because they imagine that everything can be put right by altering the *shape* of society; once that change is effected, as it sometimes is, they see no need for any other. — George Orwell, *Inside the Whale*, 1940

3248. The most radical revolutionary will become a conservative the day after the revolution. — Hannah Arendt, in *New Yorker*, September 12, 1970

3249. A mark of many successful revolutionaries is their distaste for construction projects once the smoke has cleared. — Alistair Cooke, *Six Men*, 1977

3250. A revolutionary party is a contradiction in terms. — R. H. S. Crossman, *New Statesman*, 1939

3251. Fortunately for me, in America even revolutionaries are subject to the blessed reign of law, order, and nonviolent politics. They came at me with Op-Ed pieces instead of axes. — David A. Stockman, *The Triumph of Politics*, 1987

# Rights

## See also Constitution; Equality; Natural Law

3252. Rights that do not flow from duty well performed are not worth having. — Mohandas K. Gandhi, *Non-Violence in Peace and War*, 1948

3253. The modern state no longer has anything but rights; it does not recognize duties any more. — George Bernanos, *The Last Essays of George Bernanos*, "Why Freedom?," 1955

3254. I believe that every right implies a responsibility; every opportunity, an obligation; every possession, a duty. — John D. Rockefeller Jr., speech, July 8, 1941

3255. Property has its duties as well as its rights. — Thomas Drummond, letter, May 22, 1838

3256. What men value in this world is not rights but privileges. — H. L. Mencken, *Minority Report*, 1956

3257. Right. . . is the child of law; from real laws come real rights; but from imaginary laws, from laws of nature, fancied and invented by poets, rhetoricians, and dealers in moral and intellectual poisons, come imaginary rights, a bastard blood of monsters. — Jeremy Bentham, in J. Bowring, ed., *Works, Vol. II*, "Anarchical Fallacies," 1843

3258. Nobody talks more passionately of his rights than he who, in the depths of his soul, is doubtful about them. — Friedrich Wilhelm Nietzsche, *Human, All Too Human*, 1878

3259. The primary social goods, to give them in broad categories, are rights and liberties, opportunities and power, income and wealth. — John Rawls, *A Theory of Justice*, 1971

3260. It is fair to judge peoples by the rights they will sacrifice most for. — Clarence Day, *This Simian World*, 1920

3261. I am the inferior of any man whose rights I trample under foot. — Robert G. Ingersoll, *Prose-Poems and Selections*, 1884

3262. There is no security for the personal or political rights of any man in a community where any man is deprived of his personal or political rights. — Benjamin Harrison, speech, September 3, 1892

3263. They have rights who dare maintain them. — James Russell Lowell, "The Present Crisis," 1845

3264. We have talked long enough in this country about equal rights. We have talked for a hundred years or more. It is time now to write the next chapter, and to write it in the books of law. — Lyndon B. Johnson, speech, November 27, 1963

3265. America did not invent human rights. . .human rights invented America. — Jimmy Carter, speech, January 14, 1981

3266. Human beings have an inalienable right to invent themselves; when that right is pre-empted it is called brain-washing. — Germaine Greer, in *The Times*, February 1, 1986

3267. The country, with its institutions, belongs to the people who inhabit it. Whenever they shall grow weary of the existing government, they can exercise their constitutional right of amending it, or their revolutionary right to dismember or overthrow it. — Abraham Lincoln, inaugural address, March 4, 1861

3268. The republican is the only form of government which is not eternally at open or secret war with the rights of mankind. — Thomas Jefferson, letter, March 11, 1790

3269. Let the word go forth from this time and place, to friend and foe alike, that the torch has been passed to a new generation of Americans — born in this century, tempered by war, disciplined by a hard and bitter peace, proud of our ancient heritage — and unwilling to witness or permit the slow undoing of those human rights to which this nation has always been committed, and to which we are committed today at home and around the world. — John F. Kennedy, inaugural address, January 20, 1961

**3270.** It is the purpose of the government to see that not only the legitimate interests of the few are protected, but that the welfare and rights of the many are conserved. — Franklin D. Roosevelt, speech, September 21, 1932

**3271.** The individual who refuses to defend his rights when called by his Government deserves to be a slave, and must be punished as an enemy of his country and friend to her foe. — Andrew Jackson, proclamation, September 21, 1814

**3272.** When public excitement runs high as to alien ideologies, is the time when we must be particularly alert not to impair the ancient landmarks set up in the Bill of Rights. — Luther W. Youngdahl, *United States v. Lattimore,* May 2, 1953

**3273.** During war we imprison the rights of man. — Jean Giraudoux, *Tiger at the Gates,* 1935

**3274.** It astounds us to come upon other egoists, as though we alone had the right to be selfish, and to be filled with eagerness to live. — Jules Renard, *Journal,* 1887

**3275.** The right to be wrong is as important as the right to be admired. — Edward R. Murrow, speech, June, 1954

**3276.** The greatest right in the world is the right to be wrong. — Harry Weinberger, in *New York Evening Post,* April 10, 1917

**3277.** One has the right to be wrong. — Claude Pepper, in *Reader's Digest,* December, 1987

# Rulers and Ruling

## See also Aristocracy; Despotism; Monarchy

**3278.** What millions died — that Caesar might be great! — Thomas Campbell, *Pleasures of Hope,* 1799

**3279.** So long as men worship the Caesars and Napoleons, Caesars and Napoleons will duly rise and make them miserable. — Aldous Huxley, *Ends and Means,* 1937

**3280.** Place in the hands of the King of Prussia the strongest possible military power, then he will be able to carry out the policy you wish; this policy cannot succeed through speeches, and shooting matches, and songs; it can only be carried out through blood and iron. — Otto von Bismarck, speech, January 28, 1886

**3281.** God must have loved the People in Power, for he made them so much like their own image of Him. — Kenneth Patchen, *Some Little Sayings and Observations,* 1956

**3282.** I am your anointed queen. I will never be by violence constrained to do anything. I thank God that I am endued with such qualities that if I were turned out of the realm in my petticoat, I were able to live in any place in Christome. — Elizabeth I, speech, November 5, 1566

**3283.** The king is truly *parens patriae,* the polite father of his people. — James I, speech, March 21, 1610

**3284.** I will make you shorter by the head. — Elizabeth I, in F. Chamberlain, *Sayings of Queen Elizabeth,* 1923

**3285.** I will govern according to the common weal, but not according to the common will. — James I, statement, December, 1621

**3286.** We are not amused. — Victoria, attributed

**3287.** *L'état c'est moi.* (I am the state.) — Louis XIV, remark to parliament, April 13, 1655

**3288.** When I want to know what France thinks, I ask myself. — Charles de Gaulle, in *Time,* December 17, 1965

**3289.** One had the sense that if [Charles de Gaulle] moved to a window, the center of gravity might shift, and the whole room might tilt everybody into the garden. — Henry Kissinger, in *Time,* October 15, 1979

**3290.** My people and I have come to an agreement which satisfies us both. They are to say what they please, and I am to do what I please. — Frederick the Great, attributed

**3291.** The state of monarchy is the supremest thing upon earth; for kings are not only God's lieutenants upon earth, and sit upon God's throne, but even by God himself they are called gods. — James I, speech, March 21, 1610

**3292.** Every noble crown is, and on earth will forever be, a crown of thorns. — Thomas Carlyle, *Past and Present,* 1843

**3293.** Uneasy lies the head that wears a crown. — William Shakespeare, *Henry IV, Part II,* 1597

**3294.** Let me tell you quite bluntly that this king business has given me personally nothing but headaches. — Mohammad Reza Pahlavi, in *New York Times,* September 25, 1967

**3295.** All my games were political games; I was, like Joan of Arc, perpetually being burned at the stake. — Indira Gandhi, in *New York Times,* November 5, 1971

**3296.** It is much safer to obey than to rule. — Thomas à Kempis, *De Imitatione Christo,* ca. 1427

**3297.** Kings are like stars — they rise and set, they have The worship of the world, but no repose. — Percy Bysshe Shelley, *Hellas,* 1821

**3298.** What is a King? — a man condemned to bear The public burden of the nation's care. — Matthew Prior, *Solomon,* 1718

**3299.** It is not by whining that one carries out the job of king. — Napoleon I, letter, August 13, 1809

**3300.** A prince who gets a reputation for good nature in the first year of his reign, is laughed at in the second. — Napoleon I, letter, April 4, 1807

**3301.** Every ruler is harsh whose rule is new. — Aeschylus, *Prometheus Bound,* ca. 490 B.C.

**3302.** The foremost art of kings is the power to endure hatred. — Seneca, *Hercules Furens,* ca. 50

**3303.** The prince is the first servant of the state. — Frederick the Great, *Memoirs of the House of Brandenburg,* 1758

**3304.** The good of subjects is the end of kings. — Daniel Defoe, *The True-Born Englishman,* 1701

**3305.** I have found it impossible to carry the heavy burden of responsibility and to discharge my duties as king as I would wish to do, without the help and support of the woman I love. — Edward VIII, radio broadcast, December 11, 1936

**3306.** History has taught me that rulers are much the same in all ages, and under all forms of government; that they are as bad as they dare to be. The vanity of ruin and the curse of blindness have clung to them like an hereditary leprosy. — Samuel Taylor Coleridge, letter, April, 1798

# Scandal *see* Gossip and Publicity

# Security

## *See also* Decisions; Future

**3307.** Since, in the main, it is not armaments that cause wars but wars (or the fears thereof) that cause armaments, it follows that every nation will at every moment strive to keep its armaments in an efficient state as required by its fear; otherwise styled security. — Salvador de Madariaga, *Morning Without Noon,* 1974

**3308.** For mere vengeance I would do nothing. This nation is too great to look for mere revenge. But for the security of the future I would do everything. — James A. Garfield, speech, April 15, 1865

**3309.** A councilor ought not to sleep the whole night through, a man to whom the populace is entrusted, and who has many responsibilities. — Homer, *The Iliad,* ca. 700 B.C.

**3310.** He that is too secure is not safe. — Thomas Fuller, M.D., *Gnomologia,* 1732

**3311.** We are not certain; we are never certain. If we were, we could reach some conclusions, and we could, at last,

make others take us seriously. — Albert Camus, *The Fall,* 1956

**3312.** The public...demands certainties.... But there are no certainties. — H. L. Mencken, *Prejudices, First Series,* 1919

**3313.** We live in a fantasy world, a world of illusion. The great task in life is to find reality. — Iris Murdoch, in *The Times,* April 15, 1983

**3314.** Security is when everything is settled, when nothing can happen to you; security is the denial of life. — Germaine Greer, *The Female Eunuch,* 1970

**3315.** Security is a kind of death. — Tennessee Williams, in *Esquire,* September, 1971

**3316.** The chains which men bear they have imposed upon themselves; strike them off, and they will weep for their lost security. — John Passmore, *The Perfectibility of Man,* 1970

---

# Slavery

## See also Freedom; Tyranny

**3317.** He who is by nature not his own but another's man, is by nature a slave. — Aristotle, *Politics,* 4th c. B.C.

**3318.** He loves his bonds, who when the first are broke, Submits his neck unto a second yoke. — Robert Herrick, "To Love," 1648

**3319.** Either be wholly slaves or wholly free. — John Dryden, *The Hind and the Panther,* 1687

**3320.** If you cannot be free, be as free as you can. — Ralph Waldo Emerson, *Journals,* 1836

**3321.** Fetters of gold are still fetters, and the softest lining can never make them so easy as liberty. — Mary Astell, *An Essay in Defense of the Female Sex,* 1696

**3322.** Lean liberty is better than fat slavery. — Thomas Fuller, M.D., *Gnomologia,* 1732

**3323.** Men would rather be starving

and free than fed in bonds. — Pearl S. Buck, *What America Means to Me,* 1943

**3324.** I believe that no people ever yet groaned under the heavy yoke of slavery but when they deserved it. — Samuel Adams, *Independent Advertiser,* 1748

**3325.** Free people, remember this: You may acquire liberty, but once lost it is never regained. — Jean-Jacques Rousseau, *The Social Contract,* 1762

**3326.** How is it that we hear the loudest yelps for liberty among the drivers of negroes? — Samuel Johnson, *Taxation No Tyranny,* 1775

**3327.** We fight not to enslave, but to set a country free, and to make room upon the earth for honest men to live in. — Thomas Paine, *The American Crisis,* 1776–83

**3328.** Freedom has a thousand charms to show That slaves, howe'er contented, never know. — William Cowper, *Table Talk,* 1782

**3329.** If you put a chain around the neck of a slave, the other end fastens itself around your own. — Ralph Waldo Emerson, *Essays: First Series,* "Compensation," 1841

**3330.** No man can put a chain about the ankle of his fellow man without at last finding the other end fastened about his own neck. — Frederick Douglass, speech, October 22, 1883

**3331.** Whenever I hear anyone arguing for slavery, I feel a strong impulse to see it tried on him personally. — Abraham Lincoln, speech, March 17, 1865

**3332.** He who desires in liberty anything other than itself is born to be a servant. — Alexis de Tocqueville, *The Old Regime,* 1856

**3333.** In giving freedom to the slave, we assure freedom to the free — honorable alike in what we give and what we preserve. We shall nobly save, or meanly lose, the last, best hope of earth. — Abraham Lincoln, message to Congress, December 1, 1862

**3334.** Where slavery is, there liberty cannot be; and where liberty is, there slavery cannot be. — Charles Sumner, speech, November 5, 1864

**3335.** There are many things more horrible than bloodshed; and slavery is one of them. — Padraic Pearse, *The Coming Revolution,* 1913

**3336.** When a prisoner sees the door of his dungeon open, he dashes for it without stopping to think where he shall get his dinner outside. — George Bernard Shaw, *Back to Methuselah,* 1921

**3337.** Slaves lose everything in their chains, even the desire of escaping from them. — Jean-Jacques Rousseau, *The Social Contract,* 1762

**3338.** It's often better to be in chains than to be free. — Franz Kafka, *The Trial,* 1925

**3339.** Man is born free, and everywhere he is in chains. — Jean-Jacques Rousseau, *The Social Contract,* 1762

**3340.** The moment the slave resolves that he will no longer be a slave, his fetters fall. He frees himself and shows the way to others. Freedom and slavery are mental states. — Mohandas K. Gandhi, *Non-Violence in Peace and War,* 1948

**3341.** For every man who lives without freedom, the rest of us must face the guilt. — Lillian Hellman, *Watch on the Rhine,* 1941

**3342.** None who have always been free can understand the terrible fascinating power of the hope of freedom to those who are not free. — Pearl S. Buck, *What America Means to Me,* 1943

**3343.** While it is true that an inherently free and scrupulous person may be destroyed, such an individual can never be enslaved or used as a blind tool. — Albert Einstein, *Impact,* 1950

**3344.** So efficient are the available instruments of slavery — fingerprints, lie detectors, brainwashing, gas chambers — that we shiver at the thought of political change which might put these instruments in the hands of men of hate. — Bernard Baruch, *A Philosophy for Our Time,* 1954

**3345.** Man alone can enslave man. — Simone Weil, *Oppression and Liberty,* 1958

**3346.** A man is either free or he is not. There cannot be any apprenticeship for freedom. — LeRoi Jones, in *Kulcher,* "Tokenism," Spring, 1962

**3347.** Freedom is indivisible, and when one man is enslaved, all are not free. — John F. Kennedy, speech, June 26, 1963

**3348.** In a consumer society there are inevitably two kinds of slaves: the prisoners of addiction and the prisoners of envy. — Ivan Illich, *Tools for Conviviality,* 1973

**3349.** Only free men can negotiate; prisoners cannot enter into contracts. — Nelson Mandela, in *Time,* February 25, 1985

**3350.** There is a grand deletion of our history as Americans, a gaping hole in our culture. Others came to drop their chains; we were issued chains on arrival. — Jesse Jackson, in *New York Times,* January 11, 1989

# Socialism

## See also Government, Forms of; Welfare

3351. Socialism can only arrive by bicycle. — José Antonio Viera Gallo, in Ivan Illich, *Energy and Equity,* 1974

3352. Socialism is the abolition of human self-alienation, the return of man as a real human being. — Erich Fromm, *Marx's Concept of Man,* 1961

3353. Without socialism, democracy tends to wither...but without democracy, socialism is impossible. — Irving Howe, *Essential Works of Socialism,* 1971

3354. The language of priorities is the religion of Socialism. — Aneurin Bevan, speech, June 8, 1949

3355. As with the Christian religion, the worst advertisement for Socialism is its adherents. — George Orwell, *The Road to Wigan Pier,* 1937

3356. Under capitalism man exploits man; under socialism the reverse is true. — Polish proverb

3357. Socialism is nothing but the capitalism of the lower classes. — Oswald Spengler, *The Hour of Decision,* 1934

3358. To the ordinary working man, the sort you would meet in any pub on Saturday night, Socialism does not mean much more than better wages and shorter hours and nobody bossing you about. — George Orwell, *The Road to Wigan Pier,* 1937

3359. You don't make the poor richer by making the rich poorer. — Winston S. Churchill, in *To the Point International,* November 1, 1976

3360. Current experience suggests that socialism is not a stage beyond capitalism but a substitute for it—a means by which the nations which did not share in the Industrial Revolution can imitate its technical achievements; a means to achieve rapid accumulation under a different set of rules of the game. — Joan Robinson, *Collected Economic Papers,* 1960

3361. Every reasonable human being should be a moderate Socialist. — Thomas Mann, in *New York Times,* June 18, 1950

3362. The typical Socialist is...a prim little man with a white-collar job, usually a secret teetotaller and often with vegetarian leanings. — George Orwell, *The Road to Wigan Pier,* 1937

# Speech

## See also Freedom of Speech; Gossip and Publicity; Language

3363. They tell me I say ill-natured things. I have a weak voice; if I did not say ill-natured things, no one would hear what I said. — Samuel Rogers, attributed

3364. Liberty doesn't work as good in practice as it does in Speech. — Will Rogers, *There's Not a Bathing Suit in Russia,* 1927

3365. A people's speech is the skin of its culture. — Max Lerner, *America as a Civilization,* 1957

3366. A prince should...be very careful that nothing ever escapes his lips which is not replete with...mercy, good faith, integrity, kindliness, and religion...because men...judge rather by the eye than by the hand, for all can see but few can touch. Everyone sees what you seem, but few know what you are. — Niccolò Machiavelli, *The Prince*, 1513

**3367.** It is generally better to deal by speech than by letter. — Francis Bacon, *Essays*, "Of Negotiating," 1625

**3368.** The true use of speech is not so much to express our wants as to conceal them. — Oliver Goldsmith, *The Bee*, 1759

**3369.** Persuasion is the resource of the feeble; and the feeble can seldom persuade. — Edward Gibbon, *Decline and Fall of the Roman Empire*, 1776–88

**3370.** The object of oratory alone is not truth, but persuasion. — Thomas Babington, in *Knight's Quarterly Magazine*, August, 1824

**3371.** He who wants to persuade should put his trust, not in the right argument, but in the right word. The power of sound has always been greater than the power of sense. — Joseph Conrad, *A Personal Record*, 1912

**3372.** Men of few words are the best men. — William Shakespeare, *Henry V*, 1599

**3373.** The world would be happier if men had the same capacity to be silent that they have to speak. — Baruch Spinoza, *Ethics*, 1677

**3374.** If a politician has a choice between listening and talking, guess which one he will choose. — James Abourezk, in *Playboy*, "Life Inside the Congressional Cookie Jar," March, 1979

**3375.** The most difficult thing of all, to keep quiet and listen. — Aulus Gellius, *Attic Nights*, ca. 150

**3376.** The most precious thing a man can lend is his ears. — Dagobert D. Runes, *Treasury of Thought*, 1966

**3377.** Friends, Romans, countrymen, lend me your ears. — William Shakespeare, *Julius Caesar*, 1599

**3378.** If a thing goes without saying, let it. — Jacob M. Braude, *Treasury of Wit and Humor*, 1964

**3379.** Speech is the small change of silence. — George Meredith, *The Ordeal of Richard Feverel*, 1859

**3380.** I regret often that I have spoken; never that I have been silent. — Publilius Syrus, *Sententiae*, ca. 43 B.C.

**3381.** One never repents of having spoken too little, but often of having spoken too much. — Philippe de Commynes, *Memoires*, 1524

**3382.** Monkeys... very sensibly refrain from speech, lest they should be set to earn their livings. — Kenneth Grahame, *The Golden Age*, 1895

**3383.** Amplification is the vice of the modern orator. Speeches measured by the hour die by the hour. — Thomas Jefferson, letter, April 20, 1824

**3384.** He that hath the worst cause makes the most noise. — Thomas Fuller, M.D., *Gnomologia*, 1732

**3385.** Continuous eloquence is tedious. — Blaise Pascal, *Pensées*, 1670

**3386.** Plenty of eloquence, but little wisdom. — Sallust, *The War with Catiline*, ca. 40 B.C.

**3387.** Eloquence may exist without a proportional degree of wisdom. — Edmund Burke, *Reflections on the Revolution in France*, 1790

**3388.** Many have been the wise speeches of fools, though not so many as the foolish speeches of wise men. — Thomas Fuller, D.D., *The Holy State and the Profane State*, 1642

**3389.** Be silent always when you doubt your sense. — Alexander Pope, *An Essay on Criticism*, 1711

**3390.** Sometimes you have to be silent to be heard. — Stanislaw Lec, *Unkempt Thoughts*, 1962

**3391.** Don't keep jingling in the course of your conversation any intellectual money you may have. — Joseph Farrell, *Lectures of a Certain Professor*, 1877

**3392.** The unluckiest insolvent in the world is the man whose expenditure of speech is too great for his income of ideas. — Christopher Morley, *Inward Ho!*, 1923

**3393.** Every man is born with the faculty of reason and the faculty of speech, but why should he be able to speak before he has anything to say? — Benjamin Whichcote, *Moral and Religious Aphorisms*, 1703

**3394.** We shall probably have nothing to say, but we intend to say it at great length. — Don Marquis, *The Almost Perfect State,* 1927

**3395.** Blessed is the man who, having nothing to say, abstains from giving in words evidence of the fact. — George Eliot, *Impressions of Theophrastus Such,* 1879

**3396.** He's a wonderful talker, who has the art of telling you nothing in a great harangue. — Molière, *Le Misanthrope,* 1666

**3397.** Let thy speech be short, comprehending much in few words. — Bible: Apocrypha, *Ecclesiasticus 32:8*

**3398.** I'll speak in a monstrous little voice. — William Shakespeare, *A Midsummer Night's Dream,* 1595

**3399.** Every man has the right to be heard; but no man has the right to strangle democracy with a single set of vocal cords. — Adlai Stevenson, speech, August 28, 1952

**3400.** Half the world is composed of people who have something to say and can't, and the other half who have nothing to say and keep on saying it. — Robert Frost, in *Kansas City Star,* July 14, 1977

**3401.** What is the short meaning of the long speech? — Friedrich von Schiller, *Die Piccolomini,* 1799

**3402.** Miss not the discourse of the elders. — Bible: Apocrypha, *Ecclesiasticus 8:9*

**3403.** A heavy and cautious responsibility of speech is the easiest thing in the world; anybody can do it. That is why so many tired, elderly, and wealthy men go in for politics. — Gilbert K. Chesterton, *All Things Considered,* "The Case for the Ephemeral," 1908

**3404.** Politicians' minds are rarely narrow but often flat.... Distrustful even of an audience of friends because he knows that every sentence from his mouth may be taken some day by itself and used to harm him, he is bound to the formula for dullness: accuracy and completeness about details and vagueness about general ideas. — Stimson Bullitt, *To Be a Politician,* 1977

**3405.** There is no such thing as a nonpolitical speech by a politician. — Richard M. Nixon, speech, September 14, 1955

**3406.** I think this is the most extraordinary collection of talent, of human knowledge, that has ever been gathered together at the White House — with the possible exception of when Thomas Jefferson dined alone. — John F. Kennedy, statement at a dinner for American Nobel Prize laureates, April 29, 1962

**3407.** One of the...greatest writers of political prose...Thomas Jefferson...was also easily the worst public speaker of his time, perhaps of any time. — D. W. Brogan, *The American Character,* 1944

**3408.** Hyperbole was to Lyndon Johnson what oxygen is to life. — Lance Morrow, in *New York Times,* April 3, 1966

# Spoils *see* Office

# *State*

## *See also* Government; Monarchy; Nationalism

**3409.** The state exists for the sake of a good life, and not for the sake of life only. — Aristotle, *Politics,* 4th c. B.C.

**3410.** Our ship of state, which recent storms have threatened to destroy, has come safely to harbor at last. — Sophocles, *Antigone,* ca. 442 B.C.

**3411.** In the youth of a state arms

do flourish; in the middle age of a state, learning; and then both of them together for a time; in the declining age of a state, mechanical arts and merchandise. — Francis Bacon, *Essays*, "Of Vicissitude of Things," 1625

**3412.** States, like men, have their growth, their manhood, their decrepitude, their decay. — Walter Savage Landor, *Imaginary Conversations*, "Leonora di Este and Panigarola," 1824–53

**3413.** The nations which have put mankind and posterity most in their debt have been small states — Israel, Athens, Florence, Elizabethan England. — William Ralph Inge, *Outspoken Essays: Second Series*, "States, Visible and Invisible," 1922

**3414.** Because he is a sociable creature, man would form a state even if he foresaw no advantage beyond the knitting together of human relations.... The state is a community that makes possible a better, fuller life than could be attained without it. — M. Judd Harmon, *Political Thought*, 1964

**3415.** Man owes his entire existence to the state, and has his being within it alone. Whatever worth and spiritual reality he possesses are his solely by virtue of the state. — Georg Wilhelm Friedrich Hegel, *Lectures on the Philosophy of World History: Introduction*, 1830

**3416.** Any state is better than none at all. — M. Judd Harmon, *Political Thought*, 1964

**3417.** While the state exists there is no freedom; when there is freedom there will be no state. — Lenin, *The State and Revolution*, 1917

**3418.** Where the State begins, individual liberty ceases, and vice versa. — Michael Bakunin, *Federalism, Socialism and Anti-Theologism*, 1868

**3419.** A democracy is a state which recognizes the subjection of the minority to the majority, that is, an organization for the systematic use of violence by one class against the other, by one part of the population against another. — Lenin, *The State and Revolution*, 1917

**3420.** A state which dwarfs its men, in order that they may be more docile instruments in its hands even for beneficial purposes, will find that with small men no great things can really be accomplished. — John Stuart Mill, *On Liberty*, 1859

**3421.** I saw that the State was half-witted, that it was timid as a lone woman with her silver spoons, and that it did not know its friends from its foes, and I lost all my remaining respect for it, and pitied it. — Henry David Thoreau, *Civil Disobedience*, 1849

**3422.** Where the state is weak, the army rules. — Napoleon I, remark, January 9, 1808

**3423.** When the State intervenes to insure the indoctrination of some doctrine, it does so because there is no conclusive evidence in favor of that doctrine. — Bertrand Russell, *Sceptical Essays*, 1928

**3424.** Democracy is but one form of *state*, and we Marxists are opposed to *all* and every *kind* of state. — Lenin, *The Task of the Proletariat*, 1917

**3425.** The State is not "abolished," it *withers away*. — Friedrich Engels, *Anti-Duhring*, 1878

**3426.** States do not prosper through ideology. — Napoleon I, letter, April 24, 1805

**3427.** A nation may be said to consist of its territory, its people, and its laws. The territory is the only part which is of certain durability. — Abraham Lincoln, message to Congress, December 1, 1862

**3428.** No man has a right to fix the boundary of the march of a nation; no man has a right to say to his country — thus far shalt thou go and no further. — Charles S. Parnell, speech, January 21, 1885

**3429.** Every State must conquer or be conquered. — Michael Bakunin, *Federalism, Socialism and Anti-Theologism*, 1868

**3430.** Each State can have for enemies only other States, and not men; for between things disparate in nature there can be no real relation. — Jean-Jacques Rousseau, *The Social Contract*, 1762

3431. A state worthy of the name has no friends—only interests. —Charles de Gaulle, in *Newsweek,* October 1, 1962

# Taxes

## *See also* Budgets; Economics

3432. Render therefore unto Caesar things which are Caesar's; and unto God the things that are God's. —Bible, *Matthew 22:21*

3433. In this world nothing can be said to be certain, except death and taxes. —Benjamin Franklin, letter, November 13, 1789

3434. Man is not like other animals in the ways that are really significant: animals have instincts, we have taxes. —Erving Goffman, in *New York Times,* February 12, 1969

3435. Taxes, after all, are the dues that we pay for the privileges of membership in an organized society. —Franklin D. Roosevelt, speech, October 21, 1936

3436. The wisdom of man never yet contrived a system of taxation that would operate with perfect equality. —Andrew Jackson, "Proclamation to the People of South Carolina," December 10, 1832

3437. To tax and to please, no more than to love and to be wise, is not given to men. —Edmund Burke, *On American Taxation,* 1775

3438. It was as true...as taxes is. And nothing's truer than them. —Charles Dickens, *David Copperfield,* 1850

3439. Taxation without representation is tyranny. —James Otis, statement, ca. 1761

3440. Taxation and representation are inseparable...whatever is a man's own, is absolutely his own; no man hath a right to take it from him without his consent either expressed by himself or representative. —Charles Pratt, speech, February 10, 1766

3441. An old tax is a good tax. —Political maxim

3442. *Excise.* A hateful tax levied upon commodities. —Samuel Johnson, *A Dictionary of the English Language,* 1755

3443. The power to tax involves the power to destroy. —John Marshall, statement, 1819

3444. There is no art which one government sooner learns of another than that of draining money from the pockets of the people. —Adam Smith, *Wealth of Nations, Vol. V,* 1776

3445. The art of taxation consists in so plucking the goose as to obtain the largest possible amount of feathers with the smallest possible amount of hissing. —Jean Baptiste Colbert, in *Time,* April 17, 1978

3446. Riches are for spending. —Francis Bacon, *Essays,* "Of Expense," 1625

3447. Government expands to absorb revenue and then some. —Tom Wicker, in *New York Times Magazine,* March 17, 1968

3448. There's no getting blood out of a turnip. —Frederick Marryat, *Japhet, in Search of a Father,* 1836

3449. A minister of finance is a legally authorized pickpocket. —Paul Ramadier, in *Quote,* October 7, 1956

3450. The current tax code is a daily mugging. —Ronald Reagan, speech, September 2, 1985

3451. Neither will it be, that a people overlaid with taxes should ever become valiant and martial. —Francis Bacon, *Essays,* "Of the True Greatness of Kingdoms," 1625

3452. The heart of the supply-side synthesis rested on the notion of "push-pull" economic dynamic. Hard money policies would "pull down" the rate of inflation and nominal GNP growth. The tax cut and whole range of supply-side economic policy would "push up" the rate of real output and employment expansion. —David A. Stockman, *The Triumph of Politics,* 1987

**3453.** These unhappy times call for the building of plans that. . . build from the bottom up and not from the top down, that put their faith once more in the forgotten man at the bottom of the economic pyramid. — Franklin D. Roosevelt, radio address, April 7, 1932

**3454.** When everybody has got money they cut taxes, and when they're broke them raise 'em. That's statesmanship of the highest order. —Will Rogers, *The Autobiography of Will Rogers,* 1949

**3455.** [A tax loophole is] some-thing that benefits the other guy. If it benefits you, it is tax reform. —Russell B. Long, in *Time,* November 10, 1986

**3456.** Even Albert Einstein reportedly needed help on his 1040 form. —Ronald Reagan, speech, May 28, 1985

**3457.** The Income Tax has made more Liars out of the American people than golf has. —Will Rogers, *The Illiterate Digest,* 1924

**3458.** The king's cheese is half wasted in parings; but no matter, 'tis made of the people's milk. —Benjamin Franklin, *Poor Richard's Almanac,* 1733–58

**3459.** I see it is impossible for the King to have things done as cheap as other men. —Samuel Pepys, *Diary,* July 21, 1662

# Theory

## See also Belief; Thought

**3460.** The theory of our modern technic shows that nothing is as practical as theory. —J. Robert Oppenheimer, in *Reflex,* July, 1927

**3461.** One good head is better than a hundred strong hands. — Thomas Fuller, M.D., *Gnomologia,* 1732

**3462.** People prefer theory to practice because it involves them in no more real responsibility than a game of checkers, while it permits them to feel they're doing something serious and important. — Leo Stein, *Journey Into the Self,* 1950

**3463.** No one can be a great thinker who does not recognize that as a thinker, it is his first duty to follow his intellect to whatever conclusions it may lead. —John Stuart Mill, *On Liberty,* 1859

**3464.** One of the functions of intelligence is to take account of the dangers that come from trusting solely to the intelligence. — Lewis Mumford, *The Transformation of Man,* 1956

**3465.** As a rule we disbelieve all facts and theories for which we have no use. —William James, *The Will to Believe,* 1897

**3466.** An attack upon systematic thought is treason to civilization. — Alfred North Whitehead, *Adventures of Ideas,* 1933

**3467.** To become a popular religion, it is only necessary for a superstition to enslave a philosophy. —William Ralph Inge, lecture, May 27, 1920

**3468.** Freedom of thought is the only guarantee against an infection of people by mass myths, which, in the hands of treacherous hypocrites and demagogues, can be transformed into bloody dictatorships. — Andrei Dmitrievich Sakharov, *Progress, Coexistence, and Intellectual Freedom,* 1968

**3469.** As often as a study is cultivated by narrow minds, they will draw from it narrow conclusions. —John Stuart Mill, *Auguste Comte and Positivism,* 1865

**3470.** An honest man can never

surrender an honest doubt. — Walter Malone, *The Agnostic's Creed*, 1886

**3471.** No great improvements in the lot of mankind are possible, until a great change takes place in the fundamental constitution of their modes of thought. — John Stuart Mill, *Autobiography*, 1873

**3472.** Without a revolutionary theory there can be no revolutionary movement. — Lenin, "What Is to Be Done?," 1902

**3473.** The cold metal of economic theory is in Marx's pages immersed in such a wealth of streaming phrases as to acquire a temperature not naturally its own. — Joseph A. Schumpeter, *Capitalism, Socialism and Democracy*, 1942

**3474.** To a great extent the validity of a political theory is relative to the circumstances in which it is formulated. — M. Judd Harmon, *Political Thought*, 1964

**3475.** General propositions are seldom mentioned in the huts of Indians: much less are they to be found in the thoughts of children. — John Locke, *An Essay concerning Human Understanding*, 1690

**3476.** Amid the pressure of great events, a general principle gives no help. — Georg Wilhelm Friedrich Hegel, *Philosophy of History*, 1832

**3477.** It is not with the words and explanations of theory that nations are governed. — Napoleon I, letter, January 9, 1810

**3478.** The general will rules in society as the private will governs each separate individual. — Maximilien Robespierre, *Lettres à ses commenttans*, January 5, 1793

**3479.** From the standpoint of the employee, it is coming to make less and less practical difference to him what his country's official ideology is and whether he happens to be employed by a government or commercial corporation. — Arnold J. Toynbee, in *Harvard Business Review*, September/October, 1958

**3480.** It is a far, far better thing to have a firm anchor in nonsense than to put out on the troubled sea of thought. — John Kenneth Galbraith, *The Affluent Society*, 1958

**3481.** Often a liberal antidote of experience supplies a sovereign cure for a paralyzing abstraction built upon a theory. — Benjamin N. Cardozo, *The Paradoxes of Legal Science*, 1928

**3482.** Most men think dramatically, not quantitatively. — Oliver Wendell Holmes Jr., *Speeches*, "Law and the Courts," 1913

**3483.** A principal problem for a theory of democratic systems is: Under what conditions can a society have sufficient participation to maintain the democratic system without introducing sources of cleavage which will undermine the cohesion? — Seymour Martin Lipset, *Political Man*, 1981

**3484.** The only interesting answers are those which destroy the questions. — Susan Sontag, in *Esquire*, July, 1968

**3485.** Like all weak men, he laid an exaggerated stress on not changing one's mind. — W. Somerset Maugham, *Of Human Bondage*, 1915

**3486.** It is more important that a proposition be interesting than that it be true. — Alfred North Whitehead, *Adventures of Ideas*, 1933

**3487.** The great tragedy of Science — the slaying of a beautiful hypothesis by an ugly fact. — T. H. Huxley, *Collected Essays*, "Biogenesis and Abiogenesis," 1895

---

# *Thought*

## See also **Knowledge; Language; Theory; Truth; Wisdom**

**3488.** Except our own thoughts, there is nothing absolutely in our power. — René Descartes, *Discourse on the Method*, 1637

**3489.** It takes a nonentity to think of everything. — Honoré de Balzac, *Pierre Grassou,* 1839

**3490.** To think correctly is a condition of behaving well. It is also in itself a moral act; those who would think correctly must resist considerable temptations. — Aldous Huxley, *The Olive Tree,* "Words and Behavior," 1937

**3491.** May God prevent us from becoming "right-thinking men" — that is to say men who agree perfectly with their own police. — Thomas Merton, in *New York Times,* December 11, 1968

**3492.** The last taboo of mankind, avoiding forbidden and dangerous thoughts, must be removed. There are no illegitimate thoughts. — Theodor Reik, *The Need to Be Loved,* 1963

**3493.** We must dare to think about "unthinkable things" because when things become "unthinkable," thinking stops and action becomes mindless. — J. William Fulbright, speech, March 26, 1964

**3494.** Don't you see that the whole aim of Newspeak is to narrow the range of thought? In the end we shall make thoughtcrime literally impossible, because there will be no words in which to express it. — George Orwell, *1984,* 1949

**3495.** When we all think alike, no one is thinking. — Walter Lippmann, in *Poughkeepsie Journal,* March 26, 1978

**3496.** Although the proportion of those who *do* think be extremely small, yet every individual flatters himself that he is *one* of the number. — Charles Caleb Colton, *Lacon,* 1820–22

**3497.** Mediocre minds usually dismiss anything which reaches beyond their own understanding. — François de La Rochefoucauld, *Maxims,* 1665

**3498.** He can't think without his hat. — Samuel Beckett, *Waiting for Godot,* 1955

**3499.** Our life is what our thoughts make it. — Marcus Aurelius Antoninus, *Meditations,* 2nd c.

**3500.** The stream of thinking is only a careless name for what, when scrutinized, reveals itself to consist chiefly of the stream of my breathing.

— William James, *Essays in Radical Empiricism,* 1912

**3501.** The number of those who undergo the fatigue of judging for themselves is very small indeed. — Richard Brinsley Sheridan, *The Critic,* 1779

**3502.** Practice and thought might gradually forge many an art. — Virgil, *Georgics I,* ca. 30 B.C.

**3503.** Orthodoxy means not thinking — not needing to think. Orthodoxy is unconsciousness. — George Orwell, *1984,* 1949

**3504.** A king can stand people's fighting, but he can't last long if people start thinking. — Will Rogers, *The Autobiography of Will Rogers,* 1949

**3505.** But this is slavery, not to speak one's thoughts. — Euripides, *The Phoenician Woman,* 411–409 B.C.

**3506.** This then is the final triumph of thought — that it disintegrates all societies, and at last destroys the thinker himself. — Will Durant, *On the Meaning of Life,* 1932

**3507.** Let no man imagine that he has no influence. Whoever he may be, and wherever he may be placed, *the man who thinks* becomes a light and a power. — Henry George, *Social Problems,* 1884

**3508.** The only real security for social well-being is the free exercise of men's minds. — Harold J. Laski, *Authority in the Modern State,* 1919

**3509.** Every real thought on every real subject knocks the wind out of somebody or other. — Oliver Wendell Holmes Sr., *The Autocrat of the Breakfast-Table,* 1858

**3510.** A chief event of life is the day in which we have encountered a mind that startles us. — Ralph Waldo Emerson, *Essays: Second Series,* "Character," 1844

**3511.** To think hard and persistently is painful. — Louis D. Brandeis, *Business — A Profession,* 1914

**3512.** It is love of candor that makes men radical thinkers. — Eric Bentley, *Thirty Years of Treason,* 1971

**3513.** The only means of strengthening one's intellect is to make up one's mind about nothing — to let the mind be a thoroughfare for all thoughts. Not a select party. — John Keats, letter, September 17, 1819

**3514.** There is no state of mind, however simple, which does not change every moment. — Henri Bergson, *Introduction to Metaphysics*, 1903

**3515.** The mind of man is like a clock that is always running down and requires to be as constantly wound up. — William Hazlitt, *Sketches and Essays*, 1839

**3516.** No truth so sublime but it may be trivial tomorrow in the light of new thoughts. — Ralph Waldo Emerson, *Essays, First Series*, "Circles," 1841

**3517.** "The true," to put it briefly, is only the expedient in the way of our thinking, just as "the right" is only the expedient in the way of our behaving. — William James, *Pragmatism*, 1907

**3518.** I am a fellow citizen of all men who think. Truth; that is my country. — Alphonse de Lamartine, *Marseillaise de la Paix*, 1841

**3519.** Only the mind cannot be sent into exile. — Ovid, *Expistulae ex Ponto*, ca. 5

**3520.** Liberty of thought is the life of the soul. — Voltaire, *Essay on Epic Poetry*, 1727

**3521.** There are two good things in life — freedom of thought and freedom of action. — W. Somerset Maugham, *Of Human Bondage*, 1915

**3522.** To think is not enough; you must think of something. — Jules Renard, *Journal*, 1899

**3523.** Think of yourself as you wish others to think of you. — Dagobert D. Runes, *Treasury of Thought*, 1966

**3524.** Stupidity is no excuse for not thinking. — Stanislaw Lec, *Unkempt Thoughts*, 1962

**3525.** We haven't got the money, so we've got to think! — Ernest Rutherford, in *Bulletin of the Institute of Physics*, 1962

**3526.** Wit is a happy and striking way of expressing a thought. — William Penn, *Some Fruits of Solitude*, 1693

## *Tolerance*

### *See also* Extremism

**3527.** Tolerance always has limits — it cannot tolerate what is itself actively intolerant. — Sidney Hook, *Pragmatism and the Tragic Sense of Life*, 1975

**3528.** The only true spirit of tolerance consists in our conscientious toleration of each other's intolerance. — Samuel Taylor Coleridge, *The Friend*, 1809

**3529.** The degree of tolerance attainable at any moment depends on the strain under which society is maintaining its cohesion. — George Bernard Shaw, *Saint Joan*, 1924

**3530.** Laws alone cannot secure freedom of expression; in order that every man present his views without penalty there must be a spirit of tolerance in the entire population. — Albert Einstein, *Out of My Later Years*, 1950

**3531.** I could never divide myself from any man upon the difference of an opinion, or be angry with his judgment for not agreeing with me in that from which, perhaps within a few days I should dissent myself. — Thomas Browne, *Religio Medici*, 1643

**3532.** The peak of tolerance is most readily achieved by those who are not burdened with convictions. — Alexander Chase, *Perspectives*, 1966

**3533.** In every age of transition men are never so firmly bound to one way of life as when they are about to abandon it, so that fanaticism and intolerance reach their most intense forms just before tolerance and mutual acceptance come to be the natural order of things. — Bernard Levin, *The Pendulum Years,* 1970

**3534.** If tolerance of diversity involves an admitted element of risk to national unity, intolerance involves a certainty that unity will be destroyed. — Alan Barth, *The Loyalty of Free Men,* 1951

**3535.** Commandment No. 1 of any truly civilized society is this: Let people be different. — David Grayson, *The Countryman's Year,* 1936

**3536.** If we cannot end now our differences, at least we can help make the world safe for diversity. — John F. Kennedy, speech, June 10, 1963

**3537.** If a man be gracious and courteous to strangers, it shows he is a citizen of the world. — Francis Bacon, *Essays,* "Of Goodness, and Goodness in Nature," 1625

**3538.** I've always felt that a person's intelligence is directly reflected by the number of conflicting points of view he can entertain simultaneously on the same topic. — Lisa Alther, *Kinflicks,* 1977

**3539.** The highest result of education is tolerance. — Helen Keller, *Optimism,* 1903

**3540.** Understanding a person does not mean condoning; it only means that one does not accuse him as if we were God or a judge placed above him. — Erich Fromm, *Man for Himself,* 1947

**3541.** There is no room in this country for hyphenated Americanism.... The one absolutely certain way of bringing this nation to ruin, of preventing all possibility of its continuing to be a nation at all, would be to permit it to become a tangle of squabbling nationalities. — Theodore Roosevelt, speech, October 12, 1915

**3542.** What is objectionable, what is dangerous about extremists is not that they are extreme, but that they are intolerant. The evil is not what they say about their cause, but what they say about their opponents. — Robert F. Kennedy, *The Pursuit of Justice,* "Extremism, Left and Right," 1964

**3543.** I have seen gross intolerance shown in support of toleration. — Samuel Taylor Coleridge, *Biographia Literaria,* 1817

**3544.** Toleration is not the *opposite* of intoleration, but is the *counterfeit* of it. Both are despotisms. The one assumes to itself the right of withholding liberty of conscience, and the other of granting it. — Thomas Paine, *The Rights of Man,* 1791

**3545.** If Jesus Christ were to come today, people would not even crucify him. They would ask him to dinner, and hear what he had to say, and make fun of it. — Thomas Carlyle, in D. A. Wilson, *Carlyle at His Zenith,* 1927

---

# Tradition

## See also Future; History

**3546.** A great statesman is he who knows when to depart from traditions, as well as when to adhere to them. — John Stuart Mill, *Representative Government,* 1861

**3547.** People will not look forward to posterity, who never look backward to their ancestors. — Edmund Burke, *Reflections on the Revolution in France,* 1790

**3548.** Great nations write their autobiographies in three manuscripts — the book of their deeds, the book of their words, and the book of their arts. — John Ruskin, *St. Mark's Rest,* 1877

**3549.** Originality and genius must be largely fed and raised on the shoulders of some old tradition. — George Santayana, *The Life of Reason,* 1905–06

**3550.** Tradition is a guide and not a jailer. — W. Somerset Maugham, *The Summing Up*, 1938

**3551.** The past is at least secure. — Daniel Webster, speech, January 26, 1830

**3552.** The past is only the present become invisible and mute; and because it is invisible and mute, its memorized glances and its murmurs are infinitely precious. We are tomorrow's past. — Mary Webb, *Precious Bane*, 1924

**3553.** Imagination continually frustrates tradition; that is its function. — John Pfeiffer, in *New York Times*, March 29, 1979

**3554.** The endeavor to keep alive any hoary establishment beyond its natural date is often pernicious and always useless. — Mary Wollstonecraft, *The French Revolution*, 1794

**3555.** Why doesn't the past decently bury itself, instead of sitting waiting to be admired by the present? — D. H. Lawrence, *St. Mawr*, 1925

**3556.** Into the dustbin of history! — Leon Trotsky, *The Russian Revolution*, 1933

**3557.** A government is not legitimate merely because it exists. — Jeane J. Kirkpatrick, in *Time*, June 17, 1985

**3558.** Nations, like men, have their infancy. — Henry St. John, *On the Study of History*, 1809

**3559.** Even a god cannot change the past. — Aristotle, *Nicomachean Ethics*, 4th c. B.C.

**3560.** We cannot reform our forefathers. — George Eliot, *Adam Bede*, 1859

**3561.** When man has wiped the slate clean and tries to write his own message, the past which lives in him and has moulded him will bring back the very things he has tried to obliterate. — Lewis Namier, *Avenues of History*, 1952

**3562.** I am sure that the mistakes of that time will not be repeated; we shall probably make another set of mistakes. — Winston S. Churchill, speech, June 8, 1944

**3563.** The past is a foreign country: they do things differently there. — L. P. Hartley, *The Go-Between*, 1953

**3564.** What is amusing now had to be taken in desperate earnest once. — Virginia Woolf, *A Room of One's Own*, 1929

**3565.** Don't talk to me about naval tradition. It's nothing but rum, sodomy, and the lash. — Winston S. Churchill, in Peter Gretton, *Former Naval Person*, 1968

**3566.** Tradition means giving votes to the most obscure of all classes, our ancestors. It is the democracy of the dead. — Gilbert K. Chesterton, *Orthodoxy*, 1908

# Trust

## See also Office

**3567.** I repeat . . . that all power is a trust; that we are accountable for its exercise; that, from the people, and for the people, all springs, and all must exist. — Benjamin Disraeli, *Vivian Grey*, 1826

**3568.** The basis of effective government is public confidence. — John F. Kennedy, message to Congress, April 27, 1961

**3569.** A man who trusts nobody is apt to be the kind of man nobody trusts. — Harold Macmillan, in *New York Herald Tribune*, December 17, 1963

**3570.** We have to distrust each other. It's our only defense against betrayal. — Tennessee Williams, *Camino Real*, 1953

**3571.** I wonder men dare trust themselves with men. — William Shakespeare, *Timon of Athens*, 1607

3572. My opinion is, that power should always be distrusted, in whatever hands it is placed. — William Jones, letter, October 5, 1782

3573. *Doverey no proverey.* (Trust but verify.) — Russian proverb

3574. Put your trust in God, my boys, and keep your powder dry. — Valentine Blacker, in E. Hayes, *Ballads of Ireland,* 1856

3575. Distrust all in whom the impulse to punish is powerful. — Friedrich Wilhelm Nietzsche, *Thus Spake Zarathustra,* 1883–92

3576. Beware of the man who will not engage in idle conversation; he is planning to steal your walking stick or water your stock. — William Emerson, in *Newsweek,* October 29, 1973

# ———— *Truth* ————

## *See also* Facts; Justice; Knowledge; Lies; Opinion; Reason; Thought

3577. If you ever injected truth into politics you have no politics. — Will Rogers, *The Autobiography of Will Rogers,* 1949

3578. The river of truth is always splitting up into arms which reunite. Islanded between them the inhabitants argue for a lifetime as to which is the mainstream. — Cyril Connolly, *The Unquiet Grave,* 1944

3579. As scarce as truth is, the supply has always been in excess of the demand. — Josh Billings, in *Rocky Mountain News,* June 5, 1980

3580. It takes two to speak the truth — one to speak and another to hear. — Henry David Thoreau, *A Week on the Concord and Merrimack Rivers,* "Wednesday," 1849

3581. The truth that makes men free is for the most part the truth which men prefer not to hear. — Herbert Agar, *A Time for Greatness,* 1942

3582. The truth is generally seen, rarely heard. — Balthasar Gracián, *The Art of Worldly Wisdom,* 1647

3583. Truth is tough. It will not break, like a bubble, at a touch; nay, you may kick it about all day, like a football, and it will be round and full at evening. — Oliver Wendell Holmes Sr., *The Professor at the Breakfast-Table,* 1860

3584. Truth generally lies in the coordination of antagonistic opinions. — Herbert Spencer, *Autobiography,* 1904

3585. A truth does not become greater by frequent repetition. — Maimonides, *Tehiyat Hamethim,* "Responsa," ca. 1200

3586. A platitude is simply a truth repeated until people get tired of hearing it. — Stanley Baldwin, speech, May 29, 1924

3587. Whenever truth stands in the mind unaccompanied by the evidence upon which it depends, it cannot properly be said to be apprehended at all. — William Godwin, *An Enquiry concerning Political Justice,* 1793

3588. Irrationally held truths may be more harmful than reasoned errors. — T. H. Huxley, *Science and Culture and Other Essays,* "The Coming of Age of the Origin of Species," 1881

3589. The truth is often a terrible weapon of aggression. It is possible to lie, and even to murder, for the truth. — Alfred Adler, *The Problems of Neurosis,* 1929

3590. Crooked things may be as stiff and unflexible as straight: and men may be as positive in error as in truth. — John Locke, *An Essay concerning Human Understanding,* 1690

3591. But it is not enough to possess a truth; it is essential that the truth possess us. — Maurice Maeterlinck, *The Treasure of the Humble,* "The Deeper Life," 1896

**3592.** Absolute truth is incompatible with an advanced state of society. — Joaquim Maria Machado de Assiz, *Epitaph of a Small Winner,* 1881

**3593.** It is error alone which needs the support of government. Truth can stand by itself. — Thomas Jefferson, *Notes on the State of Virginia,* 1781–85

**3594.** The spirit of truth and the spirit of freedom — they are the pillars of society. — Henrik Ibsen, *Pillars of Society,* 1877

**3595.** The truth is found when men are free to pursue it. — Franklin D. Roosevelt, speech, February 22, 1936

**3596.** Chase after truth like all hell and you'll free yourself, even though you never touch its coat-tails. — Clarence Darrow, *Voltaire,* 1916

**3597.** If we want truth, every man ought to be free to say what he thinks without fear. If the advocates of one side are to be rewarded with miters, and the advocates on the other with rope or stake, truth will not be heard. — Desiderius Erasmus, letter, December 6, 1520

**3598.** Crushing truths perish by being acknowledged. — Albert Camus, *The Myth of Sisyphus,* 1955

**3599.** The truth may be one, final, determined, but my apprehension of it can never be anything of the kind; it is changing continuously. — Bede Jarrett, *Meditations for Layfolk,* 1915

**3600.** There are no whole truths; all truths are half-truths. It is trying to treat them as whole truths that plays the devil. — Alfred North Whitehead, *Dialogues,* 1954

**3601.** All truth is equilibrated. Pushing any truth out very far, you are met by a counter-truth. — Henry Ward Beecher, *Proverbs from Plymouth Pulpit,* 1887

**3602.** Nobody speaks the truth when there's something they must have. — Elizabeth Bowen, *The House in Paris,* 1935

**3603.** No man thoroughly understands a truth until he has contended against it. — Ralph Waldo Emerson, *Essays: First Series,* "Compensation," 1841

**3604.** Truth has rough flavors if we bite through. — George Eliot, *Armgart,* 1871

**3605.** The truth sticks in our throats with all the sauces it is served with: it will never go down until we take it without any sauce at all. — George Bernard Shaw, *Saint Joan,* 1924

**3606.** Follow not truth too near the heels, lest it dash out thy teeth. — George Herbert, *Jacula Prudentum,* 1651

**3607.** The truth is cruel, but it can be loved, and it makes free those who have loved it. — George Santayana, *Little Essays,* 1920

**3608.** I speak truth not so much as I would, but as much as I dare, and I dare a little more as I grow older. — Michel Eyquem de Montaigne, *Essays,* 1580

**3609.** The first reaction to truth is hatred. — Tertullian, *Apologeticus,* ca. 197

**3610.** Intense feeling too often obscures the truth. — Harry S Truman, speech, October 19, 1948

**3611.** All great truths begin as blasphemies. — George Bernard Shaw, *Annajanska,* 1917

**3612.** Heresies are experiments in man's unsatisfied search for truth. — H. G. Wells, *Crux Ansata,* 1944

**3613.** It is the customary fate of new truths to begin as heresies and to end as superstitions. — T. H. Huxley, *Science and Culture and Other Essays,* "The Coming of Age of the Origin of Species," 1881

**3614.** What late was Truth, now turn'd to Heresie. — Michael Drayton, *Legends,* 1596

**3615.** Truth always lags last, limping along on the arm of Time. — Balthasar Gracián, *The Art of Worldly Wisdom,* 1647

**3616.** There are no new truths, but only truths that have not been recognized by those who have perceived them without noticing. — Mary McCarthy, *On the Contrary,* 1961

**3617.** Speak your truth quietly and clearly; and listen to others, even the dull and ignorant; they too have their story. — Max Ehrmann, *Desiderata*, 1927

**3618.** Truth is the cry of all, but the game of the few. — George Berkeley, *Siris*, 1744

**3619.** Truth, sir, is a profound sea, and few there be that dare wade deep enough to find out the bottom on't. — George Farquhar, *The Beaux' Stratagem*, 1707

**3620.** God offers to every mind a choice between truth and repose. Take which you please — you can never have both. — Ralph Waldo Emerson, *Essays: First Series,* "Intellect," 1841

**3621.** The great obstacle to truth is the common man's lethargic reluctance to make a thorough house-cleaning of his mind. — Dagobert D. Runes, *Treasury of Thought,* 1966

**3622.** The cause of truth counts not the number of adherents. — Samson Raphael Hirsch, *Nineteen Letters,* 1836

**3623.** Truth hath a quiet breast. — William Shakespeare, *Richard II,* 1595

**3624.** The essential thing is not to find truth but to investigate and search for it. — Max Nordau, *Paradoxes,* 1885

**3625.** Truth is the most valuable thing we have. Let us economize it. — Mark Twain, *Following the Equator,* 1897

# Tyranny

## See also Despotism; Freedom; Majority and Minority; Power; Revolution; Slavery

**3626.** Duke Ting [d. 495 B.C.] said, Is there any one phrase that could ruin a country? Master K'ung [Confucius] said... here is one that comes near to it. There is a saying among men: "What pleasure is there in being a prince, unless one can say whatever one chooses, and no one dares to disagree?" — Confucius, *The Analects of Confucius,* 1938

**3627.** All men would be tyrants if they could. — Daniel Defoe, *The Kentish Petition,* 1712–13

**3628.** Destiny, *n.* A tyrant's authority to crime and a fool's excuse for failure. — Ambrose Bierce, *The Devil's Dictionary,* 1906

**3629.** Any excuse will serve a tyrant. — Aesop, *Fables,* "The Wolf and the Lamb," ca. 550 B.C.

**3630.** Tyrants seldom want pretexts. — Edmund Burke, *Letter to a Member of the National Assembly,* 1791

**3631.** To be a great autocrat you must be a great barbarian. — Joseph Conrad, *The Mirror of the Sea,* 1906

**3632.** I shall be an autocrat: that's my trade. And the good Lord will forgive me: that's his. — Catherine the Great, attributed

**3633.** O, it is excellent To have a giant's strength; but it is tyrannous To use it like a giant. — William Shakespeare, *Measure for Measure,* 1604

**3634.** As soon as the prince sets himself up above the law, he loses the king in the tyrant; he does to all intents and purpose unking himself. — Jonathan Mayhew, *A Discourse concerning Unlimited Submission and Non-Resistance to the Higher Powers,* 1750

**3635.** Wherever Law ends, Tyranny begins. — John Locke, *Second Treatise of Government,* 1690

**3636.** If a sovereign oppresses his people to a great degree, they will rise and cut off his head. There is a remedy in human nature against tyranny, that will keep us safe under every form of government. — Samuel Johnson, in James Boswell, *Life of Samuel Johnson,* 1791

**3637.** The only legitimate right to govern is an express grant of power from the governed. — William Henry Harrison, inaugural address, March 4, 1841

**3638.** "The consent of the governed" is more than a safeguard against ignorant tyrants: it is an insurance against benevolent despots as well. — Walter Lippmann, *A Preface to Politics,* 1914

**3639.** It is not easy for a person to do any great harm when his tenure of office is short, whereas long possession begets tyranny. — Aristotle, *Politics,* 4th c. B.C.

**3640.** Make men large and strong, and tyranny will bankrupt itself in making shackles for them. — Henry Ward Beecher, *Proverbs from Plymouth Pulpit,* 1887

**3641.** In a healthy nation there is a kind of dramatic balance between the will of the people and the government, which prevents its degeneration into tyranny. — Albert Einstein, *Out of My Later Years,* 1950

**3642.** Enlighten the people generally, and tyranny and oppression of body and mind will vanish like evil spirits at the dawn of day. — Thomas Jefferson, letter, April 24, 1816

**3643.** Tyrants never perish from tyranny, but always from folly. — Walter Savage Landor, *Imaginary Conversations,* 1824–53

**3644.** Tyrants have not yet discovered any chains that can fetter the mind. — Charles Caleb Colton, *Lacon,* 1820–22

**3645.** I have sworn upon the altar of God, eternal hostility against every form of tyranny over the mind of man. — Thomas Jefferson, letter, September 23, 1800

**3646.** God Himself has no right to be a tyrant. — William Godwin, *Sketches of History,* 1784

**3647.** What I find most repulsive in America is not the extreme freedom reigning there, but the shortage of guarantees against tyranny. — Alexis de Tocqueville, *Democracy in America,* 1835

**3648.** None can love freedom but good men; the rest love not freedom but

license, which never hath more scope than under tyrants. — John Milton, *Tenure of Kings and Magistrates,* 1649

**3649.** The more a regime claims to be the embodiment of liberty the more tyrannical it is likely to be. — Ian Gilmour, *Inside Right,* 1977

**3650.** If the world knew how to use freedom without abusing it, tyranny would not exist. — Tehyi Hsieh, *Chinese Epigrams Inside Out and Proverbs,* 1948

**3651.** Kings will be tyrants from policy, when subjects are rebels from principle. — Edmund Burke, *Reflections on the Revolution in France,* 1790

**3652.** Whoever puts his hand on me to govern me is a usurper and a tyrant; I declare him my enemy. — Pierre Joseph Proudhon, *Confessions of a Revolutionary,* 1849

**3653.** Every successful revolution puts on in time the robe of the tyrant it has deposed. — Barbara W. Tuchman, attributed

**3654.** They that are discontented under *monarchy,* call it *tyranny;* and they that are displeased with *aristocracy,* call it *oligarchy:* so also, they which find themselves grieved under a *democracy,* call it *anarchy,* which signifies the want of government; and yet I think no man believes, that want of government, is any new kind of government. — Thomas Hobbes, *Leviathan,* 1651

**3655.** Revolutions have never lightened the burden of tyranny; they have only shifted it to another shoulder. — George Bernard Shaw, *Man and Superman,* 1903

**3656.** It is this — the "positive" conception of liberty: not freedom from, but freedom to — which the adherents of the "negative" notion represent as being, at times, no better than a specious disguise for brutal tyranny. — Isaiah Berlin, *Two Concepts of Liberty,* 1958

**3657.** Whoever has power in his hands wants to be despotic; the craze for domination is an incurable disease. — Voltaire, letter, October 16, 1765

**3658.** They who study mankind with a whip in their hands will always go wrong. — Frederick Douglass, speech, August 1, 1860

**3659.** People tolerate those they fear further than those they love. — Edgar Watson Howe, *Country Town Sayings,* 1911

**3660.** If you have but a single ruler, you lie at the discretion of a master who has no reason to love you; and if you have several, you must bear at once their tyranny and their divisions. — Jean-Jacques Rousseau, *A Discourse on Political Economy,* 1758

**3661.** The freest form of government is only the least objectionable form. The rule of the many by the few we call tyranny: the rule of the few by the many is tyranny also; only of a less intense kind. — Herbert Spencer, *Social Statics, Part II,* 1851

**3662.** The tyrant grinds down his slaves and they don't turn against him; they crush those beneath them. — Emily Brontë, *Wuthering Heights,* 1847

**3663.** Tyrants are but the spawn of Ignorance, Begotten by the slaves they trample on. — James Russell Lowell, "Prometheus," 1843

**3664.** Of all the tyrannies of humankind, The worst is that which persecutes the mind. — John Dryden, *The Hind and the Panther,* 1687

**3665.** The most tyrannical governments are those which make crimes of opinions, for everyone has an unalienable right to his thoughts. — Baruch Spinoza, *Tractatus Theologicus-Politicus,* 1670

**3666.** Death is better, a milder fate than tyranny. — Aeschylus, *Agememnon,* ca. 458 B.C.

**3667.** The face of tyranny Is always mild at first. — Jean Racine, *Britannicus,* 1669

**3668.** A tyrant. . . is always stirring up some war or other, in order that the people may require a leader. — Plato, *The Republic,* ca. 370 B.C.

**3669.** For how can tyrants safely govern home, Unless abroad they purchase great alliance? — William Shakespeare, *Henry VI, Part III,* 1592

**3670.** No one can terrorize a whole nation, unless we are all his accomplices. — Edward R. Murrow, broadcast, March 7, 1954

**3671.** When a nation has allowed itself to fall under a tyrannical regime, it cannot be absolved from the faults due to the guilt of that regime. — Winston S. Churchill, message, July 28, 1944

**3672.** I suspect that in our loathing of totalitarianism, there is infused a good deal of admiration for its efficiency. — T. S. Eliot, "The Idea of a Christian Society," 1939

**3673.** Tyranny is always better organized than freedom. — Charles Péguy, *Basic Verities,* 1943

**3674.** Tyranny is a habit; it may develop, and it does develop at last, into a disease. — Fyodor Dostoyevski, *The House of the Dead,* 1862

**3675.** It has been discovered that the best way to insure implicit obedience is to commence tyranny in the nursery. — Benjamin Disraeli, speech, June 15, 1874

**3676.** The more complex the despotism, the more smoothly all things move on the surface. — Elizabeth Cady Stanton, *History of Woman Suffrage,* 1881

# U.S. Presidency

## See also Leaders; Leadership; Office

**3677.** Presidency, *n.* The greased pig in the field game of American politics. — Ambrose Bierce, *The Devil's Dictionary,* 1906

**3678.** There is something behind the throne greater than the King himself. — William Pitt (I), speech, March 2, 1770

**3679.** All Presidents grow in office.

—Earl Schenck Miers, in *Saturday Review*, August 29, 1959

**3680.** The presidency has made every man who occupied it, no matter how small, bigger than he was; and no matter how big, not big enough for its demands. — Lyndon B. Johnson, in *New York Times*, March 26, 1972

**3681.** In America any boy may become president and I suppose it's just one of the risks he takes. — Adlai Stevenson, speech, September 26, 1952

**3682.** Becoming president is an utterly personal business between the man who offers himself as national leader and the Americans who judge him. — Theodore H. White, *The Making of the President 1960*, 1961

**3683.** What makes a great President is the ability to take certain actions the public might not agree with, and still maintain their trust. — Frank Donatelli, in *New York Times*, January 18, 1989

**3684.** Most of the problems a President has to face have their roots in the past. — Harry S Truman, *Memoirs*, 1955

**3685.** I think the president is the only person who can change the direction or attitude of our nation. — Jimmy Carter, in *Encore America & Worldwide News*, June 21, 1976

**3686.** It isn't wisdom or intelligence that influences a president, it's opportunity. — Bill Moyers, in *Newsweek*, April 17, 1978

**3687.** A President either is constantly on top of events or, if he hesitates, events will soon be on top of him. I never felt that I could let up for a single moment. — Harry S Truman, *Memoirs*, 1955

**3688.** It is the duty of the President to propose and it is the privilege of the Congress to dispose. — Franklin D. Roosevelt, press conference, July 23, 1937

**3689.** The President cannot, with success, constantly appeal to the country. After a time he will get no response. — Calvin Coolidge, *Autobiography*, 1929

**3690.** I think the presidency is an institution over which you have temporary custody. — Ronald Reagan, in *Time*, April 7, 1986

**3691.** The presidency has many problems, but boredom is the least of them. — Richard M. Nixon, interview, January 9, 1973

**3692.** All the President is, is a glorified public relations man who spends his time flattering, kissing and kicking people to get them to do what they are supposed to do anyway. — Harry S Truman, letter, November 14, 1947

**3693.** We have exchanged the Washingtonian dignity for the Jeffersonian simplicity, which was, in truth, only another name for the Jacksonian vulgarity. — Henry C. Potter, *Bishop Potter's Address*, 1890

**3694.** The Presidency hovers over the popular American imagination almost as a sacerdotal office, a priestly role for which normal political standards are invalid. — Theodore H. White, *The Making of the President 1960*, 1961

**3695.** When a president does it, then it is not illegal. — Richard M. Nixon, on CBS television, May 19, 1977

**3696.** While the people retain their virtue and vigilance, no administration, by any extreme of wickedness or folly, can very seriously injure the government in the short space of four years. — Abraham Lincoln, inaugural address, March 4, 1861

**3697.** The American people are not going to elect a seventy-year-old, right wing, ex–movie actor to be president. — Hamilton Jordan, statement, 1980

**3698.** There have been five Aquarian presidents, the most famous being Lincoln, F.D.R. and Reagan. All three were formidable communicators. — Joan Quigley, *What Does Joan Say,* 1990

**3699.** My own view is that taping of conversations for historical purposes was a bad decision on the part of all the presidents. I don't think Kennedy should have done it. I don't think Johnson should have done it. And I don't think we should have done it. — Richard M. Nixon, in *New York Times*, March 16, 1974

**3700.** By the time a man gets to be Presidential material he's been bought ten times over. — Gore Vidal, in *Newsweek*, November 18, 1974

**3701.** Great men are not chosen (as American) presidents, firstly, because great men are rare in politics; secondly, because the method of choice does not bring them to the top; thirdly, because they are not, in quiet times, absolutely needed. — James Bryce, "Why Great Men Are Not Chosen Presidents," 1888

**3702.** No candidate for the Presidency ought ever to remain in the Cabinet. He is an unsafe advisor. — James K. Polk, *Diary*, February 21, 1848

**3703.** All I have I would have given gladly not to be standing here today. — Lyndon B. Johnson, speech, November 27, 1963

**3704.** Frankly, I don't mind not being president. I just mind that someone else is. — Edward M. Kennedy, speech, March 22, 1986

**3705.** How do they know? — Dorothy Parker, responding to news of the death of Calvin Coolidge, in Malcolm Cowley, *Writers at Work*, 1958

**3706.** Well, I have one consolation — no candidate was ever elected expresident by such a large majority. — William H. Taft, statement, 1912

**3707.** If I'd known how much packing I'd have to do, I'd have run again. — Harry S Truman, in *Time*, January 26, 1953

**3708.** If you are as happy, my dear sir, on entering this house as I am in leaving it and returning home, you are the happiest man in this country. — James Buchanan, remark to Abraham Lincoln upon leaving the White House, March, 1861

**3709.** Oh, that lovely title, expresident. — Dwight D. Eisenhower, in *New York Post*, October 26, 1959

**3710.** The vice-presidency isn't worth a pitcher of warm piss. — John Nance Garner, in O. C. Fisher, *Cactus Jack*, 1978

# Violence

## See also Conflict; Force; War

**3711.** Power and violence are opposites; where the one rules absolutely, the other is absent. — Hannah Arendt, *Crisis of the Republic*, 1972

**3712.** Many of our own cities and towns are mini–Sarajevos every night of the week. We cannot offer hope and succor to the rest of the world if we cannot bring hope and relief to our own crime-ridden streets. — H. Ross Perot, *United We Stand*, 1992

**3713.** I say violence is necessary. It is as American as cherry pie. — H. Rap Brown, speech, July 27, 1967

**3714.** The urge for destruction is also a creative urge! — Michael Bakunin, *Yearbook for Knowledge and Skill*, 1842

**3715.** In violence, we forget who we are. — Mary McCarthy, *On the Contrary*, 1961

**3716.** Every normal man must be tempted at times, to spit on his hands, hoist the black flag, and begin slitting throats. — H. L. Mencken, *Prejudices, First Series*, 1919

**3717.** Keep violence in the mind Where it belongs. — Brian Aldiss, *Barefoot in the Head*, 1969

**3718.** He who would be free must strike the first blow. — Frederick Douglass, *My Bondage and My Freedom*, 1855

**3719.** Assassination is the extreme form of censorship. — George Bernard Shaw, *The Showing Up of Blanco Posnet*, "The Rejected Statement," 1911

**3720.** Assassination is the quickest way. — Molière, *Le Sicilien*, 1668

**3721.** History is a bath of blood. — William James, *Memories and Studies*, 1911

3722. If you look closely at most of the ideas expressed with violence, you begin to see that, once you've scraped away the terminology, you're usually left with the worst platitudes. — Françoise Giroud, *I Give You My Word,* 1974

3723. Kill a man, and you are an assassin. Kill millions of men, and you are a conqueror. Kill everyone, and you are a god. — Jean Rostand, *Thoughts of a Biologist,* 1939

3724. He knew that the essence of war is violence, and that moderation in war is imbecility. — Thomas Babington, *Essays Contributed to the Edinburgh Review,* 1843

3725. So long as governments set the example of killing their enemies, private individuals will occasionally kill theirs. — Elbert Hubbard, *Contemplations,* 1902

3726. The highest and ultimate instrument of political power is capital punishment. — Philip Melanchthon, *Philosophiae Moralis Epitomes,* ca. 1530

3727. The State calls its own violence law, but that of the individual crime. — Max Stirner, *The Ego and His Own,* 1845

3728. Government is an association of men who do violence against the rest of us. — Leo Tolstoy, *The Kingdom of God Is Within You,* 1893

3729. Thou wilt show my head to the people: it is worth showing. — Georges Jacques Danton, statement to his executioner, April 5, 1794

3730. Fascism is not defined by the number of its victims, but by the way it kills them. — Jean-Paul Sartre, remark, June 22, 1953

3731. Fascism is Capitalism plus Murder. — Upton Sinclair, *Singing Jailbirds,* 1924

# Virtue and Vice

## See also Character; Corruption; Ends and Means; Justice; Morality

3732. The greatest art of a politician is to render vice serviceable to the cause of virtue. — Henry St. John, comment (ca. 1728), in Joseph Spence, *Observations, Anecdotes, and Characters,* 1820

3733. The just man having a firm grasp of his intentions, neither the heated passions of his fellow man ordaining something awful, nor a tyrant staring him in the face, will shake him in his convictions. — Horace, *Odes,* 1st c. B.C.

3734. Anyone entrusted with power will abuse it if not also animated with the love of truth and virtue, no matter whether he be a prince, or one of the people. — Jean de La Fontaine, *Fables,* 1668

3735. If men were angels, no government would be necessary. — James Madison, *The Federalist,* 1788

3736. The world is the best of all possible worlds, and everything in it is a necessary evil. — F. H. Bradley, *Appearance and Reality,* 1893

3737. Few men have virtue to withstand the highest bidder. — George Washington, letter, August 17, 1779

3738. Eminence without merit earns deference without esteem. — Sébastien Roch Nicholas Chamfort, *Maximes et pensées,* 1805

3739. A good man would prefer to be defeated than to defeat injustice by evil means. — Sallust, *Jugurthine War,* ca. 41 B.C.

3740. To do a great right, do a little wrong. — William Shakespeare, *The Merchant of Venice,* 1596–97

3741. Life — the way it really is — is a battle not between Bad and Good, but between Bad and Worse. — Joseph Brodsky, in *New York Times,* October 1, 1972

3742. There are people who are virtuous only in a piece-meal way; virtue is a fabric from which they never make themselves a whole garment. — Joseph Joubert, *Pensées*, 1810

3743. My meaning in saying he is a good man is to have you understand me that he is sufficient. — William Shakespeare, *The Merchant of Venice*, 1596–97

3744. The way of truth is like a great road. It is not difficult to know; the evil is only that men will not seek it. — Mencius, *Discourses*, ca. 300 B.C.

3745. Liberty can no more exist without virtue and independence, than the body can live and move without a soul. — John Adams, in *Boston Gazette*, February 6, 1775

3746. If men were born free, they would, so long as they remained free, form no conception of good or evil. — Baruch Spinoza, *Ethics*, 1677

3747. Liberty does not always have clean hands. — André Malraux, speech, November 12, 1966

3748. Liberty, next to religion, has been the motive of good deeds and the common pretext of crime. — John E. E. Dalberg, speech, February 26, 1877

3749. Wickedness is the root of despotism as virtue is the essence of the Republic. — Maximilien Robespierre, statement, May 7, 1794

3750. Every vice you destroy has a corresponding virtue, which perishes along with it. — Anatole France, *The Garden of Epicurus*, 1894

3751. Our virtues are most often but our vices disguised. — François de La Rochefoucauld, *Maxims*, 1665

3752. Successful and fortunate crime is called virtue. — Seneca, *Hercules Furens*, 1st c.

3753. The virtues of society are vices of the saint. — Ralph Waldo Emerson, *Essays: First Series*, "Circles," 1841

3754. Curse on his virtues! they've undone his country. Such popular humanity is treason. — Joseph Addison, *Cato*, 1713

3755. Every political good carried to the extreme must be productive of evil. — Mary Wollstonecraft, *The French Revolution*, 1794

3756. Power gradually extirpates from the mind every human and gentle virtue. Pity, benevolence, friendship, are things almost unknown in high stations. — Edmund Burke, *A Vindication of Natural Society*, 1756

3757. The highest virtue is always against the law. — Ralph Waldo Emerson, *The Conduct of Life*, "Worship," 1860

3758. Men never forgive those in whom there is nothing to pardon. — Edward Bulwer-Lytton, *Weeds and Wild Flowers*, 1826

3759. Virtue is not always amiable. — John Adams, diary, February 9, 1779

3760. I prefer an accommodating vice to an obstinate virtue. — Molière, *Amphitryon*, 1666

3761. No good deed will go unpunished. — Walter Annenberg, *Poughkeepsie Journal*, March 26, 1978

3762. The chief cause of our misery is less the violence of our passions than the feebleness of our virtues. — Joseph Roux, *Meditations of a Parish Priest*, 1886

3763. The difference between a good man and a bad one is the choice of the cause. — William James, letter, December 24, 1895

3764. Power tends to confuse itself with virtue and a great nation is peculiarly susceptible to the idea that its power is a sign of God's favor. — J. William Fulbright, speech, April 21, 1966

3765. The prince of darkness is a gentleman. — William Shakespeare, *King Lear*, 1605–06

3766. The devil, depend on it, can sometimes do a very gentlemanly thing. — Robert Louis Stevenson, *New Arabian Nights*, 1882

3767. He preaches well who lives well. — Miguel de Cervantes, *Don Quixote*, 1615

3768. Honor is like a match: you can only use it once. — Marcel Pagnol, *Marius*, 1946

3769. Thou strong seducer, opportunity! — John Dryden, *The Conquest of Granada*, 1670

3770. Temptation is not always invitation. — Oliver Wendell Holmes Jr., *Erie Railroad v. Hilt,* 1917

3771. The only thing necessary for the triumph of evil is for good men to do nothing. — Edmund Burke, attributed

3772. People are beginning to see that the first requisite to success in life is to be a good animal. — Herbert Spencer, *Education,* 1861

3773. A man has generally the good or ill qualities which he attributes to mankind. — William Shenstone, *Essays on Men and Manners,* 1764

3774. Virtue can only flourish amongst equals. — Mary Wollstonecraft, *A Vindication of the Rights of Men,* 1790

3775. Men imagine that they communicate their virtue or vice only by overt action, and do not see that virtue or vice emit a breath every moment. — Ralph Waldo Emerson, *Essays: First Series,* "Self-Reliance," 1841

3776. The purest treasure mortal times afford Is spotless reputation. — William Shakespeare, *Richard II,* 1595

3777. Silver and gold are not the only coin; virtue too passes current all over the world. — Euripides, *Oedipus,* 5th c. B.C.

# Voting and Elections

## See also Campaigns

3778. The right of election is the very essence of the constitution. — Junius, in *Public Advertiser,* April 24, 1769

3779. Where the annual elections end, there slavery begins. — John Adams, *Thoughts on Government,* 1776

3780. One man shall have one vote. — John Cartwright, *The People's Barrier Against Undue Influence,* 1780

3781. The vote is the most powerful instrument ever devised by man for breaking down injustice and destroying the terrible walls which imprison men because they are different from other men. — Lyndon B. Johnson, speech, August 6, 1965

3782. At the bottom of all the tributes paid to democracy is the little man, walking into the little booth, with a little pencil, making a little cross on a little bit of paper — no amount of rhetoric or voluminous discussion can possibly diminish the overwhelming importance of the point. — Winston S. Churchill, speech, October 31, 1944

3783. Voting is a civic sacrament. — Theodore M. Hesburgh, in *Reader's Digest,* October, 1984

3784. A man without a vote is in this land like a man without a hand. — Henry Ward Beecher, *Proverbs from Plymouth Pulpit,* 1887

3785. Voting is simply a way of determining which side is the stronger without putting it to the test of fighting. — H. L. Mencken, *Minority Report,* 1956

3786. Ballots are the rightful and peaceful successors to bullets. — Abraham Lincoln, message to Congress, July 7, 1861

3787. The more frequent the changes of Government, the more numerous are the bright ideas; and the more frequent the elections, the more benevolent they become. — Winston S. Churchill, *Maxims and Reflections,* 1947

3788. A group will have a higher rate of voting if (1) its interests are strongly affected by government policies; (2) it has access to information about the relevance of political decisions to its interests; (3) it is exposed to social pressures demanding voting; (4) it is not pressed to vote for different political parties. — Seymour Martin Lipset, *Political Man,* 1981

3789. Those who stay away from the election think that one vote will do no good: 'Tis but one step more to think one vote will do no harm. — Ralph Waldo Emerson, *Journals*, 1854

**3790.** The apathy of the modern voter is the confusion of the modern reformer. — Learned Hand, speech, March 8, 1932

**3791.** Nobody will ever deprive the American people of the right to vote except the American people themselves — and the only way they could do that is by not voting. — Franklin D. Roosevelt, radio address, October 5, 1944

**3792.** Bad politicians are sent to Washington by good people who don't vote. — William E. Simon, in *A Guide to the 99th Congress*, 1985

**3793.** It is possible that nonvoting is now, at least in the Western democracies, a reflection of the stability of the system, a response to the decline of major social conflicts, and an increase in cross-pressures, particularly those affecting the working class. — Seymour Martin Lipset, *Political Man*, 1981

**3794.** A person may be driven by shame to vote but not to inform himself or to take part in other ways. And where some informed votes are cast abstention does less harm than uninformed voters. — Stimson Bullitt, *To Be a Politician*, 1977

**3795.** The ignorance of one voter in a democracy impairs the security of all. — John F. Kennedy, speech, May 18, 1963

**3796.** Fifty per cent of [people] won't vote, and fifty per cent don't read newspapers. I hope it's the same fifty per cent. — Gore Vidal, in *Emmy*, May / June, 1991

**3797.** When the political columnists say "Every thinking man" they mean themselves, and when candidates appeal to "Every intelligent voter" they mean everybody who is going to vote for them. — Franklin P. Adams, *Nods and Becks*, 1944

**3798.** No amount of charters, direct primaries, or short ballots will make a democracy out of an illiterate people. — Walter Lippmann, *A Preface to Politics*, 1914

**3799.** When the vote is low, this almost always means that the socially and economically disadvantaged groups are underrepresented in government. — Seymour Martin Lipset, *Political Man*, 1981

**3800.** A whore's vote is just as good as a debutante's. — Sam Rayburn, in *D Magazine*, June, 1979

**3801.** Give the vote to the people who have no property, and they will sell them to the rich, who will be able to buy them. — Gouverneur Morris, speech, August 7, 1787

**3802.** Don't buy a single vote more than necessary. I'll be damned if I'm going to pay for a landslide. — Joseph P. Kennedy, attributed by John F. Kennedy, March 15, 1958

**3803.** A straw vote only shows which way the hot air blows. — O. Henry, *Rolling Stones*, "A Ruler of Men," 1913

**3804.** More men have been elected between sundown and sunup than ever were elected between sunup and sundown. — Will Rogers, *The Illiterate Digest*, 1924

**3805.** "Vote early and vote often" is the politishun's golden rule. — Josh Billings, *Josh Billings' Wit and Humor*, 1874

**3806.** As long as I count the votes what are you going to do about it? — William Marcy ("Boss") Tweed, remark during New York City election, 1871

**3807.** It's not the voting that's democracy, it's the counting. — Tom Stoppard, *Jumpers*, 1972

**3808.** Votes should be weighed, not counted. The State must sooner or later be wrecked where the majority rules and ignorance decides. — Friedrich von Schiller, *Demetrius*, 1798

**3809.** Elected officials are totally frightened of "none of the above." It's a powerful tool. Can you believe how insulting it is to be beaten by "none of the above"? — Ralph Nader, in *USA Today*, December 2, 1991

**3810.** Elections are won by men and women chiefly because most people vote against somebody, rather than for somebody. — Franklin P. Adams, *Nods and Becks*, 1944

3811. Hell, I never vote *for* anybody. I always vote *against*. — W. C. Fields, in Robert Lewis Taylor, *W. C. Fields*, 1950

3812. We'd all like t'vote fer th' best man, but he's never a candidate. — Frank McKinney Hubbard, *The Best of Kin Hubbard*, 1984

3813. Vote for the man who promises least; he'll be the least disappointing. — Bernard Baruch, in Meyer Berger, *New York*, 1960

3814. An election is a bet on the future, not a popularity test of the past. — James Reston, in *New York Times*, October 10, 1984

3815. An election is a moral horror, as bad as a battle except for the blood: a mud bath for every soul concerned in it. — George Bernard Shaw, *Back to Methuselah*, 1921

3816. Except in one-party states, general elections for important offices tend to be statistically close. The majority often does not exceed the scientific opinion polls' margin of error, so that there is yet no certain way to foretell the result. Until the moment of truth, a candidate does not know whether he is the bullfighter or the bull. — Stimson Bullitt, *To Be a Politician*, 1977

3817. Researches on historical variations in the voting behavior of American states may be summed up in the epigram "As your state goes, so goes the nation," and are demonstrations of the basic cohesion of American society. — Seymour Martin Lipset, *Political Man*, 1981

3818. No subject is more intensely discussed in the privacy of any campaign headquarters, either state or national, than the ethnic origins of the American people and their bloc-voting habits. — Theodore H. White, *The Making of the President 1960*, 1961

3819. Voters don't decide issues, they decide who will decide issues. — George Will, in *Newsweek*, March 8, 1976

3820. I've suggested we have an interactive "Electronic Town Hall" so that as a nation we can lay out the issues... and reach a consensus. — H. Ross Perot, *United We Stand*, 1992

3821. If it is true...that the existence of many parties accentuates differences and reduces consensus, then any electoral system which increases the chance for more rather than fewer parties serves democracy badly. — Seymour Martin Lipset, *Political Man*, 1981

3822. One of the evils of democracy is, you have to put up with the man you elect whether you want him or not. — Will Rogers, *The Autobiography of Will Rogers*, 1949

3823. The voters are the people who have spoken — the bastards. — Morris K. Udall, in *Chicago Sun-Times*, July 14, 1976

---

# *War*

## *See also* Diplomacy; Enemies; International Relations; Peace; Winners and Losers

3824. War cannot for a single minute be separated from politics. — Mao Zedong, lecture, 1938

3825. Probably the battle of Waterloo was won on the playing-fields of Eton, but the opening battles of all subsequent wars have been lost there. — George Orwell, *The Lion and the Unicorn*, 1941

3826. War is the trade of kings. — John Dryden, *King Arthur*, 1691

3827. Aggression unopposed becomes a contagious disease. — Jimmy Carter, speech, January 4, 1980

**3828.** In More's *Utopia* the people waged war for three purposes: to defend their own territory when invaded, to deliver the territory of an ally from invaders, and to free an oppressed nation from tyranny. — Stimson Bullitt, *To Be a Politician,* 1977

**3829.** War is a blessing compared with national degradation. — Andrew Jackson, letter, May 2, 1845

**3830.** If we heed the teachings of history, we shall not forget that in the life of every nation emergencies may arise when a resort to arms can alone save it from dishonor. — Chester A. Arthur, message to Congress, December 6, 1881

**3831.** War is too serious a matter to entrust to military men. — Georges Clemenceau, attributed

**3832.** I have never met anyone who wasn't against war. Even Hitler and Mussolini were, according to themselves. — David Low, in *New York Times Magazine,* February 10, 1946

**3833.** I have seen war...I hate war. — Franklin D. Roosevelt, speech, August 14, 1936

**3834.** War always finds a way. — Bertolt Brecht, *Mutter Courage,* 1939

**3835.** All wars are planned by old men In council rooms apart. — Grantland Rice, "The Two Sides of War," 1955

**3836.** Older men declare war. But it is youth who must fight and die. — Herbert Hoover, speech, June 27, 1944

**3837.** A bayonet is a weapon with a worker at each end. — Anonymous, 1940

**3838.** A man may build himself a throne of bayonets, but he cannot sit on it. — William Ralph Inge, *Philosophy of Plotinus,* 1923

**3839.** War is a game in which princes seldom win, the people never. — Charles Caleb Colton, *Lacon,* 1820–22

**3840.** When the rich wage war, it's the poor who die. — Jean-Paul Sartre, *The Devil and the Good Lord,* 1951

**3841.** There is many a boy here today who looks on war as all glory, but, boys, it is all hell. — William Sherman, speech, August 11, 1880

**3842.** Never in the field of human conflict was so much owed by so many to so few. — Winston S. Churchill, speech [speaking of England's debt to the Royal Air Force for its victory over the Luftwaffe], August 20, 1940

**3843.** Two armies fighting each other are one great army in the act of suicide. — Henri Barbusse, *Under Fire: The Story of a Squad,* 1917

**3844.** We hear war called murder. It is not: it is suicide. — Ramsey MacDonald, in *Observer,* May 4, 1930

**3845.** In war, whichever side may call itself the victor, there are no winners, but all are losers. — Neville Chamberlain, speech, July 3, 1938

**3846.** Accurst be he that first invented war. — Christopher Marlowe, *Tamburlaine the Great,* 1590

**3847.** It is well that war is so terrible, or we should grow too fond of it. — Robert E. Lee, statement, December, 1862

**3848.** All delays are dangerous in war. — John Dryden, *Tyrannic Love,* 1669

**3849.** The quickest way of ending a war is to lose it. — George Orwell, *Polemic,* May, 1946

**3850.** In politics, it seems, retreat is honorable if dictated by military considerations and shameful if even suggested for ethical reasons. — Mary McCarthy, *Vietnam,* 1967

**3851.** War is, after all, the universal perversion...war stories, the pornography of war. — John Rae, *The Custard Boys,* 1960

**3852.** As you know, God is usually on the side of the big squadrons against the small. — Roger de Bussy-Rabutin, letter, October 18, 1677

**3853.** God is on the side not of the heavy battalions, but of the best shots. — Voltaire, "The Piccini Notebooks," ca. 1750

**3854.** The sinews of war, unlimited money. — Cicero, *Philippic,* 1st c. B.C.

**3855.** We can manage without butter but not, for example, without guns. If we are attacked we can only defend ourselves with guns, not with butter. — Joseph Goebbels, speech, January 17, 1936

**3856.** One should always have one's boots on, and be ready to leave. —Michel Eyquem de Montaigne, *Essays,* 1580

**3857.** In war there is no second prize for the runner-up. —Omar Bradley, in *Military Review,* February, 1950

**3858.** What is our aim?...Victory, victory, at all costs, victory in spite of all terror; victory, however long and hard the road may be; for without victory, there is no survival. —Winston S. Churchill, speech, May 13, 1940

**3859.** The War That Will End War. —H. G. Wells, book title, 1914

**3860.** At eleven o'clock this morning came to an end the cruelest and most terrible war that has ever scourged mankind. I hope we may say that thus, this fateful morning, came to an end all wars. —David Lloyd George, speech, November 11, 1918

**3861.** History is littered with the wars which everybody knew would never happen. —Enoch Powell, speech, October 19, 1967

**3862.** After each war there is a little less democracy to save. —Brooks Atkinson, *Once Around the Sun,* "January 7," 1951

**3863.** We are in an armed conflict; that is the phrase I have used. There has been no declaration of war. —Anthony Eden, speech, November 1, 1956

**3864.** The mother of battles. —Saddam Hussein, speech, January 6, 1991

**3865.** Today, a generation raised in the shadows of the Cold War assumes new responsibilities in a world warmed by the sunshine of freedom but threatened still by ancient hatreds and new plagues. —Bill Clinton, inaugural address, January 20, 1993

**3866.** The mood is that of Jihad: war not as an instrument of policy but as an emblem of identity, an expression of community, an end in itself. Even where there is no shooting war, there is fractiousness, secession, and the quest for ever smaller communities. —Benjamin R. Barber, in *Atlantic,* "Jihad vs. McWorld," March, 1992

# Welfare

## See also Poverty

**3867.** It is a reproach to religion and government to suffer so much poverty and excess. —William Penn, *Some Fruits of Solitude,* 1693

**3868.** Government is a continuance of human wisdom to provide for human wants. —Edmund Burke, *Reflections on the Revolution in France,* 1790

**3869.** Social prosperity means men happy, the citizen free, the nation great. —Victor Hugo, *Les Misérables,* 1862

**3870.** The object of government is the welfare of the people. The material progress and prosperity of a nation are desirable chiefly as far as they lead to the moral and material welfare of all good citizens. —Theodore Roosevelt, *The New Nationalism,* 1910

**3871.** Would you rather have butter or guns?...[P]reparedness makes us powerful. Butter merely makes us fat. —Hermann Goering, speech, 1936

**3872.** The health of the people is really the foundation upon which all their happiness and all their power as a state depend. —Benjamin Disraeli, speech, July 24, 1877

**3873.** There is no finer investment for any community than putting milk into babies. —Winston S. Churchill, radio broadcast, March 21, 1943

**3874.** Anyone who has ever struggled with poverty knows how extremely expensive it is to be poor. —James Baldwin, *Nobody Knows My Name,* "Notes for a Hypothetical Novel," 1961

3875. If a free society cannot help the many who are poor, it cannot save the few who are rich. —John F. Kennedy, inaugural address, January 20, 1961

3876. A compassionate government keeps faith with the trust of the people, and cherishes the future of their children. —Lyndon B. Johnson, *My Hope for America,* 1964

3877. The living need charity more than the dead. —George Arnold, "The Jolly Old Pedagogue," 1866

3878. The poor don't know that their function in life is to exercise our generosity. —Jean-Paul Sartre, *The Words,* 1964

3879. We have the opportunity to move not only toward the rich society and the powerful society, but upward to the Great Society. —Lyndon B. Johnson, speech, May 22, 1964

3880. The most melancholy of human reflections, perhaps, is that on the whole, it is a question whether the benevolence of mankind does most good or harm. —Walter Bagehot, *Physics and Politics,* 1869

3881. No people do so much harm as those who go about doing good. —Mandell Creighton, *Life,* 1904

3882. Welfare is hated by those who administer it, mistrusted by those who pay for it and held in contempt by those who receive it. —Peter C. Goldmark Jr., in *New York Times,* May 24, 1977

3883. And having looked to the Government for bread, on the very first scarcity they will turn and bite the hand that fed them. —Edmund Burke, *Thoughts and Details on Scarcity,* 1800

3884. There's no such thing as a free lunch. —Anonymous, 1960's

3885. If any would not work, neither should he eat. —Bible, *II Thessalonians 3:10*

3886. Blessed is he who expects nothing, for he shall never be disappointed. —Alexander Pope, letter, October 16, 1927

3887. There is a fundamental paradox of the welfare state: that it is not built for the desperate but for those who are already capable of helping themselves. —Michael Harrington, *The Other America,* 1962

3888. All the measures of the government are directed to the purpose of making the rich richer and the poor poorer. —William Henry Harrison, speech, October 1, 1840

3889. In general, the art of government consists in taking as much money as possible from one class of citizens and giving it to the other. —Voltaire, *Philosophical Dictionary,* "Money," 1764

3890. The triumphant welfare state principle means that economic governance must consist of a fundamental trade-off between Capitalist prosperity and social security. As a nation we have chosen to have less of the former in order to have more of the latter. —David A. Stockman, *The Triumph of Politics,* 1987

3891. A government which robs Peter to pay Paul can always depend on the support of Paul. —George Bernard Shaw, *Everybody's Political What's What?,* 1944

------------ *Winners and Losers* ------------

See also **Campaigns; Voting**

3892. Given a government with a big surplus, and a big majority and a weak Opposition, and you could debauch a committee of Archangels. —John

A. Macdonald, in *Colombo's Canadian Quotations,* 1974

3893. The saddest life is that of a political aspirant under democracy. His failure is ignominious and his success is disgraceful. — H. L. Mencken, in *Baltimore Evening Sun*, December 9, 1929

**3894.** It's not whether you win or lose, but how you place the blame. —John Peers, *1,001 Logical Laws*, 1979

**3895.** It isn't important who is ahead at one time or another, in either an election or a horse race. It's the horse that comes in first at the finish that counts. —Harry S Truman, speech, October 17, 1948

**3896.** We shall fight on the beaches, we shall fight on the landing grounds, we shall fight in the fields and in the streets, we shall fight in the hills; we shall never surrender. —Winston S. Churchill, speech, June 4, 1940

**3897.** There are not fifty ways of fighting, there's only one, and that's to win. Neither revolution nor war consists in doing what one pleases. —André Malraux, *L'Espoir*, 1937

**3898.** Each success only buys an admission ticket to a more difficult problem. —Henry Kissinger, in *Wilson Library Bulletin*, March, 1979

**3899.** Merit envies success, and success takes itself for merit. —Jean Rostand, *De la vanite*, 1925

**3900.** The gods are on the side of the stronger. —Cornelius Tacitus, *Histories*, ca. 95

**3901.** The toughest thing about success is that you've got to keep on being a success. —Irving Berlin, in *Theatre Arts*, February, 1958

**3902.** Being frustrated is disagreeable, but the real disasters of life begin when you get what you want. —Irving Kristol, in *Newsweek*, November 28, 1977

**3903.** Nothing is an unmixed blessing. —Horace, *Odes*, 1st c. B.C.

**3904.** The problems of victory are more agreeable than those of defeat, but they are no less difficult. —Winston S. Churchill, speech, November 11, 1942

**3905.** Educated risks are the key to success. —William Olsten, in *Success*, February, 1988

**3906.** When there is no peril in the fight, there is no glory in the triumph. —Pierre Corneille, *Le Cid*, 1636

**3907.** When times get tough, it just gets down to who can outdo the other fellow. —W. Duke Kimbrell, in *Forbes*, November 2, 1987

**3908.** Another such victory and we are ruined. — Pyrrhus, in Plutarch, *Lives*, "Pyrrhus," ca. 279 B.C.

**3909.** I cannot give you the formula for success, but I can give you the formula for failure, which is: Try to please everybody. —Herbert B. Swope, speech, December 20, 1950

**3910.** What is the use of being elected or reelected unless you stand for something? —Grover Cleveland, remark, 1887

**3911.** Popularity? It is glory's small change. — Victor Hugo, *Ruy Blas*, 1838

**3912.** Popularity's bad for you. I try and avoid it like the plague. And I've been reasonably successful. —Brian Mulroney, news summaries, May 3, 1992

**3913.** All you need in this life is ignorance and confidence, and then success is sure. —Mark Twain, letter, December 2, 1878

**3914.** Every man meets his Waterloo at last. —Wendell Phillips, speech, November 1, 1859

**3915.** We see men fall from high estate on account of the very faults through which they attained it. —Jean La Bruyère, *Characters*, "Of the Court," 1688

**3916.** I brought myself down. I impeached myself by resigning. —Richard M. Nixon, interview, May 4, 1977

**3917.** Victory has a hundred fathers, but defeat is an orphan. — Galeazzo Ciano, *Diary*, "September 9, 1942," 1946

**3918.** We are not interested in the possibilities of defeat. — Victoria, letter, December, 1899

**3919.** Good people are good business because they've come to wisdom through failure. We get very little wisdom from success, you know. —William Saroyan, in *New York Journal-American*, August 23, 1961

**3920.** He who has never failed somewhere, that man cannot be great. — Herman Melville, in *The Literary World,* August, 1850

**3921.** It is more difficult to be an honorable man for a week than to be a hero for fifteen minutes. — Jules Renard, *Journal,* 1907

**3922.** It is better to fail in originality than to succeed in imitation. — Herman Melville, in *The Literary World,* August, 1850

**3923.** There is the greatest practical benefit in making a few failures early in life. — T. H. Huxley, *On Medical Education,* 1870

**3924.** Don't persist in a losing cause unless you truly know you can turn it into a winning one. — Robert Heller, *The Super Managers,* 1984

**3925.** A friend cannot be known in prosperity; and an enemy cannot be hidden in adversity. — Bible: Apocrypha, *Ecclesiasticus 12:8*

**3926.** Post-mortems on defeat are never very useful unless they say something about the future. — James Reston, in *New York Times,* July 15, 1964

**3927.** If at first you don't succeed, you may not be encouraged to try again. — Edwin McDowell, in *New York Times,* April 25, 1988

**3928.** There is a rough rule-of-thumb in American politics, never verified, that the man at whom the crowd throws eggs or tomatos is usually marked as the loser. — Theodore H. White, *The Making of the President 1960,* 1961

**3929.** The conduct of a losing party never appears right: at least it never can possess the only infallible criterion of wisdom to vulgar judgments — success.

— Edmund Burke, *Letter to a Member of the National Assembly,* 1791

**3930.** There is no loneliness greater than the loneliness of a failure. The failure is a stranger in his own house. — Eric Hoffer, *The Passionate State of Mind,* 1954

**3931.** Although he's regularly asked to do so, God does not take sides in American politics. — George J. Mitchell, statement, July 13, 1987

**3932.** Few things are more shocking to those who practice the arts of success than the frank description of those arts. — Logan Pearsall Smith, *Reperusals and Re-collections,* 1936

**3933.** The politicians of New York . . . see nothing wrong in the rule, that to the victor belong the spoils of the enemy. — William L. Marcy, speech, January 25, 1832

**3934.** Rats and conquerors must expect no mercy in misfortune. — Charles Caleb Colton, *Lacon,* 1820–22

**3935.** In war: resolution. In defeat: defiance. In victory: magnanimity. In peace: goodwill. — Winston S. Churchill, *The Second World War, Vol. I,* 1948

**3936.** Men should be either treated generously or destroyed, because they take revenge for slight injuries — for heavy ones they cannot. — Niccolò Machiavelli, *The Prince,* 1513

**3937.** A man can be destroyed but not defeated. — Ernest Hemingway, *The Old Man and the Sea,* 1952

**3938.** Nothing in life is so exhilarating as to be shot at without result. — Winston S. Churchill, *The Malakand Field Force,* 1898

---

# *Wisdom*

## See also Fools; Knowledge; Truth

**3939.** The punishment which the wise suffer, who refuse to take part in the government, is to live under the government of worse men. — Plato, *The Republic,* ca. 370 B.C.

**3940.** It is not enough to acquire

wisdom, it is necessary to employ it. — Cicero, *De Finibus,* ca. 45 B.C.

**3941.** Dost thou know, my son, with how little wisdom the world is governed? — Axel Oxenstierna, letter, 1648

**3942.** Is this the wisdom of a great minister? or is it the ominous vibration of a pendulum? — Junius, in *Public Advertiser,* May 30, 1769

**3943.** Nine-tenths of wisdom is being wise in time. — Theodore Roosevelt, speech, June 14, 1917

**3944.** True wisdom consists not in seeing what is immediately before our eyes, but in foreseeing what is to come. — Terence, *Adelphi,* 160 B.C.

**3945.** Wisdom consists of the anticipation of consequences. — Norman Cousins, in *Saturday Review,* April 15, 1978

**3946.** Wisdom is an affair of values, and of value judgments. It is intelligent conduct of human affairs. — Sidney Hook, in *Saturday Review,* November 11, 1967

**3947.** Magnanimity in politics is not seldom the truest wisdom; and a great empire and little minds go ill together. — Edmund Burke, *On Conciliation with America,* 1775

**3948.** The wise man would rather see men needing him than thanking him. — Balthasar Gracián, *The Art of Worldly Wisdom,* 1647

**3949.** Oppression makes a wise man mad. — Frederick Douglass, speech, July 5, 1852

**3950.** The wise man questions the wisdom of others because he questions his own, the foolish man because it is different from his own. — Leo Stein, *Journey Into the Self,* 1950

**3951.** All free governments are managed by the combined wisdom and folly of the people. — James A. Garfield, letter, April 21, 1880

**3952.** In action Wisdom goes by majorities. — George Meredith, *The Ordeal of Richard Feverel,* 1859

**3953.** Force without wisdom falls of its own weight. — Horace, *Odes,* 1st c. B.C.

**3954.** No man is wise enough nor good enough to be trusted with unlimited power. — Charles Caleb Colton, *Lacon,* 1820–22

**3955.** The wise become the unwise in the enchanted chambers of Power, whose lamp makes every face the same color. — Walter Savage Landor, *Imaginary Conversations,* "Demosthenes and Eubulides," 1824–53

**3956.** We thought, because we had power, we had wisdom. — Stephen Vincent Benét, *Litany for Dictatorships,* 1935

**3957.** Great men are not always wise. — Bible, *Job 32:9*

**3958.** Nothing doth more hurt in a state than that cunning men pass for wise. — Francis Bacon, *Essays,* "Of Cunning," 1625

**3959.** Many would be wise if they did not think themselves wise. — Balthasar Gracián, *The Art of Worldly Wisdom,* 1647

**3960.** All this worldly wisdom was once the unamiable heresy of some wise man. — Henry David Thoreau, *Journal,* 1853

**3961.** It is the wisdom of the crocodiles, that shed tears when they would devour. — Francis Bacon, *Essays,* "Of Wisdom for a Man's Self," 1625

**3962.** It's bad taste to be wise all the time, like being at a perpetual funeral. — D. H. Lawrence, *Pansies,* "Peace and War," 1929

**3963.** Pessimism is only the name that men of weak nerves give to wisdom. — Bernard De Voto, speech, December, 1935

**3964.** Doubt is the beginning, not the end, of wisdom. — George Iles, *Jottings,* 1918

**3965.** A wise skepticism is the first attribute of a good critic. — James Russell Lowell, *Among My Books,* 1870

**3966.** Sometimes it proves the highest understanding not to understand. — Balthasar Gracián, *The Art of Worldly Wisdom,* 1647

**3967.** It is of the highest advantage for one that is wise not to seem to be wise. — Aeschylus, *Prometheus Bound,* ca. 490 B.C.

**3968.** Whoever is not too wise is wise. — Martial, *Epigrammata,* 93

**3969.** Wisdom is knowing when you can't be wise. — Paul Engle, *Poems in Praise,* 1959

**3970.** An ounce of discretion is worth a pound of learning. — Thomas Adams, *Sermons,* 1629

**3971.** The art of being wise is the art of knowing what to overlook. — William James, *The Principles of Psychology,* 1890

**3972.** A wise man recognizes the convenience of a general statement, but he bows to the authority of a particular fact. — Oliver Wendell Holmes Sr., *The Poet at the Breakfast-Table,* 1872

**3973.** The subtlest wisdom can produce the subtlest folly. — François de La Rochefoucauld, *Maxims,* 1665

**3974.** The good Lord set definite limits on man's wisdom, but set no limits on his stupidity—and that's not fair! — Konrad Adenauer, in *The Churchman,* January 15, 1957

**3975.** The latter part of a wise man's life is taken up in curing the follies, prejudices, and false opinions he had contracted in the former. — Jonathan Swift, *Thoughts on Various Subjects,* 1711

**3976.** A wise man needes not blush for changing his purpose. — George Herbert, *Outlandish Proverbs,* 1640

**3977.** It does not matter one whit whether you lack wisdom teeth if you only possess wisdom. — Earnest Albert Hooton, *Twilight of Man,* 1939

**3978.** A man should never be ashamed to own he has been in the wrong, which is but saying, in other words, that he is wiser today than he was yesterday. — Jonathan Swift, *Thoughts on Various Subjects,* 1711

**3979.** Wisdom is the principal thing; therefore get wisdom: and with all thy getting get understanding. — Bible, *Proverbs 4:7*

**3980.** Wisdom is never dear, provided the article be genuine. — Horace Greeley, speech, May 23, 1871

**3981.** The price of wisdom is above rubies. — Bible. *Job 28:18*

**3982.** Wisdom outweighs any wealth. — Sophocles, *Antigone,* ca. 442 B.C.

**3983.** Let me smile with the wise, and feed with the rich. — Samuel Johnson, in James Boswell, *Life of Samuel Johnson,* 1791

# Women in Politics

**3984.** In the administration of a State neither a woman as a woman nor a man as a man has any special function, but the gifts of nature are equally diffused in both sexes. — Plato, *The Republic,* ca. 370 B.C.

**3985.** Women ought to have representatives, instead of being arbitrarily governed without any direct share allowed them in the deliberations of government. — Mary Wollstonecraft, *A Vindication of the Rights of Women,* 1792

**3986.** In the new code of laws which I suppose it will be necessary for you to make I desire you would remember the ladies, and be more generous and favorable to them than your ancestors. Do not put such unlimited power into the hands of the husbands. Remember all men would be tyrants if they could. — Abigail Adams, letter, March 31, 1776

**3987.** The appointment of a woman to office is an innovation for which the public is not prepared; nor am I. — Thomas Jefferson, letter, January 13, 1807

**3988.** The queens in history compare favorably with the kings. — Elizabeth Cady Stanton, *History of Woman Suffrage,* 1881

**3989.** There aren't many women now I'd like to see as President — but there are fewer men. — Clare Booth Luce, in *Newsweek,* October 22, 1979

**3990.** In politics, if you want anything said, ask a man. If you want anything done, ask a woman. — Margaret Thatcher, in *People,* September 15, 1975

**3991.** Though she be but little, she is fierce. — William Shakespeare, *A Midsummer Night's Dream,* 1595–96

**3992.** Toughness doesn't have to come in a pinstripe suit. — Dianne Feinstein, in *Time,* June 4, 1984

**3993.** What Britain needs is an iron lady. — Margaret Thatcher, campaign slogan, in *Newsweek,* May 14, 1979

**3994.** No one can make you feel inferior without your consent. — Eleanor Roosevelt, in *Catholic Digest,* August, 1960

**3995.** True equality can only mean the right to be uniquely creative. — Erik H. Erikson, *The Woman in America,* 1965

**3996.** Thus if, say, men are favored in the assignment of basic rights, this inequality is justified . . . only if it is to the advantage of women and acceptable from their standpoint. — John Rawls, *A Theory of Justice,* 1971

**3997.** Damn it, you can't have the crown of thorns *and* the thirty pieces of silver. — Aneurin Bevan, in Michael Foot, *Aneurin Bevan,* 1962

**3998.** If this is a Great Society, I'd hate to see a bad one. — Fannie Lou Hamer, in *The Worker,* July 13, 1975

**3999.** Any society that categorically excludes half its members from the processes by which it rules itself will be ruled in a way that is less than fully human. — Kathleen Newland, *Women in Politics, A Global Review,* 1975

**4000.** The worker is the slave of capitalist society, the female worker is the slave of that slave. — James Connolly, *The Re-conquest of Ireland,* 1915

**4001.** Women, children and revolutionists hate irony, which is the negation of all saving instincts, of all faith, of all devotion, of all action. — Joseph Conrad, *Under Western Eyes,* 1911

**4002.** Women — one half of the human race at least — care fifty times more for a marriage than a ministry. — Walter Bagehot, *The English Constitution,* "The Monarchy," 1867

**4003.** For woman is "by birth a Tory" has often been said — by education a "Tory," we mean. — Florence Nightingale, "Cassandra," 1852

**4004.** I can conceive of nothing worse than a man-governed world — except a woman-governed world. — Nancy Astor, *My Two Countries,* 1923

**4005.** The suffragette . . . is a woman who has stupidly carried her envy of certain of the superficial privileges of men to such a point that it . . . makes her blind to their valueless and often chiefly imaginary character. — H. L. Mencken, *In Defense of Women,* 1922

**4006.** She remained an outsider, by origin, by attitude, and above all by sex. Disraeli could be baptized an Anglican; there was nothing Margaret Thatcher could do about being a woman. — Geoffrey Wheatcroft, in *Atlantic,* "'That Woman' Versus the Chattering Classes," December, 1991

**4007.** The ERA [Equal Rights Amendment] came to be seen as an issue that pitted . . . women of the Right against women of the Left. Once the ERA lost its aura of benefitting all women and became a partisan issue, it lost its chance. — Jane J. Mansbridge, *Why We Lost the ERA,* 1986

**4008.** I suppose I could have stayed home, baked cookies and had teas, but what I decided was to fulfill my profession. — Hillary Clinton, in *Washington Post,* March 17, 1992

**4009.** I find it incredibly offensive for anyone to tell me as a woman that I'm going to vote for a woman because of her gender. — Marilyn Quayle, speech, July 22, 1992

# INDEX OF PERSONS

*References are to entry numbers, not pages.*

Graham, Billy (U.S. evangelist) 605
Graham, Ron (Canadian journalist)
2691
Grahame, Kenneth (Scottish writer)
3382
Grant, Albert A. (U.S. businessman)
143
Grant, George (Canadian educator)
1713
Grant, Ulysses S. (U.S. president)
1907, 2380, 3218
Grayson, David (U.S. writer) 3535
Greeley, Horace (U.S. journalist and
politician) 3980
Greene, Graham (English journalist
and writer) 590, 2116
Greer, Germaine (Australian feminist)
3266, 3314
Grey, Edward (English politician) 2238
Guazzo, Stefano (Italian writer) 1616
Guedalla, Philip (English writer) 846,
1471
Guérard, Albert (U.S. educator and
writer) 1592
Guevara, Antonio de (Spanish preacher
and writer) 1096
Guggenheimer, Richard H. (U.S. artist
and writer) 1961
Gumilev, Nikolai (Russian poet) 1155


Hägglund, Joel see Hill, Joe
Haldeman, H. R. (U.S. presidential
assistant) 815
Hale, Edward Everett (U.S. clergyman)
1998
Hale, Nathan (U.S. revolutionary
soldier) 2572
Hamer, Fannie Lou (U.S. political ac-
tivist) 3998
Hamilton, Alex (English journalist) 168
Hamilton, Alexander (U.S. lawyer and
politician) 69, 184, 665, 1358, 1881,
2218, 2366
Hamilton, Edith (U.S. writer) 925,
1043
Hamilton, Edward K. (U.S. economist
and writer) 180
Hand, Learned (U.S. jurist) 668, 832,
1065, 2063, 2081, 2103, 2378, 2478,
2759, 3049, 3790

Harbrecht, Douglas (U.S. journalist)
1840
Hardin, Garrett (U.S. educator) 422
Harding, Warren G. (U.S. president)
1316, 1528, 2311
Hardy, Thomas (English poet and
writer) 659, 2475
Harington, John (English writer) 3162
Harkness, Richard (U.S. journalist) 204
Harmon, M. Judd (U.S. educator) 128,
510, 547, 1889, 2775, 3414, 3416,
3474
Harriman, W. Averell (U.S. diplomat)
774
Harrington, James (English political
scientist) 2803
Harrington, Michael (U.S. writer) 3887
Harris, Richard (U.S. journalist) 2837
Harris, Sydney J. (U.S. journalist)
1622, 3078
Harrison, Benjamin (U.S. president)
777, 1707, 2452, 3262
Harrison, William Henry (U.S. presi-
dent) 1307, 2983, 3001, 3637, 3888
Hartley, L. P. (English writer) 3563
Havel, Vaclav (Czech president) 47
Hawkins, Anthony Hope see Hope,
Anthony
Hawthorne, Nathaniel (U.S. writer)
1512
Hayek, Friedrich A. von (Austrian
educator and writer) 3116
Hayes, Rutherford B. (U.S. president)
71, 2561, 2676
Hazlitt, William (English writer) 334,
732, 977, 1381, 1506, 1775, 2092,
2098, 2200, 2213, 2216, 2270, 2447,
2984, 3008, 3011, 3515
Hearst, William Randolph (U.S.
newspaper publisher) 2584
Heath, Edward (English prime
minister) 275, 2863
Hecht, Ben (U.S. playwright and
writer) 3013
Hegel, Georg Wilhelm Friedrich (Ger-
man philosopher) 1151, 1453, 1958,
2295, 2472, 2667, 3090, 3415, 3476
Heine, Heinrich (German poet) 1212
Heisenberg, Werner (German physicist)
1867
Heller, Joseph (U.S. writer) 229
Heller, Robert (U.S. educator) 3924

# INDEX OF KEY WORDS
# IN CONTEXT

*References are to entry numbers, not pages.*

applesauce: all politics is a. 2901
application of reason 3152
applied science 1333
appointment: by the corrupt few 594; create an a. 2395; of a woman 3987
apprehended at all 3587
apprehension of it 3599
apprenticeship: for freedom 3346; shorter 2564
approach to political problems 2035
archangels: committee of a. 3892
archbishop: get it from their a. 2810
ardor for liberty 2048
argue against a new idea 1568
argument: box on the ear is an a. 2744; convincing a. 106; main a. 115; not in the right a. 3371; of conservatism 562; of the broken window 819; of tyrants 2364; only a. available 488; worth making 234
arguments: before a court 1237; convince others by our a. 107; good a. 1499; more value than his a. 2441
aristocracies: intellectual a. 2190
aristocracy: American a. 118; absentee a. 2711; brains in an a. 123; displeased with a. 3654; every a. that has ever existed 124; in a republic 122; is always cruel 120; is like cheese 121; means government 119; monied a. 185; natural a. among men 116; of birth 669; society without an a. 127; the most democratic 117; to what is decent 395; true a. 3245
aristocrat: is the democrat 543; who loathes 1690
aristocratic and a democratic 2182
aristocratical council 729
arm of time 3615
armaments that cause wars 3307
armed forces 2662
armies: fighting each other 3843; invasion of a. 1559; large a. 893
armor of a righteous man 2274
arms: bear a. 2761; do flourish 3411; entrusted with a. 1116; race 2347; resort to a. 3830; splitting up into a. 3578; we need 2761; world in a. 2632
army: discipline 738; in the act of suicide 3843; rules 3422; thinking of an a. 2494

arranged: so tidily a. 3170
arrival in the United States 2735
arrogance of power 2738
arrows: ideas are great a. 2910
arsenal of democracy 692
art: forge many an a. 3502; highest a. 1627; lie with a. 2113; not a science ... but an a. 2890; not an a. 2896; of a politician 3732; of being honest 1501; of being wise 3971; of governing 1926, 1976; of government 1328, 1344, 3889; of honeyed words 2378; of kings 3302; of knowing 3971; of making men ethical 2295; of making men live together 1333; of politics 2894; of seeing things 1245; of taxation 3445; of telling you nothing 3396; of the possible 2885, 2886; or policy 2354; perfected the a. 2510; politics is an a. 2895; politics is the a. 2885, 2891, 2892, 2893; politics is truly the a. 2917; which one government ... learns 3444; work of a. 1383
article: be genuine 3980; grade of the a. 1625; of my faith 2642; of my political creed 729
artillery of abuse 1265
arts: and merchandise 3411; book of their a. 3548; crooked a. 1385; description of those a. 3932; mother of a. 2703; of power 2988; of success 3932
ashes: bucket of a. 1477
aspects of human life 1458
aspirant under democracy 3893
ass: shot in the a. 1935; such an a. 1917
assassin: you are an a. 3723
assassination: from ambush 1081; is not an impossibility 412; is the extreme form of censorship 3719; is the quickest way 3720; moderated by a. 2720; worthy of a. 2692
assemblies: at our a. 1178
assembly: is to watch 1979; member of the a. 1978; popular a. 729
assert: safe to a. 1289
assignment of basic rights 3996
association of men 3728
assumes: blandly a. 1694

bastards: people who have spoken the
b. 3823
bath: for every soul 3815; of blood
3721
battalions: side of the heavy b. 3853
battle: a method for untying 1117; bad
as a b. 3815; between bad and worse
3741; borne the b. 2302; call to b.
2761; graveyards of b. 3032; great b.
1875; half the b. 495; last b. 2879;
of Waterloo 3825; wins the first b.
2126
battle-cry which best rallies 2280
battles: mother of b. 3864; opening b.
3825
bayonet is a weapon 3837
bayonets: chains are worse than b.
2616; throne of b. 3838
beaches: fight on the b. 3896
beacons of wise men 1108
beam of a searchlight 3043
bear: the burden 2761; the public
burden 3298; their tyranny 3660
beasts of prey 2780
beaten by none of the above 3809
bedfellows: never be b. 1047; strange
b. 811, 812
bedrooms: privacy of their b. 1970
bees working in a glass hive 1257
beggar: amidst great riches 1435; be
not made a b. 186
beggars: and thieves 1438; none 1436
begin: as heresies 3613; by saying
2756; let us b. 2767, 2768
beginning: and end 2779; at the b.
3199; bold b. 2754; is the most important part 2763; not the end 3964;
of a change 2598; of all freedom
1638; of any great matter 3082; of
the end 2636; ridiculous b. 1566
behaving: way of our b. 3517
behavior: human b. 951; standards of
b. 323
being: has his b. 3415; reasonable b.
708
belief: any b. in particular 573; based
on the b. 1332; deluded into the b.
2813; forced into b. 165, 3135; in
God 305; in facts 1036; in our own
guidance 1076; in truth 163; is going
beyond 147; matter of b. 174; of
mine 2647; person with a b. 144;

that fashion 1267; that present
trends will continue 1730
beliefs: contradictory b. 1576; fixed by
authority 840; grounds for our b.
152; intuitive b. 153; of eighteen
158; popular b. 1445; transfer my b.
172
believe: as much as we can 154;
brought up to b. 1033; do not b.
185; easier to b. 155; every day 2520;
everything if we could 154; how insulting 3809; in what we must do
1529; it is my duty 855; man
possesses 3153; most easily 2205;
politicians who b. 1481; ready to b.
1854; that a just and good society
must wait 875; that every right
3254; that foreign policy 1710; that
government is the problem 3067;
that literature 2919; that no people
3324; that politics 2841; that
without 2540; the people 1275; this
I b. 1650; those who are seeking 169;
those who b. 1379; those whom we
do not know 1492; what is pleasant
159; what men b. 173; what they
read 1278; will agree 2500
believer in culture 2020
believes: no man b. 3654
believing that he acts 1648
bell: funeral b. is already rung 550
belly comes before the soul 379
benefit: every human b. 466; my own
b. 2375; of an individual 2370; of
the people 2369; practical b. 3923;
protection and security 1351
benefits: earned by a few 1765; inestimable b. 1208; of the unknown
547; personal b. 2398; they confer
2396
benevolence: bottom of b. 1775; of
mankind 3880
benevolent: despots 3638; more b.
they become 3787
best: equality with the b. 1003;
government 1336; looks the b. 2569;
men 3372; of all possible worlds
636; of us 2078; politics is no
politics 2854; use of laws 1902
bet on the future 3814
betrayal: defense against b. 3570
better: part of valor 1736; red than

bottom: of all human knowledge 1633;
of all the tributes 3782; of
benevolence 1775; of the economic
pyramid 3453
bought: he's been b. 3700
bound to one way of life 3533
boundary: of the march 3428; that
divides 470
bounds: out of all b. 1643; out of b.
2083
bourgeois: always bounces back 393;
are other people 398; horrible invention the b. 399; horror of the b.
392; is an epithet 395; mind 447;
prefers comfort 395; you must shock
the b. 397
bourgeoisie: existence of the b. 1688;
flower of the b. 1669; small-town b.
2524; stops the revolution half way
the b. 3196; whole b. 389
bow: there has to be a b. 2910
box on the ear 2744
boy: any b. may become president
3681; many a b. 3841
boys: are not going to be sent 3102;
are still there 1074; in the back room
2563; ought to be doing for
themselves 3103; send American b.
3103; teenage b. 1314
brain: and soul of man 2097; damage
899; dead 2000
brains: more brass than b. 123
branch of economics 2290
branches: three b. 1230
brand of ideas 1181
bravado of ignorance 1275
brave: good and the b. 2149
bread: and butter 1444; of man's spirit
2111; looked to the government for
b. 3883; steal b. 1418
breast: quiet b. 3623
breath: emit a b. 3775; of self-respect
2333
breathing: stream of my b. 3500
breeding: bad b. 2838; different b.
1403
breezes: generating b. 2482
bribe: taking of a b. 598
bridge: be a b. 34
bridges: sleep under b. 1418
brief: strive to be b. 1839
briefcase: lawyer with his b. 1911

briefcases: available b. 244
brier patch 2793
bright ideas 3787
brilliance without wisdom 2633
broke: if it ain't b. 1; we'll keep ye b.
2515
brothel: intellectual b. 3060
brother: big b. 763
brotherhood: broadened into a b.
1726; freedom, equality, b. 2299;
table of b. 3031
brothers: feel they are b. 2594; live
together as b. 3036
brow: right man's b. 1567
Browning: safety-catch on my b. 2210
brunt of life 531
brutality: police b. 2490
bubble: break like a b. 3583
buck stops here 2319
bucket of ashes 1477
buckle which fastens 1292
budget: except the federal b. 195; is a
mythical bean bag 188; is a statement 180; on paper 190; which remains 2527
bull: bullfighter or the b. 3816; moose
2308; rushes like a b. 1012
bullets: successors to b. 3786
bullfighter or the bull 3816
bulwark: of continuing liberty 1357;
main b. 3114
bulwarks of liberty 1197
bunk: history is more or less b. 1474
burden: bear any b. 2065; carry the
heavy b. 3305; of a long twilight
struggle 2761; of the nation's care
3298; of tyranny 3655
burdened with convictions 3532
bureaucracies are designed 222
bureaucracy: God will forgive you but
the b. won't 216; defends the status
quo 209; efficient 223, 241; government b. 227; is established 222; is
what we all suffer from 200; may
mean less 214; saves us from the b.
223; tedium of the b. 232; the rule
of no one 199; thought in a b. 245;
within the b. 234
bureaucrat: like a b. scorned 239;
make everybody a b. 233; makes a
mistake 210; perfect b. 201; that
does not like a poem 211

bureaucratic: expansion 1657; way of life 235

bureaucratization means 214

bureaucrats: are the only people 202; guidelines for b. 228; write memoranda 224

burglar: honest b. 1482

bushspeak 1840

business: American b. 2553; and industrial world 2900; and political decisions 1237; background in b. 1237; big b. 906, 2524; chief b. 888; difficult b. 1004; dirty b. 2817; good b. 3919; I learned in b. 225; it is your b. 421; no b. in politics 1921; nor technology 1333; of everybody 415; of government 2144; of the citizens 372; of the very few 1147; on their hands 226; personal b. 3682; public b. 1995, 2862; self-canceling b. 721; society 2209; spring of b. 1294; support b. 1359; this king b. 3294; totter on in b. 2832

busy: appear to be b. 224; too b. doing good 2743

butchers: rich b. 1876; shepherds and b. 1290

butter: bread and b. 1444; or guns 3871; we can manage without b. 3855

butterflies are free 1122


cabals: struggle of c. 1995

cabbage: smells better than a c. 1558

cabinet: is a combining committee 1292; remain in the c. 3702

cake: and eat it too: 2182; piece of c. 2795

calculate the worth 1383

calculations: political c. 2448

calf: can't expect the fatted c. 3173; lion and the c. 2411

caliber of the Congress 1999

call: answer the c. 2762; to bear arms 2761

calls to action 2759

calm: rather than to excite 1356; remember to keep c. 18

calmness and light 2055

calumnies are answered 501

camel: easier for a c. 1487; is a horse designed by a committee 207

camera: press and c. 1966

campaign: activity 2399; contributors 2807; effort put into a c. 2398; headquarters 3818; in poetry 246; is a revolving circus 250; issue in a c. 340; issue in this c. 271; political c. 264; presidential c. 247; slogans 2328; wasn't sufficiently slick 256; work 2399

campaigning: charge and countercharge of c. 248

campaigns: funding of c. 259; political c. 251

campaign's tone 56

campus politics 2853

cancer: malignant c. 869

candid: things that were so c. 3055

candidacy for any office 265

candidate: against or for a c. 250; bullheaded c. 56; does not know 3816; each c. is stalled 263; feels like a steer 253; for consul 2575; for office 1849; for the presidency 3702; never a c. 3812; no c. was ever elected 3706; stands for 340

candidates: appeal 3797; don't chew gum 270; hear the c. 263; merchandise c. 254; personality of the c. 2022; unable to be c. 804

candle: burns a c. 2464

candor: and confession 679; love of c. 3512

cannibal uses knife and fork 3091

cap: and his c. 1996

capable: he is c. 1764; of exercising 2153; of helping themselves 3887

capacities: intellectual c. 1818

capacity: and willingness 2230; any other c. 2124; for one adventure 571; moral c. 2918

capital: and labor 381; denounce c. 280; intellectual c. 2368; is the first requisite 280; punishment 3726; sufficient c. 879

capitalism: and altruism 284; and democracy 273; face of c. 275; inevitably 282; is a necessary condition 272; is the product 2024; monopoly stage of c. 285; needs 283; of the lower classes 3357; plus murder

learn is to c. 311; love your life
enough to c. it 3233; means of c.
304; necessary to c. 290; point is to
c. 309; political c. 3344; possibilities
of c. 2943; reckless c. 315; relief in
c. 318; slow to accept c. 2036; small
c. 3379, 3911; social c. 302; stupidity
against c. 2280; takes place 3471; the
direction 3685; the mentality 2338;
the past 3559; the truth 2130; thing
that does not c. 298; torrent of c.
560; turbulence and c. 1788; unable
to c. 1927
changes: begin c. 292; great c. 2166; of
circumstances 2416; of government
3787; we fear 303
chaos: and ineptitude 100; brings c.
2082; makes only c. 1043; often
breeds life 3226
chapter: write the next c. 3264
character: appearance of c. 338; content of their c. 3031; demands 354;
fellow's c. 321; imaginary c. 4005; is
best formed 344; issue 326; limitations of his own c. 329; of liberty
2090; of the censored press 1211; of
the person 340; politics ruins the c.
803; sufficient c. 1486; tend to live
in c. 1488
characteristic: distinctive c. 2837; of
the English monarchy 2257
characteristics: of a popular politician
2838; of a vigorous intellect 1671
characters: are ... agreeable 2213; bad
c. 3243; composed of two c. 607;
great c. 351
charge: and countercharge 248; when
in c. 228
charisma becomes the undoing 1927
charity: does not even allow 443; for
all 2302; must begin at home 2062;
living need c. 3877; patriotism is
like c. 2585
charlatanism of some degree 1965
charm: know what c. is 451
charms: thousand c. 3328
charters: amount of c. 3798
chase after truth 3596
chastity of the intellect 628
chateaux would never have been burnt
1422
cheating: period of c. 2609

check: drawn on a bank 1865; is in the
mail 1994; trusted without a c. 2947;
upon your rulers 3001
checkers: game of c. 3462
checks and balances 1230
cheese: aristocracy is like c. 121; kinds
of c. 2707; king's c. 3458
cherry pie 3713
chicanery: sophistry and c. 1856
chicken: like a c. 122; voting for Colonel Sanders 2506
chickweed: get the c. out of your lawn
2519
child: governed by a c. 1950; illegitimate c. 2722; is known 342; little c.
1500; of ignorance 3008; of law 3257
childbirth: pain and peril of c. 1565
children: consumption of c. 1447;
devour in turn each of her c. 3210;
future of their c. 3876; he reappears
in your c. 393; hopes of its c. 2632;
little c. 3031; should acquire 1446;
thoughts of c. 3475; women, c. and
revolutionists 4001
Chinese: written in c. 607
chivalry is gone 2233
chloroform of the Irish people 2712
choice: between listening and talking
3374; between truth and repose
3620; government of our own c.
3219; independent c. 1143; in
politics 801; method of c. 3701; of
his enemies 965; of the cause 3763;
of working or starving 2089
choices: hard c. 642
choose: guess which one he will c. 3374
chosen to have less 3890
Christian theology 434
Christianity: was subversive 1592;
without hell 277
church: alien c. 2711; politics 2853;
route of the ... c. 3212
cigar: really good 5-cent c. 1651
circle: be drawn around it 838; in the
water 1049
circles: goes around in c. 2736
circumstances: blaming their c. 341;
changes of c. 2416; of justice 1751;
present c. 386; relative to the c.
3474; rule men 658; social c. 1563
circus: no right in the c. 1523; parade
2522; revolving c. 250

cities: and towns 3712; dead c. 2343; great c. 1385; large metropolitan c. 2524; size of c. 373
citizen: American c. 807; duty of every c. 367; duty of the good c. 516; first in war 1387; free 3869; function of the c. 374; good c. 361; humblest c. 2274; is influenced 365; keep the c. 374; of all men who think 3518; of the world 3537; who criticizes his country 366
citizenry: responsible c. 600
citizens: American c. 2785; among its c. 1605; business of the c. 372; class of c. 3889; classes of c. 364; discourse to his fellow-c. 1192; enable its c. 1712; fellow c. 1443; first and second class c. 990; good c. 3870; majority of the c. 2153; members and c. 2566; of Berlin 2714; of the middle class 394; of this democracy 368; ordinary c. 2817; other c. 2145; scars to the c. 2575; to its own c. 1298
city: happy is the c. 2612; that goes around in circles 2736; what is the c. 2648
city-states of Greece 1344
civic sacrament 3783
civil: and property rights 2012; government 1420; liberties 524, 3024; political and religious rights 1196; rights 2025, 2034; servant doesn't make jokes 213; service 198, 241, 2399; society 427
civilians: that of c. 1335
civilities of the great 1389
civilization: advances 212, 2495; and profits 859; has advanced 3093; has from time to time 3201; is nothing more 1115; culture and c. 2259; farmyard c. 3223; has advanced 3093; has from time to time 3201; ideal of c. 2713; is nothing more 1115; state of c. 1608; test of c. 373; treason to c. 3466; undermine c. 280
civilizations: all the c. 2190; don't advance 3088
civilized: called c. 1340; state 2946; force another to be c. 1715
claim: competing c. 220
claims: parochial c. 557; to the division 1751

class: adversaries of that c. 390; against the other 3419; any one c. 383; born into the c. 1669; citizens of the middle c. 394; criminal c. 2002; differences 2022; educated c. 1584; every Harvard c. 2507; every c. is unfit to govern 377; lower 387; middle 386; of citizens 3889; one c. overthrows another 3191; particular c. 377; power of one c. 2997; real working c. 388; ruling c. 376; status 2732; struggle 382, 1409, 1698; struggles 378; upper c. 386; working c. 3793
class-welfare rhetoric 2023
classes: against the c. 2177; lower c. 1423, 3357; most obscure of all c. 3566; of citizens 364; of people 1251; people of all c. 2186; two c. 1689; working c. 379
classified: best c. 1337
clay: feet of c. 1966
clean hands 3747
cleanness of its hands 2583
clear-sighted who rule the world 1397
cleavage: democracy needs c. 700; sources of c. 3483
clergyman: bookie or of a c. 2696
clerks: statesmen or of c. 1341
clever: does not seem too c. 1947
cliches: operative c. 2140
clock: cuckoo c. 2719; that is always running down 3515
close: statistically c. 3816; to the United States 2727
closeness to power 2953
cloth: sight of the red c. 1012
clothed: cold and are not c. 2632
club contest 253
clumsy: most c. 709
coal: flour out of a c. sack 279; made mainly of c. 2699
coalitions: does not love c. 2694
coat-tails: touch its c. 3596
cobwebs: like c. 1914
cock crowing on its own dunghill 2593
code: of ethics 333; of laws 3986
coercion: and caprice 1657; manifested by c. 1973
coffee . . . makes the politician wise 2806
cohesion: maintaining its c. 3529; of

American society 3817; undermine the c. 3483

coin: not the only c. 3777; of the realm in politics 1479

cold war 3865

collapse has called forth 442

collateral: lowest form of c. 2531

collection: of facts 1041; of people 2178; of prejudices 3010; of talent 3406

college undergraduates 3123

collision: foreign c. 1722; is very real 1723

colonies: do not cease 1717; wretched c. 1716

color: every face the same c. 3955; forbidden c. 3012; gray isn't such a bad c. 2845; line 3030; no matter what c. you are 3034; of their skin 3031

columnist: call a c. 3059

columnists: political c. 3797

comfort: conservatism goes for c. 565; or money 1135

comforts and hopes 1070

command: armies 2193; government is not c. 1346; not a bigger tent but c. 2985; of language 1849; power at c. 2494; the rain 2255; word of c. 516; words of c. 2284

commander: be a good c. 140

commandment: must be one c. 668; no. 1 of ... society 3535

commands: what counts is who c. 1940

comment is free 1026

commerce: free c. 1169; is the greatest 882; more brilliant than c. 672

commercial corporation 3479

commission from God 1707

commitment: independent c. 1598

commitments: keep such c. 143

committed to the task 2681

committee: accomplished by a c. 208; carry out by c. 206; combining c. 1292; dealing with 328; designed by a c. 207; for managing 389; get out of c. 1992; never met a c. he didn't like 205; of archangels 3892; what is a c. 204

committees: a group of men 203; for a country 751

commodities: levied upon c. 3442; market 2739

commodity: best distributed c. 939; it exports 783

common: agreement 2656; enemies 2761; folk 1690; good 2034; interest 381, 417; law of England 3150; man's ... reluctance 3621; man 1352, 2316; not already c. 2427; nothing in c. 982; people 720; pretext of crime 3748; property 1582; rather c. 1876; sense 293, 939, 940, 1928, 3010; to all men 3134; to everyone 3136; will 3285

commonplace: seldom more c. 1399

commonwealths: raise up c. 2266; uniting into c. 3111

communicate: their ideas 1179; their virtue 3775

communication: hazard in that c. 1266; means agreeing 1021

communicators: formidable c. 3698

communism: anti–Christ of c. 439; is a hammer 433; is a Russian autocracy 430; is governed 407; is like prohibition 432; is not love 433; is Soviet power 431; is the corruption 429; is the exploitation 3115

communism's collapse 442

communist: call anybody they don't like a c. 436; can be a c. 3117; charity 443; country 445; governments 440; has no right 403; must grasp the truth 435; objection to a c. 437; what is a c. 983; world 402, 441

communists abroad 438

communities: and our country 2325; smaller c. 3866

community: any c. has a right 1715; civilized c. 1880; cooperation in the c. 3087; establishes a new c. 3195; expression of c. 3866; intelligence c. 1139; investment for any c. 3873; is like a ship 375; man in a c. 3262; nation or c. 1351; political c. 394; power of a c. 2093; shatter the c. 3195; small anarchist c. 97; state is a c. 3414; that persists 3195; unite into a c. 427; world c. 1724

companionship: mere c. 370

company: tell me thy c. 2509

compass: smaller the c. 2145

competition: is mild 67; is the only form 872; of ideas 1181; with other groups 909

complain of the age we live in 1234
completeness about details 3404
complex: human c. 3154
complexity: overwhelming in its c. 1919
compliance with reason 3143
compliment: regard that as a c. 256
composed: positive and c. 2055
compromise: and barter 466; is but the
    sacrifice 462; is the oil 464; may be
    man's best friend 463; reason for c.
    2552
compromises: of various types 2873;
    what are facts but c. 1038
compulsion: glib c. 1687; without c.
    1145
conceive of nothing worse 4004
concentration: produces c. 496
concept: of progress 3092; of the dig-
    nity 826; of the ideal republic 1528;
    word or c. 1867
conception: of good or evil 3746; of
    justice 978; of liberty 3656
conceptions: triumph of c. 1601
concepts: thoughts and c. 1687
concern: most c. 1514; to voters 2022
concerned with others 1274
conclusion: deciding upon the c. 1499
conclusions: narrow c. 3469; reach
    some c. 3311; there are no c. 656;
    whatever c. it may lead 3463; wrong
    c. 2863
concrete: fixed in c. 1842
condition: age and every c. 1545;
    evolving c. 1127; for democracy 698;
    formal c. 2472; indispensable c. 1170,
    2449; intolerable c. 1467; necessary
    c. 272; of behaving well 3490; of
    liberty 984; of mind 1156; of politics
    2805; of the country 1232; peculiar
    c. 1586; to impel man 314; upon
    which 2049; which is called war 2778
conditions: changing c. 3101; insight
    into the c. 2927; of moderate scar-
    city 1751; social c. 993; under what
    c. 3483
conduct: anti-social c. 1183; commands
    a certain c. 2269; convert itself into
    c. 2753; of a losing party 3929; of
    human affairs 3946; of their work
    2895; perilous to c. 3171; rottenness
    begins in his c. 2387
cone: inverted c. 735

conference: born in a c. 1587; press c.
    3057, 3058
conferences at the top level 774
confession: candor and c. 679
confidence: ignorance and c. 3913; pa-
    tient c. 2672; public c. 3568; show
    some c. 2918
confirmed: sufficiently c. 785
conflict: and disagreement 689; armed
    c. 3863; civil rights c. 2025; field of
    human c. 3842; international c.
    1712; of interest 2016; of opinions
    114; some kinds of c. 2551
conflicts: major social c. 3793; settling
    c. 238
conform: not to c. 514
conformist: and ignoble system 518;
    frightened c. 513
conformists: live c. 512
conformity: is the jailer of freedom
    508; is the philosophy 507; ruined
    by c. 517; rule of c. 2074
confused: hopelessly c. 1800
confusion: fundamental c. 1361;
    general c. 3243; of the modern
    reformer 3790; of tyranny 1211
Congress: angry at c. 2000; business in
    c. 1995; caliber of the c. 1999;
    everybody hates c. 1991; except c.
    2002; function of c. 1986; get
    through c. 1992; has become 1990; is
    deadlocked 1994; is messed up 559;
    member of c. 2008; members of c.
    1489, 2384; privilege of the c. 3688;
    votes mythical beans 188
congressman: act like a c. 192; loves
    their c. 1991
congressmen: are guided 2033
conjectures: high price upon c. 1541
connection between 1584
conquer or be conquered 3429
conqueror: you are a c. 3723
conquerors: rats and c. 3934;
    tumultuous c. 1448
conquest of the world 844
conscience: against c. 525; cut my c.
    349; freedom of c. 1168; freely ac-
    cording to c. 533; has no more 528;
    iron c. 523; is but a word 521; is the
    best divinity 522; its own c. 2013;
    liberty of c. 3544; live with a good
    c. 534; power without c. 2633; quiet

2280; of the indefensible 1845; of
the rich 1420
deference without esteem 3738
defiance: defense not d. 2304; to all
the forces 3109
deficits shrink 252
defined: by one word: 2874; fascism is
not d. 3730
definite: anything d. 2769
definition: of liberalism 2014; of liberty
2076; of politics 2904; of the idiot
2785; of the individual 1645; of the
left 2026; viable d. 2792
degeneration into tyranny 3641
degradation: and want 864; national d.
3829; of the idea 1201
degree: he cannot read: 942; in any d.
2797; of ability 2735; of culture
2259; of happiness 1350 1351; of
non-conformity 511; of submission
2732; of tolerance 3529; of wisdom
3387; some d. 1965; to a d. 2732; to
a great d. 3636; yield in some d.
1682
delay action 612
delays: are dangerous 3848; have
dangerous ends 2750
delegates in control 261
deletion of our history 3350
deliberations of government 3985
deliver: more than we can d. 2518; the
territory 3828
deliverance: liberation is not d. 2094
delusion: that a change 2902;
widespread d. 1410
demagogues: easily led by d. 364;
hypocrites and d. 3468; spring up
1882
demand: created by popular d. 1394;
in excess of the d. 3579
demands: big enough for its d. 3680;
it makes upon us 3155; legitimacy of
the d. 2033; of its own convenience
1367
democracies: English-speaking d. 2258;
great d. 1494; in d. it is the only
sacred thing 887; in the Western d.
3793; tendencies of d. 694; vice of
d. 2459; western d. 1724, 2231
democracy: and socialism 954, 982;
arsenal of d. 692; aspirant under d.
3893; at its ugliest 696; basis of d.

671; be great or a d. 673; can afford
1605; can be no more 669;
capitalism and d. 273; capitalist d.
670; citizens of this d. 368; claim it
is a d. 716; condition for d. 698;
cured by more d. 663; cycle d. is
built on 2963; death of d. 1081;
delusion . . . that we have a d. 1410;
denied 1748; depends upon ideas
1583; doesn't work 687; egg of d.
678; elitist d. 2187; evil of d. 2156;
evils of d. 3822; experience of d.
674; extremes of d. 2218; five hundred years of d. 2719; formed by d.
2686; fullness of d. 697; grieved
under a d. 3654; grows from the
bottom 702; has degraded 2814; has
never existed 675; ills of d. 663; imprudence of d. 665; in a complex
society 704; in a hurry 702; in a d.
685, 825, 2147, 2153, 2446; is a form
710; is a phoney word 717; is a state
3419; is brain dead 2000; is but one
form 3424; is by the nature of it
721; is clearly most appropriate 874
is good 711; is hypocrisy 1517; is
more 426; is not a fragile flower 714;
is not a static thing 705; is not only
712; is not so much a form 715; is
that system 724; is the form of
government 703; is the greatest
revenge 756; is the most difficult 706,
713; is the name 719; is the only
form 709; is the recurrent suspicion
569; is the superior form 708; is the
theory 720; is the worship of jackals
722; is the worst 683, 709; keep our
d. 668; liberty and d. 1415; little less
d. 3862; loses its touch 693; make a
d. 3798; makes d. necessary 667;
material of d. 2189; means government 119, 718; moderate social d.
276; must be progressive 673; my
anchor is d. 664; nature of our d.
751; needs cleavage 700; not the
voting that's d. 3807; obstacles to d.
1410; of direct action 717; of the
dead 3566; of the streets 717; offers
you d. 752; our d. 2376; participatory d. 717; passes into
despotism 727; perfect d. 723;
political d. 676; politician under d.

1482; pollution of d. 808; power machinery with d. 754; pretends that d. is perfect 683; requires institutions 689; rulers of our d. 666; safe for d. 691; secret weapon of d. 679; seeks equality 982; seems to be 2258; serves d. 3821; sick d. 681; smugly disdainful 681; socialist d. 670; strangle d. 3399; substitutes election 594; such as ours 2473; taste of d. 697; tends to wither 3353; that is a government 2684; the practice of self-government 707; tributes paid to d. 3782; two cheers for d. 684; under d. 686; voter in a d. 3795; was the most aristocratic 117; what chance has d. 726; which is a charming form 973; which shuts the past 680; without d. 3353

democrat: I am a d. 2512; is a young conservative 543; to rescue it 2507

democratic: call a country d. 716; class struggle 1698; depended on than a d. 2531; disease 695; dominance 2524; federation 401; freedoms 2015; government 682, 688, 2545; impulses 702; institutions 677, 979, 1231; left and right 2231; movement 2176; nation 2817; nations 701, 2668; not truly d. 690; party 2513, 2554; procedure 490; render the kingdom d. 699; society 2182, 2732; state 2087; system 2566; systems 3483; way 1955

democrats: are . . . the party 2519; believe 2520; don't understand 2014; few d. 2508; have been famous 2516; Jeffersonian d. 2503; must learn 2516; need to seek out 702; no less than the d. 2527; problem with d. 2518; republicans and d. 2503; southern d. 2510; think 981

demonstrations of the basic cohesion 3817

denial: of free speech 1577; of life 3314

deny: a license 1187; believe than to d. 155; the facts 1040

depend: for its existence 1713; on politicians 2230; on the support 3891; on your judgment 1735

depends: evidence upon which it d. 3587; on the unreasonable man 3086

depositories: only safe d. 2655

depository: of power 2959; safe d. 2664

depression when you lose 903

deprivation: cycle of d. 3072

depth of his ignorance 1632

depths of his soul 3258

description of those arts 3932

desert: through the d. 2716

design: pursuit of some d. 2909

designs: crooked d. 2578

desirable: that which is d. 1533

desire: creates 345; for glory 1046; for knowledge 1822; of escaping 3337; of knowledge 1793; of power 1793; strange d. 2999; to know 1814; universal d. 295

desolation: of war 2622; slaughter and d. 1908

desperate: built for the d. 3887

desperation: quiet d. 2215

despot: benevolent d. 726, 731; governed by a d. 735; make a d. 733; of thought 1554

despotic: wants to be d. 3657

despotism: accomplishes great things 736; can no more exist 1205; degenerates into d. 728; every d. 746; failed 726; found in d. 2218; modern form of d. 199; more complex the d. 3676; of the majority 2816; or unlimited sovereignty 729; passes into d. 727; root of d. 3749; tempered by epigrams 2704; to liberty 725; whatever crushes individuality is d. 1635; whether with d. 730

despotisms: both are d. 3544; most horrid of all d. 98

despots: benevolent d. 3638

destination: no d. 2241

destiny: a tyrant's authority 3628; of the . . . model 2046; surrender our d. 1076

destroy: every vice you d. 3750; power to d. 3443; threatened to d. 3410

destroyed: but not defeated 3937; person may be d. 3343; treated generously or d. 3936; unity will be d. 3534

destroyers of nations 620

destroys the thinker 3506

destruction: causes of its d. 319;

e. 54; played by e. 2895; whispers in the e. 2375

ears: lend me your e. 3377; man can lend ... his e. 3376; persuade others with your e. 108

earth: hell on e. 461; hope of e. 3333; joys of e. 493; level of the e. 997; lieutenants upon e. 3291; on e. will forever be 3292; peace upon e. 2622; power on e. 985; powers of the e. 492; room upon the e. 3327; supremest thing upon e. 3291; what on e. 2217; worst discrimination on e. 1405

easier to make war 2610

easy: for a person 3639; free and e. 1130; to accuse a government 1296

eat: neither should he e. 3885

eccentricity is a matter of reproach 519

echoes: manufacturing of e. 908

economic: controls 869; dynamic 3452; events 993; foundation 885; governance 3890; health 2031; insufficiency 874; interests 1712; law 1658; liberty 871; mainstream 864; modern life is e. 883; ones are incomprehensible 897; pie 2014; policy 3452; production 883; pyramid 3453; surplus 874; terrain 881; theory 3473; wisdom 898

economics: as taught 899; bad e. 862; branch of e. 2290; don't know about e. 896; is the science 951; remedial e. 218; Republican e. 895; voodoo e. 193

economist: political e. 1676; who had to worry 901

economy: American e. 906; control over ... an e. 3128; even its e. 2338; free e. 864; instability of the e. 900; is going without 902; political e. 2675; there can be no e. 894; watch over the e. 182; world e. 2347

edge: lost their e. 1869; of a new frontier 2322; of the sword 1835

edges: rougher e. 276

editor of one of the leading ... newspapers 2730

editorials: reads well in e. 357

educated: badly e. 119; only the e. are free 1137; risks 3905

educates and subsidizes 282

education: aim of e. 910; almost all e. 909; and catastrophe 911; appears to be the thing 929; by e. a tory 4003; classical e. 942; fact that e. 931; high level of e. 698; higher e. 1409; intellectual e. 852; is a process 311; is a state-controlled 908; is the art 2295; is the result 924; makes a people 913; of the people 914; or of wealth 994; political e. 2779; poor risk for e. 3121; public e. 991; result of e. 3539; that rulers ought to have 915

effect: cannot be produced 1789; has been to embody 1366; natural and necessary e. 386; of boredom 3223; of power 2989; than the cause 1300

effectiveness of a generation 3225

effects: signs and e. 1563

efficiency: administrative e. 2022; admiration for its e. 3672; there is no e. 894; total e. 103

efficient: and well-arranged 1762; are the available instruments 3344

effort: by the establishment 1577; put into a campaign 2398; redoubling your e. 1014; to reduce 1115

efforts: combined e. 2259

egg of democracy 678

eggs or tomatos 3928

egoist: any man who thinks ... is an e. 3093

egoists: come upon other e. 3274

elders: discourse of the e. 3402

elect: man you e. 3822; not going to e. 3697

elected: after he is e. 2812; can't get e. 2514; ex-president 3706; officials 3809; or reelected 3910; serve if e. 268; they get e. 2834; unless they get e. 2514

electing: who does the e. 260

election: is a bet 3814; is a moral horror 3815; is coming 638; or a horse race 3895; right of e. 3778; stay away from the e. 3789; substitutes e. 594; win an e. 1585; winning the e. 2562

elections: annual e. 3779; are won 3810; carrying e. 2156; for important offices 3816; more frequent the e. 3787

life, liberty, and e. 3107; put out of this e. 2658

esteem: deference without e. 3738

ethical: infants 2633; reasons 3850

ethics: code of e. 333; is not a branch of economics 2290; sea of e. 1884

ethnic origins of the American people 3818

eunuch: prerogative of the e. 2006

event of life 3510

events: controlled e. 1457; course of e. 659, 3208; economic e. 993; future e. 1237; great e. 1449; human e. 492; important e. 1857; march of e. 1602; narration of e. 1469; of history 404; on top of e. 3687; outcome of the greatest e. 3207; pressure of great e. 3476; will soon be on top of him 3687

ever been able to bring 2024

ever-changing topography 2848

everybody: can tell you 40; has a little bit 605; has got money 3454; hates Congress 1991; knew 3861; likes planning 1224; try to please e. 3909; who is going to vote 3797

everyone: approved by e. 943; exempts himself 1614; has an unalienable right 3665; he meets 1971; in a crowd 2200; is bound 454; is really responsible 2674; kill e. 3723; sees what you seem 3366; with a garden 2315; within reach of e. 1267

everything: above or below 977; begins in mysticism 2857; belongs to the fatherland 2573; calculates e. 2445; can be put right 3247; don't take e. 2960; explain e. 1687; express e. 1694; he wants 307; I would do e. 3308; in it is a necessary evil 3736; in our political life 1532; is black or white 3012; is settled 3314; is under federal control 195; know e. 1617; moderation in e. 2224; oppose e. 2537; risk e. 3233; settles e. 2451; should fear e. 1061; slaves lose e. 3337; that is really great 865; think of e. 3489; thinks he knows e. 2839; understand e. 1800

everywhere: he is in chains 3339; whispered e. 1254

evidence: concealing e. 1213; new e. 2009; no conclusive e. 3423; of the fact 3395; upon which it depends 3587

evil: any particular e. 2566; doing e. 616, 1757; done real e. 1214; good or an e. 654; good or e. 2125, 3746; government 744; government . . . is an e. 1364; is only that men will not seek it 3744; just as e. 592; magistrate corruptible is e. 2657; means 3739; men never do e. 145; necessary e. 1322, 2016, 3736; prevailing e. 2156; productive or e. 3755; root of all e. 877, 878, 2925; spirits 3642; subjugate e. 948; sum of e. 1338; totality of e. 1012; triumph of e. 3771

evils: among the e. 2155; existing e. 539; greatest of e. 2941; in government 1302; inevitable e. 1208; of democracy 3822; threatening e. 676

evolution: of a new generation 906; revolution as a whole . . . to e. 3216

ex-president: by such a large majority 3706; lovely title, e. 3709

exact science 1317

examination: decent and manly e. 1307

examined: well e. 631

example: by its e. 1331; good e. 2217; is always more efficacious 657; results of his own e. 454; set the e. 3725

exasperation: exhaustion and e. 1982

excellence: hope to obtain e. 1005; makes people nervous 454

excellent: in their way: 2791; never so e. 2753; to have a giant's strength 3633

exception: admits not some e. 1897; possible e. 3406

excess: carried to an e. 3176; in e. of the demand 3579; moderation even in e. 2225; poverty and e. 3867

excise a hateful tax 3442

excited in our opposition 113

excitement: motion and e. 2915; runs high 3272

excuse: any e. 3629; for failure 3628; for not thinking 3524; history never accepts 1454

excuses: several e. are always less convincing 3

faced by the armed forces 2662
faces: take their f. 2175
fact: absurd f. 2258; equality in f. 984;
  evidence of the f. 3395; kept alive by
  the f. 1243; merely marks the point
  1038; of a man's having proclaimed
  2124; paradoxical f. 991; particular f.
  3972; plain f. 656; set it down as a f.
  1261; turn it into a f. 985; ugly f. 3487
faction: liberty is to f. 2091; party f.
  1856; whisper of a f. 2560
facts: archivists of f. 1037; are never
  neutral 1039; are sacred 1026; are
  stubborn things 1025; are ventriloquists' dummies 1942; ask for f. 1029;
  baffled by the f. 1030; belief in f.
  1036; claim to be f. 632; collection of
  f. 1041; deny the f. 1040; disbelieve
  all f. 3465; dispenses with f. 1043; do
  not cease 1027; dozen f. 1029; eternal
  f. 1028; have been supplied 1035; ignoring f. 2877; in politics 1023; knew
  th' f. 1011; knowledge not of f. 910;
  notebooks of f. 1795; practice by f.
  1031; shown by f. 2002; speak for
  themselves 1024; superiority in its f.
  562; that are needed 1035; they marshall f. 625; to which they refer 1044;
  trouble with f. 1032; very few f. 1023;
  what are f. 1038; which become lies
  1473; words may varnish f. 1861;
  wrong in his f. 1045
faculties: according to his f. 984; of
  men 3108
faculty: of reason 3393; of speech 3393
fail: freedom to f. 873; in originality
  3922; I would sooner f. 1390;
  nothing can f. 2483
failed to make the adjustment 2545
failing: common f. 751
failure: excuse for f. 3628; formula for
  f. 3909; is a stranger 3930; is
  decisive 2866; is ignominious 3893;
  last refuge of the f. 63; loneliness of
  a f. 3930; penalties of f. 776;
  wisdom through f. 3919
failures: few f. 3923; human f. 3033;
  to understand 1384
fain to explore 2583
fair: in the breathing spaces 950; that's
  not f. 3974; to judge 3260
fairness: is . . . justice 1750; or justice 2110

faith: act of f. 825, 2918; and discipline
  2768; article of my f. 2642; in
  human beings 2176; in that f. 949;
  is in religion 2603; is rewarded 2918;
  let us have f. 949; lost f. 2789; of all
  f. 4001; of tomorrow 630; of yesterday 630; with the trust 3876
faithful to his principles 2270
faiths: political f. 2242
fall: by dividing we f. 471; under a
  tyrannical regime 3671
fallacy: daring f. 1545
false: entirely f. 1280; on the other
  1521; that which is f. 1827; to his
  friends 1491; true or f. 2266
false-face for the urge to rule 3179
falsehood: and errors 3054; and truth
  2126; has a perennial spring 1276; of
  the pretext 1210; idealism is f. 1536;
  truth with f. 2125
fame: and tranquillity 1047; contempt
  of f. 1050; hall o' f. 1483; is so sweet
  1048; struggle for its fame 2336; usually
  comes to those 1052
families in the world 1402
family: institution of the f. 1411; one
  big f. 425
famous: for dividing the pie 2516;
  make you f. 2491
fanatic: enslaved as the f. 1015; is a
  man 1011
fanaticism: and intolerance 3533; consists 1014; nature of f. 1012; to barbarism 1019
fanatics: foolish f. 1013; making f.
  1016; play a prominent role 3238
fancies: jokes and f. 2430
fangs: bites with keener f. 748
far: goes too f. 3130
farce: history . . . is a f. 1475
farm: committed to a f. 1123; vote
  yourself a f. 2328
farming looks mighty easy 1697
farms: robbed of their f. 1860
fascism: has now no meaning 1868; is
  capitalism plus murder 3731; is not
  defined 3730; was a counter-revolution 3197; that is f. 745
fashion: alone should dominate 1267;
  in America 2732; this year's f. 349
fat: butter merely makes us f. 3871;
  too f. to run 544

fate: determine our f. 1178; indicates
his f. 2471; milder f. 3666; of
idealists 1556; of mankind 806; of
new truths 3613; of this country 914
father of his people 3283
fatherland: is in danger 2573; workers
have no f. 2341
fathers: brought forth 2305; victory has
a hundred f. 3917
fatigue of judging 3501
fatted calf 3173
faults: account of the very f. 3915; are
not in our constitution 582; conceal
f. 1213; due to the guilt 3671; he
could have mentioned 59
favor: doing someone a f. 1020; sign of
God's f. 3764
favorable: generous and f. 3986
fear: and danger 2781; begins in f.
2847; changes we f. 303; chronic f.
1058; corrupts 1059; everything 1061;
exempt from f. 1068; is the foundation 1057; it would make me 3124;
of a fall 82; of a loss 1059; of life
1065; of the police 2286; out of f.
2318; reason to f. 3210; reasoning as
f. 1066; respect based on f. 1062; say
what he thinks without f. 3597;
tempered by f. 545; that they might
have to stop 716; the only thing we
have to f. 1067; those they f. 3659;
to be feared is to f. 1060
fears: and distastes 1070; required by
its f. 3307
feast to which all the guests 1978
feasting: dinner and f. 43
feathers: largest possible amount of f.
3445
feature: redeeming f. 2942
features of the present 2209
fed: hunger and are not f. 2632
Federalists: social bases of the f. 2503
federation: democratic f. 401
feeble: resource of the f. 3369
feebleness of our virtues 3762
feed with the rich 3983
feel: permits them to f. 3462
feeling: intense f. 3610
feelings: deep f. 1531; determined by
the f. 2440; of disgust 1086;
thoughts and f. 1403
feet: are guided 1233; die on your f.

23; firmly planted 3126; of clay
1966; under their f. 1902
fellow: man 3733; other f. 1202, 3907;
other f. just blinked 413; young f.
1103
fellow-men better 3180
fellows: liberties of their f. 707; opinions of their f. 1275; superior to his
f. 974; who heaved dead cats 3119
fence: sit on a f. 644
fetter the mind 3644
fetters: break their f. 3159; his f. fall
3340; of gold 3321
few: can touch 3366; corrupt f. 594;
die and none resign 2383; earned by
a f. 1765; gain of a f. 2533, 2534;
game of the f. 3618; governed by
the f. 2184; grossly as the f. 2152;
have the capacity 915; know what
you are 3366; led . . . by the f.
2186; rule of the f. 3661; should be
governed 675; there be that dare
3619
fibers: multitude of f. 823
fiction: continuous f. 3062; heroes and
villains from f. 1446; part f. 2919
field: game of American politics 3677;
in the f. 934; level f. 881; of human
conflict 3842; of knowledge 1631; of
politics 2221; of public education
991; of truth 1739; of world policy
1705
fields: fight in the f. 3896
fierce: she is f. 3991
fife and drum 516
fight: and die 3836; begun to f. 2298;
chance to f. 2436; for freedom 738;
in the fields 3896; in the hills 3896;
men will f. 3219; on the beaches
3896; on the landing grounds 3896;
peril in the f. 3906; refuse to f.
2643; through to victory 1529; too
cowardly to f. 544; without
ideologies 1698
fighting: periods of f. 2609; test of f.
3785; ways of f. 3897
fights for the right 2786
figure: many a public f. 1488; mythical
f. 3150; of the reasonable man 3150
figures: facts and f. 2002
file: on which my future depends 231;
rank and f. 2489, 2527

fool's excuse 3628
foot: trample under f. 3261
football: kick it about . . . like a f. 3583
footnotes: silent f. 1448
forbearance: mildness and f. 1298
forbidden . . . thoughts 3492
force: and fraud 1119; another 1715;
    brute f. 3146; government is f. 1109;
    government of f. 1110; great f. 2856;
    has no place 1112; in law 1887; is not
    a remedy 1120; lacking in f. 1949;
    limitations of f. 1113; maintained by
    f. 2090; more than our f. 768; na-
    tions use f. 2697; of numbers 2160;
    or fraud 2156; power not based on f.
    1114; spiritual f. 2339; use of f. 1115;
    without wisdom 3953; works on ser-
    vile nations 1111
forced into belief 3135
forces: are shaking 286; armed f. 2662;
    hidden f. 1658; not of men but of f.
    2888; of a capitalist society 274; of
    the crown 3109; outer f. 1956
forefathers: reform our f. 3560
foreign: affairs 797; correspondents
    3056; country 3563; nations 2588;
    policy 1708, 1709, 1710, 2022, 2625;
    relations 780; wars 3102; what is f.
    2347
forest: carry timber to the f. 243; of
    skepticism 629
forgers: liars and f. 2127
forget the world's dreadful injustice
    1424
fork: knife and f. 3091
form: a new one 3158; in which the
    masses 2459; no conception 3746; of
    addiction 1546; of brain damage
    899; of censorship 3719; of class
    struggle 1409; of continuous fiction
    3062; of freedom 1170; of govern-
    ment 683, 703, 708, 709, 710, 715,
    973, 1342, 1345, 1583, 3268, 3636,
    3661; of incest 2345; of misgovern-
    ment 3185; of organization 872; of
    sound words 1870; of state 3424; of
    tyranny 3645; which destroys 1556;
    change in f. 2902; lowest f. 2531;
    objectionable f. 3661
former imposes his will 2829
formidable: most f. 2780
forms: of bias 3017; of government

706, 1338, 1351, 2663, 3165; of
    mistake 1249; of political organiza-
    tion 2551; most intense f. 3533
formula: for dullness 3404; for failure
    3909; for success 3909
fortitude: higher f. 355
fortnight: beyond the next f. 619;
    hanged in a f. 618
fortress: like a f. 198
fortune: hostages to f. 2793; make a f.
    896; make your f. 419
forum: open f. 1171
forward: walk f. 538
fossilism: inertness and f. 3174
foundation: economic f. 885; of all
    good things 2484; of all morality
    2285; of government 1760; of law
    1885; of most governments 1057;
    upon which all their happiness 3872
foundations: are laid far back 3206; of
    political liberty 691
fountain of honor 1294
four freedoms 2929
fourth estate of the realm 3037
fox-hunting the wisest religion 546
foxes: have a sincere interest 638; tie
    firebrands to f. 3213
foxholes: atheists in the f. 148; or
    graveyards 3032
fractiousness, seccession, and the quest
    3866
frame: human f. 2986; of government
    1339
framework: of loyalty 2409; within a f.
    993
fraud: force and f. 1119; force or f.
    2156; god . . . was a f. 3119
free activity 853; again 2960; all are
    not f. 3347; always been f. 3342; an
    oppressed nation 3828; and active
    1530; and easy 1130; and firm 2591;
    and independent 2351; and uncom-
    mitted 1123; are rulers 703; as they
    want to be 1163; as you can 3320;
    association with others 875; being
    1648; born f. 2350, 3339, 3746;
    breathe f. 2307; butterflies are f.
    1122; cannot be f. 3320; chains than
    to be f. 3338; citizen f. 3869; com-
    merce 1169; confused the f. 1120;
    country 1459, 2535; covenant among
    f. men 707; democratic government

gallows: youth to the g. 1340
game: anarchism is a g. 92; can't stop playing the g. 2795; enjoy the g. 2510; football g. 2865; has become so expensive 258; know the g. 2865; of American politics 3677; of checkers 3462; of life 2790; of the few 3618; pursue their g. 2199; rules of the g. 3360; war is a g. 3839
games were political games 3295
gang of robbers 1703
gangsterism is worse 749
gangsters: acted like g. 1720
gap: bridge the g. 778
garb: reason's g. 3137
garden: everyone with a g. 2315; tilt everybody into the g. 3289
garment: whole g. 3742
gasoline is much more likely 1712
gates of Hades 1503
gauntlet of the mob 1692
geese: seeme a flock of g. 1105
gender: because of her g. 4009
general: and abstract ideas 1590; confusion 3243; elections 3816; good g. 1579; mass 1350; prize of the g. 2985; who tells his troops 738
generalities: glittering g. 1866
generalization: one safe g. 3209
generals: same occupational hazard as g. 2879
generation: each new g. 2668; effectiveness of a g. 3225; less for this g. 2244; no g. has had to do 1219; of Americans 2669, 3269; of critics 483; of mammals 906; opinions of one g. 2429; raised in the shadow 3865; rising g. 2243, 2244; to generation 1280, 3072
generations: former g. 1767; future g. 905; in three g. 391
generosity: exercise our g. 3878
generous and favorable 3986
genius: appears in the world 458; function of g. 3076; grace of g. 1928; instantly recognizes g. 459; is dangerous 2192; is that in whose power a man is 2955; of a good leader 1928; of its scientists 2632; of the constitution 585; one is a g. 1852; organizing g. 2699; originality and g. 3549; political g. 1958; rules 2188; talent and g. 457

gentleman: as well as any g. 2084; he is not a g. 437; is to a gent 1684; prince of darkness is a g. 3765; real English g. 1676
gentlemanly thing 3766
gentlemen: political g. 1555
genuflexion: grudge a g. 48
genuine: article be g. 3980
gestures: words and g. 2183
giant: use it like a g. 3633
giants: nuclear g. 2633; or dwarfs 2216
gift: work by g. and by theft 1438
gifts: all the g. 2705; of nature 3984
girls and roses 786
give: up the task: 3169; what we g. 3333
glances and its murmurs 3552
*glasnost* will go 405
glass eyes 2808
global village 1725
gloom: retrospective g. 2866
glory: desire for g. 1046; half-remembered g. 1242; in the triumph 3906; is like a circle 1049; is nothing 1626; long for g. 1056; love of g. 69; no g. 15; of Europe 2234; of rulers 1352; true g. 3082; war as all g. 3841
glory's small change 3911
gloves: silk g. 3203
gluttony: adultery or g. 1507
goaded: sufficiently g. 2698
goal: become the g. 510; not reaching your g. 1240
goals: national g. 3035; political g. 915
God: almighty 2043, 2354; and the politicians 2638; as if we were g. 3540; authority from g. 142; belief in g. 305; circumvent g. 2822; commission from g. 1707; does not take sides 3931; even by g. himself 3291; gives us to see 2302; goodness of g. 1168; grants liberty 2052; hath given liberty 2049; himself has no right to be a tyrant 3646; honest g. 1497; is just 1780; is on the side 3853; is usually on the side 3852; man with g. 2171; may have been waiting 1611; must have loved the people 3281; obedience to g. 3161; offers to every mind 3620; prevent us 3491; principle of g. 3245; put your trust in g. 3574; sin against g. 216; so far from

g. 2727; sworn upon the altar of g. 3645; thank g. that I am endued 3282; voice of g. 2451; who gave us life 2041

god: even a g. cannot change the past 3559; great g. 1663; in the sanctuary 3119; is on everyone's side 893; of nature 129; you are a g. 3723

goddess: powerful g. 12

God's: favor 3764; lieutenants upon earth 3291; mercy 2933; throne 3291; things that are g. 3432

gods: are on the side 3900; drag down the g. 2195; laughter of the g. 1739; leave the outcome to the g. 848; people of g. 682; they are called g. 3291; wish to destroy 91

going: gets rough 18; gets tough 19

gold: fetters of g. 3321; filling 2265; religion of g. 385; silver and g. 3777; standard 895

golden: age 2232; rule 3805

golf: made more liars than g. has 3457; music and g. 2913

good: a cause 1186; accomplish g. 1087; and an evil 654; and the brave 2149; bad and g. 3741; common g. 2034; distant g. 1226; doing g. 2743; enough 2310, 3241; extremely g. 2220; for America 3074; for me too 2526; for the public g. 2764; general g. 423; go about doing g. 3881; government 1329, 1343; greater g. 2016; in slavery 1088; is furthered 2147; judgment 1734; just and g. 875; license to be g. 1152; man 3763; moderately 2226; national g. 2526; neighbor 1705; of his country 792; of man 2840; of subjects 3304; of the country 2370; of the people 1879; of the state 2112; or bad 1203; or evil 2125, 3746; or for ill 1331; or harm 3880; supreme g. 1154; they inculcate 3182; to be on your guard 793; to be silly 1102; to do g. 1355; will 1776; with the bad 1209; wise and g. 313

goodness of God 1168

goods: and services 401; are indivisible 423; primary social g. 978, 3259

goose: plucking the g. 3445

Gospels: throughout the g. 2239

gossip unlike river water 1264

govern: a country 2707; a nation 1925; another man 2659; easy to g. 913; government cannot g. 3041; great number should g. 675; hand on me to g. 3652; he that would g. 1945; ideal way to g. 2478; in prose 246; laws which g. 1037; right to g. 3637; safely g. home 3669; society by episodes 3043; states 2193; the state 2745; the world 129, 1833; themselves 1077, 2666; think they g. 2653; those that toil 1968; those who g. 226; to g. is always to choose 1297; unfit to g. 377; wrong 2249

governance: economic g. 3890; I was learning 1293

governed: ability among the g. 2735; arbitrarily g. 3985; be g. 1077; by a child 1950; by a despot 735; by an elite 407; by higher ... considerations 2797; by the few 2184; by the same laws 1403; consent of the g. 3638; every well-g. state 887; few should be g. 675; nations are g. 3477; power from the g. 3637; their rude age 2257; they will be g. 2653; well g. 835; world is g. 3941

governing: the nation 2562; according to the common weal 3285; art of g. 1926, 1876; function of g. 1979; is a tougher deal 248; lack of it among the g. 2735; officials 704; pleasure of g. 1308; power 1347

government: abandon a g. 2591; ability of g. 3075; accountancy that is g. 1315; accuse a g. 1296; acts of g. 1307; adopted by our g. 1708; aim of g. 2037; all g. 466; and co-operation 101; art of g. 1328, 1344, 3889; art which one government ... learns 3444; attempts to handle 1310; attitude of g. 2665; autocratic g. 2460; bad g. 2460; basis of effective g. 3568; basis of g. 1752; best g. 1318, 1336; best practical g. 128; big g. 906; bureaucracy 227; business of g. 2144; by compulsion 1172; by discussion 718; by our wickedness 1324; by the uneducated 119; called by his g. 3271; can be no better 2450; can do it worse 1312; can easily exist 1893; can make you richer 2519; cannot be stronger 2681; cannot endure 491; cannot govern 3041; changes of g. 3787; civil g. 1420; compassionate g. 3876; confusion that g. 1361; conservative g. 1516; constitutions of g. 2661; control over its g. 1357; control the g. 1979; councils of g. 1295; deception by the g. 2139; degenerates 2655; deliberations of g. 3985; democratic g. 688, 2545; denounces it 1656; does not acquire 3001; doesn't work 2523; easier to run a revolution than a g. 3189; efficient g. 737; employed by a g. 3479; encounter in g. 453; end of g. 1349, 1355, 1742; English g. 2690; essence of g. 2950; even in its best state 1322, 1364; every other g. 1702; everybody in g. 65; evil g. 744; evils in g. 1302; exist without a g. 2771; existing g. 3158, 3267; expands to absorb 3447; exploitation and g. 2887; first duty of g. 852; form of g. 426, 683, 703, 708, 709, 710, 715, 973, 1342, 1345, 1348, 1583, 3268, 3636, 3661; forms of g. 706, 1338, 1351, 2663, 3165; foundation of g. 1760; frame of g. 1339; free g. 502, 2370; French g. 2690; from our g. 2325; function of a g. 1356; function of g. 1367; function of our g. 374; giving money and power to g. 1314; good g. 1283, 1285, 1286, 1329, 1343, 1354, 2488; good works of g. 557; greatest need . . . is for g. 1283; guilt of a g. 1301; had better get out 2637; has a tendency 1311; has become a Stop and Shop 2497; has gone beyond its limits 1363; hereditary g. 2264; honor in g. 2273; I'm from the g. 62; implies the power 1881; important thing for g. 1362; in g. you don't have to worry 225; in which all the people 1286; inherit a g. 2264; initiative without g. 1313; injure the g. 3696; institution of g. 1350; intelligible g. 2245; is a continuance 3868; is a trust 2369; is a very simple thing 1316; is absolute 1325; is an association of men 3728; is an ex-

pedient 1323; is based 1332, 2445; is begotten of aggression 1327; is best 1319; is doing 2749; is everywhere 2181; is force 1109; is founded 2660; is free 2161, 2651; is immoral 2291; is in some respects 1702; is instituted 1351; is less progressive 2680; is more than the sum 600; is neither business 1333; is not an exact science 1317; is not best 1320; is not legitimate 3557; is organized 2460; is the exact symbol 1299; is the political representative 3147; is the problem 3067; is the teacher 1331; is transformed 728; it deserves 37; just g. 994; keep the g. 374; kick the g. 1305; kind of g. 713, 3654; less g. 1309; live under a g. 3042; looked to the g. 3883; make every g. 597; measures of the g. 3888; minimalist g. 557; model of g. 2046; never come from g. 2045; never loses anything 1298; no g. can be long secure 2538; no g. has ever been beneficent 2665; no g. is better 339; no g. ought to be without censors 3040; no g. proper 1289; no g. would be necessary 3735; not a g. 1368; nothing so weakens a g. 1655; object of g. 1352, 3108, 3870; objectives of a g. 744; of all the people 2684; of checks and balances 1230; of force 1110; of laws 587, 1895; of man by man 1326; of our own choice 3219; of statesmen 1341; of the United States 281; of the day 480; of the people 2682; of worse men 3939; office of g. 1353; officers of the g. 2369, 2376; officials 666; operations of the g. 2384; oppressed by their g. 3218; orderly g. 1210; ourselves 1336; parliamentary g. 2540; people and the g. 3641; people's g. 2683; pillars of g. 1291; policies 3788; popular g. 1343, 2158; powers of g. 2018; practice of self-g. 707; practices it 1656; prevents the g. 481; principle of g. 2016; program 2748; purpose of the g. 3270; religion and g. 3867; representative g. 1985; republic is a g. 2260; republican g. 1346; responsible only 2013; resting on a valua-

nations 1720, 3548; objection 1775; obstacle to truth 3621; offices 1374; party 2567; personages 1388; political parties 2543; power 1386, 2158, 2629, 3007; president 3683; principles 2166; privilege of the g. 1396; reality 2120; right 3740; road 3744; robbery 1761; silent majority 2326; society 3879, 3998; states 1706; statesman 3546; step 1805; stumbling block 3025; talents 1374; task in life 3313; thing 932; things 3420; thinker 3463; thoughts 1566; to be g. 1382; too g. for his income 3392; tragedy of science 3487; truly g. 1391, 1530; truths 3611

greatest: among the g. 1390; need 1283

greatness: essence of g. 1378; idea of g. 1381; is not manifested 955; is usually the result 1373; knows itself 1380; of soul 1370; past g. 1242; power with g. 1400; stirred humanity into g. 1665; test of g. 1391; without g. 806

Greece: city-states of g. 1344

greed: American g. 2525

Greeks took the beating 2545

grief: comes to g. 2275

ground: drive yourself into the g. 2863; of liberty 2047

grounds: for our beliefs 152; landing g. 3896

group: interests 417; of people 2026; of the unwilling 204; will have a higher rate of voting 3788; strengthening some g. 909

groups: against public funding 259; can attain their ends 712; conservative g. 2258; disadvantaged g. 3799; interest g. 2033; linguistic or religious g. 700; of individuals 2178; which have to push 3217

grow too fond of it 3847

growth: bring about g. 307; enemy of g. 508; full g. 845; is a leap in the dark 301; of every superior mind 923; state of g. 2038; states . . . have their g. 3412

guarantee against an infection 3468

guaranteed: absolutely g. 1585

guarantees against tyranny 3647

guaranty of freedom 3116

guard: and defend 2052; be on its g. 2155; we have changed the g. 2762

guarded: carefully g. against 2646

guests: all the g. 1978

guidance: belief in our own g. 1076

guide: and not a jailer 3550; of human life 2428

guideposts and landmarks 1371

guilt: face the g. 3341; of a government 1301; of that regime 3671

guilty: rewarding the g. 2917

guinea: I would not give half a g. 1348

gulf between politics 2817

gun: barrel of a g. 435; every g. that is made 2632

guns: butter or g. 3871; defend ourselves with g. 3855; men with g. 1529, 1911; not . . . without g. 3855

gutter: straight into the g. 1547

guy: benefits the other g. 3455; who wants 2498

gymnasium: life's g. 676


habit: break the h. 2325; order breeds h. 3226; tyranny is a h. 3674

habits: bloc-voting h. 3818; men's h. 2463; of the poor 1417; thoughts and feelings 1403

hack: make a h. out of him 602

Hades: gates of h. 1503

hair: twisted round her h. 231

half: a truth 2855; its members 3999

half-truths: all truths are h. 3600

hall: hire a h. 1192; o' fame 1483

hallmark of the educated 651

halls of the politicians 2792

hallucinations: visions and h. 1544

halo: jealousy with a h. 2279

halves: to be both h. 1673

hammer which we use 433

hand: bite the h. 3883; difficult to take in h. 3171; drawn to the h. 797; eye than by the h. 3366; heavy 1932; makes the h. bleed 3149; man without a h. 3784; on the one h. 1689; puts his h. on me 3652; that rules the press 3049

handles on a reality 1919

handmaidens of legislative decisions 1982

hearts: alleys in their h. 1385; best h. 2981; first in the h. 1387; human h. endure 2788; many h. 2159; of men and women 2063

heat: laws of h. 755; light and not h. 650

heaven: equality would be a h. 980; kingdom of h. 1487; knows 1252, 1262; though h. fall 1745; thrown out of his h. 1549

heels: drag its h. 1986; too near the h. 1460, 3606

height of their power 325

held: in contempt 3882; more tightly h. 2564

hell: chase after truth like all h. 3596; Christianity without h. 277; give them hell 2327; go to h. without perspiring 3014; hath no fury 239; ideal out of h. 1549; if Hitler invaded h. 1997; it is all h. 3841; of a fright 1329; on earth 461; tell you to go to h. 771; to belong 2162

helm: hold the h. 1931; prepared to take the h. 375

help: and support 3305; here to h. 62; the many who are poor 3875; with God's h. 2762

herd: level of the h. 695; resigns momentarily from the h. 827; vulgar h. 2532

herds: flocks and h. 2264

here: it can't happen h. 762

heresie: turn'd to h. 3614

heresies: are experiments 3612; begin as h. 3613

heresy: of one age 176; of some wise man 3960; run the risk of h. 832; signifies no more 2426

heretic: oppressor or a h. 3246

heritage: ancient h. 3269; cultural h. 2930

hermits: Egyptian h. 1262

hero: for fifteen minutes 3921; needs a h. 1936; show me a h. 1395

heroes: and villains 1446; are created 1394; villains or h. 3012; who are h. 2871

heroism: madness or h. 1597

hide: from us 1532; two feet thick 2825

high: estate 3915; moral principle 2740; office 2381; stations 3756

highways of the world 3119

hills: fight in the h. 3896; of Georgia 3031

hindrance: no greater h. 2542

hindsight is always twenty-twenty 45

hissing: smallest possible amount of h. 3445

histhry always vindicates 2517

historian: first requisite of the h. 1627; or a traveler 2803; were to relate truthfully 640

historians: honored by the h. 2702; of opinion 404

historical purposes 3699

histories: many h. 1458

history: all recorded h. 901; American h. 2328; as a book 1977; breathing spaces of h. 950; can be well written 1459; compels to hurry 530; deletion of our h. 3350; does not unfold 1462; dust-heap called h. 1476; dustbin of h. 3556; events of h. 404; excuse h. never accepts 1454; gets thicker 1461; has taught me 3306; human h. 911, 1588; is a bath of blood 3721; is a distillation of rumor 1464; is a gallery of pictures 1465; is a vast early warning system 1451; is facts 1473; is far too criminal 1446; is just dirty politics 1447; is littered 3861; is more or less bunk 1474; is narration 1469; is only one long story 493; is past politics 2897; is the crystallisation 1445; is the study of . . . mistakes 1471; is the transformation 1448; is the world's judgment 1466; known to h. 407; knows no resting places 1442; large scale in h. 3223; learned anything from h. 1453; liberalized by h. 821; lies which become h. 1473; locomotives of h. 3188; make more h. 2725; men are free to make h. 1463; more to shape h. 1470; occur in h. 2166; of American freedom 1131; of all 378; of class struggles 378; of crimes 1449; of ideas 1588; of liberty 2045; of mankind 1458; of political power 1458; of procedure 1131; of progress 3085; of resistance 2045; of the great events 1449; of the world 1444, 1458, 1475, 3090; of their own 2549; page of h. 1391; political h. 1667;

politics is present h. 2897; power in
h. 1563; queens in h. 3988; rather
than for h. 640; rattling good h.
2475; second time in our h. 2619;
study in natural h. 1257; suggests
272; teaches us 1440; teachings of h.
3830; throughout h. 1601; what is h.
1473; will tell lie 2141; with h. one
can never be certain 1478; world's h.
1857; writing a modern h. 1460;
written h. 1427
history-making creature 1450
hit man 1660
hive: working in a glass h. 1257
hockey: reason h. exists 2693
hole in our culture 3350
holidays: rituals and h. 2337
home: and around the world 3269;
away from h. 327, 3103; begin at h.
2062; begins at h. 2585; I suppose I
could have stayed h. 4008; in your
mind 926; like them at h. 438; or
abroad 2112; returning h. 3708; safely
govern h. 3669; take it h. 1604;
tranquility at h. 2301
homeless: hungry and the h. 2930; orphans and the h. 1415; tempest-
tossed to me 2307
honest: and rather dull 2691; art of being h. 1501; burglar 1482; debate
2434; differences 2412; doubt 3470;
fundamentally h. 333; God 1497;
heart 1816; likely to be h. 1494; man
2361, 3470; men 32, 1484, 2412,
3327; patriot 2591; politician 2835;
remain h. 1480; save what is h. 1496
honesty: in public life 1493; intellectual h. 1479; is praised 1502; not
more than h. 601; stimulates h. 2286
honor: abide with h. 1304; fountain of
h. 1294; in government 2273; in h.
clear 779; is like a match 3768; is
not the exclusive property 2559;
knowledge and h. 1792; maintained
with h. 2617; national h. 3113; of
the press 1200; peace I hope with h.
2618; peace with h. 2619; property
or h. 2214; talked of his h. 1511;
without money 336
honorable: it is to die 2570; man 3921;
retreat is h. 3850
hope: and relief 3712; and succor 3712;

energy and h. 2768; in the world
2672; liveth in h. 1235; of better
things 3220; of earth 3333; of
freedom 3342; of posterity 2513;
only the glimmering h. 3233; rejoicing in h. 2761; that keeps the people
alive 622; there can be h. 425; to
make men 802
hopes: and dreams 1543; comforts and
h. 1070; extreme h. 1429; high h.
2686; of its children 2632; of the
future 1234
horizon of ignorance 1631
horn: blow your own h. 49
hornets break through 1914
horror: matter of h. 3024; moral h.
3815
horse: look funny on a h. 1952; race
3895; runaway h. 1018; that comes
in first 3895
horse-laugh is worth 3119
horses: cannot ride two h. 1523; stealing h. 1753
horse's foreshoulder 2833
hospitality: welcomed with h. 2564
hospitals: mental h. 2739
host of friends 1971
hostages to fortune 2793
hostility against ... tyranny 3645
hosts of error 2274
hot air 3803
hour: measured by the h. 3383; only
for an h. 2123; present h. 3239; to
hour 1472
hours: shorter h. 3358
house: buy a h. 2739; divided 491;
entering this h. 3708; in a slave state
1304; man who owns his h. 3117;
stranger in his own h. 3930
house-cleaning of his mind 3621
House of Commons 1989, 1997
House of Lords 2003, 2005, 2006
houses: just as big 3181; legislative h.
1230
Houses of Parliament 1996
human: affairs 2048, 2184, 3209, 3946;
and gentle virtue 3756; behavior
951; being 648, 827, 2691, 2927,
3352, 3361; beings 1064, 2176, 2330,
3266; blessings 1285; blunders 1470;
complex 3154; conflict 3842; creature
733; dignity 746; experience 713,

1560; failures 3033; follies 3180;
frame 2986; freedom 1127, 1456,
2364; grows not more h. 79; hands
2960; happiness 2110, 2891, 2926;
heart 2260; hearts 2788; history
1588; individual h. 1650; institutions
994, 3174; knowledge 1633, 1789,
3406; less than fully h. 3999; life
744, 1121, 1458, 2428, 2928; malice
839; mind 3119; minds 2996; nature
279, 1345, 1564, 2119, 2354, 2358,
2779, 3636; organization 992; power
1789, 2418; problem 3068; race
1923, 2346, 2607, 4002; reason
2260; reflections 3880; relations 780,
2116, 3414; relationship 215; rights
3265, 3269; self-alienation 3352;
society 1128, 1364; stupidity 839;
wants 3868; we are h. 2419;
wickedness 1470; will 2467; wisdom
3868
humanity: essential to h. 2115; friend
of h. 2776; in the higher 1423; over
humanity 1417; popular h. 3754;
progress of h. 3089; religion of h.
2176; save h. 3131; stirred h. into
greatness 1665; teach governments h.
1306; thinks in terms of h. 1284;
urge to save h. 3179
humankind: tyrannies of h. 3664
humbug or humdrum 1341
humdrum: humbug or h. 1341
humiliation: pain and h. 2996
hunger: is the mother of anarchy 94;
of ambitious minds 88; theft from
those who h. 2632
hungry: and the homeless 2930; man
2929, 2931; men 2928; tigers are
getting h. 759
hunters: attract the h. 1640
husbands: hands of the h. 3986
hut: palace than in a h. 1406
huts of Indians 3475
hyphen which joins 1292
hypocrisy: is the most difficult 1507; is
the royal road 1515; organized h.
1516; vice that cannot be forgiven is
h. 1506; without limitation 1517
hypocrite: be a h. 1504; in his pleasures
1518; see far enough into a h. 1519
hypocrites: and demagogues 3468;
called priests 1509

hypothesis: slaying of a beautiful h.
3487


I: am a Democrat 2783; am a free man
2783; am a senator 2783
ice: skating over thin i. 22
iconoclasm: rough work i. 634
idea: being called an i. 1595; can turn
into dust 1570; constricting i. 1598;
degradation of the i. 1201; die for an
i. 1540, 1541; entertain an i. 1604;
fixed i. 1597; formulated i. 1531;
good i. but it won't work 432; grand
i. 1587; has something 1565; is accepted 1571; never was an i. 1578;
new i. 1564, 1565, 1567, 1568, 1569,
2529, 3177; nothing is more
dangerous than an i. 1596; of a corporation 2656; of a law 1881; of a
people 2656; of greatness 1381; of
what the public will think 2447; old
i. 1586; only one i. 1596, 1599; opposition to some i. 113; powerful i.
1562; reject the i. 323; religion or
government 1650; some people's i.
1188; that if you leave things alone
560; that is not dangerous 1595; that
its power is a sign of God's favor
3764; that you can merchandise candidates, 254; value of an i. 1580;
whose time has come 1559, 1561
ideal: is a port 1534; pacifist i. 2713;
perfection 1535; service of an i.
1530; suitable i. out of hell 1549;
way to govern 2478
idealism: American i. 2525; bow of i.
2910; dogmatism and proselytizing
zeal 839; gone sour 623; is falsehood
1536; is the despot 1554; is the noble toga 1555; morphine or i. 1546;
springs from deep feelings 1531; to
political realism 1537
idealist: is incorrigible 1549; is one
1558; man is an i. 1524; people call
me an i. 1527
idealists: are apt to walk straight 1547;
fate of i. 1556
ideals: and principles 2873; are an imaginative understanding 1533; are
threatened 1542; destroys their i.

out of focus 1735; of men 2083; only
is concerned 2133; places of the i.
1584; popular American i. 3694
imbecility: moderation in war is i.
3724
imitation: great by i. 1377; succeed in
i. 3922
immigrants: talented young i. 3035
immoral: essentially i. 2291; or ugly
905
immorality is what they dislike 2277
immortal: men are i. 1572
immortality: approach to i. 227
impact: of a new idea 3177; of spiritual
force 2339
impatience: is fatal in politics 3194;
with fools 1086
impatient: become the more i. 2984
imperative is categorical 2269
imperialism: is the monopoly 285; sane
imperialism 2599; wild-cat i. 2599
impertinence: arrant i. 977
importance: decisions of i. 652; feel his
own i. 2355; great i. 599; of a work
1383; of more i. 1790; of the country
2401; of the point 3782
important: as the pursuit 2115; decisions 2827; for its own sake 2493; in
the exercise of power 1695; more i.
2562; operations 2495; serious and i.
3462; that a proposition 3486; thing
in life 2867; things 2827; think it is
i. 2865; who's ahead 3895
impossibility of controlling 1657
impossible: for the king 3459; government is i. 2540; ignorant enough of
the i. 1611; literally i. 3494; socialism
is i. 3353; that a man 1491; to
arouse 3208; to earn a living 2437
imposters: invented by i. 2578
impotent: all-powerful to be i. 1288
impression: permit the i. 1498
improve: freedom to i. 2106
improvement: arises from leisure 1670;
political i. 2852
improvements in the lot of mankind
3471
impulse: I feel a strong i. 3331; one i.
1015; to punish 3575
impulses: great i. 523; irrational i. 3151
inaccuracy: little i. 2117
inactionary: they are i. 2789

incest: form of i. 2345
inches: gained in i. 2047
incidents and interruptions 3043
inclination: have the i. 2200; to injustice 667
inclined to believe 1492
incognito: elegant i. 2536
income: and wealth 3259; increased i.
1409; live beyond its i. 295; meet i.
189; of ideas 3392
incompetent: and the corrupt 600;
election by the i. 594
inconsistency: little i. 2281; the only
thing 568; vacillation and i. 777
incorrigible: idealist is i. 1549
increase in cross-pressures 3793
incumbent party 2497
incumbents: blame . . . on the i. 2566
indecision: nothing is habitual but i. 648
indefensible: defense of the i. 1845
independence: individual i. 883; maintained by force 2090; virtue and i.
3745
independent: all be i. 1716; because
they are i. 1717; free and i. 2351;
free, equal, and i. 2658; is the guy
2498; of public opinion 2472; to be
i. 1147
indifference: and undernourishment
1081; of the majority 2146;
philosophy of i. 507; stupid i. 1578
indignation: feel the same i. 588;
moral i. 2279
individual: any one i. 1978; can get
wealth 1438; can never be enslaved
3343; definition of the i. 1645;
destroys the i. 1650; flatters himself
3496; freedom of the i. 826, 872;
governs each separate i. 3478; happiness of an i. 1348; human 1650;
independence 883; injustice done to
an i. 1755; is not accountable 1642;
liberty 2093, 2102, 3418; liberty of
the i. 2075; must remain 2012; no
sane i. 1001; or a party 2370; power
2093; power over any i. 2660; rights
of the i. 2012; that of the i. 3727;
wants to be a leader 167; who can
labor 865; who refuses to defend
3271; with a principle 1958
individualism: is rather like innocence
1647; rugged i. 1636

individualists: true i. 513
individuality: breaks out 1643; has no
    play 1643; is the aim 1637; whatever
    crushes i. 1635
individuals: are doing 1362; are not ex-
    posed 2943; composing a majority
    2145; composing them 1530; fears
    the i. 2176; have to limit 1701; many
    i. 1978; number of i. 417; numbers
    of i. 423; or groups 2178; pride of i.
    1007; private i. 3725; several i. 2408;
    who were capable 1574
indivisible: freedom is i. 3347
industrial world 2900
industries rise and fall 307
industry: and all the virtues 456; free i.
    1169
inefficient: most i. 709
inequality: has the natural and
    necessary effect 386; is as dear 989;
    is justified 3996; is the inevitable
    consequence 987; no greater i. 995;
    to their own advantage 1007
inertness and fossilism 3174
inevitable: arguing with the i. 488
infallibility: convinced of their own i.
    1927; unbroken i. 3235
infallible: none of us is i. 3033
infancy: nations . . . have their i. 3558
infants: ethical i. 2633
infection of people 3468
inferior: make you feel i. 3994; of any
    man 3261
inferiors: revolt 1006; social i. 1002
infidels: lives of i. 3085
inflation: is a great conservatizing issue
    1659; is as violent 1660; is like sin
    1656; might be called prosperity
    1653; persistent i. 1655; rate of i.
    3452; steel prices cause i. 1654;
    won't cure 2528
influence: and honor 1200; and its ex-
    istence 2336; disturbing i. 2242; he
    has no i. 3507; on the minds 404;
    permeating i. 2463; unwarranted i.
    1295
influences a president 3686
inform: not to i. himself 3794
information: access to i. 3788; drowning
    in i. 1832; in the hands 2954; in the
    world 1033; on which he has based it
    1733; persuasive i. 2807; without i. 2467

information's pretty thin stuff 1034
informed: better i. 3054; well enough
    i. 1357
ingrate: one i. 2395
ingredients: two prime i. 1010
inhabitants: argue for a lifetime 3578;
    of different planets 1403
inherited class status 2732
initiative: fruitful i. 1313; wipe out
    private i. 233
injure the government 3696
injuries: and attempts 3107; slight i.
    3936
injustice: anywhere 1774; breaking
    down i. 3781; defeat i. 3739; done
    to an individual 1755; dreadful i.
    1424; greatest i. 1769; in the greater
    benefits 1765; inclination to i. 667;
    national i. 1773; suppress i. 1366; to
    do any i. 1757
injustices: established i. 1766
ink: hide himself . . . in his own i.
    1843
innocence: rather like i. 1647
innocent: indicting the i. 2917; most i.
    of men 1277; reign and be i. 1946
innocents: children and other i. 1447
innovate is not to reform 3178
innovation for which the public is not
    prepared 3987
inquiry: free i. 3142; leads to i. 506
insanity: our i. 2345
insensitiveness: certain i. 2765
insolence: dose of i. 3004
insolent: apt to be i. 3003
insolvent: unluckiest i. 3392
inspiring: great and i. 865
instability: mark of i. 2242; of the
    economy 900
instinct: keen and hostile i. 746; of the
    people 2671; political i. 2334
instincts: animals have i. 3434; justify
    our i. 152; predatory i. 879; saving i.
    4001; true to your i. 2294
institution: is the lengthened shadow
    1375; of government 1350; of the
    family 1411; presidency is an i. 3690;
    which does not suppose 2657
institutions: aim and end of our i.
    1177; are just 220; are reasonably
    just 599; bureaucratic i. 238; country
    with its i. 3267; critic of our i. 2005;

67; will probably be right 3144; wise
j. 1938; world's j. 1466
judgments: serve but to declare 1732;
too quickly formed 1737; value j.
1039, 3946; vulgar j. 3929
judiciary is the safeguard 580
jungle: law of the j. 2907
junket and a mimeograph machine
2008
junto: oligarchical j. 729
juries: trial by j. 579
jurisdiction: SEC had j. 218
just: and good society 875; because he
is j. 2798; God is j. 1780; laws are j.
1758; men will be j. 1758; no man
can be j. 1781; nothing is j. 1496;
our cause is j. 3164; reasonably j.
599; scrupulous and the j. 3240
justice: acts of j. 1756; administration
of j. 1760; and good will 1776; as
fairness 978; authority without j.
1763; be done 1744, 1745; capacity
for j. 667; circumstances of j. 1751;
consistent with j. 709; contrary to j.
2798; delayed 1748; demanding j.
1768; denies freedom 1783; dream of
j. 429; fairness or j. 2110; government without j. 1761; how fond men
are of j. 1767; in a sinful world
2914; inequality is j. 3996; is like a
train 1747; is the end 1742; is the
first virtue 1762; is the sanction
1766; is the wish 1749; is truth
17453; liberty and j. 891; mocks at j.
1783; more devoted to order than to
j. 3025; not pity 1752; or human
happiness 2110; plucks j. 1784; price
of j. 1207; pursuit of j. 2227; really
is 1750; reason and j. 2366; severest
j. 1770; strictest j. 1769; think j. requires 3144; thou shalt not ration j.
668; threat to j. 1774; to all 1798;
ultimate j. 2672; way of j. 1779;
without j. 1782
justifiers: motivators and j. 839
justly: dealing j. 1746


keen as their resentment 1089
keep: on being a success 3901; quiet and
listen 3375; your powder dry 3574

kettle and the earthen pot 472
key: minor k. 3245; of knowledge
1804; to success 3905; to wisdom 136
kick it about all day 3583
kids and a dog 3064
kill: and be killed 2579; they do not k.
1834
kind: anything of the k. 3599; do not
ask me to be k. 1505; less intense k.
3661; of death 3315; of dramatic
balance 3641; of government 713
3654; of loyalty 2586; of man 3569;
of pain 2105; of patriotism 2342; of
politician 2918; of regime 716; of
state 3424; of thing I'm good at
2796; of truth 1521
kindness: and lies 2116; decency and k.
744
kinds: of aspects 1458; of cheese 2707;
of conflict 2551; of morality 1508; of
slaves 3348; of wrong 1754
king: anointed k. 2250; by your own
fireside 1412; can do no wrong 2261;
can least afford 54; can stand people's fighting 3504; duties as k.
3305; esteem of a k. 2255; greater
than the k. 3678; hedge a k. 2247;
impossible for the k. 3459; in the
tyrant 3634; is truly *parens patriae*
3283; job of k. 3299; man who
would be k. 2252; never dies 2248;
of England cannot enter 3109; one
k. 2246; peasant may become k.
699; reigns 2666; sided with the k.
2267; still the k. 2256; this k.
business 3294; what is a k. 3298;
who loses his rights 95; would sit
safely 1172
kingdom: of heaven 1487; render the
k. democratic 699
kings: and ministers 182; are like stars
3297; are not only God's lieutenants
3291; art of k. 3302; can cause 2788;
compare favorably with the k. 3988;
dominion of k. 2048; done against
k. 2267; end of k. 3304; hands of
the k. 3280; heart of k. 2254; heroic
k. 2257; is mostly rapscallions 2268;
keep k. in awe 1888; madness k.
commit 2545; misfortune of k. 2262;
must indulge in 1970; priests and k.
129; right divine of k. 2249; ruin k.

I am their l. 1073; is a stimulus
1943; make the l. possible 1079;
must have the courage 55; must
keep looking 1074; national l. 3682;
of a political party 2124; of the opposition 2004; of whom it is said
1948; people may require a l. 3668;
political l. 1920; quality in a l. 1949;
real l. 1934; should not get too far
1935; test of a l. 1959; wants to be a
l. 167; war l. 2140; worthy of
assassination 2692
leaders: are merely following 1075;
betrayed by their l. 2026; good l.
1071; help personify 1919; ineffective
l. 52; job of party l. 1078; knew a
little psychology 2568; make
mistakes 1953; may be humiliated or
unseated 262; national l. 1963; of a
revolution 3240; of many unbureaucratic organizations 214; often
just do not realize 1498; people and
their l. 2086; political l. 2421; produce more l. 1957; requires of its l.
3235; undoing of l. 1927; whose
fitness 1949
leadership: and learning 1967; as high
drama 1977; effective l. 1965; essence
of l. 1956; function of l. 1957; is
demonstrated 1974; is not
manifested 1973; should be born
1942; training for l. 1962; what
makes l. 1960
leanings: often with vegetarian l. 3362
leap in the dark 301, 1830
learn: how to produce wealth 2516;
never l. anything 938, 941; ready to
l. 927
learners go to sleep 934
learning: can be packed 1090; is discovering 920; leadership and l. 1967;
little l. 1797; long in l. 936; ostentation of l. 930; pound of l. 3970;
prevent people from l. 935; prevented
our l. 1857; without liberty 2085
leave: ready to l. 3856
leaves on a tree 1644
left: and center 2031; and right 2231;
definition of the l. 2026; is benefited
2022; right and the l. 2221; women
of the l. 4007
leftist blames 2209

legal: institutions 993; powers 881
legends are lies 1473
legislation: English l. 1535; permissive
l. 1891
legislative part of the state 1292
legislator: true l. 2663
legislators of the world 1987
legislature: professional l. 1990
legislatures that bring higher prices 603
legitimacy: and consensus 689; test of
l. 2337
legitimate: government is not l. 3557;
most l. 2033; power is l. 2946
legitimation of the lust for power 2978
legs: perfectly good l. 538; to hang
ideas on 1873
leisure: arises from l. 1670
leprosy: hereditary l. 3306
less: counts for l. 2717; than fully
human 3999
lesson: better l. 1360
lessons of paternalism 1360
letter: better to deal by speech than by
l. 3367
level: down to a l. 2354; federal l. 799;
higher l. 818; highest l. 1961; of
education 698; of incompetence 196;
of the earth 997; of the herd 695;
their own l. 2195; top l. 774
lever: Archimedes' l. 1871
liability: no greater l. 1849
liable to abuse 2950
liar: best l. 2122; proved l. 2567;
should have a good memory 2132;
who has broken his promises 3101
liars: and forgers 2127; made more l.
out of the American people 3457
libel: laws of l. 2848
liberal: American l. 2034; and progressive 999; antidote 3481; cease
from being l. 2027; duty of the l.
2015; emphasizing rights 2012;
enemies 1876; I am a l. 2011, 2020;
institutions 2027; is a conservative
2028; is a man 2021; mind 2017;
nothing l. 2014; or conservative
2367; outlook 2009; party 2530;
philosophy 2012; tempered by experience 2020; the term applied
2034; they are not l. 2789; tired l.
2023; who was mugged 536; who
wishes to replace 539

liberalism: definition of l. 2014; equals l. 2010; interest group l. 2016; is trust 2019; word l. 2035

liberals: and conservatives 2033; are the flying saucers 2032; have been able 2018; have learned 2979; have never been able 2024; I have known 2025; in the house 2025; no more l. 2029; old-school l. 541; opposed to l. 2036; talk about 2030

liberation: is not deliverance 2094; of the diverse energies 844; of the human mind 96, 3119

liberator: thanks the shepherd as his l. 2076

liberties: above all l. 533; are taken 741; civil l. 524, 3024; individual l. 2034; loss of l. 2086; of all 2074; of the country 185; of their fellows 707; preserve its l. 2044; rights and l. 3259; takes l. 1202; with liberty 2064

liberty: a release 2077; absolute l. 1204; abstract l. 2042; achieved through l. 2078; aim of government is l. 2037; all l. is individual 2102; and authority 128; and democracy 1415; and justice 891; and monopoly 870; and prosperity 1513; ardor for l. 2048; basis of a democratic state is l. 2087; becomes license 2067; blessings of l. 2054; breeds iron conscience 523; bulwarks of l. 1197; but its satellite 3000; can no more exist 3745; cannot be 1820, 3334; cannot lie apart 586; cannot long exist 589; cause of l. 743; champions of l. 2040; character of l. 2090; coined l. 863; conceived in l. 2305; conception of l. 3656; condition of l. 984; consequence of l. 987; consists in doing 2056; constitutional l. 593; contend for their l. 2652; continuing l. 1357; convenience to l. 395; cost of l. 761; dangers to l. 739; defense of l. 2227; definition of l. 2076; deserve neither l. nor safety 2069; desires in l. 3332; despotism to l. 725; destroys l. 2926; does not always have clean hands 3747; does not consist 2755; doesn't even go 735; doesn't work as good 3364;

don't care about l. 2930; done nothing for l. 970; easy as l. 3321; economic l. 871; embodiment of l. 3649; enemies of l. 971; enemy of l. 2998; enjoy l. 743; equality in l. 982; essential l. 2069; exists in proportion 2071; extinguish l. 860; fire of l. 2046; free world understands l. 402; gave us l. 2041; give me l. or give me death 2043; God grants l. 2052; greatest threat to l. 223; ground of l. 2047; has been the motive 3748; has never come 2045; history of l. 2045; idea of l. 1201; if l. has any meaning 2106; if l. means anything 2107; in my view 2068; in the mouth 2053; individual l. 510, 2093, 3418; is a beloved discipline 2108; is a different kind of pain 2105; is a product of order 2492; is called license 2066; is given 2038; is its own reward 2101; is liberty 2110; is little more 2089; is never out of bounds 2083; is not a means 2095; is not collective 2102; is not license 2068; is precious 2080; is safe 3001; is secure 1176; is so much latitude 2103; is the bread 2111; is the hardest test 2104; is the means 2100; is the most jealous 2097; is the only true riches 2092; is the possibility 2109; is the right 2088; is the soul's right 2096; is to faction 2091; itself 989; knows nothing but victories 2057; lean l. 3322; liberties with l. 2064; lies in the hearts 2063; life and l. 2351; life, l., and estate 3107; life, l., and the pursuit of happiness 2352; like charity 2062; lose l. 2999; love of l. 2098; makes his own l. secure 960; means responsibility 2079; natural l. 427, 2349; obtain l. 2073; of action 2072; of conscience 3544; of each 2074; of speech 1165; of the individual 2075; of the press 1196, 1202, 1204, 1205, 1208, 1209; of thought 3520; oh liberty 2050; one of imagination's 2099; political l. 691, 1637, 3002; produces wealth 868; proof of l. 3046; provoketh l. 1165; qualities of l. 2058; real l. 2218; regulated l. 2084; relies upon

capitalists 1713; of patriotism 1713; some sort of l. 1082
luck: greatest good l. 1392
lunatic: asylum 2240; fringe 1013
lunch: free l. 3884
lust for power 2978
lying: given to l. 2128; meddle with l. 2131; privilege of l. 2112; smallest amount of l. 2122

Macbeth without the murder 359
machinery: cannot power m. 754
McWorld: forces of m. 1727
Madisonian government 1230
madman: he isn't a m. 1020
madness: of many 2533, 2534; or heroism 1597; whatever m. 2545
magazine: farspread m. 3049
magic: dust or m. 1570
magician: watching a m. 797
magistrate: chief m. 2373; corruptible 2657; should obey the laws 2487
magnanimity in politics 3947
mail: check is in the m. 1993
main stream 1693
mainstream: economic m. 864; which is the m. 3578
maintain their trust 3683
maintaining his authority 943
majesty: intrinsic m. 1347
majorities: building m. 2144; goes by m. 3952; minorities and m. 2054
majority: are wrong 2166; big enough m. 2150; big m. 3892; can do anything 2151; can never replace 2170; composing a m. 2145; easygoing or wobbly m. 418; ever in a m. 2149; exercise 2158; in the m. 2159, 2171; in the United States 2816; indifference of the m. 2146; is a m. 2172; is best repartee 2143; minority to the m. 3419; never rule 2186; not always the m. 2156; of men 2214; of one 2168; of the citizens 2153; of the whole 2145; often does not exceed 3816; one a m. 2169; opinion 2068; principles of the m. 694; right of the m. 527; rules 2157, 3808; same in a m. 729; self-indulgent m. 2188; should deprive 2160; silent m. 2326; such a large m. 3706; then and there

2277; tyranny of the m. 2154, 2155, 2156; will of the m. 2148
make up one's mind 3513
maladministration: danger of m. 1351
malcontents: hundred m. 2395
malice: and stupidity 839; human m. 839; toward none 2302
mammals: new generation of m. 906
man: able-bodied m. 2315; adapts himself 3086; against every man 2778; ain't got no right 2454; almost any m. 733; alone can enslave man 3345; always adores 1623; ambitious m. 77, 1056; amuses himself 1545; and nation 2125; another's m. 3317; as a man 3984; as a real human being 3352; as a reasonable being 708; ask a m. 3990; at whom the crown throws eggs 3928; authority of m. 2349; average m. 2114, 2470; be gracious 3537; being all free 2658; blessed is the m. 3395; brain and soul of m. 2097; can a m. truly 876; can be destroyed 3937; can be just 1781; can become famous 1054; can climb out 329; can draw the breath 2333; can feel no pleasure 1443; can normally muster 251; can perform 1646; can pursue 1507; can put a chain 3330; cannot be great 3920; cannot be too careful 965; civilized m. 632, 2577; clever m. 1494; coexist in m. 284; common m. 1352, 2316; condemned 3298; conflicting in one m. 358; consistently moral m. 570; converted a m. 747; deadly as a hit m. 1660; degradation of m. 905; devised by m. 3781; divide myself from any m. 3531; enables a m. 929; enemies of m. 2761; enslave m. 3345; equality of m. 974; every m. is born 3393; every m. loves 448; every m. meets his Waterloo at last 3914; every m. seeks 1145; every other m. 1190; every prominent m. 1255; every thinking m. 3797; exploits man 3356; fellow m. 3330, 3733; flatters a m. 1272; followers of a great m. 1072; fool of a m. 1085; foolish m. 3950; for any considerable period 1512; forgotten m. 3453; free m. 1304, 1606, 2714, 2783, 2931,

3169; fury of a patient m. 348; gazing on the stars 1548; gets to be
president 3700; given liberty to m.
2049; good m. 361, 1376, 3743;
good of m. 2840; govern another m.
2659; government of m. 1326;
greatest m. 2532; guilty m. 1777;
happiest m. 3708; hard upon a m.
476; has a right 1045, 1190; has cast
a longing eye 2387; has good or ill
qualities 3773; has made great progress 1947; has only one idea 1596;
has the right 3399; has the talents
455; has wiped the slate clean 3561;
hasn't discovered 1539; hath by
nature a power 3107; he is a m.
1524; he's a nice m. 1948; heart of
m. 467; honest m. 2361, 3470;
honorable m. 3921; hungry m. 2929,
2931; ignorant m. 1606; impel m.
314; in his shirt 1118; in political life
71, 1279; in quest 1444; in whose
power a m. is 2955; indispensable
m. 1929; insurmountable for a m.
1128; intellectual m. 1668; intelligent m. 1092; is a damn fool 1099;
is a dangerous creature 2987; is a
history-making creature 1450; is a
hypocrite 1518; is a masterpiece
1648; is a rebel 514; is a reformer
3172; is a social . . . animal 2771; is
about the same 730; is an animal
635; is an idealist 1524; is ashamed
of 324; is born free 3339; is burdened by power 1956; is by nature a
political animal 2770; is convinced
939; is cured of ambition 70; is
deprived 3262; is easy to serve 1964;
is either free or he is not 3346; is
genuinely superior 974; is in a minority 2173; is most haunted 1810; is
not like other animals 3434; is not
necessarily intelligent 1579; is not
the sum 449; is said to have a right
3110; is simply the most formidable
2780; is truly great 1391; is wise
1100; judge a m. 520; judge of a m.
966; just m. 2798 3733; just upright
m. 2276; kill a m. 3723; kind of m.
373; known to us 2804; let no m.
imagine 3507; liberty of m. 2349;
life of m. 2781; little m. 3782; living

m. 2616; make m. ridiculous 2936;
makes a m. appear 2415; makes a m.
more conservative 553; mark of a
civilized m. 161; may be in good
spirits 2922; may build 3838; may
wear it on both sides 1520; mind of
m. 3515, 3645; more right 2168;
mortal m. 477; must be certain 1199;
must be tempted 3716; must not do
2365; never replace the m. 2170; no
great m. 1393; no m. believes 3654;
no m. can be a politician 2803; no
m. can smile 16; no m. has a right
3428; no m. has the right 3399; no
m. hath a right 3440; no m. is good
enough 2659; no m. is great enough
1076; no m. is justified 616; no m.
should 942; no m. thoroughly
understands 3603; no m. was ever
great 1377; no such thing as an
honest m. 352; no m. is wise 3954;
nobody trusts 3569; nothing makes a
m. 937; of active intellect 2805; of
controversy 2242; of genius 2188; of
ideas 1594, 1692; of timid peace
2615; offers you 752; one m. in a
million 1658; one m. is enslaved
3347; one m. must be supreme
1937; one m. shall have one vote
3780; one wise m. 2170; one-m.
power 2067; only becomes wise
1632; or woman 2506; ordinary m.
1530; ordinary working m. 3358;
ought to be free 3597; ought warily
to begin 292; owes his entire existence 3415; place for a just m.
1304; poor m. 3106; poorest m.
3109; possesses an avenue 3153;
praise any m. 267; present his views
3530; prim little m. 3362; private
m. 74, 2785, 2786; public m. 2454,
2786; public relations m. 3692; rarely
an ambitious m. 78; reasonable m.
3150; remains free 1141; renounce
being a m. 851; renounces everything else 2769; republic of m. 1344;
requiring the whole m. 1926; right
of every m. 915; rights of any m.
3262; rights of m. 3273; robbed a
m. 2960; save a m. 2536; says of the
affairs of state 2773; scarce m. 2598;
seduce a m. 602; sent to lie 792;

shadow of one m. 1375; should be allowed 2646; should never be ashamed 3978; single m. 1978; so ignorant 1619; strong 1972; stupid m. 1494; teaching every m. 918; thank heaven for a m. 439; that does what he thinks 1011; that has a mind 643; that studieth revenge 497; that system 518; thing a m. can lend 3376; thinks differently 1406; thinks he has 106; thinks of himself 2471; to be a sound politician 2797; to be strong 343; to enter the kingdom of heaven 1487; to fall 1793; to know 1799; to see 2871; to whom the populace is entrusted 3309; to whom they are least dangerous 1594; unjust m. 2798; unreasonable m. 3086; vote fer th' best m. 3812; was formed by society 1408; weapons m. has ever forged 1600; what a m. believes 166; what m. wants 1143; when a m. knows 618; when a stupid m. 854; when he comes 2355; where no m. has gone before 1220; who can stand prosperity 476; who contradicts 1562; who does not know 1581; who doesn't have 36; who first said them 3136; who has a real concern 542; who has always submitted 738; who has nothing to lose 1428; who has so much 1798; who hides one thing 1503; who holds it 1012; who is denied 652; who is deprived 863; who is false 1491; who is good enough 2310; who is not radical 3121; who is selling newspapers 1996; who is the real risk-taker 236; who is too cowardly 544; who knows 461, 2350; who lives by his own work 1144; who lives without freedom 3341; who makes no mistakes 2757; who manages 201; who never alters 2422; who never looks 3054; who occupied it 3680; who offers himself 3682; who owns his house 3117; who promises least 3813; who raises new issues 3170; who says no 3166; who says them later 3136; who stands 2058; who tells other people 2021; who thinks 637, 3093, 3507; who trusts nobody 3569; who under-

stands 2828; who walks alone 1639; who wants to act 2275; who will not engage 3576; who would be king 2252; whose expenditure of speech 3392; whose life 230; whose rights I trample 3261; will begin 922; wisdom of m. 3436; wise m. 995, 1978, 3948, 3949, 3950, 3960, 3972, 3976; with God 2171; with a host of friends 1971; with both feet 3126; with two perfectly good legs 538; without a hand 3784; without a vote 3784; work of m. 1497; worked at that 460; worth of a m. 1383; would form a state 3414; would like to be true 149; would prefer 3739; you don't like 3101; you elect 3822; you like 3101

man-governed world 4004

manage: to manipulate 2446; without butter 3855

managed by the combined wisdom 3951

management of a balance of power 1704

manager: warehouse m. 1999

manhood: of living man 2616; states their m. 3412; there is a more valuable thing m. 1320

manipulate the demanding 2446

mankind: and posterity 3413; are warranted 2072; attributes to m. 3773; benevolence of m. 3880; disorders of m. 640; end to m. 2630; errors of m. 1590; ever scourged m. 3860; fate of m. 806; greater part of m. 1234; have been created 916; history of m. 1458; justified in silencing m. 1180; leading m. 2283; lot of m. 3471; mass of m. 2245; minus one 1180; miseries and credulities of m. 75; must put an end to war 2630; nationality is m. 2348; opinions of m. 492; portion of m. free 235; power among m. 998; rest of m. 2596; rights of m. 3268; service of m. 2377; sovereignty of m. 527; study m. 3658; taboo of m. 3492; when left to themselves 1287; whole of m. 2782

mankind's most terrible misdeeds 1846

manner: vulgar m. 2838

distinguished m. 2816; do not rule circumstances 658; done as cheap as other m. 3459; dread it 2079; dwarfs its m. 3420; easy for m. to rise 2921; effect on all m. 2989; enter local politics 2821; entertained by public m. 1515; equally to all m. 2104; faculties of m. 3108; fall from high estate 3915; feeble m. 2462; fellow-m. 3180; few great m. 1369; fewer m. 3989; fond m. are of justice 1767; for all men 2674; forget 2381; free m. 844, 2434, 2714; generally decide 2220; get into trouble 1544; get m. to do 1960; give m. opportunity 1353; given to all m. by nature 3134; good m. 1485, 2433, 3648, 3771; government of m. 3042; great m. 1371, 1372, 1385, 1401, 3957; group of m. 203; grow old 1976; had the rack 3061; hands of m. 3213; happy 3869; hate what they cannot understand 3020; have been elected 3804; have struggled 493; have virtue 3737; honest m. 32, 2412, 3327; hopeful m. 2902; hungry m. 2928; if all m. knew 1261; if m. had the same capacity 3373; if m. were angels 3735; imagination of m. 2083; imagine 3775; in jail 1206; indispensable m. 1930; insist most vehemently 175; irrationalities of m. 2894; it is for m. to choose 1077; judge rather by the eye 3366; kill millions of m. 3723; know m. 2197; laws and not m. 1895; lead lives 2215; leading m. 2393; live in a condition 1053; live together 1333; live without a common power 2778; looking upon m. as virtuous 1759; make m. large and strong 3640; makes m. free 3581; makes m. radical thinkers 3512; makes slaves of m. 2986; makes women love old m. 2973; making first-class m. 676; making m. ethical 2295; masses of m. 2459; may be as positive 3590; may be converted 3141; may be popular 78; mediocre m. 574; military m. 3831; misguided m. 956; more originality . . . in m. 1641; most innocent of m. 1277; move

other m. 2909; must not obey 526; nations like m. 2344, 3558; natural aristocracy among m. 116; nature of m. 2396; never do evil 145; never forgive 3758; not given to m. 3437; not of m. 587; obsolete or m. are 2631; of all social disciplines 2242; of few words 3372; of hate 3344; of knowledge 1486; of most renowned virtue 1900; of power 3005; of weak nerves 3963; of zeal 739; old m. are sent 262; only free m. 3349; other m. 1959; pain among m. 1791; participate 1889; planned by old m. 3835; prefer not to hear 3581; president's m. 2397; privileges of m. 4005; proving to all m. 3119; public m. 323, 2446, 3056; races of m. 3030; refuse to fight 2643; responsible to all m. 2674; right-thinking m. 3491; rights of m. 2755; ruled by m. 2724; same m. 2413; saying among m. 3626; see m. needing 3948; should be . . . treated generously 3936; skillful and spirited m. 518; small m. 3420; so long as m. worship 3279; so many m. 2403; so powerfully elude 1855; society of honest m. 1484; soft m. 2340; speeches of wise m. 3388; states and not m. 3430; states like m. 3412; still want the crutch 840; straw m. 2871; struggle not of m. 2888; subjecting all m. 572; teach m. 1902; teaching m. 2594; think dramatically 3482; trust themselves with m. 3571; two m. judge 2413; understand 40; understanding m. 2800; vain hope to make m. happy 802; violent m. 1022; virtue where m. 1051; walls which imprison m. 3781; want to be always in office 2382; weak m. 3485; wealthy m. 3403; well armed 1118; were born free 3746; what m. believe 173; what m. value 3256; what m. want 875; when bad m. combine 498; who agree 3491; who are inside 1996; who by their attractions 1923; who compose it 339; who died 1601; who do the work 2563; who do violence 3728; who form the lunatic fringe 1013; who have on

923; testicles of my m. 3016; that someone else is 3704; that startles us 3510; trained m. 917; truth stands in the m. 3587; violence in the m. 3717; watches itself 1673; withdraws into itself 1043

mindless: action becomes m. 3493

minds: are like parachutes 921; are naturally affirmative 155; are rarely narrow 3404; by weak m. 3176; corrupt the m. 1883; great m. 924, 1398; greatest m. 1681, 1682; human m. 2996; little m. 3947; making up their m. 1029; mediocre m. 3497; men's m. 1172, 3508; narrow m. 3469; no m. but their own 3006; of men 404; shutting our m. 1573; weak m. 1189

minions: power and its m. 2988

minister: great m. 3942; no m. ever stood 2476; of finance 3449

ministers: foreign m. 774

ministries: made many m. 3051

ministry: blunder of a m. 775; more for a marriage than a m. 4002; politics or the m. 2818

minorities: and majorities 2054; are individuals 2178; competing m. 2147; powerful m. 2181; rights of m. 2163

minority: are right 2166, 2167; deprive a m. 2160; efficient m. 2188; elite m. 127; guarantees to the m. 2161; has usually prevailed 418; is always right 2165; make a m. 2174; of one 2173; oppressions upon the m. 2153; possesses rights 2148; respectable m. 2164; suppressed m. 2162; to the majority 3419

minute: for a single m. 3824

minutes: at least five m. 1099; hero for fifteen m. 3921

miracle: yesterday's m. 1467

miracles: fictitious m. 129

mirror: before a m. 2464

misconception: popular m. 3123

misdeeds: terrible m. 1846

miserable: rise and make them m. 3279

miseries: of life 2418; two-thirds of our m. 839

misery: always more m. 1423; cause of our m. 3762; extreme m. 1429; is abated 3237

misfortune: mercy in m. 3934; of kings 2262; voluntary m. 1612

misfortunes: of poverty 2936; recital of m. 3023

misgovernment: form of m. 3185

missiles: guided m. 956

missions: fly more m. 229

mistake: first m. 2862; forms of m. 1249; great m. 1759; making a m. 2109; to believe 875; to look too far ahead 1229; when I make a m. 2882

mistaken: for truth 3012; pronounce him to be m. 2442; way of teaching 2594

mistakes: another set of m. 3562; make m. 1953; makes a m. 210; makes no m. 2757; of that time 3562; other people's m. 1471; political m. 2363

mistress: jealous and exacting m. 2097; worst m. 380

mistrusted by those who pay 3882

misunderstood: to be great is to be m. 1382

misuse of words 1842

miters: rewarded with m. 3597

mob: a small m. 124; builds on the m. 2194; do what the m. do 2203; gauntlet of the m. 1692; governors the m. 2198; that of the m. 1335; violence 2490; what the m. regards 2207; whisper to a m. 2223

mobilization of bias 2551

mobs: two m. 2203; will never do 2193

mode: of associated living 426; of grasping reality 2858; of half the world 1344

model of government 2046

moderate: governments 2218; policies 2230; scarcity 1751; socialist 3361; white m. 3025

moderates: socialists and m. 2231

moderation: even in excess 2225; in everything 2224; in politics 2223; in principle 2226; in temper 2226; in the affairs of the nation 2228; in the pursuit of justice 2227; in war 3724

modern politics 2888

modes: and forms 1351; of thinking 2500; of thought 3471

modification: admits no m. 1223

modified in practice 1031

1333; love p. 2616; make p. 591, 2610; more destructive 2616; more perfect p. 2613; must be planted 691; no longer p. 2617; of mind 1060, 2425; of the world 905; people want p. 2637; retrenchment and reform 2530; so sweet 2043; that is p. 2625; times of p. 2612, 3238; timid p. 2615; trouble with p. 237; universal p. 638; upon earth 2622; upon the world 2638; with all nations 2300; with honor 2619; without victory 2624; work is p. 2635

peak of tolerance 3532

peasant may become king 699

peasants: are robbed 1860; playing cricket with their p. 1422

peculiarity of knowledge 1815

pedantry: is the dotage 1803; is the unseasonable ostentation 930

pedants on the other 1689

pedestals: save the p. 3231

penalties: of failure 776; severe p. 598

penalty: for overachievement 86; or punishment 1881; without p. 3530

pencil: little p. 3782; plow is a p. 1697

pendulum: vibration of a p. 3942

penetrate: deeper we p. 2504

pens: make use of our p. 1214; with office p. 197

pension pay given 2385

pensions: old-age p. 2730

people: ability of p. 3075; agents of the p. 2372; all the p. 1286; alone can act 2675; American p. 888, 1875, 2046, 2086, 2312, 2322, 2553, 3457, 3697, 3791, 3818; among p. 784; among the p. 1820; and governments 1453; and its laws 3427; and outer forces 1956; anywhere 3158; are a party to the laws 2651; are afraid 1069; are always blaming 341; are always in the wrong 2662; are angry 2000; are as free as they want to be 1163; are beginning to see 3772; are corrupted 3046; are free 1140; are generally better persuaded 3138; are good business 3919; are ignoramuses 1626; are least sure 842; are more easily led 1080; are oppressed 3218; are the masters 2654;

are the safest 2670; are thrown out of work 904; arouse the p. 3208; ask the difference 1933; authority of the p. 2504; backs of the p. 581; be nice to p. 9; believe that no p. 3324; belongs to the p. 3267; benefit of the p. 2369; bourgeois are other p. 398; builds on the p. 2647; burden the p. 1365; buy th' p. 2236; by all the p. 2684; by the p. 669, 2683, 2685, 2686; call me an idealist 1527; can be both strong and free 1332; can be truly happy 524; can only agree 649; chloroform of the Irish p. 2712; classes of p. 1251; cleverest p. 669; collection of p. 2178; come back 2912; compel p. 1984; completely consistent p. 576; contend for their liberty 2652; contracts with the p. 2550; crushed by law 1903; debauch her p. 1513; deceiving their own p. 791; demand freedom 2961; distrust of the p. 545; do so much harm 3881; don't ask for facts 1029; don't resent 2937; doomed p. 2344; doubted his word 2140; down the line 1615; dying p. 1242; easy to lead 913; enlighten the p. 3642; erratic and brilliant p. 2705; father of his p. 3283; fleece the p. 892; flock thither 1878; for all the p. 2684; for the p. 2683, 2685, 2686, 3567; formed two nations 2179; free p. 1891, 3325; from the p. 3567; free to the p. 2651; freedom of the p. 1138; generally corrupt 589; get tired of hearing it 3586; good for the p. 1087; good of the p. 1879; govern themselves 2666; government under which the p. 724; great p. 924, 1167; half of the p. 569; hath a revolting 3160; hating p. 3021; have an answer 2211; have got to know 809; have kindly said 1944; health of the p. 3872; hold 2468; however long 647; I interviewed 2736; idea of a p. 2656; illiterate p. 3798; in power 3281; in the mass 2190; in the United States 2723; incites p. 3220; infection of p. 3468; inflict on a p. 2104; inherit the p. 2264; insignificant p. 2213; instinct of the p.

peopled never 3839

peoples: happiness of p. 1514; judge p. 3260

people's: affairs 1260; fighting 3504; government 2683; judgment 2152; milk 3458; misconceptions 1471; mistakes 1471; opinions 926, 2469; pain 1414; revolutions 3208; secret virtues 1259; speech 3365; state 2650; values 1686

perception that virtue is enough 1378

*perestroika* defined as privatization 405

perfect: equality 3436; has one grave defect 450; our union is p. 3164

perfection: out of human nature 279; think of p. 330; unattainable 1627

perform: at a higher level 818; more than you can p. 3096; part they have to p. 2213

peril: always in p. 2085; in the fight 3906; of childbirth 1565; risk and hazard 1214; to the peace 905

person: another p. 110; any other p. 2355; broadminded p. 3101; does not deserve 1086; educated p. 651; educated 2180; freedom of p. 579; goes to a country 1206; in whom one impulse 1015; last p. they talked to 52; may be driven by shame 3794; mediocre p. 331; no p. but himself 1642; one p. 2260; only one p. 1180; politician was a p. 2830; running for office 340; scrupulous p. 3343; selecting a good p. 255; to do any great harm 3639; understanding a p. 3540; who can change 3685; who can tell you to go to hell 771; who is fundamentally honest 333; who keeps his mouth shut 28; with a belief 144; with predatory instincts 879; young p. 1611

personages: great p. 1388

personal or political rights 3262

personality of the candidates 2022

personally: tried on him p. 3331

personnel: pass p. 1369

persons: and not on property 141; made between p. 220; most conservative p. 3123; not so fortunate 1765; of some substance 1116; ordinary p. 1641; put forward 1751; ten guilty p. 1772; than with

their p. 372; two or three p. 1386; who when they cease to shock 1263; whom we love 3219; with bad judgment 1731

person's intelligence 3538

persuade: he who wants to p. 3371

persuaded by the reasons 3138

persuasion is the resource 3369

perversion: of the normal order 3000; universal p. 3851

pessimism: is only the name 3963; when you get used to it 164

pessimist: fears 636; what a p. is 637

pestilence: desolating p. 2986

petticoat: turned out of the realm in my p. 3282

phenomenon: explain this p. 2199

philanthropies: despises the p. 3237

philosophers: have only interpreted 309; poets and p. 1987

philosophies to explain 1367

philosophy: enslave a p. 3467; is the study 1471; liberal p. 2013; mathematics and p. 2842; of indifference 507; of one century 940; reason in my p. 3151; trained in p. 1696

phrase I have used 3863

phrases: streaming p. 3473; words or p. 1846

physical: or moral 1880; storms in the p. 3157

physicks: as well as of p. 2747

pickpocket: legally authorized p. 3449

pictures: gallery of p. 1465; mental p. 1860

pie: as American as cherry p. 3713; dividing the p. 2516; economic p. 2014

piece: of cake 2795; of land 2641

pieces: of silver 3997; Op-Ed p. 3251

piety of the skeptic 1672

pig: greased p. 3677

pillars: of government 1291; of society 3594

pinches: functions in the p. 1334

pins: row of p. 1275

pinstripe suit 3992

piss: pitcher of warm p. 3710

pit: bottomless p. 1913

pitcher of warm piss 3710

pity: it is 2571; justice not p. 1752; kills 503

tion runs low 1265; analysis 1724;
and economic health 2031; and legal
institutions 993; and religious rights
1196; and social change 302; and
social slavery 1662; animal 2770,
2771; argument 484; aspirant 3893;
bolter 2180; bonds 492; calculations
2448; campaign 264; campaigns 251;
career 2839; change 3344; columnists
3797; community 394; conservative
3131; courage 357; creed 729; crises
609; culture 2337; decisions 785,
1237, 3788; democracy 676; discussion 2140; division 2022; document
180; economist 1676; economy 2675;
education 2779; end 2095; even p.
2109; extremism 1010; faiths 2242;
freedom 272, 558, 1231; games
3295; genius 1958; gentlemen 1555;
goals 915; good 3755; history 1446,
1667; idealism 1537; ideas 1584,
2875; idols 839; improvement 2852;
instinct 2334; institutions 885, 1232;
interests 882; is replacing the
metaphysical 2858; issues 820; journalists 3056; judgment 1730; knot
1117; language 813; leader 1074,
1920, 2692; leaders 2421; liberty 691,
1637, 3002; life 71, 614, 1279, 1532,
2505, 2603, 2816; mistakes 2363;
mode 1344; motive 909; necessities
2363; nothing that is not p. 2776;
office 704; ones are insoluble 897; or
ideological difference 411; order
2338; organization 2551; participation 3217; parties 2543, 2556, 3788;
party 2124, 2497, 2553, 2557, 2559,
2562, 2568; power 435, 1458, 2658,
2997, 3213, 3726; principles 2880;
prisoners 754; problems 2035; programs 1127; prose 3407; purposes
271; question 1894; questions 132;
realism 1537; reality 357; remains
2549; reportage 2848; representative
3147; rights 3262; rule of p. life 6;
situation 365; society 370; soul 679;
speculations 2155; speech 1845; spirit
2856; standards 3694; structures
2952; struggle 546; system 134, 704,
1585, 1919, 2485, 2661; systems
2485; task 612; theory 3474; thinking 1499; thought 2706; true of the

p. 2864; understanding 249;
weapons 1600; what is p. 2776;
world 3157
politically: advance p. 2446; skilled
2951
politician: alarming as president-p.
2140; art of a p. 3732; becomes a
statesman 2812; call a p. 3059;
danger for a p. 509; from their p.
2810; good p. 1482; has a choice
3374; has few friends 53; have to be
a p. 2815; he is no p. 2803; honest
p. 2835; in my country 2820; instead of the p. 1227; is a man 2828;
is a statesman 2811; is an acrobat
2836; is by nature 307; it deserves
2918; it takes a p. 2828; knowing
every p. 2796; listen to a p. 2137;
lurks a p. 2809; makes the p. wise
2806; master p. 2482; may yield
347; must get along 41; never
believes 1490; no man can be a p.
2803; oldest, wisest p. 79; one that
would circumvent God 2822; ought
to sacrifice 3143; popular p. 2838;
proper memory for a p. 11; scurvy p.
2808; sound p. 2797; speech by a p.
3405; statesman and a p. 2829;
statesman is a p. 2828; status of a p.
3056; successful p. 2837; title of p.
1086; to lay aside disguise 1487; tops
his part 2113; true p. 2802; virtue of
a p. 2824; was a person 2830; what
a p. does today 258; who places
himself 2811; who says 2375; will do
anything 2584; wise p. 48; wouldn't
dream 3059
politicians: among p. 31, 337; are ambitious 2827; are disposed 2800; are
like the bones 2833; are not over a
year behind 2480; are promiscuous
327; are sent to Washington 3792;
are to serve 90; can make analogies
2693; degraded into p. 2814; depend on p. 2230; distasteful to p.
3170; fascinate 2831; fault of our p.
66; God and the p. 2638; halls of
the p. 2792; have a right 2799; have
the same occupational hazard 2879;
I do not admire p. 2791; influence
p. 2807; leave politics to p. 2675;
left to the p. 2844; neither love nor

2031; office p. 2853; one who chooses p. 1696; organized into p. 2551; ought to be 2314; out of politics 2498; party p. 2565; passion for p. 2819; person whose p. 2830; play p. 2853; post p. 2231; power p. 2907; practical p. 821, 2877; practices of p. 1270; prepared for p. 1237; progressive in p. 2034; purification of p. 1109; rare in p. 3701; resistance to p. 2499; revolution in p. 3185; ruins the character 803; science of p. 2840; seems like provincial struggles 2906; seldom think of p. 2794; separated from p. 3824; some stay in p. 2793; stony road of p. 2793; student of p. 2843; than it has to do with p. 528; the American citizen 807; the middle way 2219; this p. thing 2569; those who enter p. 1615; took part in p. 2782; topography of American p. 2848; views of p. 1409; what are your p. 2011; what is p. 2908; where fat, bald, disagreeable men 804; who gets what, when, how 2903, 2904; win anything in p. 818; with bloodshed 2905; without ideology 2010; you should always 46; your work is 47; zeal in p. 2860

politishun's golden rule 3805

polls: cannot stay at 91 per cent in the p. 2474; opinion p. 2464

pollster tells him 340

pollution of democracy 808

poor: and weak 1405; are Europe's blacks 3022; are our equals 999; delusion among the p. 1410; don't know 3878; don't make the p. richer 3359; expensive to be p. 3874; give me your p. 2307; grind the p. 1912; habits of the p. 1417; have little 1436; have no right 1426; help the many who are p. 3875; how apt the p. are to be proud 2944; laboring p. 2677; like the p. 1186; make the rich richer and the p. poorer 274; making the p. poorer 3888; man is deprived 3106; not to be p. 2941; property of the p. 1426; rich against the p. 1420; rich and the p. 1403; rich as well as the p. 1418; second

are the p. 364; t'be p. 2934; virtuous p. 2935; who die 3840

poorer: making the rich p. 3359; richer and not p. 3035

populace: doesn't want to be fed 858; drag down 2195; is entrusted 3309; ways for the p. to escape 3212

popular: government 2158; humanity 3754; opinion 2455; religion 3467; whether it is p. 2446

popularity: is a crime 1051; it is glory's small change 3911

popularity's bad for you 3912

population: entire p. 3530; exists in the p. 1342; of capable voters 726; part of the p. 704, 3419; starving p. 2711; transfer of p. 1860

pornography of war 3851

port: ideal is a p. 1534

portion of the press 3065

position: advanced p. 2034; certain of our own p. 113; shift one's p. 318

positions: appointive p. 1486

positive: and composed 2055; in error 3590

possess: do not p. 2341; what they do not p. 1434

possession: begets tyranny 3639; every p. 3254; is intolerable 1433

possessions: most precious p. 2099

possibilities: of change 2943; of defeat 3918; of error 2135; overexaggerate the p. 3217

possibility: no longer any p. 2756; of anything 627; of doubting 2109; of merit 2394; preventing all p. 3541

possible: art of the p. 2885, 2886; for man 1799; future events 1237; makes p. 3414; progress is p. 3089; that which is p. 1533

post: sleep at their p. 934

post-mortems on defeat 3926

posterity: divest their p. 2351; hope of p. 2513; is likely 1221; look forward to p. 3547; mankind and p. 3413; planning for p. 1222

potential for the disastrous rise 1295

Potomac: all quiet along the p. 2640

poultry: lives of the p. 638

pound: of learning 3970; of privilege 1439

poverty: ambitious p. 2940; and excess

3867; bear p. 1437; degraded by p. 3213; endure harsh p. 353; feature of p. 2942; is a great enemy 2926; is the worst of all snares 2925; misfortunes of p. 2936; shameful as p. 2924; stable p. 2943; struggled with p. 3874; talent that p. has stimulated 2923; thwarted by p. 2921; tyranny p. disease and war 2761; wealth persuade p. 558; worst of crimes is p. 2941
poverty's catching 2932
powder: keep your p. dry 3574
power: absolute p. 93, 729; absolutely in our p. 3488; acquisition of p. 2994; act of p. 126; among mankind 998; and energy 2379; and publicity 2989; and violence 3711; anyone entrusted with p. 3734; arbitrary p. 214; arrogance of p. 2738; arts of p. 2988; as a state 3872; at command 2494; avarice of p. 64; balance of p. 1704; based on p. 2952; because we had p. 3956; being out of p. 2975; burdened by p. 1956; can be exercised 1880; cancer of state p. 869; cared for is p. 2985; chambers of p. 3955; closeness to p. 2953; communicates some of its p. 1562; concentrated p. 2998; confided p. 1309; confused p. with greatness 1400; corridors of p. 2964; corrupts 2975, 2976, 2979; depository of p. 2959; diffusion of p. 3002; does not corrupt 1059; essence of government is p. 2950; executive p. 2051; exercise of p. 1695, 2673; fascinating p. 3342; feels itself 745; friend in p. 2965; from the governed 3637; getting p. 2967; governing p. 1347; gradually extirpates 3756; great p. 2629, 3007; greater the p. 2980; greatest p. 2984; grows out of the barrel 435; has the p. 179; hath by nature a p. 3107; having the p. 3158; height of their p. 325; hopes but from p. 1903; human p. 1789; if he had the p. 1180; in a man's p. 2955; in any shape 3004; in excess 1793; in his hands 3657; in history 1563; in p. I look only at one thing 2962; in the hands 3213; in trust 2945; in whose p. 2955; individual p. 2093; intoxicated with p. 2982; invariably means danger 2948; is a sign 3764; is a trust 3567; is conservative 1230; is ever grasping 2987; is given only to him 2958; is in inflicting pain 2996; is in tearing human minds 2996; is legitimate 2946; is nominated 578; is not a means 757; is not happiness 2992; is so apt to be insolent 3003; is the great aphrodisiac 2972; is wedded 1058; it is not p. itself 2978; keep wealth in p. 558; knowledge but no p. 1791; knowledge is p. 1786, 1787, 1788; lay in his p. 360; less p. 2983; light and a p. 3507; like a desolating pestilence 2986; lodged as it must be 2950; lodgement of p. 2670; lose most of their p. 2258; loss of p. 1059; love of p. 2098; lust for p. 2978; makes you attractive 2973; means the p. 1576; men of p. 3005; men with great p. 2158; military p. 3280; misplaced p. 1295; money and p. 1314; monuments of p. 2993; more p. 2206; must never be trusted 2947; no longer in your p. 2960; not based on force 1114; of a community 2093; of crowds 2190; of endurance 2418; of making laws 1881; of one class 2997; of resistance 496; of sense 3371; of sound 3371; of words 1857; on earth 985; one-man p. 2067; opportunities and p. 3259; or for friendship 2819; over any individual, 2660; over his fellow citizens 1443; over people 2960; over taste 2209; pains of p. 2990; party in p. 1419; people in p. 3281; people who have p. 3006; plus legitimacy 139; political p. 1458, 2658, 2997, 3726; politics 2907; possessed by the leaders 214; possessors of p. 1234; pride and for p. 1142; problem of p. 3005; quantum of p. 2949; quest for p. 2826; responsibility without p. 2006; rich have p. 3106; say in p. 10; scientific p. 956; secret of p. 2957; seek p. 2539, 2999; seizure of p. 612; sense of p. 2995; should always be distrusted 3572; social p.

representation: taxation and r. 3440; taxation without r. 3439

representative: expressed by r. 3440; of a natural equilibrium 3147; of custom 3147; of inertia 3147; of reason 3147; owes you 1729

representatives: elected r. 41; women ought to have r. 3985

repression: price of r. 761; seed of revolution is r. 3205

reproach to religion 3867

reptiles of the mind 2422

republic: aristocracy in a r. 122; essence of the r. 3749; ideal r. 1528; is a government 1895, 2260; of man 1344; of mediocrity 2192; Roman r. 2575; the governing power 1347

republican: economics 895; form of government 1345; government 1346; is the only form 3268; model 2046; party 2524, 2525, 2528, 2529; promise 2531; quarrel 2527; vote r. this year 2506

Republicans: and Democrats 2503; are the party 2523; believe 2520; have found a way 2526; we are r. 2521

republics weak because they appeal 2260

reputation: for good nature 3300; for power 1114; spotless r. 3776

requirement of a statesman 788

requirements: adjustment to the r. 2545

requisite: first r. 362; of the historian 1627; to success in life 3772

researches on historical variations 3817

resentment: at a reproach 1778; keen as their r. 1089

resign: none r. 2383

resigning: impeached myself by r. 3916

resistance: history of r. 2045; of the adversaries 390; power of r. 496; spirit of r. 2044; to politics 2499

resort: last r. 1115; to arms 3830

resource of the feeble 3369

resources: available 2494; great r. 523

respect: affection and r. 2820; based on fear 1062; for antiquity 563; for law 2928; for man 708; for the law 1905; healthy r. 3075; its flag 855; only those who resist me 494; remaining r. 3421; to the opinions 492; you fail to get r. 40

response: he is also a r. 1943; he will get no r. 3689; to the decline 3793

responsibilities: assumes new r. 3865; who has many r. 3309

responsibility: and danger 2948; as a free man 3169; burden of r. 3305; escape all r. 201; is the first step 2060; liberty means r. 2079; no more real r. 3462; of directing their activity 841; of speech 3403; of the great states 1706; places of r. 2564; power without r. 2971; right implies a r. 3254; sense of r. 2593; take more r. 2325; take r. 3033; without power 2006

responsible: to ourselves 1153; use 3005; who is r. 2563

rest: body at r. 2747; of mankind 2596; of the world 3712; of us must face the guilt 3341; of your life 1604

restlessness for a rejection 751

restoration: not revolution but r. 2311

restrain: abolish or r. 1890

restraint: and servitude 982; exert r. 1355; impatient of any r. 2984; need no r. 1332; self-denial and r. 369; wholesome r. 2071

restraints: government r. 3087

restriction of free thought 1173

result: foretell the r. 3816; net r. of zero 721; of a natural equilibrium 1373; of contact 924; of education 3539; of human organization 992; shot at without r. 3938; squalid r. 988

retains the feelings 2257

retaliate: they want to r. 1142

retreat: is honorable 3850; no r. 3060

retrenchment: peace, r., and reform 2530

return of man 3352

revenge: best r. 1785; for slight injuries 3936; greatest r. 756; man that studieth r. 497; mere r. 3308

revenue: absorb r. and then some 3447

revenues: public r. 2382

reverence: held in r. 2451

reverse is true 3356

revolt: incites people to r. 3220; successful r. 3198; those who have nothing to lose r. 3211

revolution: a parent of settlement

3230; and reformation 579; as a whole 3216; beginning r. 3222; compromised r. 3195; day after the r. 3248; delayed 3237; in politics 3185; in the state 3239; intellectual r. 1665; is a transfer of power 3168; is an insurrection 3191; is as natural a growth 3206; is not a dinner party 3202; is not a painting 3202; is not a piece of embroidery 3202; is not an easy thing 3186; is not the uprising 3193; justify r. 2160; leaders of a r. 3240; like Saturn 3210; make a r. 3203, 3232; makes the r. 757; missed r. 3195; nor war 3897; not r. 2311; of rising expectations 3221; only lasts fifteen years 3225; or dictatorship 3194; peaceful r. 3214; Reagan r. 276; relation to r. 3216; requires of its leaders 3235; right of r. 3218; run a r. 3189; safeguard a r. 757; seed of r. 3205; shot after the r. 3238; social r. 3212; stop a r. 3199; stops the r. 3196; successful r. 3195, 3653; takes a r. 3227; termed a r. 3198; that never took place 3197; thinkers prepare the r. 3242; veterans of the r. 2328; violent r. 3214; volcano of r. 3201

revolutionaries: are more formalistic 564; are potential Tories 3247; are subject 3251; reformers and r. 3174; successful r. 3249

revolutionary: duty of every r. 3232; every r. ends 3246; most radical r. 3248; movement 3472; movements 3241; party 3250; periods 3236; right 3267; spirit 3244; successful r. 3234; theory 3472; times 1421; to be a r. 3233; true r. 3237

revolutionists: and rebels 830; hate irony 4001

revolutions: always destroy themselves 3209; are born 3208; are not made 3187, 3206; are the cause 291; are the locomotives of history 3188; cause of r. 3223; do not go backward 3200; experiments mean r. 2846; future r. 3230; have never lightened 3655; invariably encourage 3243; modern r. 3190; quality of r. 3192

reward: in itself 3081; its own r. 2101

rewards: nor punishments 2752; of success 776

rhetoric: no amount of r. 3782; this new r. 1577

rhetoricians and dealers 3257

rich: against the poor 1420; and powerful 1405; and successful 3026; and the poor 1403; are most afraid 1421; as well as the poor 1418; can always get r. 861; consoling the r. 1688; feed with the r. 3983; feels so r. 1193; few who are r. 3875; first are the r. 364; have no right 1426; have power 3106; loved and the r. 2163; makes the r. richer 274; making the r. poorer 3359; making the r. richer 3888; man 1487; men rule 1912; men 1790; property of the r. 1426; sell them to the r. 3801; soaking the r. 2023; society 3879; terror among the r. 1410; too much 1436; very r. 1404; wage war 3840

richer: and not poorer 3035; don't make the poor r. 3359

riches: are a good handmaid 380; are for spending 3446; great r. 1435; knowledge and honor 1792; only true r. 2092; thirst of r. 1822

riddle wrapped in a mystery 2721

ridicule: public r. 3028

right: always be in the r. 2588; always r. 1745, 2165; always the r. 2489; and law 1151; and the left 2221; anything not r. 2157; argument 3371; constitutional r. 2160, 3267; dissent is a r. 826; divine of kings 2249; do what is r. 1150; equality may perhaps be a r. 985; ever been r. 2004; exclusively in the r. 1379; fights for the r. 2786; firmness in the r. 2302; God-given r. 1305; government of the r. 557; great r. 3740; greatest r. 3276; has no r. 403; implies a responsibility 3254; in the circus 1523; in the r. 2287; inalienable r. 3266; intellectual of the r. 557; is only the expedient 3517; is preempted 3266; is the child of law 3257; judgment will probably be r. 3144; left and r. 2231; legitimate r. 3637; Lenin was r. 1658; makes might 949; matter of r. 132; might

sanguinary: most s. 1335
sap in a tree 2331
satellite: liberty but its s. 3000
satire: rather than for history 640; write s. 641
satisfactions in past greatness 1242
satisfy: can never s. 979; endeavoring to s. 1337
sauces it is served with 3605
saucy: liberty to be s. 3003
sausages: laws are like s. 1918
save: democracy to s. 3862; it from dishonor 3830; the few who are rich 3875; we shall nobly s. 3333
say: what they please 3290; whatever one chooses 3626
saying: among men 3626; goes without s. 3378; revise the old s. 239
scaffold to scaffold 3083
scale: large s. in history 3223
scandal: by a woman of easy virtue 2567; no s. like rags 2924; public s. 350
scapegoat: servant or a s. 1667
scarce as truth is 3579
scarcity: very first s. 3883
scarecrows of fools 1108
scars: expose his wound s. 2575
scepticism is the chastity 628
schedule is already full 613
schemes of political improvement 2852
scholars: useful chiefly to s. 2549
school: training s. 676
schools in a society 2182
science: applied s. 1333; dismal s. 880; exact s. 1317, 2883; great tragedy of s. 3487; life or in s. 2472; not a s. 2890; of liberty 2884; of politics 2840; politics is the s. 2884; which studies human behavior 951
scientists: genius of its s. 2632
scope: never hath more s. 3648
scorn: laughed to s. 2276
scoundrel: first refuge of a s. 2392; last refuge of a s. 2390
scoundrels: last refuge of s. 2391
scruples: frees one from all s. 3244
scrupulous and the just 3240
sea: is calm 1931; islands of the s. 3030; of ethics 1884; of thought 3480; profound s. 3619; rough rude s. 2250; very much at s. 2402

search: for truth 826, 3612; investigate and s. 3624
searchlight: beam of a s. 3043
seat: firm s. 1932
seats of politeness 1908
second class citizens 990
secrecy: and a free 688; bond of s. 1179; in government 2139
secret: dirty little s. 2545; know that's a s. 1254; of power 2957; penetrate to the s. 1037; weapon 2715
secretary of state 2008
sect or party 2536
sector: private s. 799, 1312
secularized: wholly s. 1347
secure: he that is too s. 3310
security: economic s. 1409; is a kind of death 3315; is when everything is settled 3314; learns to think s. 131; not only for s. 1136; of all 3795; of the future 3308; of the people 1351; only real s. 3508; otherwise styled s. 3307; social s. 3890; there is no s. 3262; weep for their lost s. 3316
seducer: strong s. 3769
seed of revolution 3205
seeds: grown from its s. 1344
segment of the human complex 3154
segregation now 3029
self-alienation: human s. 3352
self-criticism is the secret weapon 679
self-interest: heedless s. 862
selfish: and so hard 2243; men are s. 1110; right to be s. 3274
selfishness: euphemism for s. 555; hatred and s. 3127; makes government needful 597
senate: United States s. 1834
senators: and congressmen 666; pray for the s. 1998
sensation of ignorance 1629
sense: common s. 293, 939, 940, 1928, 3010; current s. 3131; doubt your s. 3389; of duty 850; of limitation 1810; of power 2995; of purpose 2810; of responsibility 2593; of what is right 3134; one had the s. 3289; organs 2790; power of s. 3371
sentence: every s. from his mouth 3404; simply declarative s. 234
sentences written by the most innocent 1277

silly at the right moment 1102
silver: and gold 3777; pieces of s. 3997
simple: ignorant and the s. 590
simplicity: complicate s. 3094; Jeffersonian s. 3693
simplification: totalitarianism spells s. 750
sin: against God 216; deadly 624; in secret 350; in which we never forgive 2444; inflation is like s. 1656
sincerity: even his s. 1519; rehearses his s. 2464; respect s. 478; smallest quantity of s. 2282
sinews of war 3854
single dogmatic creed 844
sit down together 3031
situation: leave behind him a s. 1928; of persons 1765; of power 2379
situations: worsens s. 1311
size is not grandeur 2329
skeptic: always rhymes 626; piety of the s. 1672; too much of a s. 627
skeptical: about the ability of government 3075; obligation to be s. 632
skepticism: forest of s. 629; is therefore the first step 631; of the powers 2918; riddling the faith 630; wise s. 3965
skill: is a superb and necessary instrument 1961; need of s. 1112; taste or s. 2804
skin: color of their s. 3031; hang the tiger's s. 410; of its culture 3365; thick s. 2522
sky: broad and peaceful s. 2317; lifts his head to the s. 635
slate: wiped the s. clean 3561
slaughter and desolation 1908
slave: begins by demanding 1768; by nature a s. 3317; deserves to be a s. 3271; freedom to the s. 3333; half s. 491; has but one master 77; moment the s. resolves 3340; neck of a s. 3329; no longer be a s. 3340; of capitalist society 4000; of that s. 4000; state 1304
slavery: arguing for s. 3331; begins 3779; cannot be 3334; chains and s. 2043; equal in s. 2731; fat s. 3322; freedom and s. 3340; good in s. 1088; instruments of s. 3344; is one of them 3335; of labor 867; of whatever nature 1662; social s. 1662;

there is no s. 1607; this is s. 3505; voluntary v. 3164; where s. is 3334; yoke of s. 3324
slaves: and taskmasters 2121; creed of s. 2364; grinds down his s. 3662; lose everything 3337; masters and the s. 2092; never know 3328; of men 2986; sons of former s. 3031; they trample on 3663; two kinds of s. 3348; wholly s. 3319
sleep: get much s. 2411
slippery slope 2086
slow to turn 1330
small: against the s. 3852; change 3379, 3911; extremely s. 3496; no matter how s. 3680; reach the s. 1941; weak and s. 2564
smart: enough 2865; when you're s. 1610
smear: expect the s. 1279
smell of common folk 1690
smile with the wise 3983
smoke: and wealth 2718; has cleared 3249
smoothly: more s. 3676
snares: worst of all s. 2925
sneer: killed by a s. 1567; refute a s. 112
snobs: impudent s. 1691
sober: drunk or s. 2589
social: advantages 1751; animal 2771; conditions 993; conflicts 3793; conscience 3181; disciplines 2242; existence 1407; goods 3259; institutions 1762; order 2485; pressures 3788; program 866; progress 2449; prosperity 3869; revolution 3212; security 3890; slavery 1662; system 3000; unrest 282; well-being 3508
socialism: can only arrive by bicycle 3351; democracy and s. 954, 982; does not mean much more 3358; is capitalism of the lower classes 3357; is impossible 3353; is the abolition 3352; language of s. 3354; Marxian s. 404; seeks equality 982; under s. 3356; without s. 3353; worst advertisement for s. 3355
socialist: democracy 670; moderate s. 3361; typical s. 3362
socialists: and moderates 2231; proletarian s. 3026

terms: contradiction in t. 3250;
  familiar t. 3056; speakin' t. 2511;
  upon good t. 3003
terrace: from the t. 1396
terrible: war is so t. 3847
territory: consist of its t. 3427; defend
  their own t. 3828; does not make a
  nation 2329; is the only part 3427;
  of an ally 3828
terror: among the rich 1410; in spite of
  the t. 3858; reigns of t. 3165; strike
  t. into others 1060; warfare, t.,
  murder, bloodshed 2719
terrors of the future 3092
test: acid final t. 2562; hardest t. 2104;
  martyrdom is the t. 1190; of a leader
  1959; of a political party 2562; of
  civilization 373; of fighting 3785; of
  greatness 1391; of intelligence 1575;
  of legitimacy 2337; of political institutions 1232; of the past 3814
testicles of my mind 3016
theft: from those who hunger 2632;
  work by gift and by t. 1438
theme of a political campaign 264
theology is the grandmother 434
theories for which we have no use 3465
theory: abstraction built upon a t.
  3481; as practical as t. 3460;
  democracy is the t. 720; economic t.
  3473; explanations of t. 3477;
  however elegant 1762; of democratic
  systems 3483; of our modern technic
  3460; political t. 3474; revolutionary
  t. 3472; to practice 3462
thief doth fear each bush 532
thieves: get so much 1438; union of
  two t. 1721; will join 1484
thing: about success 3901; always the
  same t. 361; any damn fool t. 2960;
  barren t. 566; call a t. immoral 905;
  consensus is a fine t. 490; dangerous
  t. 1797; delightful t. 330; easiest t.
  in the world 3403; easy t. 3186; far
  far better t. 3480; first t. he believes
  974; first t. we do 3204; goes
  without saying 3378; great t. 932;
  greatest t. 335; hard-bought t. 1160;
  important t. 1362; in the world
  1256; in which men are consistent
  568; is to use it well 933; leave a t.
  alone 560; more valuable t. 1320;

most difficult t. 3375; most exciting
  t. 453; most important t. 546; most
  precious t. 3376; most useful t. 615;
  most valuable t. 1650, 3625; nastiest
  t. 769; no such t. 3405, 3884; not a
  static t. 705; one t. alone 531; one t.
  better 1286; one t. we have 861; only
  t. necessary 3771; only t. we have to
  fear 1067; only t. worth doing 1033;
  sacred t. 887; shameless t. 723;
  slowest t. 1094; some damned silly t.
  2728; tell the same t. 773; that does
  not change 298; that enables a man
  929; that saves 223; this politics t.
  2569; to do 650, 1279, 1611; to remain undone 33; uncomfortable t.
  1830; very simple t. 1316; want of a
  t. 1433; wisdom is the principal t.
  3979; wisest t. 1192
things: about youth 551; accomplishing
  small t. 736; all mortal t. 1296; all
  possible t. 2969; all t. 3676; almost
  unknown 3756; are at risk 1663; are
  getting worse 639; believed six impossible t. 178; better t. 3220; ceased
  to need t. 876; crooked t. 3590;
  disparate in nature 3430; do t.
  differently 3563; done as cheap
  3459; enslaved by the very t. 1434;
  equal in all t. 981; few t. are more
  shocking 3932; get worse 2514; great
  t. 3420; he has tried to obliterate
  3561; hundred t. 2565; ill-natured t.
  3363; in life 3521; invisible 1245;
  more horrible 3335; more t. 324;
  more vital 1186; natural order of t.
  3533; new order of t. 3171; quite
  other 1161; small t. 322; state of t.
  308; stubborn t. 1025; tendency of t.
  998; that are God's 3432; that are
  brought 230; that were so candid
  3055; too many t. 420; unspeakably
  precious t. 1168; unthinkable t.
  3493; untruthful t. 1041; very
  laughable t. 2852; we do many t.
  799; which are Caesar's 3432; which
  enable its citizens 1712; which we
  most desire 72; won't get worse 2514
think: about the future 1238; alike
  2406, 3495; as I think 2431; as you
  like 932; cannot t. 2186; correctly
  3490; dare to t. 3493; don't t. we

should have done it 3699; for
himself 918; freely 1199; hard and
persistently 3511; he is a martyr
3028; him worth flattering 1272; it
done 33; it is hell 2327; it is important 2865; it is the voice of God
2451; men who t. 3518; men's
thoughts 2463; needing to t. 3503;
no man believes 3654; not to t.
2869; of everything 3489; of perfection 330; of politics 2794; of
something 3522; of yourself 3523;
otherwise 1661; people t. 2526;
public will t. 2447; read, t., speak
and write 919; stopping to t. 3336;
that a stupid man 1494; that an
opinion 1280; that one vote will do
no good 3789; the presidency 3690;
the president 3685; themselves wise
3959; they govern 2653; they know
1616; those that t. 1968; those who
do t. 3496; to t. is not enough 3522;
too much 266; used to t. 291; we've
got to t. 3525; what they t. best
1731; what we like 1177; what you t.
932; without his hat 3498; you look
funny 1952
thinker: as a t. 3463; consistent t. 570;
deep t. 1696; destroys the t. 3506;
great t. 3463; lets loose a t. 1663;
new t. 1581; puts some new portion
1664
thinkers: prepare the revolution 3242;
radical t. 3512
thinking: about something else 1052;
at all 2447; consists in deciding
1499; effort of t. 2204; excuse for
not t. 3524; man 3797; modes of t.
2500; no one is t. 3495; not t. 3503;
of an army 2494; people start t.
3504; stream of t. 3500; that they
can be 1759; trouble of t. 840; vexation of t. 2536; way of our t. 3517;
without t. 2495
thinks: differently 1649; for himself
827; he is guiding 65; he knows
everything 2839; in terms of
humanity 1284; man who t. 3507; of
war 2612; say what he t. 3597
thirst of riches 1822
thirty pieces of silver 3997
thorns: crown of t. 3292, 3997; no t. 15

thoroughfare for all thoughts 3513
those: they love 3659; who administer
it 3882; who are already capable
3887; who disagree 1577; who do
not display 1260; who do think
3496; who go about doing good
3881; who like to play 1687; who
never retract 2417; who undergo the
fatigue 3501; who want 2751
thought: activity by t. 840; because we
had power 3956; contradictions of t.
1577; despot of t. 1554; enemy of t.
2746; every real t. 3509; expressing a
t. 3526; free t. 1173, 1178; freedom
of t. 931, 1175, 3468, 3521; in a
bureaucracy 245; inmost t. 2504; is
not free 2437; is viscous 1850; liberty
of t. 3520; makes t. unnecessary
1267; modes of t. 3471; of political
change 3344; original t. 1574;
political t. 2706; practice and t.
3502; progress of t. 2542; range of t.
3494; schools of t. 475; systematic t.
3466; systems of t. 1762; that is
silenced 1174; triumph of t. 3506;
troubled sea of t. 3480; world of t.
925
thoughtcrime literally impossible 3494
thoughts: and concepts 1687; and feelings 1403; are beyond the reach
1572; control our t. 2293; dangerous
t. 3492; except for our own t. 3488;
great t. 1566; illegitimate t. 3492;
light of new t. 3516; limits on t.
1178; men's t. 2463; misleading
1859; of children 3475; our t. make
it 3499; right to his t. 3665; second
t. 171; speak one's t. 3505;
thoroughfare for all t. 3513; to one
another 1176
thread: form the t. 1858
threat: of censorship 1187; to justice 1774
threatened: ideals are t. 1542; not t.
2258
throat: cutting each other's t. 381; find
its t. cut 313; sheep's t. 2076
throats: begin slitting t. 3716; sticks in
our t. 3605
throne: monarch in his t. 1412; no t.
15; of bayonets 3838; safely on his t.
1172; sit upon God's t. 3291;
something behind the t. 3678

United States 411, 2638, 2783
units of power 750
unity: and peace 1082; is desirable 510;
    risk to national u. 3534; understands
    u. 402; will be destroyed 3534
university: best u. 1692
unjust: if they are u. 1762
unknown: benefits of the u. 547
unlimited power 733
unlovable: congenitally u. 2920
unnecessary: do the u. 204
unorthodoxy or dissent 831
unpalatable: disastrous and the u. 2886
unpopular: always u. 2959; safe to be
    u. 834; with friends 2798
unpractical: most u. 709
unreasonable: being u. 3148
unselfish and the intelligent 3240
unstable: weak and u. 1114
untaught to bear poverty 1437
unthinkable: as an honest burglar
    1482; things 3493
untrue: revised if it is u. 1762
untruths: unfashionable u. 2135
unwisdom: wisdom and u. 1299
unwise: still be u. 1896
uprising: point of the u. 612
urge: creative u. 3714; for destruction
    3714; to rule 3179; to save humanity
    3179
use: of blunt objects 2911; of freedom
    2493; of his powers 2805; of our in-
    tellect 1680; of power 2951; of
    speech 3368; of violence 3419
used as a blind tool 3343
useless: always u. 3554
uses: alternative u. 951
usurpations: sudden u. 1138
usurper and a tyrant 3652


vacillation and inconsistency 777
vague: short and v. 577
vagueness about general ideas 3404
vain: always in v. 2085
valets: best v. 54
validity of a political theory 3474
valor: better part of v. 1736
valuation of property 3106
value: depends 1865; high v. 2438;
    highest v. 3113; judgments 3946;

more v. than his arguments 2441; no
    v. at all 2469; of an idea 1580; of
    popular judgment 2182; one v. 1015
values: affair of v. 3946; more impor-
    tant than v. 1686; not of facts but of
    v. 910
vanity: betrayed by his v. 1694; of ruin
    3306
variable: independent v. 2448
variance with the reality 906
variations in the voting behavior 3817
varieties of absolutism 2539
variety: admits v. 684; of aims 750
vegetarianism: in favor of v. 2410
vehicle: polluted v. 3045
veneration: arbitrary v. 2600
vengeance: for mere v. 3308; inspires
    v. 503
ventriloquists' dummies 1042
verify: trust but v. 3573
verity: aware of a v. 1560
vested interest in social unrest 282
veteran: consult the v. 1227; of twelve
    years 1834
veterans of the Revolution 2328
vexation of thinking 2536
vexatious: most v. 1335
vibration of a pendulum 3942
vice: American v. 695; accommodating
    v. 3760; always a v. 2226; nerve-
    racking v. 1507; no v. 2227; of
    democracies 2459; of the modern
    orator 3383; render v. serviceable
    3732; that cannot be forgiven 1506;
    unpardonable v. 2228; virtue or v.
    3775; you destroy 3750
vice-presidency isn't worth 3710
vices: disguised 3751; greatest v. 1681;
    of the saint 3753; reveal our v. 1552
victim: easily fall v. 2118; marks its v.
    2988
victims: must have its v. 3173; number
    of its v. 3730; promise easy v. 3243;
    they are its v. 3240; who respect 485
victim's sympathies 2989
victor: call itself the v. 3845; to the v .
    belong the spoils 3933
victories: nothing but v. 2057
victory: another such v. 3908; at all
    costs 3858; dig for v. 2315; fight
    through to v. 1529; get anything for
    their v. 2652; has a hundred fathers

commonly understood 805; is given
to lying 2128; keep his w. 3105; let
the w. go forth 3269; mortuary w.
1009; native w. 1551; of command
516; of mouth 1266; one w. 982; opprobrious w. 2853; or concept 1867;
phoney w. 717; plans for a new w.
1236; right w. 1871; stop using the
w. 716; that cowards use 521; whose
nuances 1876
words: abuse of w. 1856; and explanations 3477; and gestures 2183; are
pegs 1873; are slippery 1850; are
weapons 1862; book of their w.
3548; can be treasonable 1836;
disguise it as by w. 1855; exports
most is w. 783; express everything in
w. 1694; flow of w. 1171; form the
thread 1858; from loose using 1869;
giving in w. 3395; good w. 58;
honeyed w. 2378; in the English
language 62; in which to express it
3494; magic w. 1846; may varnish
facts 1861; men of few w. 3372; men's
w. 2463; misuse of w. 1842; misused
w. 1859; much in a few w. 3397; of
command 2284; of wisdom 1042;
plurality of w. 1841; power of w.
1857; pride in the w. 2714; sound w.
1870; too many w. 1843; wound 1834
work: any would not w. 3885; by gift
and by theft 1438; conduct of their
w. 2895; democracy doesn't w. 687;
don't w. at all 2845; done by people
1615; done its w. 2123; finish the w.
2302; for Uncle Sam 2399; from the
masses 2183; government doesn't w.
2523; he loves 461; importance of a
w. 1383; like the w. 2793; lives by
his own w. 1144; make institutions
w. 236; meaningful w. 875; men
who do the w. 2563; most important
part of any work 2763; my friend is
peace 2635; of development 2563; of
man 1497; of the world 3043; out
the direction 906; rough w. 634;
take his w. 640; thrown out of w.
904; until our work is done 2768;
whether it will w. 2446; worst w. is
done 1550
worker: at each end 3837; female w.
4000; is the slave 4000

workers: get so little 1438; have no
fatherland 2341; not the w. but the
robbers 1427; should get a nickel
more an hour 2730
workhouse: age going to the w. 1340
working: class 388, 3793; or starving
2089
works: means by which it w. 948
world: across the w. 756; adapts
himself to the w. 3086; ages of the
w. 971; all over the w. 1493, 3777;
all the w. 2177; any in the w. 603;
anywhere in the w. 2245; appears in
the w. 458; arms race 2347; around
the w. 3269; at peril 1664; best actors in the w. 1489; brave w. 312;
breaks through from another w.
1155; business and industrial w.
2900; caused in the w. 3078; citizen
of the w. 3537; commodity in the w.
939; Communist w. 402, 441; community 1724; complex w. 1313; conquest of the w. 844; control of the
w. 1427; crisis 2347; curse of the w.
1544; disputes in the w. 1874;
dominate the w. 1706; easiest thing
in the w. 3403; economy 2347; enter
the w. 2418; environment 2347;
events of this w. 1449; eye of the w.
1103; eyes of the w. 2415; face of the
w. 2740; families in the w. 1402;
fantasy w. 3313; free w. 402, 441;
friends in the w. 1261; front to the
w. 14; govern the w. 129, 1833;
greatest right in the w. 3276; half
the w. 1344, 2695, 3400; has achieved
brilliance 2633; has been laid waste
1601; has ever known 1186; highways
of the w. 3119; history of the w.
1444, 1458, 1475, 3090; hope in the
w. 2672; how apt 2944; how is the
w. ruled 1278; improve the w. 297;
in arms 2632; in the w. 1650, 2531;
in their w. 1498; in this w. nothing
can be said 3433; in which we live
2235; information in the w. 1033;
interpreted the w. 309; is becoming
2240; is disgracefully managed 2237;
is divided 1689, 2751; is filled 837; is
governed 3941; is moving 552; is
quickly bored 3023; is the best 3736;
is weary 2814; itself 1875; knew how